Medieval Monasteries of Great Britain

Medieval Monasteries of Great Britain

Lionel Butler and Chris Given-Wilson

Michael Joseph

London

In memory of P.F.G.-W. and L.H.B.

MICHAEL JOSEPH LTD

Penguin Books Ltd, 27 Wrights Lane, London W8 5TZ (Publishing and
Editorial) *and* Harmondsworth, Middlesex, England (Distribution and
Warehouse)
Viking Penguin Inc., 40 West 23rd Street, New York, New York 10010,
USA
Penguin Books Australia Ltd, Ringwood, Victoria, Australia
Penguin Books Canada Ltd, 2801 John Street, Markham, Ontario, Canada,
L3R IB4
Penguin Books (NZ) Ltd, 182–190 Wairau Road, Auckland 10, New
Zealand

First published in Great Britain February 1979
Second impression July 1983

First published in this edition July 1983
Second impression July 1987

Filmset and printed in Great Britain by BAS Printers Limited,
Over Wallop, Hampshire
and bound by
Dorstel Press Limited, Harlow

ISBN 0 7181 2368 9

Contents

Introduction
by Lionel Butler

Gazetteer
by Chris Given-Wilson

Acknowledgements

The authors and publisher wish to thank the sources listed below for their kind permission to reproduce the photographs which appear on the following pages:

Aerofilms Ltd: 184, 316

The Archbishop of Canterbury and the Trustees of Lambeth Palace Library: 98

Bodleian Library: 26, 30, 49

British Library: 14, 40, 55, 103, 110, 115

British Museum: 21, 23, 24, 73, 155

British Tourist Authority: 171, 173, 174, 176, 179, 180, 181, 188, 215, 216, 217, 227, 229, 230, 249, 311, 313, 328, 329, 332, 342, 353, 354, 378–9, 381, 383, 385, 386, 392, 393, 394

Cambridge University Collection (copyright reserved): 150, 168, 213, 219, 224, 239, 244, 271, 284, 299, 307, 319, 325, 350, 363, 368, 388

Country Life: 304

The Courtauld Institute of Art, and the Master and Fellows of Corpus Christi College, Cambridge: 45

Fitzwilliam Museum: 95

Hampshire Field Club: 150

A. F. Kersting: 158, 254, 273, 302, 317, 398, 399, 400

National Monuments Record: 151, 153, 225, 253, 275, 397

Reece Winstone: 157

The Master and Fellows of Trinity College, Cambridge: 64, 97

Warburg Institute: 70

The illustrations on the following pages are Crown Copyright and are reproduced with permission of the Controller of Her Majesty's Stationery Office: 140, 142, 147, 161, 163, 166, 186, 192, 194, 196, 198, 200, 203, 205, 207, 210, 221, 232–3, 235, 240, 241, 246, 257, 259, 261, 262, 265, 266, 268, 269, 278, 282, 288, 291, 292, 294, 296, 297, 305, 308, 321, 326, 334, 335, 336, 338, 340, 346, 351, 359, 360, 364, 370, 372, 376, 377, 390

The authors also record their thanks for the indispensable advice and help of Janet Christie.

Illustrations

Introduction

Gazetteer

The endpaper map was drawn by Boris Weltman; all other line drawings (apart from those on pages 226 and 369 which are Crown Copyright and are reproduced with permission of the Controller of Her Majesty's Stationery Office) were drawn by Yvonne Skargon.

Note to 1983 Edition

This is really Lionel Butler's book. Shortly after resigning his post as Professor of Medieval History at the University of St Andrews in 1973, he agreed to write this book on medieval monasteries in Britain. Initially it was to be written by him alone, but he soon realized that his new duties as Principal of the Royal Holloway College were taking up so much of his time that he would be unable to complete the work himself, so he asked me to compile the gazetteer while he wrote the introduction. Hence this book, the product of a happy co-operation stretching over two years.

Lionel's teaching and administrative duties, which he performed marvellously well, seemed to take up almost all the time that he had, with the result that little of his research found its way into print. It is therefore gratifying that he saw this book through publication and knew that it had been a success. He would have been delighted to know that it was going to be reprinted, but he died, quite suddenly, in November 1981. He has been greatly missed by many friends, and it is fitting that this reprint of *Medieval Monasteries* should be dedicated to his memory. I know too that Lionel would have wished to join with me in doing something which we should have done when *Medieval Monasteries* was first published, that is to acknowledge the debt which we owe to Jenny Dereham of Michael Joseph for all the hard work and editorial expertise which she put into the book.

Chris Given-Wilson
St Andrews, May 1983.

Introduction

by
Lionel Butler

The First Monks in England

The first Christian monks were solitaries (the Greek *monos* means 'alone'), living apart from the society of the Roman Empire in the Egyptian desert. They renounced marriage, meat and wine, good clothes and physical comforts, and devoted themselves to meditation, to prayers for the living and the souls of the departed, to works of charity and to mortifying the flesh. St. Anthony the Abbot (*abbas*: 'father') was a pioneer of this way of life from A.D. 270 to 290, attracting many disciples to it. In the next few decades, while some of these hermits remained solitary, many others gathered together into monasteries, and we learn of the first nunnery* for women, in Egypt. Monks congregated together to say their prayers and eat their meals, and their daily routine was regulated in precise detail. It included manual work. They had no individual cells but slept in dormitories. St. Basil introduced both the hermit and the monastic community to the Greek lands of the Empire and, about 340, St. Athanasius brought them to Italy.

The earliest Christian monks

In the generations after the dissolution of the Roman Empire in the West (476), St. Benedict, who founded the great abbey of Monte Cassino in the mountains between Rome and Naples, led the way to momentous developments in monasticism. The Benedictine Rule envisaged the monk not as a solitary, self-punishing ascetic and visionary, but as a brother in a family or school, devoted, under the authority of the abbot, to the service of God. At his profession, he took the vows which for the rest of time defined what a monk was: the vows of lifelong personal poverty, chastity and obedience to the abbot and the Rule, and the vow of stability, committing him to stay until death in the monastic family which had admitted him. His work, under the Rule, might take him outside the walls of the convent, but otherwise he must remain within them, and the gates were closed to all outsiders unless, as invalids or paupers, travellers or refugees, they needed succour. When Benedict died in 543, he had founded, without realising it, an order – the Benedictine Order – which was to comprehend virtually all of the monks in the Roman Church – under the rule of the Pope – for four centuries.

Benedict and the vows of religion

The paramount duty of the monastic community was to recite the seven canonical Hours or services of the liturgy (the *Opus Dei*, or work of God). The timing depended on the length of the day and the night. At

The canonical Hours

*Nonnus is Latin for 'old fellow': nonna is the feminine. However, many women became nuns when young.

14

the March and September equinoxes, when day and night each last twelve hours, the monks rose at two o'clock, from a seven-hour sleep, and the Hours were:

2 a.m.	Vigils (the 'night-watch' office) — Meditation
At first light:	Lauds ('praises')
6 a.m.	Prime, at sunrise
9 a.m.	Terce, at the end of the third hour
12 noon	Nones
4.30 p.m.	Vespers (the evening service: Vesper is the evening star)
6 p.m.	Compline, at dusk (to 'complete' the Hours)

The Hours did not include confession which a monk made in chapter, that is, in the sight and hearing of the abbot and all the brethren of the convent. Mass (the Eucharist, or Holy Communion) was not one of the Hours, but was celebrated every Sunday. In between the Hours there were periods for work, a two-hour siesta after Nones, and the one meal of the day after Vespers.

A monk vowed to follow a disciplined, ascetic life, given over to prayer and humility. It was not necessary for him to become a priest – more precisely to receive any of the seven clerical orders ascending from *hostiarius* (doorkeeper) through exorcist, reader, acolyte, subdeacon and deacon to priest. The clerical order alone administered the sacraments – baptism, absolution, confirmation (the prerogative of the bishop), ordination of clerks (clergy), matrimony, communion, unction for the sick and dying, and the casting out of evil spirits. A monk, like a clerk, received the tonsure, the shaving of a circular patch of hair from the crown of the head, to signalise his intention to serve the Church, though not necessarily to be ordained; but the view of the popes of the 6th century was that the clerical order, serving the spiritual needs of the lay people of the diocese, under the authority of the bishop and his household (or 'familia') of clerks, was distinct and apart from the monastic order, which had left the world for the cloisters, the 'closed-in' places.

Practice, however, cut across theory. The clerical order inevitably discovered some of its most energetic, capable and saintly recruits in the monasteries; and the monk who was also a priest, and even a bishop, was by 600 coming to be the most significant type of ecclesiastical leader, whether in the cloister, around the diocese, or among the heathen. Such was the experience of Gregory I, the pope who concerned himself with the conversion of the English, and began it by sending Benedictine monks there. But before crossing to England, we should pause to notice not only the penetration of the Benedictine Rule through Italy and north of the Alps into Gaul (equal approximately to modern France), but also the flourishing at this time of a different strain of monasticism – which we conveniently call 'Celtic'. It laid less stress than did Benedict on the communal life and its spiritual benefits, and more on prayer, fasting, work and severe penances as

(Opposite) The Benedictine monks of Christ Church, Canterbury, portray themselves doing homage to St. Benedict, 'father of monks and leader' (early eleventh century).

Benedictine and Celtic monks

paths to perfection for the individual; more stress also on private study, scholarship and the advance of learning. Bobbio in Italy, Luxeuil in Gaul, and Bangor in Ireland were the most influential Celtic monasteries (and for them the tonsure was the shaving of all of the top of the head, with no fringe above the forehead). But neither the Benedictines nor the Celtic monks, for all their fundamental cloistered stability, could or would keep out of the secular world, let alone of heathen lands like England and Scotland.

The Anglo-Saxons Christianity had come to the province of Britain, as the official religion of the Roman Empire, in the 4th century A.D. Other faiths, like Mithraism, co-existed with it under the Romans; but missionaries like Kentigern and Patrick carried Christianity beyond Rome's northern British frontier into Scotland and over the sea to Ireland. In the 5th century, the western Roman Empire disintegrated and Britain, from the Forth to the Channel, was taken over by pagan migrants from Germany and the Low Countries, the Angles, Saxons and Jutes. The Anglo-Saxons – more accurately known as the Old English – drove British Christianity out of England, so that Cornwall, Wales, Strathclyde, Scotland beyond the Forth and Ireland were a chain of loosely connected, sometimes internecine sovereignties, chiefly Christian. The career of Columba, the Irish monk who created the great teaching and missionary abbey on the island of Hy, or Iona, reminds us that the victory of Christianity was not yet assured in the late 6th century – when he was striving to strengthen Christian teaching among the Scots, and convert their pagan neighbours, the Picts.

Meanwhile, Christianity had perished utterly from the lands of the English, a loose nexus of pagan kingdoms – Northumbria (stretching to the Forth), Lindsey, East Anglia, Mercia (the midland kingdom), Essex, Kent, Sussex and Wessex (the populous kingdom of the West Saxons). Their kings, who from time to time recognised one of their number as 'Bretwalda', or overlord, were the guardians of the pagan faith. To win over the kings and their courts to Christianity would be the key to the success of the monks who were to attempt the conversion of the English.

Paganism The heathen faith of the Old English left no written records of its own. Its character can only dimly be discerned, and it should not be identified too closely with the comparatively sophisticated and well documented paganism of the Scandinavian peoples a few centuries later. The Old English worshipped and made blood sacrifices to gods of cosmic power (Woden), war (Tiw) and thunder (Thunor) and a goddess of spring (Frig). English place-names, especially in the midlands and the south, reveal the cults of these deities as widely spread over the countryside: scores of names like Wednesbury (Staffordshire), Tuesley (Surrey), Thundersley (Essex), Harrow ('the shrine', Middlesex) and Wye ('the sanctuary', Kent). Their holy days provided much of the calendar the Christians were to introduce. The pagans began their year on 25 December and in April they revered the goddess Eostre.

Heathenism was deeply rooted in England when the first Christian missionaries to the English arrived. No evangelists from Ireland or Wales had tried to sap its vitality. Irish monks were preaching the gospel to continental pagans. Welsh monks stayed at home. Monks from Rome were the first to attempt the conversion of the English.

They had been sent by the great Pope Gregory I, who thought of England as a long-lost province of the Roman church, its territory to be recovered and its English souls to be saved by missionaries from the see of Peter and Paul, the capital of the church. Augustine, Prior of St. Andrew's monastery in Rome, led them to the Isle of Thanet in 597, where they met Ethelbert, King of Kent, whose help was to be essential to their mission. Ethelbert's wife, Bertha, daughter of the King of Paris, was a Christian and it was probably under her influence that he allowed Augustine and his monks to preach and make thousands of converts and to restore, as monasteries, some of the derelict old churches in Kent. Augustine founded the first English monasteries, St. Peter and St. Paul, and St. Augustine's, at Canterbury. It was at St. Peter and St. Paul that he was buried, after he and his monks had established, within ten years, Christianity as the official religion of the Kingdoms of Kent and Essex and the city of London. Augustine had made a slow start in carrying out Gregory's comprehensive plans for the Church in England. He had failed in negotiations to win the co-operation of the leaders of the British church in Wales, itself mainly monastic; but he and his monks had put down roots in Canterbury, Rochester, London and elsewhere which were not to be plucked up.

The mission of Augustine

Old English Monasticism

The century which followed Augustine's death saw the conversion to Christianity of each English kingdom. By 700 paganism was a defeated and dying religion throughout the British Isles. Yet the missionary monks had a long and exacting struggle. Augustine's follower Paulinus was consecrated bishop and accompanied Ethelbert's daughter when she went to marry King Edwin of Northumbria. In 627, Paulinus converted and baptised Edwin and his thegns. This followed a debate in which the chief priest, Coifi, denounced paganism as profitless, and an unnamed thegn compared the life of man with 'the swift flight of a lone sparrow through the banqueting hall. Inside there is a comforting fire. Outside the winter storms are raging. After a few moments of comfort, he vanishes from sight, from winter into winter. Likewise, we know nothing of what went before this life, nothing of what follows. Therefore, if this new teaching can reveal any more certain knowledge, it seems only right that we should follow it.'

Clearly, paganism could no longer satisfy, spiritually and intellectually, at least some of the English now that the conquest was over and the settled kingdoms were developing. So Paulinus and his monks made York once more what it had been in Roman times, the centre of

Paulinus in the north

northern Christianity. There was a swift pagan reaction in 632, when Penda, King of Mercia, led a virtual holy war against the northern Christians, and destroyed nearly all the achievements of Paulinus. Penda was ultimately defeated in 654, but his long reign had been a continuous, powerful heathen challenge to the Christian mission.

Throughout the century, its progress was slowed down in different regions of England by relapses into paganism by royal and noble converts, the determination of a wary king, like Redwald of East Anglia, to worship both the Holy Trinity and his old gods, Woden and Tiw, and the sloth of some communities to be moved by and feel curious about the gospel of the Christians – Sussex and the Isle of Wight the last of all.

Aidan at Lindisfarne   At the time when the mission begun by Augustine seemed to flag and fail, Edwin's successor Oswald invited the monks of Iona to send his people an evangelist, and they sent the Northumbrians Aidan, who inaugurated the growth of Celtic Christianity in England. Aidan set up his monastery and his see not in Oswald's capital but on the off-shore island of Lindisfarne. He and the Irish monks who came with him divided the year between periods of ritual fasting and penitence in the wooden huts which made up their abbey and long preaching and baptising tours across Northumbria. An admirer called Aidan 'indifferent to the dignity of a bishop, but influencing all men by his humility and devotion'. The Celtic monks felt less interest than had Gregory and Augustine in organising the church territorially in dioceses and parishes. Aidan saw the Northumbrians, as Diuma and Chad saw – after Penda's death – the Mercians and Cedd the East Saxons, as flocks to be fed in the primitive apostolic tradition. They founded many new monasteries as local centres for this work, and were keen to establish nunneries. It was Aidan who had the vision to persuade Hilda of Whitby to become a nun in England, not Gaul, and to establish her abbey on the Yorkshire coast.

The Celtic mission significantly strengthened and inspired Christianity in England at a critical time; but the differences between the spirit and organisation of Celtic Christianity based on Lindisfarne and its Roman counterpart based on Canterbury – extending to details (of great importance then) such as the correct way to consecrate a bishop, tonsure a monk, and calculate the date of Easter – might have split the youthful English church tragically, as contemporaries feared. The Synod of Whitby, convened by a King of Northumbria in 663, held under Hilda's roof, and intellectually dominated by a Northumbrian monk, Wilfrid, settled the issues. Wilfrid had studied five years in Italy and Gaul. He argued against resistance by the Christians of 'the two last islands of the ocean' to the authority of St. Peter, inherited by the Church of Rome, and obeyed, said Wilfrid, by all Christians elsewhere. King Oswy pronounced that the authority – not of St. Columba of Iona, but of St. Peter of Rome, to whom Jesus gave the keys of heaven – should be obeyed thenceforward. The Celts had lost the argument, and some retired to Iona. Others stayed, to make their contribution to the missionary work of the last decades of the century – Fursa in East Anglia, Maildubh who founded Malmesbury Abbey, and above all Cuthbert of Lindisfarne.

Cuthbert, Wilfrid and their contemporary Theodore of Tarsus were the most influential monks of the era which followed the Synod of Whitby. Cuthbert was English, but was trained as a novice at Melrose Abbey, a stronghold of Celtic monasticism. As a monk at Ripon, then back to Melrose as Prior, and as Prior of Lindisfarne, he deeply affected the barbarous society of Northumbria by his ascetic life, his miracles and his long and enterprising journeys around Northumbria to preach, baptise and administer the sacraments. After his death, his body became the most sacred relic of the church in the north. Yet Cuthbert accepted Roman ways, the overall authority in England of the Archbishop of Canterbury and the need for the close and detailed administration of a diocese by its bishop. As a bishop, at the end of his days, Cuthbert, in contrast to Aidan before him, travelled about with a household retinue large enough to sustain his episcopal dignity and the administration of his diocese. This monk, who once had been a shepherd, became the patron saint of the north of England and the Scottish Borders as surely as St. James in Spain or St. Denis in France.

Wilfrid and Theodore

Wilfrid's abilities, and the favour he won at the royal court made him, after the Synod of Whitby, the most powerful churchman in Northumbria. He founded Hexham Abbey on a site given him by Queen Ethelthryth and became protector of most of the northern monasteries; but though ascetic, he was not cloistered. He acquired wide landed estates, built up a military retinue, schooled in his household both the monks and the warriors of the future and supervised the whole life of the northern church from his see of York. By encouraging the Queen to become a nun at Coldingham, he brought upon himself the anger of King Ecgfrith, who expelled him from Northumbria in 677, with the support of Archbishop Theodore of Canterbury. The rest of Wilfrid's strenuous and contentious life was devoted to his efforts to recover his lost position in Northumbria. He failed, though he was able to come back at times to his monasteries of Hexham and Ripon; but his exile and his journeys across Europe to appeal to the Pope bore their own rich fruit. He founded many monasteries in Mercia, began the conversion of the pagans of the Isle of Wight and the Netherlands, and introduced the Rule of St. Benedict to the English monastic system.

Wilfrid's fall in 677 gave Archbishop Theodore the opportunity to reorganise the northern church. Theodore, a Greek monk from Syria, had been sent by the Pope to become Archbishop of Canterbury in 669. Scholar, philosopher and legist, his concern was less with monasticism than with organising afresh and unifying the English church as a whole, the creation of new dioceses so that England had seventeen in all, and the holding of national Synods to legislate on church order and discipline, on Christian marriage, and against heathen practices. Theodore provided the framework in which English church leaders, so many of them monks at this time, could work. His vision was that of English Christendom under the undivided authority of the Archbishop of Canterbury, himself the servant of the Pope. He would have deplored the impairing of the unity of the church by the creation in 735, half a century after his death, of the separate Archbishopric of York.

English monks overseas

The vitality of English monasticism at this time may be argued from its missionary efforts overseas. England's neighbours, the Franks of Gaul, were Christians. Beyond the Rhine, in Germany and the Netherlands, were pagan tribes and kingdoms. A succession of English monks, inspired at the start by Wilfrid, worked among these heathens between 690 and 750. Willibrord, a monk of Ripon, who had studied in Irish monasteries, and eleven of his brethren (making an apostolic Twelve in all) preached with some success to the Frisians around Utrecht, and, in vain, to the Danes. At the close of a life in which he often saw resurgent pagans burn his churches and expel his priests and was all but slain for baptising Christians in the heathen holy spring on Heligoland, he had firmly set up Utrecht as a great missionary archbishopric.

His disciple Boniface was a West Saxon of noble birth who from childhood wished to live under the Benedictine Rule and become a scholar. Years of study at Exeter, Nursling in Hampshire, and Utrecht – where he learned the language and customs of the Germans – prepared him for consecration as a bishop at Rome, to convert the heathen east of the Rhine, in Hesse, Thuringia and Bavaria. The hewing down of the sacred oak of Woden in Hesse and the founding of the abbey of Fulda – which became the greatest in Germany – and the abbey of Bischofsheim – for men and women, which Leofgyth, a nun from Wimborne, came out to rule for him – epitomised his achievements. He helped to reform the Frankish church and became Archbishop of Mainz.

Willibald in Frisia, Willehad, Bishop of Bremen, among the pagans of the Weser and Elbe estuaries, and many other English monks and nuns followed in Boniface's steps. They drew significantly on the learning and evangelical zeal of the Celtic church, were well supplied with recruits from English abbeys, made pilgrimages to Rome and even Jerusalem and formed strong bonds with the Frankish monarchy. For some, including Boniface, there was the ultimate palm of martyrdom by the sword of the unconverted. Their work was the true beginning of the conversion of the Germanic peoples beyond the Rhine.

The life of monks and nuns

The English church's development through the 7th century, at first hesitant and faltering, then confident and successful, had been chiefly the work of monks. Secular clergy – priests who had not taken the strict monastic vows of religion – played a lesser part. Missionary zeal won the more ground because it set in motion a popular drive towards the monastic way of life, to some extent led by but not restricted to the Old English upper classes.

Guthlac, the warrior and hunter who left the fashionable world to start a centre of monastic life in the desolate demon-haunted fens of Crowland was a nobleman; but Cuthbert was a shepherd boy and Willibrord, who preached to the continental pagans, was a ploughman. For every great founder whom history records – from Benedict Biscop, with his foundations at Wearmouth and Jarrow in the north-east, to Aldhelm at Malmesbury, Bradford-on-Avon and Frome in the south-west – there were hundreds who came in to lead a disciplined, ascetic and contemplative life under his rule. The energy of individual founders and early abbots in sending out groups of monks to plant new houses elsewhere produced families of monasteries, like that of Medeshamstede (later Peterborough), whose daughter houses stretched from the east midlands – at Breedon in Leicestershire and Brixworth, Northamptonshire, where the church is the largest surviving Old English building of the 7th and 8th centuries – to Bermondsey and Woking in Surrey and Hoo in Kent.

Probably no houses for nuns alone were founded at this time: but England became renowned for the devoutness and scholarship of its double monasteries for men and women, each under the rule of an

The Guthlac Roll, a vellum roll containing a series of drawings, in roundels, illustrating the life of St Guthlac, who became an anchorite on the island of Crowland, in the Lincolnshire marshes, in A.D. 699. Executed at Crowland Abbey at the end of the twelfth century.

21

abbess, like Hilda's Whitby, the Ely of Queen Ethelthryth, and the houses founded by the Mercian royal sisters, Much Wenlock by Mildburg, and Minster-in-Thanet by Mildthryth; and Bardney, Barking, Coldingham, Repton and Wimborne. The double monasteries as institutions were not to survive the Danish invasions of the 9th century, and the part of women in the evolution of English monasticism was never again to be so influential and learned.

English learning and education in the two centuries after the Synod of Whitby present us with a picture vivid in some places, shadowy in most; but the monasteries can confidently be identified as their principal seat. Theodore and his friend, the North African Abbot Hadrian, who came with him to England, created in the Canterbury monasteries, including the cathedral priory, a school of higher learning which embraced theology, the interpretation of the scriptures, law, science and music – and which had no equal across the sea in Gaul. Latin was the language of scholarship, but studies in Greek also throve in Canterbury. Aldhelm of Malmesbury, poet, letter-writer and moralist, the cleverest and best educated scholar of his time, was a Canterbury product. The far north was scholarship's other luminous centre, fed by the Irish learned tradition, with its highly wrought Latin style and noble handwritings, which influenced Canterbury and Aldhelm.

However, the south also fed the north. The famous Gospel Book created by Eadfrith, Bishop of Lindisfarne from 678 to 721, is, as a work of art – its script, its figure-drawing, above all the complex decoration of the manuscript – more Old English than Celtic and reflects some influences from Canterbury. Benedict Biscop had brought back from his four continental journeys to his own northern foundations not only saints' relics and fine church ornaments, but also the books to create the superb libraries at Wearmouth and Jarrow. The scholarly achievement of Bede of Jarrow, who never went south to York, was made possible by Benedict's libraries. Bede, drawing on his studies of ancient writers and his impressive power to collate oral reminiscences, folk tradition, letters and other documentary evidence, completed in 731 the first great interpretation of English history and of the Conversion – *The Ecclesiastical History of the English Nation*. His many works were keenly studied at York which, in the 8th century, academically outshone Canterbury. The monk Alcuin, poet, lawyer and theologian, left York in mid-career to preside over the palace school and the intellectual life of the court of the Frankish Emperor Charlemagne and to create at Tours, where he was made Abbot of St. Martin's, a new learned centre on the continent.

Minsters　　The Old English churches from 597, when Augustine landed, to 865, when the Danes invaded the land in great strength, had been inspired, led and in part dominated by the monks – in the work of conversion, the founding of cathedrals, monasteries and lesser churches in towns and country, the organising and managing of the dioceses, and in education, learning and the arts.

The beginning of St. Matthew's Gospel in the Latin (Vulgate) manuscripts of the Gospels written and illuminated at Lindisfarne, Northumbria, about A.D. 698.

'Minster', the Old English word for 'monastery', was also the name for the mother-church of such a group of village churches and preaching crosses as Minster Lovell headed in the Windrush Valley of Oxfordshire. Such minsters may have been convents of monks who were the spiritual pastors of the rural communities around them; or they may have been not strictly monasteries but the headquarters of a small community of secular priests or 'clerks'. How far a parochial

The beginning of Book IV, of the *Ecclesiastical History of the English People* by the Venerable Bede (died 735) from a manuscript probably written in southern England in the later eighth century.

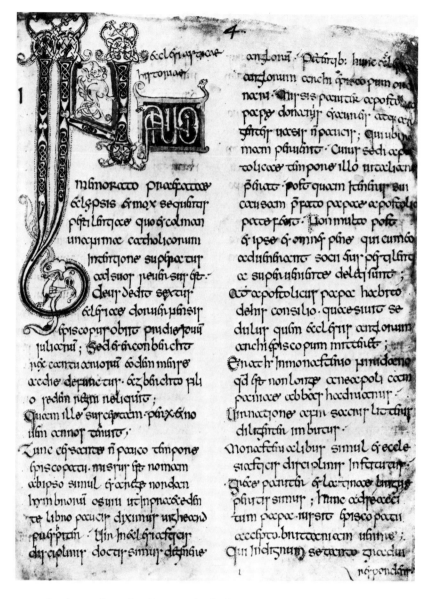

organisation of each diocese had developed by the 9th century, towards the fully evolved system we can trace in the 13th century, can never be known. Most of the evidence from this early era – vividly as we can describe it as a golden age of monasticism – has failed to survive. Much of it was clearly destroyed in the invasions of England by the pagan warriors who were now crossing the seas from Norway and Denmark.

The attack from Norway and Denmark

Almost the first Vikings to attack England were the Norse who sacked Lindisfarne in 793 and Jarrow a year later. Succeeding raiders were increasingly lured by the wealth and relative vulnerability of the monasteries. The climax of their operations was the descent upon England of the Danish Great Army in 865, against which only Wessex under King Alfred was able to stand out. After twenty-one years of destructive war, Alfred achieved a peace treaty with the leaders of the Great Army, ceding them northern and eastern England, including London, and retaining the rest himself. Scandinavian intervention in and involvement with England – and all of the British Isles – was to continue, in one way and another, for the next two hundred years; but already by 886 the Old English Heptarchy – the system of tribal kingdoms – had been destroyed, leaving Wessex as its heir. Church organisation was in ruins in some dioceses, in the others badly damaged. Every English monastery had either perished, in what were now the lands of the Danes (the 'Danelaw'), or shrunk to a community of a few monks or secular priests, with education disrupted and scholarship nearly at a standstill.

The Age of Dunstan

By 900, the number of monks and nuns, learned and devout, was pathetically small, and dwindling. English monasticism was moribund, but it was not extinct. What survived was a glow in the embers, from which strenuous efforts might kindle a revival. Monasteries still had their buildings, their lands, jurisdiction and revenues or, in the Danelaw, at least the title to them. The bones of St. Cuthbert and Eadfrith's Gospel Book – rescued from Lindisfarne by fleeing monks – epitomise what else had been saved: veneration for the founder-saints, admiring memories of the piety and culture of the golden age. Other conditions favoured revival. The Danes who settled in the boroughs and shires of the north and east accepted Christianity. Little was recorded of their conversion, but it was swift. Alfred and his descendants, an all but unbroken line of able and energetic rulers, conquered the Danelaw piecemeal and founded a unitary Kingdom of the English, with many wars against fresh Viking invaders to come, but with an intermittent, loose hegemony over all of Great Britain.

Decline and revival

These West Saxon kings made an increasingly close alliance with their clergy as well as their earls and thegns and merchants. The survival of 10th-century and early 11th-century bell-towers and sculptures, fenestration and sections of walling in so many churches of mainly later construction testifies to the energetic church-building undertaken by the Old English propertied classes from Alfred's time on. Yet though Alfred and his queen created nunneries at Shaftesbury, Wilton and Winchester, it was not until the reign of his grandson Edmund that a sustained revival of monasticism began, when Dunstan, a Somerset monk of noble family and related to the King, restored in 943 a community of monks and the Benedictine rule to Glastonbury, home of the most sacred relic in Wessex and a magnet for pilgrims from as far away as Ireland.

Abbots, archbishops and kings

During the fifty years following the return of the monks to Glastonbury, Dunstan and his well-connected associates, Ethelwold of Winchester and the Dane Oswald, brought monasticism back to full-blooded life and, in doing so, directed the whole course of the English church. Together they controlled the major dioceses – Canterbury, York, London, Winchester and Worcester. The support, sometimes the guidance of successive kings and their queens, was indispensable. King Edred sent Ethelwold to restore the decayed Abbey of Abingdon. Austere, severe but compassionate, musical and a craftsman of skill, Ethelwold brought monks from Abingdon to the Old and New Minsters of Westminster, and recreated in the Danelaw the fenland abbeys of Peterborough, Ely, Ramsey, Thorney and Crowland, recovering and increasing their vast endowments in land. His disciples reformed St. Albans and founded Eynsham. Oswald planted his monasteries in the west: at Westbury, Winchcombe, Pershore and Deerhurst; and he introduced monks into the cathedral at Worcester. The leadership was always Dunstan's: the statesman among the three, Archbishop of Canterbury, adviser of kings, he has the ultimate credit for the return of the monks to Malmesbury and Bath, Cerne and Sherborne, Christ Church and St. Augustine's at Canterbury, and Westminster.

St. Dunstan at Christ's feet from a contemporary drawing ascribed to Dunstan himself.

By the middle of the 11th century, England had about fifty monasteries and twelve nunneries, including new foundations like Burton-on-Trent, St. Benet's Holme and Coventry. Almost all were large and richly endowed with land: small, unprosperous houses like Athelney and Buckfast were few. Though nearly all the religious houses were in the southern half of the kingdom, they possessed about one-sixth of the land in England.

No king collaborated more closely with Dunstan, Ethelwold and Oswald than the devout and talented Edgar, great-grandson of Alfred; none was more generous with gifts of land to endow their monasteries. The three bishops and the king decided that a code should be drawn up embodying a common pattern of life for all English monasteries to follow, under the patronage and supervision of the king and queen. The ancient Rule of St. Benedict was not precise enough to prevent local custom, local divergence, even eccentricity developing in ebullient or merely remote centres.

The Regularis Concordia

It was in or about 970 that the English bishops, abbots and abbesses met with Edgar at his capital of Winchester and agreed on the *Regularis Concordia* – 'the monastic concord of the monks and nuns of the English nation' – originally drafted by Ethelwold. The *Concordia* was influenced by ideas which had come to England from reformed abbeys in the Frankish lands, especially Fleury in Lorraine and St. Peter's, Ghent, in Flanders, with which refounded English abbeys already had close links. The ideals of the *Concordia* were not those of early Celtic and Northumbrian monasticism. The monk was no longer envisaged as one 'called' to surrender himself wholly to God under the teaching of an inspired and saintly leader. The convent was to be a community which together brought the clerical life to perfection and strengthened the Church Militant. Its paramount task was the observance of the liturgy – with increasingly elaborate vocal prayer and chant – and intercessions for the living and the departed. The lay support and munificence enjoyed by the revived monasteries of Dunstan's time grew out of deep faith in the efficacy of the prayers of monks for the souls of benefactors and their families. Other work was secondary (it should exclude agricultural work on monastic lands, which fell to the lay tenants), and should be done within the cloister: teaching the *oblates*, the children given by their parents to become monks – with other educational duties left to the secular clergy; writing and illuminating books; handicrafts and domestic services within the convent. The *Concordia* agreed on practices peculiar to England: lay people coming to Sunday Mass in the conventual church; bells pealing and monks processing through the streets on festal days; prayers for the king and queen at nearly every service. If a cathedral was served, like Winchester and Worcester, by a convent of monks instead of a chapter of canons, the monks were to elect a bishop, if possible from among themselves, and the bishop would continue to live as a monk. The idea binding together both the *Concordia* and its subscribers, the rulers of state and church in England, is that the pursuit and support of the monastic ideal are the path to salvation.

In the Abbey of Bath, on Whitsunday 973, Edgar – who was to die the next year, still only thirty-two – had himself ceremonially re-crowned, in the presence of the congregated abbots and abbesses, monks and nuns, of England. The service, the model for many succeeding coronations, symbolised with splendour the revival of

27

Cnut and Edward the Confessor

English monarchy and English monasticism, a century after the fiercest inroads of the Danes.

From Edgar's reign until 1066, when the Norman Conquest brought in profound changes, the history of the English monasteries was continuous, the quality of conventual life relatively pure, creative and immune to change. Dunstan in old age, with Edgar's sons showing less capacity for kingship than their father, saw Viking expeditions come back against England. From 980, raids built up into a war of conquest, which put the Dane Cnut on the English throne by 1016.

This long generation of warfare harmed several monasteries, tapped the wealth of all as contributors to the Danegeld, and drew one Abbot, Wulsig of Ramsey, in arms to his death in the Battle of Ashingdon; but the monastic system survived strongly into the peace imposed by Cnut. He, a Christian, son of the convert King Sven, won favour with the English clergy by his generosity. In Dunstan's time, most lands granted to the monasteries had been gifts of kings and of a small group of noblemen, like Aethelmaer at Cerne and Eynsham, and Brihtnoth at Ely. Acting in this tradition, Cnut revived the Abbey of Bury St. Edmunds (where his heathen precursors had martyred a King of the East Angles in 870), and made it one of the half-dozen most richly landed houses in England. This special royal concern with the monasteries remained strong with the last Old English kings. Edward the Confessor, who restored the line of Alfred to the throne in 1042, revived the royal foundation at Westminster as an abbey directly and peculiarly dependent on the king – a private monastery of the royal family, on contemporary French and German models. Harold had brought monks from Lorraine to start a house at Waltham long before his brief reign began with coronation at Westminster Abbey and ended on the battlefield of Hastings.

The last Old English monks

Eadmer, a monk writing in Norman times and looking back to the last generation of Old English monasticism, of which he had no personal memory, drew a famous sketch of Christ Church, the cathedral priory of Canterbury. The monks of Christ Church, he wrote, were backsliders from the disciplined life, extravagant, and too fond of riding and hawking and music. Eadmer's account, along with some vaguer criticisms from contemporaries of his, used to be taken as the starting-point for judging the monasteries under Cnut and Edward as ill-governed and slack. Christ Church probably was lax, and not alone in that; but the sound and comprehensive verdict is that English monasteries from 980 to 1066 kept their vitality and resisted both moral decay and the encroachment of greedy laymen upon their property and revenues.

For them, it was a time of vigorous construction – of churches, conventual buildings, manor houses, mills and barns; of fen drainage and scrub clearance. Their monastic buildings were less systematically and spaciously planned than those now being put up by Italian, French and Norman monks; but English monks were creating for their own liturgical purposes illuminated service books, embroidered vestments and hangings, silver and golden vessels and lamps, paintings and carvings superior in wealth and beauty to what could be seen in the greater continental abbeys. Musically, they were inventive, using the full body of the plain chant, and enhancing it with a system of polyphony, a combination of boys' trebles with male voices, and a generous use of organ music that were characteristically English.

In their writings, they reached out to the secular world beyond the monasteries. Before 700, English had become the first Western European vernacular to develop its own literature. From Dunstan's time it was a prime instrument of monastic instruction to lay society. Aelfric, monk of Cerne and later Eynsham, used English for pastoral letters to the clergy, for paraphrases of key books of the Old Testament, and treatises on the Bible and on the virtues of clerical celibacy – which he addressed to Sigeferth of Asthall, a thegn of the Oxfordshire countryside. Aelfric was no original thinker, and he stayed diffidently in his cloister; but he was, by the written word, a powerful and imaginative teacher. Many like him flourished in the late Old English monasteries, using English (and sometimes Latin) to compose homilies, denunciations of the sins of the age, scientific compendia, books on music and medicine, lives of the saints (including the 10th-century reformers), translations of the gospels, and the Anglo-Saxon Chronicle, the history of the times kept conscientiously by monks at Winchester, Abingdon and Worcester.

The Old English monks of the 11th century produced no leader of Dunstan's apostolic stature. They drifted apart from the movements in intellectual and monastic life now taking hold of western European society. But, up to 1066 and even beyond, they built, steadily and creatively, on the achievements of the English 10th century in cultural, liturgical and spiritual fields. As archbishops and bishops, they kept their grip on high place in the English church, and their weight and pull as counsellors of their king. Overseas, in Norway, Sweden and Denmark, where paganism flourished long after the conversion of kings, monks from England were the leading evangelists to the unbelievers and were still founding monasteries in Scandinavia in the 12th century.

The Normans and the Cluniacs

The Duchy of Normandy, lying along the southern coast of the Channel, had been wrested in 911 by pagan Vikings from the Kings of the West Franks. By the 11th century, its originally Norse and Danish ruling class was identifying itself far more with France than with Scandinavia and its dukes were militant Christians, with a keen loyalty to the Papacy.

Conquest and reorganisation

William the Conqueror inherited from his father a supremacy over the revived church in Normandy which led him to appoint the bishops

Lanfranc, Prior of Bec, Abbot of Caen, and Archbishop of Canterbury (1070–89), from a twelfth-century manuscript of his reply to Berengar of Tours.

and abbots of his choice and, in combination with his own force of character, to act more as the ally than the servant of the Pope. William was personally pious and austere, an enthusiast for papal ideas on church reform, a patron of the intellectually brilliant and growing Norman monasteries of Bec, Fécamp and Jumièges, and the founder, with his duchess, of the great double monastery of Caen. He and the Archbishop of Canterbury whom he brought back to England from Caen, the Abbot Lanfranc (an Italian who had professed canon law at Pavia and theology at the distinguished Schools of Tours and Avranches before founding his own remarkable school of higher studies at Bec) governed the church in conquered England not as oppressors but as strict reformers, moving along courses acceptable at Rome. William gave thanks for his victory of Hastings by founding the rich Battle Abbey, its high altar said to cover the spot where King Harold had been killed, and his Yorkshire foundation of Selby Abbey was his contribution to monastic revival in the northern lands which he found so resistant to his rule.

But the pace at which major new abbeys were created under William and his son King William Rufus – between 1066 and 1100 – was not swift by the standards to be set in the next century. Some Norman barons created monasteries in provincial towns: Shrewsbury (the foundation of Earl Roger Montgomery), Chester, Colchester and Lewes. The Norman abbot of the little house at Cranborne re-settled most of his monks at Tewkesbury. Scores of minor houses were established in this early Norman period. Many were cells of continental monasteries which the new Norman lords in England wished to enrich with lands they had acquired as rewards from the Conqueror. Edward the Confessor had inaugurated the practice with his gifts to Norman houses.

Perhaps the most significant impact of William and Lanfranc on the English church was the replacement by Normans and Frenchmen of nearly all its native English bishops and abbots, some when they were deposed by the reforming archbishop, most when they died or retired. By 1100 the English monasteries were ruled by foreigners speaking French, with at best lukewarm sympathies for the history, language and traditions of the Anglo-Saxon monks. Yet the new abbots and priors and other officials could only attain efficiency by consulting their native-born monks; and for Edward the Confessor – who had lived, an exile, at the Norman court in his earlier years – all the Normans had a veneration which helped to protect the English elements in monasticism. Lanfranc removed from the calendar the names of many of the English saints whose cults in the older monasteries he regarded as unmerited; but his reorganisation of the dioceses led him to make wider use of an especially English practice. A few English cathedrals had been monastic before 1066. Under the Normans there were soon ten – Canterbury, Winchester, Worcester, Rochester, Durham, Norwich, Ely, Bath (co-cathedral with Wells), Coventry (co-cathedral with Lichfield) and Carlisle. Only nine English bishops and their cathedrals had chapters of secular canons – York, London, Lincoln, Lichfield, Wells, Salisbury, Exeter, Chichester, and Hereford. The close links of English monasticism with the government of the Church were thus reinforced.

Two English monks, Wulfstan, Bishop of Worcester, and his neighbour, Abbot Aethelwig of Evesham, made it their purpose from the start to support William the Conqueror, for the protection and benefit of their monks and their fellow-countrymen of the west

Revival in the north

31

midland shires. Under these two, Old English monasticism, at Worcester, Evesham, Winchcombe and Pershore, had a final flowering, spiritual and cultural, in the generation after 1066. To Evesham came many refugees from William's harrying of the rebellious north and south-west, for the food and shelter Aelthelwig would provide.

With them was one of William's Norman knights, Reinfrid, who, on campaign in Yorkshire, had been deeply stirred by the ruinous desolation of Hilda's long abandoned abbey at Whitby. North of the Humber, indeed, there had been no monastic revival from the total destruction left by the Vikings in the 9th century, except that in 995 a cathedral for the north-east, for a time monastic, and a shrine for Cuthbert's bones had been erected on the high bluff round which the River Wear curls at Durham. At Evesham, Reinfrid took his monastic vows before Aethelwig and met a fellow-monk, Aldwin of Winchcombe, who had been inspired by reading Bede to plan a pilgrimage to Cuthbert's tomb, and to lead the life of a hermit in the north. In 1074, Reinfrid, Aldwin and another Evesham monk travelled north on foot, with a donkey to carry their books and vestments. From York to Monkchester (later Newcastle) on the Tyne, they visited no monastery which was not a ruin. Though their original purpose had been to visit shrines and then settle down to a life of solitude and privation, they and their helpers, within ten years, had restored monasticism to Wearmouth, Jarrow and Whitby, and set up the important Abbey of St. Mary's at York, lying just west of the Minster. Aldwin became prior to a community of monks whom the Norman Bishop of Durham, with papal encouragement, brought to Durham to serve the cathedral in perpetuity.

One of these monks of Durham cathedral priory was Turgot, an Anglo-Dane who had been a prisoner-of-war of the Conqueror, escaped overseas from Lincoln castle, and taught sacred music at the royal court of Norway. Turgot succeeded Aldwin as prior, played a major part in the early stages of the construction of the great Norman cathedral at Durham, and formed a close relationship with St. Margaret of Scotland and the reform movement there. By 1100, northern monasticism, its memory so long kept fresh in Bede's pages, had risen, full of vitality, from its ashes.

Cluny and her daughters The monastery the Norman kings most venerated was in neither Normandy nor England, but was Cluny in Burgundy, on a main pilgrim route to Rome. The monks of Cluny, from the foundation of their house by Duke William of Aquitaine in 910, were exempt from the authority of their local bishop, and directly dependent on the Pope. Cluniac monasticism was distinguished by its overriding emphasis on the liturgy. The time given to the singing of the Office, the number of daily psalms and prayers, the elaborate ceremonies and the intercessions and masses and public almsgivings by the monks were increased far beyond what was usual elsewhere. Under a line of outstanding abbots – culminating in the long reign of St. Hugh of Cluny, from 1049 to 1109, the contemporary of the early Norman kings – Cluny gave up all educational, intellectual and artistic pursuits for the sake of its liturgy. The abbey has been called 'a world in itself, given wholly to the worship of God in a setting of incomparable splendour and untouched by secular intrigue'.

Yet Cluny was by no means isolated. In the 10th century she spread widely her ideas on the principles of monastic liturgy, and profoundly affected Fleury and Ghent, and through them Dunstan, Oswald and their circle, and the *Regularis Concordia*. In the 11th century, Cluny was building up her own monastic Order. Many monasteries founded by Cluniac monks or reformed on Cluniac lines became her daughter-houses, under the authority and discipline of her abbot the sole abbot of the Cluniac Order, who appointed all its priors. Such centralisation, hard to implement in practice, was a fundamental weakness. Cluny was important for the example she set, not the control she tried to exercise.

William I asked St. Hugh – without success – to send him twelve of the holiest Cluniac monks to reorganise the church in his newly conquered realm. William II, a foe to priests and a mocker of God, was generous in England to the Cluniacs alone. His brother Henry I staffed his great royal foundation of Reading Abbey with monks drawn from Cluny, though Reading did not come into the Cluniac Order, and paid for the completion of the vast nave of Cluny Abbey Church itself. Henry's daughter Matilda sent Cluny a big bell cast in an English foundry. Her rival for the English throne, Stephen, founded a Cluniac priory at Faversham in Kent as a burial-place for himself and his family, emphasising the belief in the Cluniacs as ferrymen of departed souls – not least on the 2nd of November, All Souls Day, a feast of the Church instituted by the Cluniacs as a fit sequel to All Saints Day.

The first Cluniac priory had been Lewes, founded by the Conqueror's baronial friend William Warenne after a visit to Cluny, when he and his wife Gundred had been overwhelmed by the beauties of the liturgy and the sumptuous hospitality. (Their contemporary, St. Peter Damian, deploring the high standard of the food and wine served there, had been told by St. Hugh that, without it, the monks would not have the sustenance to meet the demands of almost perpetual worship, standing and kneeling night and day in the choir.)

However, the Cluniac Order hardly throve in England. Its only centre to match Lewes in importance and wealth was Bermondsey Priory, founded by the London merchant Alwin Child about 1087 and handsomely enriched by William Rufus, who set a fashion for endowing it. Lewes and Bermondsey were the sources from which Anglo-Norman noble families drew monks to set up priories at Thetford and Castle Acre in Norfolk, Pontefract in Yorkshire, the refounded Wenlock in Shropshire, and Dudley, Gervase Paganel's elegant house under the frowning height of the Worcestershire castle from which he ran his lucrative iron forges, timber plantations and swine-runs in the rustic heart of the midlands. Most of the thirty-six

English Cluniac priories either had small beginnings and came to little, or were cells of priories across the sea in Normandy which took the revenues but did nothing for their development. As a youth, Anselm, Lanfranc's successor, decided to take monastic vows but not at Cluny, because there the monks prayed and chanted too long, leaving no time for studies and the pursuits of the mind. Newer forms of monasticism were to have a strong appeal in 12th-century England. By the time King Stephen was buried at Faversham in 1154, the Cluniac Order, as a growing concern, had shot its bolt.

The Cistercian Monks

Cîteaux and Bernard of Clairvaux

The new Order which was to have the deepest influence on the society of England, as of Scotland and almost every other Catholic country, was that of the white monks or Cistercians. They wore a white habit with a black apron or scapular over it, and their first house, Cîteaux (*Cistercium*) in Burgundy, was founded in 1098 by a group of monks who wished not to start a new Order but to return to the simplicity and austerity of early Benedictine monasticism. An Englishman, Stephen Harding, second Abbot of Cîteaux from 1109 to 1133, took the lead in framing the ideals of Cistercianism, and Bernard of Clairvaux, son of a French knight, one of the most influential preachers and writers of the medieval church, was the main force in expanding the Order, so that by 1200 it had 500 abbeys in Europe (and 750 by the fifteenth century). The central principle was uniformity of observance within the Order, achieved through an annual general chapter of all the abbots, meeting at Cîteaux to legislate for the white monks as a whole; and through the regular visitation of every monastery by the abbot of the house from which it had been founded. Thus the Cistercian Order was organised as one family tree, with every house branching off from the main stem, Cîteaux. One branch was Bernard's own Abbey of Clairvaux, from which half the Order's houses ultimately derived their foundation. Central Cistercian efficiency was always meant to go hand in hand with a great measure of local autonomy.

Rievaulx and Fountains

The first Cistercians in England settled at Waverley in Surrey in 1128, but it was the bringing over of thirty white monks by a famous noble monastic founder, Walter Espec, to Rievaulx in the Rye Valley in Yorkshire in 1132 which awoke the English enthusiastically to the Cistercian blend of puritanism and compassion. The first monks of Rievaulx, led by an Englishman, William, persuaded by their example a group of thirteen frustrated reformers at York to leave their abbey of St. Mary's for the desolate valley of the Skell, where Archbishop Thurstan of York, who had taken them under his wing, gave them a riverside site, an extensive tract of waste land fed by pure springs. Here they built rough huts and set up the Cistercian house of 'St. Mary at the Springs'. This was the origin of Fountains Abbey which, like Rievaulx, conformed to the second great principle of the white monks, that they should dwell 'remote from the comings and goings of the people', out in the wilderness. The bare and empty valleys of the Rye and Skell were deserts which the Cistercians were to make blossom like the rose; but that was not foreseen in the 1130s.

The white monks renounced all wealth, all luxury. They refused to follow the Benedictine practice of accepting gifts of populous and cultivated manors; or monopoly rights over local law-courts, fairs, mills, fisheries or bakeries; or the rights to the patronage, tithes, altar dues and burial fees of parish churches – or any such sources of revenue in cash and kind drawn from the society they had left in seach of God. A gift of 'desert' land, hitherto uncultivated, from which the convent could scratch a merc subsistence, was enough. They denied themselves cloaks, fur-lined boots, shirts, drawers, warm bedclothes and combs for the hair, just as they denied their abbey churches stained glass for the windows, gold and jewelled vessels for the altar, silk and embroidery and fine linen for vestments and hangings, and human and animal figures in their stone carvings. Their idea of the *Opus Dei* was the reverse of the Cluniac: no processions, no litanies, little chanting and few psalms, the simplest of ceremonial, no special services for saints' days. The cult of the local saint and his relics were not for them: all their abbeys were dedicated to St. Mary the Virgin.

The Cistercians in the wilds

Yet Cistercian puritanism was not negative. Its aim was to cut off the monk from all worldly distractions and give him the time, the peace and the discipline to pursue in equal measure and with equal zeal the three activities to which St. Benedict had directed him – not only the *Opus Dei*, but also hard work and the study of the scriptures, linked with private prayers. His spiritual life was to be devotional and meditative, not fired by the intellectual ambitions of theological exploration. Cistercian determination to shear away all ties with the world led them to decide against setting up schools for oblate children. No youth was accepted as a novice under the age of sixteen, and the noviciate was a full, exacting twelve months. Cistercian success in securing exemption from visitation by the local bishop was another means of keeping 'the world' at bay.

Bernard of Clairvaux, Ailred, Abbot of Rievaulx, and other early Cistercian leaders won for their Order admiration, recruits and gifts by planning a communal life in the wilderness not only austere and selfless but also egalitarian: the abbot strove to live more frugally than his monks and, unlike Benedictine abbots, had hardly any hierarchy of officials. Above all, they offered the monk the chance of a close and mystical union with God. For them – and their publicity, in sermons, books and conversation, in the world they were abandoning, was superb – the desert is the place where the Holy Spirit enlightens and comforts the soul. 'You will find in the woods something you never find in books', wrote Bernard in one of his letters. 'Stones and trees will teach you a lesson you never heard from masters in school. Honey can be drawn from the rock, oil from the hardest stone.'

The key to the history of England and most European countries in the 12th century is the growth of population and the associated drive to bring under cultivation and exploitation vast areas of forest, heath, marsh and flooded coastland untouched in Roman times and thereafter. This drive had begun earlier in the middle ages: it was still incomplete in the 13th century; but the era of St. Bernard was a turning-point. It is hard to take this as a coincidence. Deep down, Bernard probably sensed (as many of his secular contemporaries were beginning to grasp), that the wilderness held a potential new world. (It was to be German Cistercians who created the celebrated Golden Meadows by draining Thuringian bogs, and who invented the greenhouse there.)

Endowing a Cistercian monastery was fairly easy. Archbishop Thurstan, Dean Hugh of York, and many other rich clerics, noblemen and merchants – and simpler folk – of northern England were generous in their grants of undeveloped land. Within a generation, by 1153, Rievaulx and Fountains had grown to great size, and from them had been founded thirty daughter-houses, stretching up to Kinloss, Melrose and Dundrennan in Scotland, down through their many houses in Yorkshire (like Kirkstall and Meaux), Lincolnshire (where Ailred established Revesby in a marshy wilderness) and Suffolk, to Woburn in Bedfordshire.

In 1147 two recent major foundations were added (Furness, where the Lancashire monastic revival began in 1127; and Byland in Yorkshire) with a dozen lesser houses, when the Pope incorporated into the Cistercian Order the Grey Monks who had originated at Savigny in Normandy. Although the general chapter of the Order had said in 1152 that there must be no new foundations, the Cistercian abbeys of England and Wales went on increasing in number and there were over one hundred by the end of the 12th century. In South Wales, Anglo-Norman penetration had brought in its wake several Benedictine settlements; but Central and North Wales had hardly any monasteries until successive native princes – chiefly the Lord Rhys in the 12th century and Llywelyn the Great in the 13th – established the Cistercians at Whitland and Strata Florida, Aberconwy, Cymmer, Valle Crucis and elsewhere. As at Rievaulx, Fountains, Kirkstall and other Yorkshire sites, the white monks in Wales set most of their abbeys in valleys flanked by valuable pasture on the moors and hills. When monks came direct from Cîteaux in 1204 to found Beaulieu Abbey in the Hampshire forest for King John, it was not the last Cistercian foundation in England and Wales; but it brought to a close three-quarters of a century of intensive growth.

Lay brothers Such growth depended on changes introduced by the Cistercians into monastic organisation. The Benedictines lived amid the 'world' of estate bailiffs, free tenants and villeins who produced from the monastic lands the revenues on which their Order throve; but the Cistercians brought with them into the 'wilderness' great numbers of lay brothers (*conversi*) of their Order to build for them, grow their food and tend their flocks and herds. It was expected that lay brothers should be illiterate, and books were forbidden them so that they should remain in that state. They worshipped in the abbey church, but only at the start and finish of the working day. Otherwise the Hours for them consisted of brief and familiar prayers said at their work, and they received communion only seven times a year. As Cistercian properties grew, a way had to be found of running the remoter holdings without breaking Cistercian principles by renting them to tenants; and so they set up distant centres of agrarian management called *granges*. Each grange, in theory, had to be within a day's ride of its abbey, though some were more far-flung. The grange did not resemble a Benedictine cell, which was a 'mini-priory' with resident monks, but was a large farmstead (with a small oratory), staffed only by lay brothers.

Enthusiasm for the Cistercians caused some benefactors to give them lands which were hardly in desert places; and their desire to retain such endowments often led them to *make* them deserted, by evicting tenants and pulling down houses and even parish churches. When the Earl of Lincoln, William Roumare, endowed Revesby Abbey in 1142, the Cistercians destroyed three villages, only seven of the peasants accepting the offer of land elsewhere. Their very principles were driving the Cistercians to becoming enclosing landlords; and their exemption from paying tithes and the attractions of their Order for thousands of lay brethren who came to serve it ensured them the resources and man-power to exploit their greatest material asset – the sheep pastures of Yorkshire, Lincolnshire and Wales. Here they reared great flocks which made the most important contributions to England's chief export trade, wool and wool-fells for the weavers of Flanders and Florence, in the 13th century. The Cistercians were not the only large-scale sheep farmers in Britain, even among the religious orders. The nuns of Minchinhampton, for instance, were grazing two thousand sheep in Gloucestershire some years before the first white monks reached England. Many Benedictine abbots, many bishops, deans and chapters, and earls and barons built up large flocks; but when the Cistercians arrived, they took the lead and set the pace. In 1193, when the English government had to raise a heavy national tax to ransom King Richard the Lion Heart out of captivity in the hands of the German Emperor, the Cistercians collectively paid their share in wool – one year's yield.

During the 13th century, as the Cistercian estates were more enterprisingly exploited, the lay brothers began to decline in number and the practice of degrading villages into granges ceased. The Cistercians were acquiring and drawing profits from types of property forbidden to them by Stephen Harding and St. Bernard – villages, hamlets, mills, churches, tithes, and the proceeds of justice. They came more and more to resemble Benedictine landlords, tending to be set apart only by their concentration on producing wool and fleeces, sheepskin for parchment, ewes' milk and cheese (mutton being

White monks and their sheep

37

regarded as no more than a secondary product). Cistercianism was at first a puritanical retreat from the world. Its popularity among all classes, high and low, and the failure of its abbots to recruit novices selectively brought it too many disciples, too much potentially valuable property, and it could not escape the world it had renounced. When its earliest makeshift hutments came to be replaced by buildings in stone, the renunciation of architectural ornament and conscious elegance cleared the way for the construction of churches and cloisters of a severe beauty.

Ailred of Rievaulx   The nature of 12th-century Cistercian life can best be apprehended from the warm-hearted biography of Ailred of Rievaulx written by one of his monks, Walter Daniel. Ailred came from a family of hereditary priests of Hexham (in his own day, marriage among the secular clergy, under reforming pressure, was on the wane). He became steward at the court of David, King of Scots; but, like his friend Waldef, the Scots king's stepson, and other members of the northern ruling class, Ailred, coming back from a mission to York for his royal master, found the magnetism of the life at Rievaulx irresistible. Riding down into the valley, he presented himself at the abbey gate, and was admitted as a novice. Waldef was sent to be the first Abbot of Melrose, Ailred to be the first at Revesby. He came back to Rievaulx as Abbot in 1147, and in twenty years had developed it into a community of six hundred members. Some were highly born and, like him, had turned their backs on exalted positions and glittering prospects. Most were simple and uneducated. The abbey church on feast days, writes Walter Daniel, was packed with monks as tightly as a hive with bees, or a thronging heavenly choir with angels. It was Ailred's patience and compassion towards the weak, the poor and the spiritually afflicted which drew so many novices to Rievaulx. His concern was to lead them to a life of fruitful work, prayer and discipline, bringing them peace of mind and spirit in an atmosphere of charity and friendship. His duties often took him away from Rievaulx, far out indeed into the world, on visits to the daughter-abbeys of Rievaulx in Scotland, Yorkshire and the south, and annually across the sea on the way to and from the general chapter at Cîteaux. Ailred was a public figure, friendly with the Scots kings and Henry II of England, a sought-after arbiter in monastic disputes, like the suit about jurisdiction over Byland Abbey between Savigny and Furness. He preached at Westminster for his kinsman the Abbot, when the bones of Edward the Confessor were translated to their new shrine, and he wrote the standard life of Edward. Ailred published many sermons, and books on *Charity* (at St. Bernard's request), *Spiritual Friendship* and *The Soul*. Though not an important theologian, he wrote for the guidance of others on personal spiritual experience and the approach of the individual soul to God. His younger and intellectually more lively monks formed around him a circle to study and discuss the classics, especially Cicero, the Fathers of the Church, the legend of King Arthur. When he died in 1167, after years of pain from gout and gallstones – his sick bay at Rievaulx was a shed, with one compartment for his pallet bed, the other for his oratory, outside the abbey infirmary – he had created a living ideal for English Cistercians to follow: 'friendship's child: his whole concern to love and be loved', as Walter Daniel said.

The Carthusians

An Order which had germinated a few years before Cîteaux was founded but was slow to enter England was that of the Poor Brothers of God of the Charterhouse, the Carthusians. In 1084, St. Bruno, a canon of Rheims and a brilliant teacher in the cathedral school there, decided, with six friends, to form a community of hermits, turning from the Benedictine pattern to that of early Christian Egypt. The Bishop of Grenoble gave them a rocky and desolate site, often snowbound, in the mountains of his diocese. There they built three huts and an oratory and took to a life of prayer, harsh austerity and silence. This place was the Grande Chartreuse, the first Charterhouse, the nucleus of a religious order which since then has never needed to be reformed, because it has 'never been deformed' or departed from its initial standards. Bruno soon left, to establish other hermit communities in Italy, and it was not until 1130 that the Carthusians codified their Customs in writing, and only in 1142 that strictly they became a religious Order.

Bruno and the Poor Brothers of God

In 1168 the prior of the Grande Chartreuse visited King Henry II, who ten years later founded the first Carthusian priory in England as part of the penance for his involvement in the slaying of Archbishop Thomas Becket at Canterbury Cathedral in 1170. The Carthusians were settled at Witham in Selwood Forest on the Somerset border with Wiltshire, at that time a place remote and inhospitable enough for the purpose, as the first prior, Narbert, and his monks, all Frenchmen, soon found. Following the Carthusian Customs, they wore the roughest possible hair shirts, and their other clothes were scanty, coarse and undyed. Three days a week they lived on bread made from unbolted flour, and water; on the other four they had only slender rations of fish, cheese, eggs and vegetables. They ate no meat at all. They gathered in the priory church for only three Hours of the Office, Mattins (Vigils), Lauds and Vespers. They recited the other Hours in their cells (described by Abbot Peter the Venerable of Cluny, after a visit to the Grande Chartreuse, as 'separate little houses, like those of the ancient monks of Egypt, where the Carthusians occupy themselves continually with reading, prayer and the labour of their hands, especially the writing of books: . . . here too they boil their vegetables'). The private cell, for the Carthusians a miniature house, with a garden and a patch of cultivable land around it, was not characteristic of the greater 12th-century monastic orders, with their preference for dormitories; it was a conscious borrowing from the desert hermits of the past.

To prevent their priories from becoming large and richly endowed,

Becket's murder, from a twelfth-century manuscript – perhaps the earliest picture of it. It is followed by the text of John of Salisbury's letter 'Ex insperator . . .', the first written account.

the Carthusians restricted the numbers in each priory to a prior and an 'upper house' of twelve monks with a 'lower house' of eighteen lay brothers to look after their deliberately modest buildings and meagre arable holdings, flocks and herds. The monks themselves did no work in common and no agricultural labour. The days of the lay brothers were regulated on monastic principles: they had cells and an oratory of their own, but their life had a stronger communal element than the life of the monks. In every respect they were the 'lower house', and not allowed to rise to positions of administrative power. The Carthusians, solitary in their cells for so long each day, were vowed to silence except when speech was essential (though there were occasions, like feast days, when they were summoned to dine together and talk together).

The Witham Charterhouse, to begin with, failed. Only a few hutments were put up, the monks and the lay brothers lapsed into a communal and soon apathetic life, and the first two priors gave no leadership. Deeply troubled, Henry II persuaded Hugh of Avalon, a nobly-born monk of the Grande Chartreuse, to take over Witham as prior in 1180. In six years Hugh had set Witham on its feet, building an upper house of stone round a cloister and a lower house of wood, breathing inspiration into the community and establishing its prestige in ecclesiatical circles in England. Robert Fitz Henry retired as Prior of Winchester to spend his last years there, and the Scottish Abbot Adam of Dryburgh left his own order to spend twenty-five years as a monk at Witham, where he wrote influential books on Carthusian life and prayer. In 1184 Hugh was taken from Witham to be Bishop of Lincoln until his death in 1200. He is remembered as St. Hugh of Lincoln, the last English monk-bishop to be a saint. Hugh was a true hermit neither at heart nor in action: as bishop, he was an energetic builder, educator and preacher, a powerful moral and spiritual stay for clergy and people as he travelled his sprawling diocese, which in the middle ages stretched from the Humber to the Thames. But he brought to the work an inner balance, patience, humility and spiritual insight bred in him through the long, exacting, self-dependent years in the Charterhouses. His companion and biographer, Adam of Eynsham, said that Hugh was too aware of the constant and wonderful presence of God to be impressed by individual miracles, wonders and signs. When men and women of his own diocese told him how they despaired of their own salvation, he assured them that it was not only monks and hermits who would possess the Kingdom of God, and that only three things were demanded of a Christian – 'love in the heart, truth on the lips, and chastity in the body'. Hugh regularly revisited Witham, but it was never his thought that the Charterhouses should send great shepherds of souls into the world, as in a sense they had sent him, or that Witham should become, as he might have made it, the Rievaulx of the south, drawing great numbers to it and begetting many daughter-houses. However many might feel called to the Charterhouse, a select and tested few should be chosen. It is not surprising that during the century and a

The Carthusians in England: Hugh of Lincoln

41

half after Hugh's death, only two more English Charterhouses were founded, by William Longsword Earl of Salisbury at Hinton near Bath, in 1226, and by another nobleman, Sir Nicholas Cantelupe, at Beauvale near Nottingham, in 1320.

The Carthusians had their stern critics among the other Orders. The great Abbot Samson of Bury St. Edmunds deplored those who gave up the pastoral burden to become anchorites. Alexander of Lewes, a learned canon who became a monk at Witham and later left it in discontent for the Cluniac abbey at Reading, complained that while with the Carthusians he could not go daily to mass, only on Sundays, and that his days were dull, idle and melancholy. The Carthusians, he said, spent hours gazing at blank walls, claiming that this was the only way to heaven. Hugh's reply was that Alexander lacked the strength needed to pierce, like Moses, through the dark cloud to where God was. Alexander eventually tired of Reading Abbey and asked for readmission to Witham. St. Hugh, keeping from Lincoln a fatherly eye on the Charterhouse, saw to it that the door should not be opened a second time to Alexander's knock.

The later Carthusians   In the later medieval generations, following the first pandemic onset of the Black Death in 1348–50, enthusiasm for creating new houses of monks and nuns was all but dead; yet it affected significantly one Order, the Carthusian. This enthusiasm arose in the royal family and their circle, and its flame was keenly fanned by a devout and gifted Carthusian, John Luscote, Prior of Hinton. Sir Walter Manny, who came from Hainault in the Low Countries in the service of Philippa of Hainault, King Edward III's queen, and was prominent both at court and in the royal campaigns in France in the earlier stages of the Hundred Years War, combined with Michael Northburgh, Bishop of London, who had kept Edward III's war journal on the Crecy expedition, to persuade Luscote to co-operate in establishing a Charterhouse on a London site: for Manny had seen and admired the Paris Charterhouse. The new house was to be built alongside the ground which Manny had given outside London wall for the burial of Black Death victims in 1349. The London Charterhouse was in being by 1370. The prevailing respect for the Carthusians and for the efficacy of their prayers for souls is clear from the names of the benefactors, some of whom endowed complete cells (there were twenty-five cells in the London Carthusian community): great lords and war-captains around King Edward and his son, the Black Prince – like William Ufford, Earl of Suffolk, and Sir Robert Knollys; ladies like the Countess of Pembroke, who had already founded a Cambridge college and nunnery; the Bishops of Durham and Lincoln and London merchants like William Walworth, Mayor of London who, with a squire's help, unhorsed and killed Wat Tyler, who was leading the rebellious peasants of 1381 to confront their young King, Richard II, at Smithfield. The Carthusians had many to pray for. Later in the century, members of the higher nobility who played leading rôles in the power struggles of the reign of

Edward's grandson Richard II founded four more Charterhouses: two in the towns – Michael de la Pole's in his ancestral Hull, Lord Zouche's at Coventry – and two 'in the wilderness', Thomas Mowbray, Earl of Nottingham, planting a house at Epworth in the fastnesses of the Isle of Axholme, and Richard II's nephew Thomas Holland, Duke of Surrey, the house of Mount Grace in Cleveland.

This vogue for the Carthusians in the higher circles of a chivalric but materialistic society was no doubt an acknowledgement that they had followed their vocation more steadfastly and with more purpose than the monks of the larger orders. If modest comforts, the gifts of fond kinsfolk and admiring visitors at the guest-house, had filtered into their cells since 1200, their morality and devoutness were held in high repute and their publications, sermons and conversation show them eagerly sharing with an increasingly educated laity an appetite for the teachings and revelations of the English mystics, Richard Rolle and Walter Hilton, the authors of *The Fire of Love, The Prick of Conscience, The Ladder of Perfection, The Cloud of Unknowing*, and their continental counterparts St. Thomas à Kempis, St. Catherine of Siena, and St. Bridget of Sweden. To bring the Carthusians to urban centres was almost knowingly to disrupt their peace and their solitude, by imposing on them the need to be hospitable, to be visited in their cells by the well-born, seeking spiritual counsel and consolation, to preach, and to bury the faithful in their cemeteries.

The distinction and courage of soul of the later Carthusians – right up to their stand against Henry VIII at the Dissolution – and the integrity and worth of those they recruited as novices – such as John Blackman, Fellow of Eton and Warden of King's Hall, Cambridge, in the 15th century, and Richard Rede, London goldsmith, in the 16th – show that coming to town did not corrupt them. The latest and largest Carthusian foundation in England, the House of Jesus of Bethlehem, was the creation of the most puritanical and orthodox of medieval English kings, Henry V (1413–1422). He set his Charterhouse on the Surrey bank of the Thames at Sheen, opposite his Abbey of the Holy Saviour, St. Mary and St. Bridget (Syon House, for both nuns and monks of the new Swedish Bridgettine Order), on the Middlesex side. Both foundations, like Witham, were in expiation of a royal crime against the church: Henry V's father, Henry IV, had executed Archbishop Richard Scroope of York as a rebel in 1405, and the foundations had been the price required by the Pope for the king's exoneration. For Syon House and all the new Carthusian foundations, the Crown was able to draw for endowments on lands and other assets acquired in England by monasteries of Normandy and France in Norman times and in many instances compulsorily purchased or annexed from their abbots overseas by the English government. All the monks of all the new Charterhouses together would by no means have filled Rievaulx under Ailred, and much of their endowment was existing monastic wealth, recycled from the 'alien priories'. Yet the intellect and the spirit of English monasticism stayed healthily alive among the Carthusians to the end.

The Regular Canons

The Black Canons and the Augustinian Rule

Cluny and Cîteaux had begun as Benedictine houses, but soon became offshoots from which new Orders sprang. The Grande Chartreuse was a conscious departure from the Benedictine Order. But alongside the Benedictines there had been for decades before the Norman Conquest another great international order or family of regular clergy, the Canons of St. Augustine – the Austin Canons, as the English called them, or Black Canons, from their black outdoor cloaks. The first English house submitted to their Rule was probably St. Botolph's Priory, Colchester, in 1103 – a quarter-century before the Cistercians arrived. A canon was a clerk living according to a rule (Greek *kanòn*: 'rule'). For centuries before 1066, cathedrals and the large town and country churches known as *minsters* had been served by bodies of clerks or canons distinct from priests serving churches single-handed or monks under the vows of religion and the Benedictine Rule. Such canons had to sleep in a common dormitory and take their meals in a common refectory. They were paid stipends from a common treasury. There was always a trend towards the easing of discipline and the acquisition, by senior and better-off canons, of individual houses and lands belonging to their church but tenanted by them for life. Dunstan and his followers had replaced clerks or canons of this kind with monks in several major ecclesiastical centres.

Meanwhile, on the continent there was a growing movement to bring chapters or bodies of canons under a much stricter, more monastic rule, including the observance of the vows of personal poverty and chastity – for canons were often married. (A papal campaign for celibacy for all clergy was waged in the 11th century: it was far less an onslaught on 'sin' than a move to get rid of a social institution, clerical marriage, widely accepted and approved in Catholic countries but deplored by reforming popes). The Lateran Council of 1059 did not enforce a monastic rule on the communities of canons, but it urged upon them all the virtues of leading a monastic life, under a rule and a prior. Many a community was now adopting a rule of its own, and its members were becoming known as regular canons – thus setting themselves apart from those who followed the older, worldly (or 'secular') life, and came to be called secular canons.

(Opposite) The Law of Marriage. This illustrates a problem involving 'bigamy' – whether a lady whose betrothed had taken religious vows is free to marry another; from a twelfth-century copy of Gratian, *causa 27.*

The Rule adopted by the regular canons was based on a letter in which St. Augustine of Hippo had given advice and regulations to a new religious house in 5th-century North Africa. This document was brief. It had to be strengthened and amplified by local regulations for particular houses of Austin Canons, and by borrowing from the Benedictine Rule itself. The canons thus came under a rule in itself demanding, but falling rather short of monastic strictness and

castitatis habens desponsauit sibi u
xorem. Jua priori condicioni renun
cians transtulit se ad alium; y illi nup
sit. Jlle cui prius desponsa fuit repe
tit eam. Hic primum queritur an
coniugium possit ee. inc nouentes.
Secdo an liceat sponse a sponso disce
dere y alij nubere. Quod uero uo
uentes matrimonia contrahere non
possint mutis auctoritatib; pbatur.

De uo
uentib; an possit
nu.

uniformity. The daily Office was less protracted, food and drink and conversation were less tightly restricted, and there was more freedom of movement outside the walls. The history of the Regular Canons is more loosely knit, less easy to present as a unitary, developing drama than that of the Cluniacs or the Cistercians: but lay society's interest in them and generosity to them was strong and deep.

The Austin Canons in England   There were two kinds of foundation of Austin Canons in England. Colchester, where St. Botolph's, an existing priory of secular canons, was brought under the Augustinian Rule, typifies the first; and Holy Trinity in Aldgate, London, the second, where Henry I's queen, Matilda (mother of the more famous Matilda, who waged the war of succession against her cousin Stephen), established a completely new priory in 1107. The queen's foundation rapidly created five important daughter houses, at Oxford (where the house dedicated to the local Old English saint, St. Frideswide, was taken over), Dunstable, St. Osyth and, in the far west, Plympton and Launceston. Henry I (1100–1135) himself gave the canons their richest abbey, substituting them for a declining college of clerks, by then diminished to one priest, in the centre of the wool-trading town of Cirencester in the Cotswolds. The Austin Canons built both an abbey church at Cirencester and a parish church for the townspeople at the abbey gates. Henry also settled Austin Canons at Carlisle in 1122, and their house became in 1133 the cathedral of a new diocese on the border with Scotland. During his reign, forty houses of canons had been set up in England, and another hundred in the next eighty years. The Austin Canons were popular in lay society and new houses were still being endowed for them into the 14th century so that they had over two hundred by 1350. None was more celebrated than Walsingham Priory in Suffolk where the statue of the Virgin Mary ('Our Lady of Walsingham') was deeply venerated and thought to work miracles. Walsingham drew pilgrims to its shrine from all over England, and also from abroad, in consistent and increasing numbers – including most of the Kings and Queens of England, last of all Henry VIII – down the centuries until the Dissolution.

At root, the vocation of the Austin Canons was similar to that of the other monastic orders: to instruct and inspire other Christians by the example of their godly living, under their vows; and to serve the spiritual needs of the world by prayer and praise to God. They were popular partly because their houses were often easy to found. Despite the splendid start given them by Henry I and his queen, only thirteen of their houses held the rank of abbey. Of their two hundred priories, nearly all were of modest size, and a significant number never had the resources to house as many as ten canons or nuns. Breedon, for instance, had five canons, Buckland seven. The nucleus of some priories, established by an only moderately well-to-do founder, would be a large parish church, of which the founder owned or had bought the *advowson* (the patronage, or right to nominate the incumbent priest for the bishop to institute if suitable). The Austin Canons would share the parish church with the parishioners, and would control its revenues. Their numbers, present and future, their financial health and intellectual and spiritual vitality would depend on how far his descendants and other local people would keep adding to the endowments. Many such foundations never throve, and their solvency, morality and morale were a perennial problem for their local bishop.

The great majority of Augustinian houses were under their bishop's authority and visitation. Few enjoyed papal exemption. Innocent III, at the Fourth Lateran Council in 1215, decreed that the Canons should hold regular general chapters, where all their houses should be represented, and should reform and legislate for themselves. England thereafter had a general chapter for the Austin houses in the Province of Canterbury and another for the Province of York. However, it is variety of character and to some extent purpose which are the hallmark of the Austin Canons, as may also be said of the Benedictines. Some were great, like Merton Priory, founded in 1114 by Henry I's Sheriff of Surrey, Gilbert, with its daughter-houses in Cornwall, Scotland (at Holyrood) and Normandy; others were modest in size, some had to struggle to survive. Some dominated towns, like Cirencester, others adorned the countryside, like Bolton in Wharfedale and Lanercost. Some replaced hermitages, like Llanthony by Gloucester and Bushmead. At least six served hospitals, in remote Anglesey or in the capital, where the Austin Canons brought into being St. Bartholomew's Hospital at Smithfield and St. Thomas's Hospital at Southwark.

A significant, though never a great number of Austin Canons were seconded from their houses to be vicars of parish churches of which their priory had the patronage. They were not an evangelising or missionary order, but were ubiquitous, familiar and respected on the English medieval scene; and something more, we may reflect, following in imagination the steps of the young King Henry V, as he went on a royal progress through England in 1421 after his victories in France. He made his pilgrimage to Our Lady of Walsingham, guarded as she was by the Austin Canons, then northward to Yorkshire, where he worshipped at the shrine of the Augustinian saint, John of Bridlington. John Thwing, East Riding farmer's son, Oxford scholar, Prior of the Bridlington Augustinians, dying of the plague in 1379, left behind him a reputation (localised then, shadowy and little recorded since) for miracle-working, modesty and benevolence of spirit and austerity of life that did not leave him below Ailred. He was canonised in 1401, almost the last of the saints of medieval England. He was once asked why he did not join a stricter order than the Augustinians, and replied that the rule of any order could lead a man to perfectness of life; but which rule was the best, insisted his questioner. 'The Gospel of St. John,' replied the canon.

As well as the Augustinians, a number of separate, more centralised orders of Regular Canons established themselves in England. The Order of Arrouaise, an abbey near Bapaume in France, where the Augustinian

Arrouaise, St. Victoire, Prémontré

47

Rule was adapted to absorb many Cistercian principles, had several daughter-houses: at Great Missenden in Buckinghamshire, their first English house, colonised in Henry I's reign, in 1133; at Dorchester on Thames, in the church which once had been an Old English cathedral, where St. Birinus from Gaul had begun the conversion of the West Saxons; at Lilleshall in Shropshire and Notley in Essex. They also had a nunnery at Harrold, Bedfordshire.

The mother house of the Victorine Canons was the Abbey of Saint-Victoire in Paris, renowned for its teaching of logic, theology and philosophy. An Englishman, coming back from pilgrimage to the tomb of St. James the Apostle at Compostela in Spain, had visited Saint-Victoire and brought over three of the canons to Herefordshire, to found the Order's first English house at Wigmore. More rewarding for the Victorines was their settlement at Bristol. In Stephen's reign, Bristol, the third largest of English towns, was the military and naval headquarters of the young Henry of Anjou (later Henry II), conducting his mother Matilda's strugle for the succession. One of his chief supporters, the Bristol merchant Robert Fitz Harding, was enfeoffed by Henry with the great estate of Berkeley along the Severn estuary, and it was on his business fortune and his landed wealth that Fitz Harding was able to draw for his foundation of the major Victorine Abbey of St. Augustine's, Bristol, converted to a cathedral when Bristol diocese was created at the Reformation. Fitz Harding's descendants, the medieval Lords of Berkeley, kept up a continuing and generous interest in St. Augustine's. The Order of Canons of the Holy Sepulchre of Jerusalem, founded after the success of the First Crusade, had a few English houses, one at Warwick.

The Canons of the Order of Prémontré, the forest hamlet near Laon in France where they were first brought together in 1120 by the wandering evangelical preacher St. Norbert, arrived at Newhouse in Lincolnshire in 1143, and spread rapidly, acquiring thirty-one abbeys and three nunneries, chiefly in remote places. Norbert had modelled his Order of Premonstratensians on the Cistercians, with annual general chapters appointing visitors to inspect and report on the houses of each of the circaries or regions into which the Premonstratensians were grouped. The circary system made it possible to impose common standards of liturgy, food, dress and conduct. Although puritanical forms of monasticism had their faithful followers in England, it is probable that before the Norbertines arrived, the Cistercians had channelled away, for the rest of the century, most of this kind of zeal in their direction. Neither the individual English Premonstratensian communities nor their total number increased greatly after their early years were over.

Gilbert of Sempringham Only one monastic order originated in England, the Gilbertine Canons. In 1131, Gilbert, parish priest at the village of Sempringham in Lincolnshire, built a small convent beside his parish church at the request of seven women who wished to lead a strictly religious life.

Hugh of Saint-Victor
(fl.c. 1125–41), head of
the school of Saint-Victor
at Paris, mother house of
the Victorine
congregation of
Regular Canons; from
a thirteenth-century
manuscript of one of his
works, *De arca morali*.

Shortly afterwards, on the advice of William, the first Abbot of Rievaulx, who came to stay with him, Gilbert added lay sisters to his nunnery; and as benefactions flowed in, lay brothers on the Cistercian model were added, to cultivate the land and gather in rent and dues. In 1139, as numbers grew, Gilbert was compelled to rebuild a larger convent on fresh ground at Sempringham, with a double church, cloister and out-buildings; and other Lincolnshire monasteries, some of them double houses for monks and nuns, were putting themselves under Gilbert's protection and supervision. In 1147, he crossed the Channel and appeared at the general chapter at Cîteaux. The assembled Cistercian abbots, however, were preoccupied that year with the absorption of the Order of the Grey Monks of Savigny, and were unwilling to take the Gilbertine houses, especially the nunneries, into their order. Pope Eugenius III was present at the chapter, to supervise the annexing of Savigny to Cîteaux; and he encouraged and directed Gilbert to regard his houses as constituting an order in its own right. Gilbert accepted the commission, took the title of Master, and expanded his order with priests who were to be canons and chaplains to his nuns. The Rule he composed put the nuns under Benedictine regulations, the canons under Augustinian, and the lay brothers and sisters under Cistercian. His own contribution was a constitution for the running of an order of mixed monasteries under a Master and general chapter, with the nuns having a significant voice in its government.

The Gilbertine Canons
When Gilbert died in 1189, his order had twelve monasteries, ten of them double houses for nuns and canons. There were a thousand nuns, and five hundred lay brothers; and the order had numerous hospitals for lepers and houses for orphans. Its reputation, and without doubt its internal standards, were high. Most of the houses were in Lincolnshire – where it is probably no exaggeration to say that the Gilbertines provided fairly comprehensive rural welfare services – and nearly all the rest in neighbouring counties. Although fourteen other houses (two of them double) were to be added after St. Gilbert's death, these foundations were sporadic, usually with long intervals of years between. The Gilbertines were popular with the less exalted social classes for whom they catered, and never attracted benefactions from donors of outstanding wealth. Only two of their houses, Sempringham, and Watton in Yorkshire, were substantially well off; and Sempringham, with two hundred nuns and lay sisters to provide for, was in serious hardship when the Bishop of Lincoln visited it in 1247. Changing labour conditions in the 13th and 14th centuries – especially higher wages – steadily drew away the lay brothers and sisters, whose numbers were decisively depleted by the Black Death in 1349 and 1350. At Shouldham Priory in 1321 one of the canons, playing football, killed another player, a layman, who collided with the canon's sheathed dagger in a tackle. We should not judge Gilbert's Order by that one episode; but a fair observation might be that had the founder had his

way and brought his flock into the Cistercian fold, the subsequent history of the Gilbertine houses would have been more vigorous, more prosperous and less provincial.

The Friars

The friars – the mendicant brothers – were strictly not monks at all, and the traveller in search of their buildings will find only a few fragments surviving in England; but we must consider the friars, so important were they in the history of the religious orders, so dynamic and influential in their heyday. They arrived in England within a few years of the coming to birth of their various orders in the 13th century, in Spain, in Italy and in the Holy Land. The appearance of the mendicant orders soon after 1200 was probably much more a response to contemporary social conditions than had been the early growth of the Cluniac and Cistercian Orders. Towards 1200, the population of western Europe was growing fast, in comparison with earlier centuries, and towns, as well as agrarian society, were expanding. Among the laity, especially in the towns, intellectual, moral and spiritual standards were rising, for which the monastic orders could claim a good deal of the credit. Yet prosperity and higher standards meant greater expectations and more trenchant criticism of the church as already established. This in itself did not prove that the monks and the secular clergy were suddenly in decline; but more was wanted of them. There was an appetite and a field for a new movement, and the friars fed the appetite and moved on to the field.

The wealth of the monks was beginning to be censured by the laity which had once enriched them. The skill and vigour with which the world-losing, self-denying white monks of the Cistercian Order had made apparently barren assets richly productive brought them a reputation for avarice and obsession with money. There was also an upsurge of questioning of the articles of faith: the doctrines of the Church, debated, weighed afresh and restated as they had been for generations under papal leadership, were now subject to aggressive challenge or even dogmatic replacement by newly asserted truths. False beliefs – heresies – dangerous to the future of the soul, were preached and spread. The Catharist or Albigensian heresy, originating in the Balkans, took a strong hold on Christians in northern Italy, southern France, the Rhineland, and the Low Countries, even if in England only a few people in Oxford dabbled with it. Small wonder that successive popes and bishops and orthodox believers among the laity were alarmed: Catharism, despite its claims to be Christian, was less a heresy than a faith alternative to Christianity.

It was the need to confront heresy rather than criticise clerical and monastic wealth and worldliness which called into being the first of the mendicant brotherhoods, the Order of Preachers, the friars in black and white habits recruited by the Augustinian canon Dominic of Osma

Dominic of Osma

(1170–1221) in Spain. Dominic imposed on the members of the new order he created strict personal poverty, to make them fit for and credible in the struggle for what he saw as true beliefs against false; but for him the battle for the soul was a battle in the mind, an intellectual campaign. He drew into his order novices who were well schooled and intellectually alert, and he gave them a training in which the demands of the daily Office were lighter than in monasteries, the study of logic and theology had the central place, and lucid and cogent preaching of the true faith – in the pulpit and through the written word – was the final goal. Medieval Catholicism won the fight against the Albigensian heresy, combining the arms of the crusading knights from northern France with the persuasive power of the Dominican preachers.

Dominic had realised that the bishops and their parish clergy were under-equipped for the struggle with heresy, and the monks were too remote from the world to play an effective part in it. His friars needed a rule, to give them discipline and education: then they must go into the world, to preach and teach. Dominic had adapted monasticism to the purposes of the Church Militant among the laity.

Francis of Assisi His Italian contemporary, Francis of Assisi (1181–1224), was a rich, nobly born layman who felt himself, in manhood, called to follow the paths of humility and simplicity and to imitate Jesus Christ, to the point that he mystically received on his own body the *stigmata*, the marks of the five wounds inflicted at the crucifixion. He gave himself up to prayer in the Umbrian equivalent of the wilderness, and to a life of total poverty which took no thought for the morrow and depended for the day's food and shelter only on the alms of others, and was devoted to helping the afflicted, the sick and above all the lepers. He was concerned for all God's creatures, preaching the Gospel to birds and animals, and calling men and women to repent and be absolved while there was time. He did not want to found a religious order, and when his disciples grew swiftly in number to their hundreds and then their thousands, he declared that he did not wish to put them under any rule save that of the Lord, 'neither the rule of Augustine, nor of Benedict, nor of Bernard. The Lord has told me that he wishes me to be a 'new fool' in the world, leading you by no other way than that of his wisdom'. His friars should not become learned men, nor use books even for daily worship. They were not to touch money, acquire property, or accept privilege and the protection of the law. He never deviated from his path, and followed it to its logical end, dying still quite young, poor, solitary, broken in health, happy in mind and tranquil in soul; but he must have realised that he had indeed created a great new religious order. He was a saint, arguably 'the only perfect Christian', after whom the Church had to hasten, to make use of his work. Others had to organise the Franciscan Order, and it was more difficult than the making of the Dominican Order. One of his legacies was profound conflict within the Church itself. The claim of the Franciscans to preach, hear confessions and absolve sinners, and administer the mass and other sacraments in their churches cut across the rights and duties of bishops and parish priests. The meaning of the vow of apostolic poverty was a question dividing his followers even before he died and perplexing the Pope and the Church for a century and more after his death. Literal adherence to what Francis taught on poverty had been itself made a heresy by the 14th century.

The men and women who joined the new mendicant orders in the early 13th century (the Dominicans, correctly known as the Friars Preachers, the Franciscans and the Friars Minors, the 'little brothers' of Francis) were professed to their order as a whole, not to any particular convent. Instead of stability there was mobility, freedom to move about the world on the work of preaching and evangelising. The houses of both orders were grouped into provinces, with an annual provincial chapter, and regular general chapters of representatives of the whole order. The Dominicans, with their Master at their head and their provincial priors, tended to emphasise the authority of their high officers. The Franciscans, their houses headed by 'ministers', stressed that their governors were their servants. All were elected, all held office for limited periods, not for life. There was an element of democracy in this, but more significant was the belief that a system of elective oligarchy put the best and most efficient friars in power, under the ultimate control of the representative chapters. This was a striking departure from the monastic principle of government by paternalist local abbots.

The first mendicants

Meanwhile, there was an inevitable and on the whole healthy rivalry between the orders, which led each to model itself in part on what was best in the other. Poverty was not at the heart of the original Dominican ideal, but the Black Friars rigorously practised it. The Franciscans gave up their founder's hostility to learning, and were soon emulating the Dominicans as scholars, philosophers and theologians. The fundamental purpose of each order was a mission to the laity. Their sermons, into which they put a new training, knowledge, fervour and eloquence, attracted eager congregations and brought them into keen demand as confessors, and the fashion grew for burial in their cemeteries, often preceded by deathbed reception into their orders. The parish clergy and the monks suffered and resented severe competition from the friars for their congregations, their offerings and their legacies. Successive popes and Councils of the Church had to legislate to control the resulting problems and allay jealousy and hostility towards the mendicants. The friars were allowed to preach in their own churches and in public pulpits, but could only bury Christians in their own cemeteries if they shared the offerings and legacies with the local parish clergy. Confessions were to be heard in any diocese only by friars specially nominated by their orders and licensed by the bishop, and licences were to be carefully limited in number.

The friars reached England with speed. They included Englishmen who had sat at the feet of Francis in Italy, and two of whom had argued

The friars in England

53

with him against his more extreme views and actions; and others, like the distinguished Alexander of Hales, who had joined the Friars Preachers in Paris. Ready to welcome them were English church leaders who were widely familiar with religious developments on the continent: like the Bishop of Winchester, Peter des Roches; Alexander Stavensby, later Bishop of Lichfield, who had lectured in Toulouse with Dominic in his class; and Archbishop Stephen Langton of Canterbury, friend of Pope Innocent III (1198–1216), who had channelled the spring waters struck by Dominic's insight and the zeal of Francis down to the strongly flowing courses of the two great orders. Archbishop Langton asked one of the Dominicans, who had come by way of Dover to Canterbury, to preach a sermon in a local church instead of him: he probably cast himself in the rôle of King Ethelbert receiving Augustine and his Roman missionaries in pagan Kent six hundred years before. The Archbishop put the Black Friars under his protection, and they went on to Oxford, the centre of higher learning in England, and established their first English house there. Three years later, the first Franciscan Grey Friars to come to England followed the same route and set up their first houses in London, Oxford, Northampton and Cambridge. By the middle of the 13th century, the two orders had established seventy convents in England, and by the early 14th century one hundred. Most of them were in London, the two university towns of Oxford and Cambridge, the cathedral cities and the county towns. Both orders had houses in thirty English urban centres. Meanwhile, they were joined, mostly in the towns, where nearly all convents of friars were planted, by other new mendicant orders.

A number of communities of hermits in the mountains of Italy, having adopted the rule of St. Augustine, coalesced, in 1256, under papal supervision, into the Order of the Hermits of St. Augustine – the Austin Friars (an order distinct from the Austin Canons). Once organised, they turned away from the hermit life, and became scholars and preachers, like the Dominicans. Their order grew slowly in England, starting in small country towns – Clare in Suffolk, Cleobury Mortimer in Shropshire, Tickhill in Yorkshire – and eventually moving into the larger centres, including London, Oxford and Cambridge, with thirty-four houses in all. The Carmelites, the White Friars, were also to begin with a hermit order, located on Mount Carmel in Palestine, with settlements in Italy and the Catholic west. An Englishman, St. Simon Stock, reformed them along Dominican lines and made them into a chiefly urban and missionary order, though they remained the most contemplative of all the friars. They had thirty-seven English houses, a few remote from the towns, like Losenham and Aylesford in Kent and Hulme, Northumberland. The four major orders of friars all had convents in eleven important English towns, among them London, Oxford, Cambridge and York. Other and smaller mendicant orders appeared in England: the Friars of the Holy Cross (Crutched Friars), the Friars of the Penitential Sack, the Pied Friars. All of the orders but the

Franciscan were under the Dominican influence; and their function was to teach and preach in the English towns.

The friars worked among the laity, as priests and instructors: their work, in medieval society, was not for women to do. Francis of Assisi, however, had had women followers, their first leader a well-to-do provincial society beauty, St. Clare, who eloped nocturnally from her angry parents to profess the vows of religion before Francis himself. Clare founded the Second Order of the Franciscans, for women who joined it to worship the Trinity, intercede for mankind, and lead an

The Poor Clares

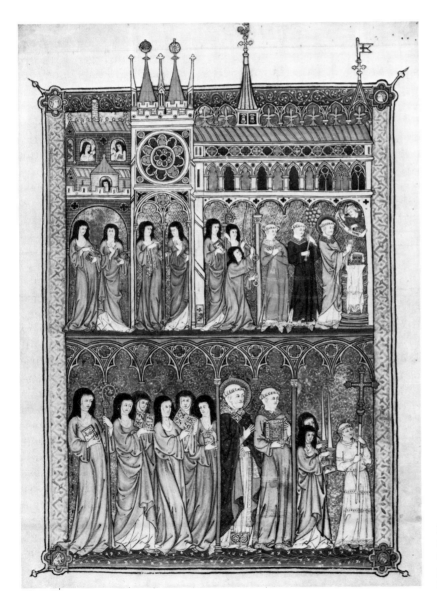

In the ideal convent, nuns attend mass (above) and follow the priest in procession. A French miniature of *c.* 1300.

55

existence of the utmost poverty in fasting and silence. The earliest of the Poor Clares needed great strength of will, for papal and episcopal concern for the welfare of nuns submitted to an extremely exacting rule amounted to disapproval of the entire venture. St. Clare got her way: the Poor Clares, the 'Minoresses', as the English called them, had a substantial convent in London, another in Northampton, and three in the East Anglian countryside.

The friars and the laity

The friars were made welcome in England. The bishops gave them places in their households, lectureships at the two growing universities, donations in cash, and sites for their convents. King Henry III was open-handedly generous to them, and set a royal fashion for choosing Dominicans as the king's confessors; and he began the practice of employing friars, like his confidant Adam Marsh, as royal envoys on diplomatic missions, a field in which the Preachers continued active until the 16th century. Edward I never visited a town without giving money to the friars. The Franciscans were perhaps not so grateful when the Queen Mother, Isabella, the 'she-wolf of France', having arranged the painful murder of her husband Edward II, dragged her son, the teenage King Edward III, to York in 1327, commandeered quarters for the royal household in the Franciscan convent there for six weeks, and one evening gave a party for sixty courtiers and their ladies in the Grey Friars' dormitory. York smiled sourly when the puritanical young king violently turned his mother and her Mortimer lover out of power in the Nottingham *coup d'état* three years later.

The friars in England based themselves upon the towns. Their buildings and their lands, which Dominic and Francis had forbidden them to own, were held in trust for them by corporations of the citizens, which frequently bought property for them. Individual benefactors, like the burgesses Richard Mulliner at Cambridge and Richard Pride at Oxford, gave them houses. The Londoners were very generous, and did not waver, though they disapproved, when the friars stood out for tolerance towards the city's Jewish community. The monks of the greater urban abbeys were less welcoming, apprehensively seeing the friars as rivals, and foes to monastic privilege. From Abingdon, a town dominated by its Benedictine abbey, the first Franciscans were turned away. At Bury St. Edmunds, the chief town of Suffolk, the monks were sufficiently powerful to keep out the Franciscans for good. Royal favour and the interest of several popes who issued bulls on behalf of the friars – who went so far as to invade Bury by night, bringing a portable altar with them, and setting up house in a farmstead on the outskirts of town – failed them in the face of the locally entrenched power of the Benedictines; and the Friars Minors had to accept a site for their house in the Suffolk countryside, ceded them as a compromise by the obdurate spiritual descendants of the great Abbot Samson. The Cistercians at Scarborough and the Austin Canons at Oxford and Dunstable, obstructed, with significant success, their arrival. Abbot John of Peterborough described the descent of the followers of St. Francis upon England as 'more than misery . . . a truculent plague'. But in most places the monks at worst were conducting a surly rearguard action: the friars came, and they stayed.

The only properties which the friars held in England were their own churches and conventual buildings. It was against their principles to acquire housing as an investment or land, rents or tithes, though eventually they were to obtain gardens and smallholdings, to grow some food of their own on the edges of towns. The friars who were excluded from Bury St. Edmunds could hardly have survived if they had not been given land to farm at Babwell. In remote Anglesey the Franciscans cultivated thirty acres at Llanfaes, and at Dunwich they had their own fishing boat. But these were exceptions. Unlike the monks, whose first task when a new monastery was founded had been to build their convent, the friars were slow to construct churches of their own. In London, Oxford, Cambridge and many other towns they obtained the temporary use of parish churches for their masses, confessionals and daily offices, in a sense thrusting their rivalry under the very noses of the secular clergy. Their early quarters were deliberately chosen for their meanness and discomfort. In the city of London, the Franciscans lived for a time in Stinking Lane, near the shambles, in Canterbury in the cellars of a school, in Cambridge in what was virtually part of the gaol, and in Lincoln, Oxford, Reading and Worcester on sites which were often flooded in winter. Admittedly, the acquisition of comfortable urban sites within the walls of a growing town was nowhere easy by the 13th century; but the Franciscans in particular went out of their way to create discomfort and poverty for themselves. In London and Shrewsbury they tore down stone-built houses which had been given them for residence, and literally put mud hutments in their place. The townspeople of Southampton were displeased when the Grey Friars knocked down a cloister which had been specially constructed and presented to them.

Within a decade or two of their coming to England, the growing size of the congregations who came to hear their sermons, and the pressing demands for burial in their cemeteries, persuaded them to seek more extensive sites and to plan churches and convents which would be on an adequate scale, and would be built to last. There was also a certain reaction away from the determination to create conditions of discomfort and squalor and towards the provision of well-proportioned buildings in an austerely attractive style. No complete friary survives in England, and there is only one complete friars' church, that of the Dominicans at Norwich, now St. Andrew's Hall. Other survivals are few and fragmentary. It is known, however, that the earlier stone churches of the friars, built about the middle of the 13th century, were single-storey buildings, with aisles long in proportion to their breadth, perhaps on average 100 feet by 22 feet, like the Franciscan church at Lincoln. The churches built later in the

The friaries

The churches and cloisters of the friars

57

century were on a more ample scale, with a broader and longer nave, with two aisles (or, in some places, only one aisle). The nave was joined to the choir by a transverse passage called the walking place, which was surmounted by a central bell tower and might have doors at either end, giving on to the cloister and the public street. A few of these bell towers still stand: Coventry has both its Franciscan and its Dominican belfry. The nave was constructed for the hearing of sermons, but the aisles must have gradually filled up with altars and the tombs of the well-to-do. The choir was reserved for the friars themselves, with stalls facing one another across its breadth, and the high altar at the square east end. The length of the newer friars' town churches may have been on average 200 feet. The Dominican church at Norwich, well lit by its fine gothic windows and clerestory, is 250 feet long, with its nave 77 feet wide, its handsome proportions and solidity of construction a virtual rejection of the mendicant ideal of poverty, as is the beautiful Franciscan chancel at Chichester. In London, the Franciscans had the biggest church of friars in England, 296 feet long, its nave 90 feet wide: its scale was modest compared with that of many of the abbey churches of the Benedictines, Cistercians and Austin Canons. However, it is difficult to reconstruct an impression of – for example – the Dominican and Franciscan churches in Cambridge, which were fine and spacious enough for the University to try (but fail) to acquire them for itself after the Dissolution. Like nearly all the buildings of the mendicants in England, they were soon to be swept away.

The friars' cloisters and other conventual buildings seem not to have been laid out on any standard plan. Even within the individual orders, there was no apparent attempt at uniformity. The Dominicans themselves observed in the 13th century that they had nearly as many different plans for their buildings, as they had houses. This variety may in part be explained by the difficulties of developing the narrow and awkward sites they were often given in the towns; but probably the early friars simply were not interested in uniformity, logic and elegance in the lay-out of their convents. The cloister was, by comparison with the monks' cloisters, small, narrow and dark, often made of timber and not used for study and writing. It was not immediately adjacent to the church, but separated from it by a courtyard. The chapter house, of simple, square design, the refectory and the dormitory were indeed grouped around the cloister, often not in their normal monastic positions. The Dominicans provided cubicles – tiny private rooms, in effect – in their dormitories for selected friars to study in and sleep in. The other members of the convent slept communally in rows of beds and in some houses, like Gloucester, their library was established at one end of the dormitory. Beyond the cloister, other buildings – the apartments of the head of the house, the accommodation reserved for the visits of the provincial head of the order, the infirmary and the guest hall – were arranged on no standard plan. The friars were no more spared the visits and demands of guests than were the monks, and guest halls survive at Canterbury and Boston. They were not landlords of great estates, and capacious tithe barns and massive gatehouses with courtrooms above the arch were not a feature of their convents. The west door of the church giving on to the street, the 'preaching interiors', the special care for books in the libraries they systematically built up, the cubicles for study, and the schools which the Dominican Chapter General in 1250 deplored as having been too lavishly provided – these appear to have been the specially distinctive features of the friars' conventual buildings, and all directly served the purposes of preaching, learning and teaching amidst lay society.

What we can learn of the history of the 13th-century friars as *The ideal of poverty* builders – from knocking down stonework to make way for clay and wattle to constructing commodious and severely beautiful town churches – to some extent epitomises the whole development of their orders at this time. The Franciscans arrived dedicated to absolute poverty. They lived on alms, but would not accept money. Each friar was restricted to a beggar's wardrobe: one habit, one girdle of cord, one pair of breeches, no shoes. They travelled barefoot even on the coldest winter days, and there are many contemporary tales of the admiration, followers and alms they won by enduring this particular hardship. The Dominicans were less interested in acting out so extreme an ideal of poverty, but they had to compete with the Friars Minors; so they restricted their brethren to a coat and three tunics each – and shoes. It was the Dominican mission – to teach and to preach, to suppress heresy, keep false doctrine at bay, inculcate the divine truths – which was in England, as elsewhere, the greatest threat to the Franciscan ideal of poverty. The training of the Dominicans in the knowledge and understanding of the Latin Bible, of the Fathers and the commentaries, and in logic, philosophy and theology, required long years of study, some in the convent, some at the universities: Oxford and Cambridge were both in vigorous existence when the friars arrived, and the University of Paris was accessible to Englishmen. To become a learned and effective preacher required time and robust health – and therefore adequate food, drink, clothing and shelter, however austerely limited; it required travel, books, writing materials – it had to be financed, which was why Francis had forbidden his own friars any books.

Paradoxically, the first party of Franciscans to arrive in England *The friars in Oxford* went within weeks to Oxford, to look for young men to recruit, and stayed there for nine months. The first link with Oxford was renewed and strengthened when lay benefactors bought for the Franciscans a permanent house, to be held for them in trust by the municipality; and there the Grey Friars set up a school and invited Robert Grosseteste, Chancellor of Oxford University, the most gifted teacher in England, to lecture to them. Grosseteste, who was a secular cleric and eventually became Bishop of Lincoln, appears to have seen the Franciscans as the group most likely to reform and transform the parishes of England, their pastors and their flocks, and better fitted to achieve the aims of the

Dominicans than the Dominicans themselves. The Grey Friars' house at Oxford swiftly became the most distinguished centre of teaching in the University. It took in pupils who were not members of the order, and eventually began sending its products to teach in cathedral schools, in Benedictine monasteries, including Christ Church, Canterbury and Worcester, and overseas. The Franciscans in England, who had arrived with a mission to the poor and the uneducated, had become a learned order and a teaching order. Roger Bacon, Adam Marsh, John Pecham, Duns Scotus, William Ockham – outstanding leaders in European intellectual life during the next hundred years – were all English Franciscans. Among all friars, the Dominican ideal was now in the ascendant, and the Black Friars, of whom the Italian Thomas Aquinas was one, had to work hard to keep up in the race. The true disciples of Francis, in England as elsewhere, were soon a minority, though energetic and active, within their own order.

Criticism of the friars   Long before the end of the 13th century, the friars were attracting merited criticism. Once they ceased to be itinerant and established themselves in their convents, the ideal of getting their living from begging alone and asking daily for only one day's sustenance was no longer a working formula. Offerings at confessions, sermons and burials, gifts of property and money to be held for them by trustees, and legacies – for few of the thousands of extant medieval wills fail to remember the friars – swelled their revenues; and begging became a profession, committed by each convent to expert mendicants known as procurators. Later, the sole right to beg for a convent was often leased to friars called limitors, who would attempt to make a profit on what they had paid for their monopoly. Rivalries and enmities troubled the orders – not only between parish priests and friars, but also between one convent and another, over the boundaries dividing their 'begging areas', and between Dominicans and Franciscans over sites for convents in the towns, over potential recruits and benefactors. At Oxford and Cambridge there was noticeable academic jealousy between the orders; and, as nearly all the leaders of the friars were chosen from among the university-trained intellectuals, a gap widened in the Franciscan Order between them and the simpler, uneducated brethren. Relations between the Dominican Robert Kilwardby and the Franciscan John Pecham, outstanding scholars who were successive Archbishops of Canterbury between 1273 and 1294, were notoriously tense. Yet, these imperfections apart, the friars were setting high standards for monks, parish clergy and lay people to follow, and were an invigorating, purifying force in the church and the secular world.

The Hospitallers and the Templars

The military orders   Among the many new orders which came into being in the 11th and 12th centuries were the military-religious orders closely involved with the crusading struggle waged by Christendom against Islam in the

Mediterranean and against the last European pagan peoples in the Baltic lands. The Spanish orders – like the Knights of St. James of Compostela, of Alcantara and of Calatrava – and the Teutonic Order of St. Mary had neither houses nor members in the British Isles; but two great international military orders had – both originating in Jerusalem in the generation following the capture of the Holy City by the crusaders in 1099 and the setting up of a Christian Kingdom of Jerusalem stretching from the far north of Syria down to the Sinai desert. They were the Knights of the Hospital of St. John of Jerusalem, whose original mission was to shelter and care for sick, poor and weary pilgrims coming to the holy places; and the Knights of the Temple, who guarded the holy places of Jerusalem, protected pilgrims and lived according to a Rule composed for them by Bernard of Clairvaux. Both orders were rapidly endowed with revenues, town properties, churches, and lands in the Kingdom of Jerusalem and its dependent fiefs, and then in almost every Catholic country in Europe.

Before many years had passed, most of their brethren, though living under the vows of religion, were conventual knights (their priests being known as 'chaplains'). The two orders played an increasingly significant part in the defence and administration of the Kingdom of Jerusalem, building and garrisoning major castles, and fighting alongside royal and baronial forces and crusaders come out from the West, in the perennial wars against the Egyptians and Turks. The one Convent of each order was situated in the Holy Land, and in Europe it had dependent upon it a score of priories, each of them holding a nexus of estates called 'preceptories' or 'commanderies'. Their headquarters in the British Isles were in London: the Temple and St. John's Priory, Clerkenwell, each with a round church in conscious imitation of the Church of the Holy Sepulchre in Jerusalem, each laid out like a major monastery. Each order had about fifty commanderies in the British Isles, and the location of many of their properties can still readily be identified from names like Temple Bruer, Temple Cowley, Temple Meads, St. John's Jerusalem (in Kent, at Sutton-atte-Hone) and St. John's Wood.

From the time of the Egyptian war-lord Saladin – who in 1187 recaptured Jerusalem itself by a campaign in which many Templars and Hospitallers perished – the Christians' cause in the Holy Land was in decline, and Acre, their last stronghold, was lost in 1291. The failure of the Templars to mobilise their European wealth and man-power in a new crusading venture cost them much sympathy when they were subjected in 1308 to attack – in France, by the French king – on the grounds of alleged heresy, sorcery, sodomy and corruption. The persecution of the French Templars led swiftly to the papal suppression of the entire Order in 1312, and though there was little antagonism to them in the British Isles, their fall was calmly accepted. Most of their properties were transferred to the Hospitallers, though in England the Crown acquired the London Temple (as did the French king the Paris

The fall of the Templars

Temple) and a good deal else. The Hospitallers had, in 1310, already created for themselves what was virtually a sovereign state (and crusading bastion) in Rhodes, Cos and other Greek islands. When they lost Rhodes to the Ottoman Turks in 1522, their Convent was set up afresh in Malta, in 1530, where it remained until 1798, when Napoleon seized the island, but lost it to the British.

The English Hospitallers The English Knights Hospitallers from 1312 until their dissolution by Henry VIII in 1540 were thus a minor – though a well-endowed – branch of an international society in which the preponderance of wealth and power lay with the French and the Spaniards. To satisfy the statutes of the order they were of noble lineage – in practice drawn partly from baronial families but mostly from the shire-knight and gentry classes. The vow of obedience to their rule and their Order was strictly kept and discipline was strong. The vow of chastity was at least outwardly observed, but the order offered a career open to talent which made the vow of poverty, for the more successful knight, something of a mockery until the order claimed nearly all his money and goods at his death.

An English knight's life, after his reception and noviciate at Clerkenwell, would follow a varied pattern: periods of several years in Rhodes, serving against the Muslim powers at sea or in coastal castles like Feraclos and Bodrum (where the carved coats of arms, signatures and graffiti of many English and Scottish knights may still be seen), alternating with spells of residence at home – with promotion to the office of Commander – to assist with the management of the order's estates and finances, and the despatch to Rhodes of newly trained Knights, lay mercenaries, and the profits of the hospitaller lands in the form of money, weapons, armour and English woollen cloth. A knight or Commander might be sent by the Grand Master of the order on a diplomatic mission to the Pope, the Doge of Venice or the royal courts of Spain. He might be 'seconded' into the king's service: Robert Hales, who served with other Hospitallers when a crusading force raided and sacked Alexandria in 1365, was Treasurer of England under Richard II, and was lynched by the rebellious peasants of Kent and Essex in the rising of 1381, when Clerkenwell Priory was burnt down and the Hospitaller manor of Highbury ransacked. John Langstrother, who helped defend Rhodes against Egyptian invasion and Bodrum against Turkish attack, was Prior of England and royal Treasurer at the time of his execution, caught on the losing side in the Wars of the Roses in 1471. John Weston commanded war galleys against the Turks in the eastern Mediterranean, and Thomas Sheffield is recorded by pilgrims on their way to Palestine as helping to administer the order's great infirmary at Rhodes.

English knights of St. John were prominent in the final defence of Rhodes against the besieging Turks in 1522, in the negotiations for a new Mediterranean base for the Convent of the order – (which included a visit to the rebuilt Clerkenwell Priory and a meeting with

Henry VIII by Philippe Villiers de l'Isle Adam, the Grand Master, in 1528) – and in the subsequent settlement in Malta, where the English knights, as in Rhodes, supervised coastal defence. A handful of English knights, after the order was dissolved in England by King Henry in 1540, remained in Malta, cut off from their own country, and deeply committed to the crusading warfare against the Turks. A few of their churches, like the round church of Little Maplestead in Essex, and fragments of their preceptories – a gatehouse, a dovecot, a medieval portion of a mainly reconstructed commander's house – survive in England, Wales and Scotland to remind us that much of their careers were spent managing lands and dispensing hospitality, medical assistance and alms.

In medieval England there were many hospitals not belonging to the Order of St. John: nearly one thousand have been traced. Without forming a monastic order, many of them were monastic, with resident priests and brothers and sisters living and working under the vows of religion. The London hospitals of St. Bartholomew's and St. Thomas's were under the aegis of the Augustinian Canons, and other major English hospitals – at Bristol, Leicester, York – were run according to a semi-conventual rule. Medieval hospitals accommodated travellers and fed the poor as well as taking in the sick. In an age which had no knowledge of (for example) the circulation of the blood or micro-biology, their theory and practice of hygiene, medicine, surgery and therapy were a world away from those of the 20th century; but they administered some drugs, performed some operations and nursed many patients with a skill which compels us not to dismiss them as merely incompetent or primitive or superstitious. The widespread establish-ment in the 12th century of isolation hospitals for lepers (lazar-houses) made possible the steady elimination of leprosy (confused though it was with other skin diseases) from the population.

Hospitals and lazar-houses

The Buildings of the Monastery

There were over a thousand English monasteries. Nearly all the richest of them were Old English foundations, which had come into possession of spacious sites (Glastonbury Abbey stood in sixty acres), in times when undeveloped land was easier to acquire than it was by the 12th century – except in the wilds where the Cistercians built their houses. The monasteries of the 13th century varied greatly in resources, in the number of their monks, and in the scale of their conventual buildings. Many of their churches were less than 100 feet in length, dwarfed five-fold by great structures like those at Winchester and St. Albans. In consequence, it is difficult to present a standard impression of the buildings of an English monastery, but the attempt should be made. The paramount need was for a fairly level site, to allow for the construction, within the ambience of the monastery walls, of the church, the cloister where the monks lived, ate, studied and slept,

Choosing a site

the abbot's house, the infirmary, guest-house, brew-house, bake-house, stables, mills, dovecot, fishpond, garden and orchard. Rochester Cathedral Priory, ancient foundation as it was, came to be excessively cramped for space. The Cluniac Priory at Thetford in Norfolk was so beleaguered by urban housing that it had to be moved out of town.

Next it was essential to ensure that the site was well supplied with water, most of all for drinking, but also for washing and drainage, building works and fishponds. There were many fast days when monks were not allowed fresh meat, and fish from the monastery's pond was in demand: carp above all, but also perch and tench, roach and bream, eels and pike. At Kirklees, the Cistercians created a series of fishponds by damming a descending stream at different levels. The most fortunate arrangement for a monastery would be to secure the supply of water from a spring, either nearby and by way of a channelled stream, as at Fountains; or within the precincts themselves, as at Haughmond, where the spring was protected and kept pure by a well-house. Leeds Priory in Kent was fed by a spring from which the water flowed through the fishpond, then through the monastery buildings as a drain,

An early plan of Christchurch, Canterbury, shows the waterworks supplying the monastic buildings by the church, with its two transepts, at the top.

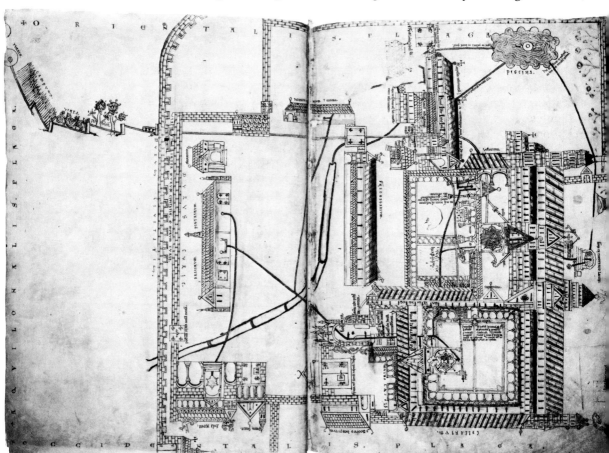

and out over a mill-wheel. Monastic kitchens and lavatories were often constructed over the course of such a stream flowing through their premises. The major urban monasteries, such as Christ Church, Canterbury, the London Charterhouse and St. Augustine's, Bristol, brought their water in by conduits and pipes from sources outside. The Franciscan friars, in towns like Cambridge, Coventry and Lincoln were the leading experts in developing supplies of piped water, using lead conduits. A monastery's drains and sewers were often stone-clad and several feet high. The cellarer of Christ Church, Canterbury, Roger Norreys, imprisoned in the infirmary by the chapter for improper practices in 1188, escaped by the sewers: *per necessaria exivit immundus.*

Another problem, only a little less acute than the water supply, was to provide enough firewood. More than one monastery had to be moved to bring it closer to essential fuel resources. The classic example is Byland Abbey, which was shifted from place to place before the fourth choice in half a century sited the community satisfactorily.

The visitor to a monastery would approach it by the gatehouse. Splendid gatehouses have survived in considerable numbers in England. St. John's Gate in Clerkenwell, London, is, apart from the church, the only surviving part of the headquarters of the English Hospitallers. St. Augustine's Priory at Canterbury had two gatehouses because of the heavy demands on its hospitality. At the Charterhouse in London, as elsewhere, callers could be looked at through a grating and identified, before being admitted. The gatehouse entrance was vaulted and high enough to allow heavily laden carts to go through. Above the arch would be a courtroom or a schoolroom, and flanking it would be side doors for pedestrians and sometimes side rooms for guests. The gatehouse might be fortified, its roof battlemented: it might even include a small prison, as at Ely. The Cistercians, their minds on sublimer things – and on the needs of lay brothers – provided gatehouse chapels, as at Coggeshall in Essex. Some abbeys constructed parish churches, for the convenience of the lay people, outside their gatehouses – as did Westminster Abbey when St. Margaret's Church was built.

Once inside the gatehouse, the visitor would be among a cluster of buildings not arranged on any uniform plan: a great barn, perhaps 300 feet long and 100 feet wide; a malthouse, a corn garner or granary; a house with a dining hall for monastery servants; and, in every monastery, the stables. Bakery, brewery, smithy can all be added. There was no standard layout. The keynote was monastic determination to supply all the needs of life within the precincts.

At the heart of this complex was the cloister: the Latin word, *claustrum*, meant no more than a place enclosed and shut in. The cloister was a court built around an open rectangle, the garth, which was edged by a covered passage-way on all four sides. Beside and above this passage-way were the most important buildings of the monastery.

The gatehouse

The monastery church

65

The church, the biggest building, usually stood on the north side, to be a shelter against the colder winds and not to cut off the sunlight. With windows at its east end and along its northern and southern flanks, the church was illuminated by as much natural light as possible, with the choir and the chapels concentrated in the east, to catch the morning sunlight. The church was usually shaped like a crucifix: the east end short, though often elongated in the later middle ages; the arms of the cross, the transepts, short, too, and equal in length; the western shaft of the cross, the nave of the church, in proportion long.

The principal door of the church was at the west end, facing the gatehouse, and was often the centre of an imposing façade of windows and arcading, sometimes with twin towers, as at Durham, Dunstable and Llanthony in Monmouthshire. Castle Acre is a small monastery and Peterborough a greater, each with a fine west façade. At Rievaulx, Fountains and Byland the Cistercians added to the west façade a narthex or arched portico. A bell tower was built at the west front of some abbeys, like Bolton and Furness. Elsewhere – Canterbury, Gloucester, Worcester, Kirkstall, Durham, Carlisle – the bell tower rose above the crossing, where nave, chancel and transepts met. Eastwards from the main door stretched the nave, without aisles in smaller monastic churches, but in the bigger houses flanked by a north aisle and a south aisle. Each aisle was separated from the nave by arches, above which rose the triforium (or range of blind arches) and the clerestory (or range of arched windows below the roof). Some naves were of imposing length, like Fountains with eleven arches and Peterborough and Norwich with twelve. At the end of the nave, before one came to the transepts and the east end, was the rood screen, a stone partition with altars set in front of it and twin doors connecting it with the choir to the east. When the monasteries were dissolved in the 16th century, the nave was sometimes retained as a parish church, and the rood screen was transformed into its east end, the rest of the church being demolished. Above the rood screen was a loft, approached by a spiral staircase, and above the rood loft was a crucifix, with the carved wooden figure of Jesus Christ crucified, Mary and John the Evangelist. No example of the rood, the object of the most earnest devotion in medieval monasteries, survived the Dissolution. Beyond the rood screen the transepts met the nave; eastwards, across the west end of the choir ran another screen, constructed in stone and known as the *pulpitum*, with a door in the middle opening into the choir. In England, many a *pulpitum* was decorated with statues or paintings of the Kings and Queens of the realm, going back to Alfred, with a local saint sometimes in the midst. York Minster, which is not a monastery, has the finest surviving *pulpitum* in England, with fifteen sculptured kings, from William the Conqueror to Henry VI. This was the part of the church which housed the organs, sometimes in a wooden loft stretching over the crossing, between the rood screen and the *pulpitum*. (What we call an organ was known as 'a pair of organs' in the middle ages.)

East of the *pulpitum* ran the choir stalls of carved wood, on bases of stonework, to protect them from damp. They had high ornamented canopied backs, with desks in front for service books. On the undersides of their hinged seats, which were raised like cinema seats when the monk had to stand during the service, were the famous carvings known as *misericords*, depicting evangelists, angels, flowers, foliage and cockades – but also dishonest ale-wives, foxes garbed as monks preaching to the credulous, demons and sinners of every kind. The misericord was so constructed as to allow a monk who was standing, tired, during a long service, to sit, unofficially; but it often illustrated an episode on the primrose path to the everlasting bonfire. The abbot's seat, suitably carved, was at the west end of the choir, on the south side. At the west end too stood a lectern, brass, in the shape of an eagle with spread wings, on which the music books were put for the choir-leaders to see, with their enlarged lettering and musical notation. East of the choir stalls were the presbytery and the high altar, with the reredos behind, usually of carved and painted wood, showing the story of the fall and the redemption. In the bigger churches, there were chapels east of the high altar, and they were linked by a broad passage of horseshoe shape, known as the ambulatory. Tewkesbury is the finest example; Christ Church, Canterbury, and Norwich are others.

Often the main feature of the ambulatory was a Lady Chapel, dedicated to the Virgin Mary, and situated immediately behind the high altar, although the superb Lady Chapel at Ely was at the north-east corner of the monastic cathedral. Some monasteries had particular statues of the Virgin Mary which attracted pilgrims and offerings, notably the statue at Walsingham, which stood on the north side of the nave in a chapel modelled on the house of the Holy Family at Nazareth. At Hailes Abbey in Gloucestershire, the Cistercians preserved a much venerated relic of the Holy Blood, though the fragment of the True Cross at Bromholm in Norfolk was in the parish church. English monasteries were fairly rich in relics of the native saints, preserved in massive coffins set in rich canopied shrines. The bones and the shrines of the Old English saints, Edward the Confessor at Westminster and Cuthbert at Durham, have survived the crisis of the Reformation until the present day. The body and shrine of St. Thomas Becket, the martyr of Canterbury, were a powerful magnet for pilgrims from all over the British Isles and much of the continent, but Henry VIII deliberately destroyed them when the monasteries were dissolved. The cults of local saints like Birinus at Dorchester on Thames, Guthlac at Crowland and Warburg at Chester, all dating from Anglo-Saxon times and sedulously sustained by their monks, were obliterated at the same time. Saints' relics in caskets, enclosed within the structure of monastic altars, have survived into the 20th century in places as far apart as Rievaulx and Bodmin.

In the transepts, or northern and southern arms of the church, leading at right-angles from the crossing, were the side chapels, subsidiary altars and chantries where masses were said for the souls of benefactors of the monastery. Transepts were unusual in nunneries, which had no priests of their own and where masses were relatively few. From the far end of the north transept, a door in the north wall gave on to the burial ground of the monastic community. In the south transept was the dormitory door, which opened on to the spiral night staircase, leading to the first-floor level and the adjacent monks' dormitory at the west end of the transept, to enable the monks to come down to the night and early morning services by the shortest route. There might be another door in the south transept, as well as the two doors in the nave, leading to the cloister, for use in processions before high mass on Sundays and feast days.

The cloister   The cloister was usually, though not always, on the south side of the monastic church. Its centre, the garth, was a plot of ground far less likely to be a trim lawn than unturfed and laid out in vegetable beds and herb gardens with a well at the side or in the middle. Low walls surmounted by arches divided the garth from the paved cloister walk or alley. On the far side of the alley rose the lower stage of the wall of the church or other monastic buildings, and the alley was covered either with a lean-to roof or the projection above it of the upper floor of the monastic buildings. The Cistercians began with wooden cloisters, later replacing them in stone. The cloister arches were usually filled in with a combination of glass and wooden shutters. The northern cloister alley, facing south over the garth, was in especial need of natural lighting and protection from the elements, as it was a study area as well as a passage linking important parts of the monastery. Carrels were ranged along the south side: these were individual desks, sometimes provided with wooden walls, canopy, door, bench and unglazed window looking south, so that it became a tiny cabin for one man to read and write in, sheltered from draughts and damp. The pursuit of learning and scholarship might be so strong at a monastery that small carrels were also put in the eastern or western alleys. Otherwise, the cloister alley might contain a wooden cupboard built into the wall – an *armarium*, for the storage of books (fine examples of the stone recesses for book-cupboards survive at Fountains and Lilleshall); and statues of saints, set in stone niches with lights burning perpetually before them.

The chapter house   The eastern range of the monastic buildings flanking the cloister alleys consisted mainly of the chapter house. Here the convent met frequently – normally every day – to hear confessions, examine the conduct of individual monks, commemorate those who had given property or money to the house, and transact every kind of monastic business. From the cloister, the monks moved direct into the chapter house through a large ornamental doorway, flanked on either side by broad window openings, sometimes glazed, sometimes not, and in some places sweeping down to ground level. In some monasteries, a broad portico lay between and linked the cloister alley and the chapter house: in effect it pushed the chapter house further to the east, so that it could be built with windows able to catch the light on all sides. Inside the chapter house, the abbot sat on an ornate chair with its back to the eastern wall, and the monks sat in seats along the northern and southern walls, taking their places in order of seniority. In the centre of the open space of the chapter house was a lectern holding the necrology, a book in which the convent enrolled the names of its benefactors and protectors, and of its own deceased monks, and on the anniversary of their deaths, their names were read out in commemoration. Some chapter houses were rectangular, others had an apse at the eastern side. Some were circular, as at Worcester, and others twelve-sided, as at Westminster Abbey. Some had side aisles, which the Cistercians favoured, and others had simple interiors without aisles.

Between the chapter house and the south transept ran the slype, a wide roofed corridor connecting the cloister with the monks' cemetery. The monks used the slype for conversation, for talk was prohibited in the cloister itself. In some houses, the slype was eventually developed into a library, though in most houses books were normally kept in wooden cupboards, in the cloister, the choir, the sacristy and the refectory. Tombstones were rarely set above the graves in the cemetery garth. Monks who commanded special reverence might be buried in stone or leaden coffins, to ensure that the gravediggers, in a burial ground limited in area and dug for fresh graves decade after decade, would not turn up their bones and send them to the charnel house. The most distinguished members of a convent might be buried, with inscribed tombstones, even carved effigies of themselves over their bones, in the chapter house, the cloister alley, the narthex and, by the 15th and early 16th centuries, the church itself. If the monastery church was also a parish church, there would be on its north side a cemetery for the laity, and a commodious ornamental porch for weddings, as may be seen at Tewkesbury and Selby.

The upper storey on the eastern side of the cloister was the monks' dormitory: the dorter, with a long range of windows facing east and west on either side. In the 12th century, the dorter had no partitions and resembled a barrack room or hospital ward. By the 14th century there was a strong emphasis on privacy, for study, meditation, prayer and sleep, and the dorter was divided into wooden cubicles, each with its own window, desk, bookshelf, bench and bed. Below the dorter, in many Benedictine monasteries, was the warming-house. East of the dorter, on the upper-storey level, ran the rere-dorter, the monastic lavatory, with its individual cabinets along both sides of a central passage and, below, on ground level, the great drain.

Dorter and frater

On the southern side of the cloister was the refectory, or frater, usually on the upper storey, approached by a staircase from the cloister alley, and running east and west. It had high windows in its south wall, to catch the daylight. In a few houses it was on the ground level. In many abbeys, such as Rievaulx, the refectory ran at right-angles to and south from the cloister alley, and the kitchen and warming-house were closely integrated with it into the main claustral range. The refectory was roofed with timber not stone, probably to improve the acoustics for the reader who read daily during meals from the scriptures or homilies to the monks. Against the clatter and clamour of the community at dinner, he read from a pulpit which was usually built into the wall of the refectory, half-way between the entrance and the high table on its dais. Here, under a carved or painted crucifix, the abbot, prior and obedientiaries sat at their meals. The tables for the other monks ran at right-angles to the high table, down the length of the refectory. At the lower end might be a broad hatch giving on to the kitchen. The monastic kitchen in some houses was part not of the southern but the western range of the cloister, and in others it was a separate building, standing apart because of fire risks. Its fire-places, ovens and chimneys were built into the thickness of the walls, though it might also have a central open hearth with a chimney above. The best example of a monastic kitchen to survive in England is at Glastonbury – not the frater kitchen, but the private kitchen of the abbot. It is eight-sided, buttressed, two-storeyed and surmounted by a cupola which culminated in a massive chimney. The kitchen was surrounded by the pantry and buttery (which often had their own hatches into the refectory for the serving of bread, butter and beer), the bakery, brewery and bolting-house, where corn was sieved.

February in the Calendar of the St. Alban's Psalter, c. 1120. The warming-house was the only room in a monastery, apart from the kitchen and infirmary, where a fire was allowed.

70

Below the refectory was the stone-vaulted cellar, where beer and wine were stored in casks, and adjacent was the lavatorium where, early in the day and before their meals, the monks washed their hands and faces in a long, shallow basin or trough beneath a lead waterpipe with brass taps, set into the cloister wall under blind arcading often faced with marble. There might also be a barber's house and a bell-house from which the community was rung in to wash and dine.

On the fourth, the western side of the cloister, the head of the house had his accommodation (though the Cistercians used the western range entirely for lay brothers, and housed the abbot elsewhere) and there were also chambers for guests. Even the most modest apartments for an abbot or prior would include a chamber or parlour for the daytime, a bedchamber, a dining room and a chapel. The entertainment of eminent guests was a responsibility of the head of house, and extensive as his suite of chambers might seem for the use of one monk, it became necessary for many abbots and priors to arrange for dining halls of their own to be built, usually sited on the upper storey, with guest-rooms beneath. The abbot's hall had a high table at one end, with a doorway just behind it leading to the abbot's private chambers, and an oriel or 'bay' window to light it. Other tables, for the less important guests and senior clerks and retainers, ran the length of the hall to the parallel screens with doors in them, providing access to the hall for all but the select guests of the abbot and contact between the hall and the kitchen, buttery and pantry. In the greater houses the abbot had his own kitchen, but elsewhere he might draw upon the resources of the main conventual kitchen and domestic offices. The opulence of this accommodation was not necessarily the result of an abbot's deliberate choice. The Archbishops of York virtually compelled the Priors of Bridlington to maintain a sumptuous hostel, so that the prelate could rely on somewhere comfortable and spacious to stay while on his visitations of eastern Yorkshire.

The abbot's lodgings

The western range of the cloister was, however, not always made over to the head of the house and his guests. In the beginning, the Cistercians had used it to provide the lay brothers with a refectory and a common room on the ground floor and a dorter above, with its own rere-dorter and night-stair down to the church. When lay brothers declined in number in the 14th century, their accommodation in the western range was taken over by the abbot for other purposes – administration and hospitality.

East of the eastern range of the cloisters was the infirmary, with which he often shared his own kitchen, partly because the resident sick could include guests of the abbot, partly because dietary rules were relaxed and more delicate dishes and a greater abundance of flesh-meat were served both to guests and to whose who were ill. The infirmary was fundamentally for sick monks, but those who were too old, too infirm or too stricken mentally to live up to the astringent demands of the Rule were retired there and allowed more rest and a kindlier diet

The infirmary

than the conventual monk was. The infirmary had a great hall or ward, with a lofty roof, at least one big wall fireplace, a chapel at one end (a fine infirmary chapel survives at Furness Abbey), a laver and lavatories at the other end, and a range of high windows along each wall. The beds were arranged in the side aisles, set between each pair of windows, bedheads to the wall. The central nave of the infirmary would be an open walk-way, as in a modern hospital. Some monastic infirmaries were constructed on a relatively small scale: a clear idea of them can be gained from Haughmond, where the little infirmary was tall and airy, and directly connected with the abbot's house. Most of them, however, were surprisingly large in relation to the number of their monks. One explanation was the regular blood-letting, or phlebotomy, to which monks were treated for medical reasons. Blood-letting was regarded not as an unpleasant operation to be undergone, but as a pleasure to be looked forward to, and the frequency with which a monk could be bled was consequently restricted: four times a year for Cistercians, five times for Carthusians, though an Austin canon might go eight times a year. After each phlebotomy, a monk was allowed to rest in the infirmary for three days, during which he enjoyed a late rising hour, exemption from choir, plenty of meat and other rich food, and freedom to stroll in the gardens and vineyards; but he was forbidden to play at dice or chess or to hold frivolous converse, for it was believed that blood-letting made the patient talkative. At Bury St. Edmunds, according to Abbot Samson's biographer, Jocelin of Brakelond, the monks, after they had been bled, would tell one another their most intimate secrets, so that Samson had to order senior monks to go for bleeding with their juniors and control their talk and conduct.

From the 13th century onwards, there was a growing practice of moving the abbot out of the western range of the cloister and into an abbot's house specially built for him and standing on its own fairly near to the monastic dorter: it was generally a three-floored mansion with its dining hall on the middle storey, and hardly distinguishable from the rural manor-house of a noble family.

The Abbot and his Monks

The heyday of monasticism

By about 1220, the great age of monastic growth in England, a combination of Benedictine expansion after the Norman Conquest and the achievements of the new Orders, was at its end. For the monks, the 13th century was a zenith or at the least a plateau, on which they can be observed at their most numerous, most well supported, though perhaps not most revered: certainly the best time at which to assess their place in society and their contribution to it. The 13th century was a prosperous but not a golden age: marred by famine, flood and strife, the material, intellectual and spiritual acme of the middle ages, it ran on, as 'centuries' will, deep into the 1300s. Monastic history in England turned its most crucial and painful corner when the bubonic plague, the Black Death, struck England in the years 1348–1350.

How many monks were there in 13th-century England? If we count those living within the walls of a typical monastery, we shall find that one-third were monks, and the remainder were paying guests (*corrodians*), temporary visitors, and serving men and women. St. Albans had one hundred monks, the largest community in England, for in the great Cistercian abbeys, Rievaulx, Fountains, Waverley, Louth Park and Meaux, the number of monks had fallen away from the big communities of Ailred's time to between sixty and seventy. The greater Benedictine houses, like Durham, Winchester, Norwich, Peterborough and Glastonbury, had each a similar contingent of about sixty monks.

One of the earliest detailed maps of Great Britain extant, drawn about A.D. 1250 by Matthew Paris, historian, artist and monk of St. Alban's. Features emphasised are the two Roman walls, rivers, towns and the monastery of St. Alban's ('cenobuim Sancti Albani'). 'Scocia Vitramarina' is shown as an island connected with southern Scotland only by a bridge at Stirling ('Estiuelin').

No house of Austin Canons reached this level: Waltham had fifty canons, Barnwell and Cirencester only thirty each. It seems likely that in the 13th century, with a population in England of perhaps three million, the numbers of professed monks and canons were:

MONKS	
Benedictines	4000
Cluniacs	500
Cistercians	3000
Carthusians	200
CANONS	
Augustinians	3000
Premonstratensians and Victorines	800
Gilbertines	1000
NUNS (of all orders)	7000
HOSPITALLERS AND TEMPLARS	500
	20,000

The novice One member of the population in 150 was, then, a monk or a nun, and there were a great many other people in one way or another attached to the religious houses. No longer did they include the children who, in earlier years, had been 'offered' in infancy, by their parents, to monastic communities, to be educated as 'oblates' and professed as monks or nuns whatever their own wishes. 'The children of the cloister', under the pressure of Cistercian and Carthusian reform, had disappeared by 1200. The age for a postulant, one seeking admission to a monastery or nunnery, was now between seventeen and nineteen (or later), when a young man or woman would know what were his or her personal beliefs and what would be the implications of entering the cloister for life. By 1200, it was less easy for a postulant to be admitted than in the age of rapid expansion. A house of fifty monks might have only two or three vacant places a year. Once admitted, the postulant became a novice, who must give all his worldly goods to the monastery (especially if he was well off), or else to the poor. His instruction would include a close study of the Rule. His own clothes would be kept for him, in case he wished to give up his vocation or was asked to leave. He usually took the vows of religion at the end of twelve months.

Lay brothers and lay sisters Lay brothers and, with the Gilbertines, lay sisters, were still an important part of the monastic population in 1200: in the big Cistercian abbeys, fifty years before, they had outnumbered the monks by three to one, and the Carthusians, the Austin Canons and the Benedictines, following in the steps of the white monks, recruited them in considerable numbers. In the 13th century, their ranks were steadily and heavily depleted. Not only did market forces and a falling-off of their own enthusiasm draw them away: they became difficult to deal with, an embarrassment and a challenge to the monastic rule. The records of the Welsh Cistercian abbeys bring to light episodes of violence committed by the lay brothers – assaults on the cellarer at Margam, stealing the abbot's horses at Neath, going on strike at Strata Florida – none too serious in themselves but pointing to a tenser, more unmanageable relationship between convent and lay brethren than Ailred of Rievaulx could ever have expected. After 1350 they were a negligible branch of the monastic community.

A monastery where lay brothers were dwindling in number and where the legitimate tasks of the monks gave them less time to work with their hands inevitably needed domestic servants, men and women of the laity who agreed to work for wages. Even the Cistercians had to accept the need: the thin end of the wedge for them was a Cistercian statute which allowed an abbey with only eight lay brothers to hire servants, who were expected, optimistically, to take the vows of religion. The Benedictines and Augustinians had no qualms about hiring servants: for every monk at Norwich there were more than two servants, for every canon at Nostell there were three. At any one time in the 13th century, English monasteries and nunneries probably employed, paid and usually housed some 40,000 servants, many of whom brought their wives and children to live with them in the precincts. The callings of this army of servants were innumerable: porters, cresset-keepers (lamplighters) and bath-attendants; butlers, chamberlains, cooks, scullions, herring-curers; scriveners and keepers of the wax; servants in the infirmary, the stables, the brewery, bakehouse and boathouse (Worcester Cathedral Priory had a crew of five boatmen on the River Severn). Washerwomen and sewing-women appear, as might be expected, in great numbers; but it is surprising to find chaplains among the paid servants.

Servants

Domestic help was needed not only for the abbot and his monks but also for the remarkable number of guests – some lodging free, others paying their way – who used the monastery as a residential hotel and made up about one-sixth of its population. Many an abbot or prior retired when elderly and tired, and resided in the monastery with a pension, an allowance in food and clothing, and a set of rooms. Not all were as barefaced as Abbot Adam of Eynsham who, having written the life of St. Hugh of Lincoln, was removed from office in 1228 for covering up his gross financial incompetence, but stayed on in the abbey and was allocated the profits of one of its manors for his maintenance. An Abbot of Wigmore who decided to retire in 1318 was given board, lodging and clothing for himself, another canon to attend him, and two servants. Retired heads of houses sometimes lived on, at the expense of their brothers, for sixteen or twenty years or more, and a house might find itself providing for two or more successively retired priors. We learn of more than one of them who was persuaded to leave the cloister and lead the life almost of a lay squire on one of the foundation's country manors; but misconduct in old age or neglect of the Hours could bring down upon an ex-prior – as upon John Worcester of Little Malvern – the loss of his comforts and emoluments and an uncomfortable return to the austere life of the cloister, as an ordinary monk.

Corrodians The most numerous lodgers in a monastery, however, were the corrodians. A corrody was an annuity. A layman would buy it for himself, with his wife and members of his family often included, in return for an outright grant of land or money. For the monastery it was a convenient way of picking up a lump sum in a time of need; for the corrodian, it guaranteed an agreed, secure and comfortable standard of living in old age, with the possibility of entering the order itself before death and being buried in monastic habit in the priory churchyard. This might take a long time: the canons of Merton housed an old corrodian who lived among them for twenty-nine years. A corrody might be very detailed in its terms: Bayham Priory in Sussex sold a corrody to a man and his crippled invalid son, and guaranteed to make good provision for his daughters, teach his younger sons a trade, pay all his debts, and send his lawyer an annual fee. Sometimes the corrodian did not reside, but simply paid a premium for a life-long allowance of food, fuel, clothing and even the rights of pasture, wood-cutting and hunting. In return for lump sums, an imprudent abbot or prior might saddle his house with ten or twenty corrodies or more, gambling on the early (or not too long delayed) death of the corrodians for them not to sap the resources of the house too expensively. The letter-books of the bishops of the day show them as deeply concerned to restrain monasteries from mortgaging the future to too many corrodies.

Land and wealth Monks and nuns and canons in almost every English religious house were consequently surrounded by a penumbra of servants and lodgers and their families, as well as temporary visitors and guests. The ideal of St. Benedict, let alone of St. Bruno and St. Bernard, that the monastery should be a place of seclusion, solitude, even silence, was thus largely lost. In the midst of all this, the Hours were observed by the monks, the church, the library, the refectory and the kitchens were kept in good order, and well supplied and maintained. There was private study, private prayer, the composition and copying of books; but monks found it more and more difficult not to be closely involved with the worldly affairs they were vowed to shun.

Unquestionably, the problems began with their possession of the lands and other properties given them by benefactors, without which the monastic orders could never have thriven or made room for more than a handful of postulants. By the 13th century, English monastic lands were wide and wealthy. Bury St. Edmunds had 170 manors. Meaux had 20,000 acres. Crowland Abbey had land in five shires, Lewes Priory land in 223 parishes. Although these were among the especially richly endowed, nearly every house in England and Wales, in proportion to the number of its monks, had too much property, too solid a material stake in the world, not to be forced to commit a great deal of the time, energy and thought of its monks to the business of managing and defending property and extracting a satisfactory return from it.

A momentous consequence of the monastery's being a propertied corporation was the steady separation of the head of the house from his monks. Heads of houses were either abbots or priors. It is not possible to draw a sharp distinction between the two titles. All Cistercian, Premonstratensian and Victorine houses were abbeys, and all Cluniac and Carthusian houses were priories, daughter-houses of Cluny and the Grande Chartreuse (except that Cluniac Bermondsey, anomalously, was an abbey). The greater Benedictine foundations and a few of the Augustinian houses were abbeys: the majority of the houses of these two Orders, like all those of the Gilbertines, were priories. Within the walls of a monastery, it was of only marginal importance whether the head was abbot or prior: for the present purpose, let us refer to him as 'the abbot'.

The abbot

From St. Benedict's time onwards he had always been cast in something of a dual role, the two parts of which were not easily reconciled. He was the good shepherd of his flock, leading or driving them, but sharing their sufferings, familiar with them, their friend and brother – as Ailred was. Yet he was also the father of the house. His election by the monks in chapter was regarded as the result of the guidance of the Holy Spirit, expressly and fervently prayed for in the hymn *Veni, creator Spiritus* ('Come down, Creator Spirit'). His instructions came as from God, and he was the representative of Jesus within his monastery. That his monks should keep their vows and obey the Rule and his house should be well and quietly governed, efficient and secure, was his inescapable responsibility. He professed the novices and appointed the officials, granted privileges and administered discipline. Although he was required to seek the advice of the senior, wiser and more experienced monks, he was without question an autocrat, elected for life, unless he was translated elsewhere, chose in old age to retire, or had to be unseated because of a total breakdown in health, physical or mental, or grave offences against the Rule. The stronger tendency, then, was for the abbot to be treated more as a majestic father than a loving brother, to be deferential rather than familiar with him. When he came home from his travels, he would be greeted by a procession of monks, to conduct him to the altar with thanksgiving for his return. Most of his journeys arose from the need for him to undertake a ceaseless round of visits to his house's estates. He must hold court, judge in civil actions – usually disputes between his tenants, but also in criminal cases – confer with and keep close surveillance of the estate bailiffs, deal with countless petitions for justice and requests for favours. An abbot of one of the greater houses might be wanted to serve the Crown as an assize judge, to attend the royal court at Whitsuntide or the Lords' house in Parliament at Michaelmas. Travel further afield, to the Papal Curia at Rome, was sometimes necessary and could be a pleasure which could be spun out. One Abbot of Westminster, Walter Wenlock, spent a protracted vacation at Orvieto after his business at the Holy See was completed, and another, Richard Croxley, took up employment in Rome as a papal chaplain. Abbot Samson of Bury had to make an arduous journey to Rhineland Germany, though his biographer writes a little tartly that he was 'in better spirits anywhere than at Bury'.

To superintend the day-to-day life of the monastery and the welfare and conduct of the monks was a task which the abbot had to delegate to the prior of his house, his chief official, who was bound therefore to come between the abbot and the individual monk. (Where the head of a house was the prior, he had a sub-prior.) There was no more vivid symbol of that than the prior's duty of inspecting the cloister after dark and ensuring that only where necessary were any doors unlocked, any lights still burning.

At home, the abbot had the duty of hospitality to a constant flow of guests – ranging from the royal court itself, the archbishop or the local bishop and neighbouring noblemen (all these with their households) to the tenants, who might be of aristocratic or knightly rank, of the lands of the house, or the leading citizens of towns nearby, where the house would have property. The Benedictine Rule had always allowed the abbot to have a kitchen and a table of his own; and the claims of hospitality, arising so strongly from the monastery's involvement with the outside world, were probably decisive in impelling the abbot of the great majority of houses to have his own lodgings built, standing apart from the cloister. In the larger English monasteries, the abbot would retain a body of about fifty household servants, paid, fed, clothed and accommodated by him: squires (even an occasional knight) as his escort and bodyguard; clerks to manage his correspondence, valets to give him courier and postal services, look after his wardrobe and personal belongings, and manage his stable, as well as cooks, grooms, and laundresses. Such a household might stable fifty horses.

Samson (head of one of England's largest abbeys), after his election, 'setting his household in order, appointed divers servants to various duties, saying that he had decided to have twenty-six horses in his courtyard, for a child must crawl and then stand upright and walk. He enjoined his servants beyond all things that they should take heed that he be not dishonoured by a lack of meat and drink, but rather that they in all things should anxiously provide for the hospitality of the house'. Hospitality had to be paid for, and the flow of money for it was not wholly predictable. At Bury, in good times, the abbot's household on average ate daily one ox, two pigs, four geese and twenty-two chickens; in bad times we hear of the abbot dismissing nearly all his household retainers, giving up hospitality and refusing important invitations which required costly travel. Only a few abbots entertained on the scale and with the arrogance of the Cistercian Hugh of Beaulieu, who on occasion sat down to dinner with three earls and forty knights: so much for the effect of St. Bernard's teaching – but Abbot Hugh was a friend of King John's.

There was emphatically concern in high places in the Church that abbots were becoming (often because they had no choice, in some instances because it suited their inclinations) public figures, symbols of authority and administration, at least touched by worldly living, remote from their monks. The general chapters of the Benedictine monks, and archbishops and bishops on their visitations to non-exempt houses began to press abbots hard to live among their monks more frequently and continuously, and to instruct them more and more not to take important actions (such as admitting postulants, selling or leasing monastic lands, and exercising patronage) without the agreement of their own monastic chapter, or sometimes of a committee of the older and wiser. Monks and canons were in general governed by strong autocracy tempered by oligarchy.

The monastic officials working under the abbot were known as the obedientiaries. A monastery of average size probably had fifteen obedientiaries. The biggest houses would have up to twenty of them. The number of offices was such that it gave most of the monks an opportunity of taking part sooner or later in the management of their houses, and administering the lands attached to his particular office. The abbot's chief obedientiary and deputy-general was the prior, who might have one or more sub-priors responsible to him. The abbey church was in the particular care of the sacristan. He was responsible for its security and cleanliness, which included keeping a fresh and clean floor-covering of rushes and straw. He looked after the altar vessels, crucifixes and ornaments, the altar frontals and altar cloths, the reliquaries, and the vestments kept in the sacristy. The illumination of the church was another of his special responsibilities – with fine wax candles for altars and shrines, cheaper tallow candles elsewhere, and torches and cressets, which were stone lanterns with hollows drilled out and filled with mutton fat on which wicks floated. The sacristan, with many liturgical treasures, including altar paintings, to protect, warming-pans heated by charcoal or 'sea-coal' to provide for the priest at the altar on cold early mornings, punctual bell-ringing to perform and clocks to superintend, would often be required to sleep in the church. He would be assisted by at least one sub-sacristan. The precentor had charge of the liturgical books, gospels, psalters, missals (mass-books), and choir-books, written on fine vellum, often expensively illuminated, in jewelled bindings of leather on selected woods. The books in the monastery library were also in his care. His chief task was to lead the chant at services from the south side of the choir. Over the singing he had absolute authority, with the succentor leading, under him, on the north side, when antiphons were sung. The novice-master instructed the novices in the Rule and prepared them to

The obedientiaries

meet the spiritual and physical demands of the monk's life – as well as giving them lessons in reading, singing and comportment. The noviciate lasted a year, during which progress was reviewed more than once. At its close, the novice, if accepted, made his vows and swore obedience to the Rule.

There were other obedientiaries. None was more important and powerful than the cellarer, who had charge of the properties of the convent, its lands, revenues and church patronage. He supervised the kitchen, the bakery and the brewery, the maintenance and repair of all buildings, the purchase of food, drink, clothing, fuel, and farm stock, and the transport system – horses, carriages, carts, wagons and boats. Lay brethren, servants and tenants came under his authority. In a larger house there would be a need for at least one sub-cellarer. The serving of meals of suitable quality, and on time, was the responsibility of the kitchener, and the furnishing and running of the refectory that of the refectorian. The hosteller looked after the guests of the house, their rooms and their beds, for the sake of the reputation of the house, the honour of God and the increase of charity. The infirmarian had charge of all arrangements for the sick; the almoner gave money, clothing, food and drink to the poor, to lepers, pilgrims and beggars and visited those poor and old people who could not leave their beds. Some monasteries had houses for the poor within their precincts: Bermondsey, for instance, ran a house for poor boys and penurious converts from the Jewish faith.

Monastic Property and Income

Resources During the 12th century, when the monastic orders had been so widely expanded and so generously endowed with property, they began to adopt a more ambitious approach to the extraction of the maximum income from their resources. Income came in part from offerings. Even without the relics of a famous saint like Cuthbert, Edmund, Edward the Confessor or Thomas Becket, the collecting boxes in the abbey church were well filled by the laity. Novices brought in donations in cash and land; older men would frequently enter the lay fraternity of a house, vowing a life of chastity and intensive prayer outside the cloister, accepting spiritual guidance from the monks, temporarily entering the infirmary for rest and treatment, more permanently taking up a corrody, and entering the order shortly before death, to be buried at last in the monastic cemetery, and prayed for by the monks thereafter. These privileges were paid for, sometimes with all the worldly goods of the laymen. So it was also with pious laywomen and the nunneries. Sometimes a layman paid a monastery for the right to be allowed to nominate a novice – perhaps his own son, or the son of a relative or friend – when the house next had a vacancy. Sir Ralph Camays and Selborne Priory once went to law over the patronage of West Tisted Church in Hampshire. The suit was settled in favour of the monks, but

Sir Ralph was compensated by being given the right to the next vacancy at the priory. Lay piety and lay interests were thus providing the monasteries with new income every decade, but the flood of lay generosity was subsiding significantly after 1200.

Parish churches themselves were also an important source of income. A monastery might either have appropriated to it all the tithes of a parish, offset by the obligation to provide and pay for a parson to look after the spiritual needs of the people; or the incumbent of a parish might have to pay a pension of fixed amount, year in, year out, to a monastery. Nearly every monastery and nunnery drew on parish resources in these ways. St. Albans had the tithes of sixteen churches, and provision for another four; Norwich Cathedral Priory took tithes and pensions from eighty-seven, in the city and in the East Anglian countryside.

Many monasteries were situated in towns and might own town houses outside their own walls; but some included entire boroughs among their endowments, and a borough like Battle had grown up at the abbey gates, on the abbey lands. There were thirty monastic boroughs in England, twenty-five of them belonging to the Benedictines, five to the Austin Canons. Among them were major provincial centres like Burton-on-Trent, Bury St. Edmunds, Coventry, Glastonbury, Malmesbury, Peterborough and Reading, and smaller towns like Abingdon, Evesham, Faversham, Tavistock, Whitby and Winchcombe. A few of them were the property of distant monasteries: Leominster belonged to Reading Abbey, Weymouth to Winchester Cathedral Priory, and Sandwich to Christ Church, Canterbury. The monks' control of their borough, whether exercised on their behalf by the abbot, the sacrist, or the cellarer, was invariably strong.

Monastic boroughs

They appointed a lay bailiff to preside over the law-courts in the borough and to levy for them the fines with which civil disputes were composed and the 'amercements' in money inflicted on offenders. The bailiff also collected the rents and rates of the householders, the market tolls, the dues on brewing ale, and the revenues from such monopolies as grinding corn and fulling cloth. He was usually a burgess himself, but in the last century of monasticism, 1440–1540, the office was frequently conferred on members of the knightly class or gentry of the countryside around, with their growing interest in acquiring urban influence. Monastic overlordship gave the burgesses law and order and economic security; but from 1200 onwards the burgesses showed a mounting interest in self-government and tried to secure it, by petition and argument, by forming merchant gilds to attempt to take over commerce, and by force. Under pressure, the monks could always turn, successfully, to the king and secure his support and judgement in their favour in his courts.

At Bury in 1264 the younger burgesses formed a Gild of Youth, pushed the abbot and his authority out of the town, and tried to establish a municipal constitution, with aldermen and bailiffs of their own. The monks turned to the Crown, there was a royal enquiry, and the young men's movement collapsed and the gild was dissolved. Norwich, not even a monastic borough, was the scene of bitter disagreement between the monks of the cathedral and the citizens, who burnt down much of the cathedral priory in 1272 and had to pay a heavy fine of £2000.

The years 1326–7, when King Edward II was being deposed in circumstances of political violence, and 1381, the time of the general revolt of the peasants in England, provide stark examples of the tension between the monastic borough communities and the monks who ruled them. In 1327, the townspeople of St. Albans, besieging the abbey, called for a bailiff of their own, free of the jurisdiction of the abbey, an end to the monks' monopoly of the corn-mills, and representation in Parliament. At the court of a weakened king, they won their case. Seven years later, Abbot Richard Wallingford, though afflicted by leprosy which had destroyed his clarity of speech, won back in the courts all that the monks had lost. At Bury St. Edmunds, there was a local civil war. The abbey's peasant tenants joined the townsfolk in ransacking and burning the guest houses and outbuildings of the monastery and plundering grain, hay and livestock from the manors of the abbey. The abbot was compelled to grant Bury municipal self-government: even so, he was kidnapped and held captive for a time, in London and Brussels. The story was similar at Abingdon – with Oxford scholars joining the insurgents and the senior monks brought before a rebel assembly of three thousand men in Bagley Wood to seal a charter of autonomy for the townspeople. Abingdon Abbey lost 250 illuminated service books, which were pillaged and sold by the insurgents. Again at Barnstaple, Cirencester, Coventry, Dunstable, Plymouth, monks and their armed servants were killed, concessions of self-government were exacted, the local sheriff intervened successfully, using professional troops against untrained rebels, the charters and concessions exacted by the townsfolk were quashed in the royal courts, and insurgents were indicted and executed.

In 1381, the burgesses of the monastic towns took advantage of a popular rising which began among the peasants on the rural manors, and asserted their ancient grievances and aims, though with more violence than before – with the prior of Bury and one of the monk-wardens being lynched, and the monks of St. Albans only saved from massacre by the courage and masterfulness of their abbot, Thomas de la Mare, and those of Peterborough by the intervention of the Bishop of Norwich and his private army. Once again, the armed power of the Crown and the authority of the royal courts, provided the ultimate sanction against the insurgents.

Apart from Reading, where there was progress towards municipal self-government in the 15th century, the monastic borough communities steadily subsided, after 1381, in their efforts to achieve freedom from the paternalist rule of their monks.

The greater proportion of the income of nearly every abbey and priory came from its lands, which it held in perpetuity, to the end of earthly time. Land could include the lordship of an entire town, such as Abingdon, Barnstaple, Bury St. Edmunds, Cirencester, Coventry, Dunstable, Durham, Peterborough, St. Albans and others; and the monopolies, on many monastic lands, of milling, cutting timber, reeds and peat, fishing, trapping game, refining salt, and claiming wrecks washed ashore. Monasteries had lucrative markets and fairs. They might take tolls, as Blyth Abbey did on all foodstuffs, livestock, wool and timber passing through the town, and Abingdon Abbey on cargoes going past its walls up and down the river Thames between Oxford and London. The Austin Canons at Carlisle imported and sold wine. Those of Newburgh bred and sold horses. The Cistercians of Rievaulx and Louth Park produced and sold pig iron from their own mines. Even so the main substance of a monastery's income came from the crops and farm stock on its lands.

Monastic lands

The fundamental purpose of giving land to a monastery was to feed the monks and supply them with horses, fodder, fuel, beeswax, leather and timber, and to provide them with a main source of money to buy books, church ornaments, clothing, household utensils, carts and plough, spices and drugs, and salt. Some of the manors of a monastery were exploited directly as 'demesne', under a lay bailiff or reeve who was responsible to the cellarer for the delivery each year, on agreed dates, of a quota of foodstuffs and raw materials: enough to meet the monastery's needs for a stated period – two weeks or four or eight: wheat, barley and malt, cheese, butter and eggs, bacon and lard, poultry and fish, honey and fruit. Usually, most of the manors were put into the hands of lay tenants, who held them by a variety of tenures: some of them hereditary, others for a fixed term of years, some granted for an agreed annual rent, others in return for the complex of services, dues and rights known as 'knight service'.

Landlords, bailiffs and tenants

The Norman kings had imposed on the lands of many monasteries feudal obligations which included putting at the royal disposal, on occasion, a force of mounted warriors; and in consequence the abbots of the Norman era had enfeoffed many men with lands held by knight service. These knights and their descendants formed the core of the class of lesser nobility found grouped on the estates of every medieval house of significant size. The practice of committing so much of the land to lay tenants secured the income of the monastery and gave it a considerable measure of protection. As a system, it could not run itself, but needed strong and vigilant supervision by the abbot and his obedientiaries. On the other hand, it left them with much of their time and energy free to devote to their monastic calling. Economically, it was not enterprising; and even though not all monastic leaders were economically aware, the opportunities of increasing income from land became more obvious with each successive decade of the 12th century.

Economic growth   The characteristic unit of the English agrarian society conquered by the Normans was the village or hamlet community with its arable pasture, woodland and waste, growing enough for its own needs, specialising little, selling little beyond its own boundaries. The manor – the estate held by the king or a lay landlord or a bishop or a monastery – might coincide with the village; or a manor might embrace more villages than one; or a village might be divided among more manors than one; and not all of the English countryside was parcelled out in manors. Neither manor nor village should be thought of as anything like economically encapsulated; yet even though the needs of towns, and of monasteries too, created a market, and the royal requirements of services and taxes sucked resources from the village, there was a dominant element of self-sufficiency.

After 1100 came a change. Population grew and with it the towns: but rural society grew also, advancing with a new determination and improved techniques upon the forest, the heath, the marsh, the waste and scrub, to bring them more and more under exploitation. Trade expanded, in corn, in cheese, in wool, in horses and cattle; and prices rose. Abbots and convents had long been landowners – undying corporations, not like families where estates might be broken up among different heirs or pass to other families: they now began to see clearly the advantages of becoming their own estate managers as well, and turning away from a system of predictable and guaranteed revenues to the quest for an increasing income.

The monks increase their demesne land   From about 1150, monasteries pursued with purpose and success a policy of bringing as much land as possible back under their own direct supervision and exploitation. Leases expired and were not renewed, and the land was brought into demesne. Lawsuits were set on foot to acquire land which had been lost or the title to which was debatable. There was vigorous buying up of small lots needed to round out existing holdings. The monks were energetic and in many places pioneering in the work of 'assarting' – creating ploughland by clearing previously untamed forest – and in embanking, dyking and draining in marshes, meres and coastal flats. The aim was both to bring more acres under plough or pasture and to study and develop every way in which the yield of the soil could be increased: manuring, marling, rotating cereal and vegetable crops, sowing wheat instead of oats or barley. Manors were organised in interdependent groups, to co-ordinate their work and resources. Food was grown more and more for the money it would fetch on the market, with Ramsey promoting its grain sales in Colchester and Ipswich, Glastonbury its cheese in Southampton and Winchester, and scores of monasteries supplying London: while the houses in Kent exported the wheat they grew to Flemish and northern French towns and bought from other growers the cheaper corn needed to feed themselves. The most celebrated monastic cash crop of all, however, was wool.

Sheep and wool   The Cistercians, as already observed, were not the first of the monastic orders to pasture big flocks of sheep on their lands. The Benedictines of Ely were already feeding 13,000 sheep at the time of the Domesday Book (1086). Yet it was the early Cistercians who injected new vitality and new ambition into the growing and selling of English wool. Ever since the days when St. Boniface had written to the abbesses of Wearmouth and Thanet for cloaks of English wool to keep his missionaries warm in the Rhineland winter and the nuns of Coldingham had been episcopally scolded for giving less time to study and prayer than to weaving fine cloths, English wool had enjoyed European prestige. The Vikings had both raided and traded for wool and cloth from England.

By the 12th century, big and lucrative markets for English wool were appearing. With the growth of population, the chief weaving towns at home – Lincoln, Beverley, Stamford, Northampton, Leicester, York, Oxford, Winchester, London itself – were demanding more and more wool for their looms. On a much greater scale was the cloth-making industry of northern France, Flanders and Brabant, with centres like Arras, Ghent and Ypres, and with an insatiable appetite for English wool. Soon after 1200 merchants from the Italian weaving and cloth-finishing cities – Florence above all – were buying wool and semi-finished cloth in England to be shipped to Italy in the galleys of Venice and Genoa.

The Cistercians, settling well away from areas of intensive cultivation and from the complex social organisation of manor and village, felt a need for large capital sums for expensive and sometimes grandiose building schemes. They found that the assets which they could most rapidly exploit to make money were the natural, so far undeveloped, sheep pastures they had acquired: on the Northumberland and Yorkshire moors, the Lincolnshire wolds and fens, the Welsh valleys, the Cotswolds, and the Wiltshire and Dorset downlands. These broad pastures were not always on high ground. The white monks of Meaux grazed 11,000 sheep on the river flats and marsh of Holderness, on the Humber. Their abbot made the significant calculation that on these pastures he could graze five sheep for every one ox. The regular canons, Gilbertines, Premonstratensians and Augustinians, went into wholesale sheep farming with the same purpose and in the same regions. Soon the Cistercians were sending their lay brothers to buy up the wool clips of thousands of small farmers and peasants who pastured small flocks of their own. The milk, cheese and manure of the sheep were also highly valued: the mutton less so. It was the wool which brought in the high profits.

The system of granges, the employment of lay brothers in flock management, and the relative smallness of the labour force required all aided Cistercian enterprise. They were pioneers in grading their wools, which the Benedictines had preferred to sell mixed and in bulk. They studied feeding and breeding, and the possibility of grappling with the deadly disease of sheep-rot (caused by the liver fluke parasite) by keeping flocks fairly continuously on the move, and with the skin disease called scab by developing salves of mercury and alum. Their finest wools were of short staple, grown on the upland pastures of hill, moor, wold and down. Linsey-Woolsey, from the Lincolnshire wolds, Lemster Ore, Cotswold and March from the western shires, were by the 13th century famed for their strength and fineness of fibre, and prized in Flanders and Florence. The Yorkshire wools were of rather coarser fibre, but especial strength, and produced in great abundance. The wools of long staple could best be grown in England on the clay plain of the midlands, but by 1150 much of it was under plough, with the sheep put to graze on waste land and in the autumn folded on the stubble. In the fenlands and on the Romney and Somerset marshes the Benedictines grazed long-staple flocks.

The Cistercians developed sheep farming for the wool markets, domestic and overseas, on a much larger scale than had been known before. Until about 1300 they were the most powerful single wool-growing group, and they and the regular canons were producing the best fleeces in Europe, outside Spain: Cistercian Fountains, Rievaulx, Jervaulx and Louth Park; Augustinian Bridlington and Gilbertine Old Malton. The prohibitions placed by the Cistercian General Chapter on many of their activities in the wool business were in practice ignored as English Cistercian wealth grew. Yet the great bulk of the wool was far from being grown by the Cistercians and the regular canons. The greater houses of black monks built up large flocks, like Winchester Cathedral Priory with 20,000 sheep in 1320, and Christ Church, Canterbury with 14,000; and the major proportion of English wool was grown by laymen, ranging from the king, on the royal estates, through great earls, like Lancaster, Lincoln, and Norfolk, down to villeins and self-employed shepherds.

A monastery, like a lay baron, had to organise its estates as a unity for sheep-farming purposes. Flocks were concentrated on the wide pastures of moorland and marsh for the summer months, and the wool clip in June. An abbey might manage all its flocks from a single manor – as did Pershore at the manor of Broadway, with a lay stock keeper in charge of a staff of shepherds. In autum they were thinned out in number and folded in individual manors to consume stubble and winter feed and await the lambing time.

The wool trade and the cloth industry   The wool merchant, native or foreign, who was the link between the grower and the weaver, would visit the monastic sheep-walks in spring, look at the flocks, make an estimate of the June yield, offer a price and arrange for transport after the wool-shearing. Soon abbots were succumbing to the temptation of ready money by selling their wool for a period of years ahead. As early as 1165, the Flemish merchant William Cade bought the wool of the Cistercians of Louth Park for the next six years. Such contracts became common. They might be for two years, they might run to twenty. For payment in advance, the merchant was given a low price. As the quantity of wool bought in advance was precisely stated, the monastery would have to compensate the buyer for a poor yield in a future year.

In the 13th century, the buying of monastic wool from the sheep's back was increasingly dominated by Italian merchants, from Lucca, Siena and Florence. Many of them came to England as the pope's agents to collect taxes levied from time to time on the lands and incomes of the Church in order to finance crusades. Their tax-gathering duties took them to the monasteries and gave them an extra lever for manipulating a profitable bargain: they could offer to pay a monastery's tax due to the papacy in return for wool in the future. As the royal government, from 1275 onwards, was levying more and more heavy taxes on wool exported from England, the Italian exporters were also able to make a further profit from lending money to the king in return for the taxes due to be paid on export. The main effect of this system of sale and export of wool was to keep down the prices and the profits accruing to the growers, and a further result was to land many a sheep-farming religious house into debt. Fountains, Glastonbury and Westminster were among abbeys owing heavily to Italian merchants in the 1290s. Grotesquely, the Abbey of Fountains itself had been mortgaged – against all principles of law – to Italians in 1276, until King Edward I rectified the situation. In 1343 the greatest of the Florentine merchant banking houses, the Bardi and the Peruzzi, crashed mainly because of their over-involvement with England, for King Edward III repudiated his huge debts to them.

For the next two hundred years, English merchants – starting with the De la Pole family in Hull, in the heart of 'Cistercian country' – bought most of the surplus wool of the monasteries. A decreasing amount of wool went abroad, in 1450 hardly 30 per cent of what had been exported in 1275, while England made and exported more and more of her own woollen cloth, woven less in the older cloth towns and much more in numerous new centres in the Lake District, Yorkshire and the West Country. But monastic concern with growing wool was never matched by a parallel interest in the weaving, finishing and marketing of cloth. The fulling mill from Flanders, driven by water power, had been introduced into England by the Templars about 1150–80, and it has been argued that this invention alone caused English cloth manufacture to move out of the old cloth towns to places westward where there were more water power and fewer restrictions. St. Albans Abbey, indeed, constructed fulling mills and ordered all its tenants, including the townsfolk, to take their cloth there to be fulled in return for fees in cash. The townsfolk resisted and planned a protest to Edward I's Spanish Queen Eleanor when she visited the abbey. The abbot's attempt to sneak the Queen into the town by a back way was foiled by a throng of women armed with distaffs, who waylaid Eleanor with tears and anger; but later, in the royal court, the abbot won his case for a monopoly of fulling at St. Albans. Neither the Benedictine nor the Cistercian Rule would have allowed monks to become major cloth-manufacturers; but no Rule prevented them from growing, often in 'the wilderness and the solitary places', the essential raw material for the leading industry of England.

Managing the monastic estates

Wool was a speciality; but nearly all monasteries, whether they grazed flocks or not, were general farmers. The Cistercians again offered an interesting model. Their granges were self-contained demesnes, with a pattern of large fields of arable and meadows, efficient to work and not cut up into dozens of strips for individual peasant farmers to cultivate. Typical in its organisation, though exceptional in size, was Beaulieu Abbey's great grange of Faringdon, in Berkshire. The abbey owned the ploughs, harrows, tools, carts, and two resident monks managed the grange with a work force of four lay brothers and numerous wage-labourers. Faringdon sold its corn and other produce in local towns, and in London, where Farringdon Market still survives.

But the Cistercians, the Benedictines and the other orders found that direct farming presented difficult problems of management. Nowhere are these more clearly illustrated than in one of the best and most famous biographies of the middle ages, the life of Samson, Abbot of Bury St. Edmunds from 1180 to 1211, written by one of his monks, the admiring but sharp-eyed Jocelin of Brakelond (or Breckland). Samson, tall, robust, bald, red-bearded, was elected at the age of forty-seven, after seventeen years as a monk at Bury, virtually to rescue the abbey from the financial confusion and debt into which it had fallen under his unworldly predecessor. He was devout, sternly just, tacitly kind. He spoke French and Latin fluently, preached and read the scriptures impressively in English, with an East Anglian accent, and gave up meat and put on horsehair undergarments for life after Saladin captured the Holy City in 1187. Yet the welfare of his monastic community, its internal harmony and good external relations with Suffolk society, in town and country, meant more to him than the higher Benedictine ideals. He had energy and courage, toured the Bury churches and lands continually on horseback, made a voyage to Norway, and stood up to the royal government of Richard the Lion Heart on an issue of principle – whether monasteries owing knight service to the king were obliged to send either their knights or the cash payment in lieu called *scutage* to overseas campaigns.

Among his monks, he set greater store on the administrative qualities of the successful obedientiary than on the contemplative or scholarly virtues; but the building up and direct farming of estates could not safely be left to the zealous obedientiary with professional lay support or the constant surveillance of other monks. His most painful and instructive experience of the problems came from his own snap inspection of four manors of the abbey, grouped under the control of the obedientiary Geoffrey Ruffus, who led the life of a land-agent almost perpetually outside the cloister and was found to have secretly creamed off from the estate profits a fortune of 200 marks (£133.13s.4d.)

in silver and gold. Samson put the four manors, for the future, into the custody of two monks, who should watch and check each other. The abbot, whose beard by now was white, can be perceived finding his way towards a system of management and control which was to be perfected by the monasteries in the 13th century.

The abler, more energetic monks in the great majority of monasteries were likely to include few of intense spirituality or artistic or intellectual distinction, and many with the taste and capacity for administration. The 'obedientiary system' doubtless fulfilled them as individuals, satisfying the desire to serve others – feeding, clothing and supervising brother monks, looking after guests, tending the sick, giving alms to the poor; visiting manors, conferring with bailiffs and tenants, selling and buying at fairs and markets; spending many of their days away from the routine of the cloister, without needing to give up ascetic habits and austere self-discipline. The system suited contemporaries of Samson's like the remarkable run of Abbots of St. Albans – Simon, Warin and John – during the half-century from 1167 to 1214. They left administration, estates and finances largely to an oligarchy of senior monks, and devoted themselves with high success to organising, guiding and contributing to the sparkling artistic, intellectual and literary life of St. Albans, pre-eminent among English monasteries.

The obedientiary system

But the obedientiary system impeded any central policy for the estates and any profitable concentrating of flocks, dairy herds and particular crops in selected areas. At best, it held back the maximising of income, at worst it encouraged extravagance and peculation as practised by Geoffrey Ruffus. The principles of effective change were fairly easy to perceive: the setting up of a common treasury, into which all income flowed, and from which all spending proceeded; and the central auditing of all accounts by a committee of senior monks, chosen by the abbot or prior. The obedientiaries would thus fall to the level of executives. Such advance could be achieved by internal effort. At Christ Church, the cathedral priory of Canterbury, the central treasury and audit were entrusted to three monks as early as 1170. Reform was also pushed forward by papal decree and by the legislation and visitations of such zealous archbishops as the Dominican Robert Kilwardby and the Franciscan John Pecham, successively at Canterbury in the later years of the 13th century.

Christ Church, Canterbury, offers a telling example of the pattern of administrative changes, variable though they were from house to house. The head of the centralised estate administration was the prior. For the purpose he was left independent of the titular abbot, the Archbishop of Canterbury. The prior made his proposals and gave his instructions after touring the estates and consulting the senior monks, the monk-wardens, and the bailiffs. The senior monks collectively ran the priory exchequer, where they audited the accounts, issued the estimates for future working, and laid down in detail policy for land-

Centralised management of the land

purchase, corn sales, assarting and marling, brewing and the renders in kind called food-farms.

Under them were four custodies – geographically grouped networks of land – in East Kent; the Weald and Romney Marsh; Essex; and the Thames Valley counties of Surrey, Buckinghamshire and Oxfordshire. A monk-warden presided over each custody. He presented all the accounts of the manors in his custody. He appointed the bailiffs and visited each of them, on their manors, every Easter-tide and every September, accompanied by a lay clerk well trained in accountancy and law. At these times, the monk-warden prepared his instructions as to the crops to be grown, produce to be marketed, timber to be felled, new buildings to be constructed, beasts to be sold or slaughtered. Within their custodies and in collaboration one with another, the monk-wardens arranged mutual aid between all the manors of the priory. One manor supplied another with seed corn, or lent temporary help at harvest. In summer, manors with the best pastures grazed the flocks and herds of the arable-rich manors. (Under this kind of system, Westminster Abbey sent sick cows from Eye on the Thames along the river to the healthier air and superior pastures of Staines.)

Monk-wardens were expected to live in the cloister for as many days and nights as they could. Their duties and, to an extent, their inclination, often kept them continuously resident in their custodies. Archbishop Pecham, on his visitations of 1280–84, indignantly ordered them back to their monasteries: all too frequently, from his standpoint, they slipped away to their custodies, where served their bailiffs, laymen who carried out policy, handed in every Michaelmas Day, their accounts, written in Latin with roman figures in jet black ink on long yellow parchments, delivered the cash rents and the renders in kind, and offered an estimate of the profit for the coming year.

Prior Henry Eastry of Canterbury

The chief architect and most successful practitioner of the Christ Church system of estate management was Henry Eastry, Prior from 1285 to 1331. His were the golden years of high farming on the Canterbury Cathedral Priory lands. Like Samson, he was elected (at the age of thirty-five) to extricate his house from a financial plight. Christ Church was £5000 in debt: the equivalent of two years' gross revenue. Prior Eastry had a personal authority, a sure sense of the world, a firm grip on discipline. His letters suggest that he never felt drawn to the ascetic or contemplative life or to theological study, but that his compelling interest for half a century was the material prosperity of his priory.

He began by making heavy cuts in expenditure and rationalising administration and accounting. He consistently sought advice from his senior monks and expert legal guidance from outside the priory. Economic currents were running favourably, though there were many years when the weather was not, and the importunity of successive kings for corrodies and loans was a drain. No prior of Christ Church developed and exploited its lands more intensively than Eastry. He knitted the widely spread custodies and manors into a tightly unified system of production for the market, with special emphasis on cheese, corn and wool. His flocks were grouped on the sweet grasslands of the large manors of the Isle of Thanet and Romney Marsh, which he greatly extended with schemes of embankment and reclamation.

Eastry's reward was to liquidate the Christ Church debts and increase annual revenue by 25 per cent, so that he was able to pay for the building of the stone screen round the Canterbury cathedral choir and the university studies overseas of numerous young monks. When they wrote to him from Paris, Orléans or Bologna, he could resolve their financial difficulties, but referred their intellectual problems to learned doctors at Oxford. He was the assiduous counsellor of five consecutive archbishops of Canterbury, diverse personalities who were at one in the value they set on the cautious realism and wide experience of this monk who sat regularly in Parliament and entertained year after year eminent pilgrims to the shrine of St. Thomas and travellers passing through Canterbury on the route between London and the continent. When the south-east was scared by the threat in 1325 of an invasion of England by King Charles IV of France, Prior Eastry forecast, accurately, that the French would be found more eager to shake their fists than draw their swords.

Eastry was a superb estate manager, and worked strenuously and shrewdly to the end: but he had indifferent health, regularly consulting a London physician; was personally unassuming and frugal, ordering in his old age a mule from Flanders which should be 'not a big, tall beast, but a little mule, a good carrier' (*nepas grant mul et haut, mes un petit muyl bien portant*); and died, in his early eighties, while celebrating mass.

Prior Eastry should not be put on a pedestal. His contemporaries *High farmers* included other monks who were great high farmers. John Taunton, Abbot of Glastonbury (1274–90) extensively increased his abbey's demesnes, enclosed game-parks, and was a great builder in Somerset stone of farmhouses, barns, byres, dairies, dovecots and chapels; but he was also a keen student of Aquinas and an active theologian and legislator, who added many books to the Glastonbury library. Abbot Geoffrey Crowland of Peterborough (1299–1320) continually ploughed capital back into the lands of his house, reclaiming arable from uncultivated fenland, digging drains and sluices, and dykes reinforced with plantings of oak and ash, creating herb gardens, orchards, rabbit warrens and woods, and constructing windmills, stables, sheep-cotes, hen-runs and every variety of rural dwelling, from grange to shepherd's cottage. Neither his effort nor Eastry's collapsed or lost its momentum under the strain of England's notoriously bad harvests of 1315, 1316 and 1317. Crowland, Eastry and Taunton were outstanding but not exceptional; for the monastic orders as a whole had become in the 13th century a school for shrewd, enterprising landowners.

The pandemic pestilence called the Black Death swept from Asia *Plague and its* through Europe in the late 1340s. In its two forms – bubonic plague, *consequences*

91

carried by fleas on rats, and pneumonic plague, spread by direct contagion – it crossed to England in 1348. A population of about three and a half million was reduced by probably 20 per cent at once, and one-third overall by its four major visitations: 1348–50, 1361–62, 1369 and 1379. Its incidence across England and Scotland was uneven, from region to region. In the closely-knit monastic communities, its effects were dire. In 1349, St. Albans lost the abbot and forty-seven monks, Westminster the abbot and twenty-six monks – all in a few days. At Meaux, only ten survived out of a convent of forty-two monks and seven lay brothers; at Newenham in Devon, only the abbot and two monks lived to bury twenty other brethren; in Cambridge, all the Dominican Friars perished. Yet at Christ Church, Canterbury, so near to the continent, only four monks died, possibly because the priory had a remarkably pure supply of running water and outstanding hygiene. However, the annual rate at which heads of houses died increased seven-fold in 1348–49 and the number of monks, nuns and friars in England on the eve of the plague had fallen by nearly half by 1380.

A slow, never more than partial recovery in numbers had begun by 1400, and the plague never raged nation-wide again. Without comprehensive and wholly reliable statistics for the 14th century, the precise effects of 'the Death', as men and women called it, cannot be measured. English monasteries would never be so populous and vigorous again; yet, for example, monastic building schemes, though after 1350 they slowed down to some extent, were not stopped, and were eventually carried through.

Leasing the demesne   The adverse effects on the system of high demesne farming associated with names like Eastry and Taunton were decisive. Nevertheless, even before 1348, there had been some retreat from the system. No monastery had ever ceased to draw in a significant proportion of its revenues by granting leases of land, as against direct exploitation; and a return to the leasing out of parcels of demesne land and of whole manors had already set in.

To explain fully this reversal of the strong trends of the 13th century is not easy. Population was probably already slightly declining. Cycles of bad weather; bad harvests, bringing western Europe near to famine, as in 1315–17; and the inroads in the northern shires of the intermittent but savage warfare with the Scots, from 1296 onwards, shook the confidence of monastic landlords. Agricultural prices were falling, while rents rose, and the temptations to give up direct farming and lease out the land grew stronger. After the Black Death, the trend was powerful. The unfree villein peasants, or bondmen, compelled to give about half their working hours to labour on the monastic demesne in return for strip-holdings of their own, could – by law and by force – be kept on their manors; but the wage labourers – ploughmen, carters, shepherds, cowherds, swineherds, gardeners, grooms, serving maids – with little if any land of their own but freedom to move, their numbers thinned out by the plague, became mobile, scarce and highly paid.

Moreover, there were fewer monks to devote themselves to estate management, and the alternative – the steady collection of rents – was more feasible, more attractive. Some land, a shrinking proportion, on which the monasteries sought strenuously to tie down their now often resentful villeins, remained under direct exploitation until the Dissolution in 1540. Meanwhile, thriving peasant survivors of the plague, ambitious bailiffs, minor rural gentry, and townsmen with money to invest in farming, eagerly paid the entry fines and the annual rents for nine-year, fifteen-year, twenty-one-year and longer leases of monastic demesne and manors. There were still capable monastic landlords on the grand scale after the Black Death, such as Abbot Clown of Leicester; but by 1380 the age of direct high farming was over.

Generalisation is, however, perilous. Even in so relatively small and compact a society as later medieval England, the economic fortunes of the monasteries do not present a uniform picture. Durham Cathedral Priory's revenues from land were at their peak – £4500 – in 1308, and after 1350 they never surpassed £2200, falling well below that figure in the 15th century; but Durham suffered from Scottish invasions and raids over its lands for crucial periods. Westminster Abbey's direct cultivation of its estates continued strongly from 1350 to 1400, and its income rose; but Westminster, exceptionally, was still being granted new endowments of land, by royal benefactors such as Eleanor of Castile, Edward I's queen; Richard II; Henry V; and, in the Tudor age, Henry VII and his mother, Lady Margaret Beaufort. On all monastic lands, however, the monks, over the generations, had to yield a bigger share in the profits of agriculture to the peasants and the rural middle class, and the very determination and pertinacity of their efforts to resist doing so account for the rage and vindictiveness with which their properties and their persons were often attacked in the Peasants' Revolt of 1381 (as the men of Kent attacked the Hospitallers, and the East Anglian rebels the black monks of Bury).

One pronounced feature of the age of contraction and decline (which was not, however, an age of disaster) which runs from the mid-14th to the late 15th century was the centralisation of executive and financial power more and more into one man's hands in many of the greater houses. The work, independence and authority of the leading obedientiaries was taken over by the head of the house, as Prior Thomas Chillenden did at Christ Church, Canterbury, from 1391 to 1411, making enough money by his policy of granting extensive leases to reconstruct the cathedral nave; but sometimes it was delegated, as were wide administrative and financial powers to the successive bursars of Durham.

Contraction and decline on the land

Creators, Discoverers and Thinkers

At the heart of monastic intellectual life was the monastery library; yet the monks rarely, if ever, made plans or earmarked annual funds for the

The monastery library

steady collecting of books. Their libraries grew when an abbot or a scholar in their ranks had special needs for books, and when bequests and gifts of books were made, often by their own members: Prior Thomas left his medical books to Christ Church, Canterbury, and his successor Prior Eastry his law books. However, over the centuries, by sheer weight of accumulating and copying manuscripts, the monasteries gathered together libraries of remarkable range and depth. By 1500, the largest collections were at Canterbury – one in Christ Church, another in St. Augustine's – and Bury St. Edmunds: each of those houses owned some nine thousand works bound into about two thousand volumes, all in manuscript, while printed books were now coming in. Elsewhere, the size of the library dwindled steadily down from Leicester, with nearly one thousand volumes, to the fifty or eighty books in the cupboard of the smaller priory or nunnery.

The core of any library was the bibles (each bound into nine volumes), the missals, psalters and other service books; the writings of four great Fathers of the Church – the 'Latin doctors' Jerome, Augustine, Ambrose and Gregory; and the books on grammar and composition needed for teaching Latin in the earlier monastic centuries when most monks entered the cloister as boys. A good monastic library would include many classics: the poetry, plays, letters, speeches and histories of the Romans, with Virgil, Horace, Ovid, Seneca, Terence, Cicero, the elder Pliny, Suetonius and Sallust most prominent. The texts of Plautus, Livy and, surprisingly, Caesar, were rare. Catullus and Lucretius were unknown. Not so the books of the ancient Roman and Greek authorities on mathematics, geography and atronomy, agriculture and architecture, music and astrology. The Greek authors, Homer too, had to be read in Latin translations and abridgements.

Around this core grew many collections of medieval works of theology, logic and philosophy, history, law and medicine, and lighter reading. The little Premonstratensian priory at Titchfield, in Hampshire, had no books on theology, but a formidable section on English common law, forest law and statute law, and a lively set of French poems and romances. The friars' libraries were strong in contemporary biblical commentaries, theology, poetry and romances, and friars were well-known for greedily buying up books on the market. In Richard II's time, Friar John Erghum bequeathed to his Augustinian brethren at York two hundred volumes of Latin classics, English history and law, French poetry, sermons, and books on medicine, magic and fortune-telling. Syon House, founded in 1415, quickly accumulated 1500 volumes, mostly bequeathed by its own Bridgettines, and including many copies of the English mystics and printed editions of the humanists and poets of Renaissance Italy.

Scribes and painters   Most of the books collected had been copied, illustrated and bound by the monks themselves. The *scriptorium* was often the busiest department of a house. Each year there were service-books and bibles to replace, outgoing letters to be copied into registers, and manuscripts

Medieval artists sometimes signed their work in unusual ways. Here William de Brailes put his name to the small figure of a monk being saved by St. Michael on the Day of Judgment – 'W. De Brale Me Fecit'.

to transcribe and illuminate with miniature paintings of biblical themes, from Adam and Eve in Eden to the fiery events of the Apocalypse, and with decorated capital letters, some spreading

95

(Opposite) Eadwine, monk of Canterbury, had no false modesty about the excellence of the manuscript which he finished about 1149. The inscription round his portrait reads: 'I am the prince of writers; neither my fame nor my praise will die quickly: demand of my letters who I am. The Letters: Fame proclaims you in your writing for ever, Eadwine, you who are to be seen here in the painting. The worthiness of this book demonstrates your excellence. O God, this book is given to you by him. Receive this acceptable gift.'

brilliantly across a whole page. There was generous use of azure and red pigments, and gold and silver leaf, though an English speciality was the untinted drawing. Styles evolved and changed over the generations. Monastic 'book-hand' tended to be uniform nationally at any one time, though developing in form from century to century, and reaching the heights of beauty and clarity in the 12th century. Anglo-Saxon figure-drawing was fresh and light, Cnut's *Liber Vitae*, given to the monks of Winchester about 1020, contrasts radically with the boldly drawn, brightly coloured, domineering hawk-faced kings and prophets of the Winchester Bible which a group of master artists, some recruited from Sicily, illustrated for the same community only a century and a half later.

Lay scribes and painters were sometimes needed to work alongside the monks, and lived as corrodians within the walls. At the Austin priory of Worksop, the canons produced the scripts, and left the paintings to the lay artists. Some professional painters became monks, as did Walter the Painter who carved and painted the life of St. Alban for the high altar at St. Albans and later worked for Westminster Abbey. Too many of the artists – whether monks, friars or laymen – have remained anonymous. William Winchester, Henry III's favourite painter, was a monk who worked at Westminster and Windsor, and so was the St. Albans illustrator Matthew Paris, but monk-painters cannot be traced after the 13th century. Yet the Guildford Dominican, Friar John Siferwas, was illustrating liturgical books between 1380 and 1407 with beautiful and subtly observed groups of human figures, birds and animals, and a fine double portrait of himself and his patron, Lord Lovel. After his time, writing, drawing and painting lapsed more and more from the hands of monks and friars to lay professionals.

Monks as craftsmen

Carving in ivory, wood and stone, painting on panel, work in gold, silver and bronze, bell founding and organ building had been widely practised by Anglo-Saxon monks. Their jewellery and metalwork was regarded overseas as the best in western Europe. Such skills became rare among the monks of Norman times. The goldsmith Anketil, who had managed the Danish royal mint, became a monk and made a new shrine for the patron saint at St. Albans in 1129. A few years later, Hugh the sacrist carved the rood-screen and cast the bronze doors at Bury St. Edmund's. But in all these crafts, design and construction were steadily taken over by lay masters, often resident. Yet manual crafts never ceased to be taught to some of the monks, especially those who were not bookish. In 1419, Thomas Selmiston, a Canterbury monk, was said to be the cleverest embroiderer in England; and most houses would need a few residents like William Corfill, sacrist of Wenlock, who was an expert weaver, clockmaker, organ-builder and bell-founder.

Monks as physicians

Several at least of the greater monasteries of the Norman era had monks who were physicians and had usually studied medicine at Salerno University, in the Norman Kingdom of Sicily. The Frenchman Baldwin, Abbot of Bury, and the Italian Farizio, Abbot of Abingdon,

between them advised and treated five successive kings and their wives, including Henry I's queen, at childbirth, and established reputations which attracted to them as their patients archbishops of Canterbury and great barons like Geoffrey de Vere and Milo Crispin. There were celebrated consultants among the monks of Chertsey, Malmesbury, St. Albans and Worcester. The fees paid to Thomas Northwich enabled him to provide most of the money needed for the new tower at his abbey of Evesham in 1200.

Medical practice took monk physicians into well-to-do lay society and among women, and it brought them handsome rewards. Even though they gave their fees to their convents, the popes and the Church Councils forbade the profession to them. However, it was not so much legislation as the rise of the medical practices in the towns and of medical studies in the new universities which put monastic medicine into a backwater after 1200. Monasteries began to hire physicians from the secular world for their own monks; but the monks kept and studied their medical treatises, and their infirmaries gave them many patients to treat. Monasteries with saints' shrines seem usually to have had larger collections of medical books than other monasteries, no doubt because of the number of sick people who arrived there as pilgrims and needed treatment. It was probably from mixed motives that John Rothwell of Newnham Priory was allowed to practise surgery only if his patient was a brother canon.

In 1516, Erasmus complained acidly, if with exaggeration, that English monks made far too much liturgical music to have time to make anything else. Twenty years later, with the Dissolution, nearly all of their many thousands of books of music were scattered and destroyed; and it is more difficult to discover the history of music than of any other art in the monasteries. English monks were probably the first in Europe, outside Rome, to be instructed in the Gregorian chant, or plainsong, which Pope Gregory I established for the singing of the greater part of the words of the mass and other offices; though, after the worst of the Danish invasions were over, Ethelwold had to import it afresh from the continental abbey of Corbie. Thereafter, the monks enriched the chant with tropes or *melismata*, interpolations sung upon one of the vowels of the text, which were eventually developed into independent hymns. The monks of Normandy greatly elaborated the chant, but music was a field in which they did not seek to change English ways.

Meanwhile, the greater English abbeys, alongside fully troped plainsong, developed polyphonic part-singing, with highly trained soloists and much emphasis on the treble voices of boys. Monks seem to have been the leading musicians of the 12th century, as composers, performers and theorists, but after 1200 tropes went out of fashion and it was in the town communities, the cathedrals and the colleges of secular priests and scholars that the creative developments took place, notably in choral singing. The 13th-century monastic chant-books

(Opposite)
A Benedictine monk painting a statuette of the Virgin from a thirteenth-century English manuscript.

Music in the monastery

surviving at Worcester preserve a music still fundamentally of the 10th century.

The introduction in the 13th century of a second daily mass, the 'Lady Mass', with its anthem to the Blessed Virgin Mary, imposed a heavy new burden on monastic choirs at a time when 'the children of the cloister', brought up within the convent itself, had been removed and were no longer available for treble parts. Monasteries which could afford it paid adult choristers to sing, chiefly falsetto; and the larger abbeys set up song schools, under lay choirmasters, to bring back boys' voices to their choirs. By the 15th century the monks were installing the new type of organ, developed in Flanders and Germany, with its chromatic keyboard and its stops to shut off particular banks of pipes, at first to supplement, rather than replace the older organs, with their small range of notes, each rigidly operating a large number of pipes. The chance survival of original contracts of service shows Durham Cathedral Priory engaging its lay choirmaster to play the organs, sing, train the monks in plainsong, polyphony and counterpoint, and compose a new mass annually. Ironically, some of the finest musicians of Henry VIII's reign were monastery choirmasters, like Robert Fairfax at St. Albans and Thomas Tallis at Waltham.

School and university

Before 1066 monastic schools had educated both the children of the cloister – the monks of the future – and the sons of the better-off laity. After 1066 many Norman monks came to teach in English monasteries; Lanfranc and Anselm, the leading reformers of the church, had both taught in Normandy. But they did not create new systems of schooling in the English monasteries. The old monastic schools went on, even though eventually children were no longer admitted to live in the cloister. Other schools – a larger number – were run by cathedrals, houses of canons and parish priests, and were often subsidised by the monks, who gave them sites and buildings and paid their teachers' salaries.

In the earlier 12th century, monastic scholars like the historians Orderic Vitalis and William of Malmesbury believed that a monk of ability could acquire his higher education from the books in the library of his monastery. This was true for the study of scripture, classical literature and history; but the renaissance of logic, philosophy and science and the consequent advances in theology pulled monastic students for a time to the great cathedral schools, and soon to the newly established universities, especially Paris and then Oxford and Cambridge. By 1200, abbots, priors and leading monks were increasingly university-trained in the wide range of first-degree arts subjects and, in many instances, in the higher specialisms also: theology, medicine and law. In the 13th century the friars, from the outset, trained all their promising recruits in their own schools at the universities.

The monks, having arrived at Oxford and Cambridge before the friars, were slow to create their own colleges there, preferring for generations the lodging houses and small halls or hostels where nearly all university students and teachers lived. Just outside the walls of Oxford, the Cistercians founded as centres of study Rewley Abbey in 1271 and St. Bernard's College in 1446. A score of the larger Benedictine monasteries collaborated to provide for their monks an Oxford residence, Gloucester Hall, where their terrace of little houses still forms part of Worcester College. Over the years, one-tenth of the Westminster monks came to Gloucester Hall, while Durham Cathedral Priory had an Oxford college of its own, with places for eight monks and eight lay students who paid their way by working as college servants. The Austin Canons did not found their Oxford college, St. Mary's, until 1445. At Cambridge, the Benedictines had Buckingham College. Some monks still pursued their Oxford or Cambridge studies while residing in lodgings; it was hardly possible for anyone to be both cloistered and an active university man. The protracted length of the courses of study – eight years to become a Master of Arts, another nine to acquire a Doctorate – reinforced the temptations of such a life.

Typical of an abbot's worries about his monks at the universities are those which Walter Monington of Glastonbury fretted over in 1361: the young men read too little and spent too much. They went hunting and fishing and trespassing, and called on the younger nuns at Godstow up the Thames, and less reputable ladies in Oxford town. They would not repair their finances by taking private pupils. Those who mended their ways, stayed the course and achieved academic success, would have enjoyed their own rooms and control of their own daily routine too long to fit contentedly back in the cloister; and they would be eligible for influential appointments in royal or baronial service or at the papal court. What English monks and friars achieved as a result of their university studies was often paid for at a price which Bernard or Francis would have thought too high.

Something must be said of the scholarly and literary achievement of the religious orders in England: firstly, between 1066 and the arrival of the friars. To separate monastic writings from those of the secular clergy is rather artificial. For example, the great philosopher John of Salisbury was not a monk; nor was Geoffrey of Monmouth, whose prose epic, half history, half myth, on the Kings of the Britons, is the fountain-head of the study of both pre-Roman Britain and King Arthur and his knights. What characterised the monk-writers of the period was that unlike Geoffrey of Monmouth or the major Anglo-Saxon authors, they hardly wrote for a public outside the cloisters. The best of them were not Normans: Lanfranc, who gave the English the standard western text of the Vulgate – the Bible in Latin – was Italian, and so was Anselm. The monks who founded a new school of historians and biographers in England were all natives: Eadmer (Anselm's biographer), Orderic of Shrewsbury, Symeon of Durham, William of Malmesbury, Jocelin of Brakelond. Their work – along with the composition of much Latin verse, skilfully imitating classical models –

Monks as authors

101

was the main literary production of the period: an age of good
scholarship and even better style.

For most of the middle ages, monks were indeed the principal,
though never the only recorders of the history of their own time and of
the recent past. Monastic histories were almost always in the form of
the chronicle or annals, in which the events of each successive year
were narrated as they happened. The texts of important documents,
such as selected letters to the abbot from the king or the pope, or Magna
Carta, King John's Great Charter of Liberties to his subjects in 1215,
were often fully transcribed into the chronicle. Every monastery was
keeping a chronicle by 1200. Some of them were written to focus
attention on a particular chain of events, such as Battle Abbey's
chronicle of its dispute with the Bishop of Chichester or Thomas
Marlberge's account of the misdeeds of Roger Norreys, the wicked and
oppressive Abbot of Evesham. At Winchester, Richard Devizes wrote a
remarkably full history of England during the early years of King
Richard I.

St. Albans, only a day's ride from London on the main road leading
north, was the frequent resort of members of the royal family, the
baronage and the higher clergy. Early in the 13th century, its monks
began the most sophisticated and well-informed monastic history of all.
Roger Wendover gave it a distinguished start and his pupil Matthew
Paris continued it until his death in 1259. Paris's historical writing ran
in two main streams: a chronicle in which English history and St.
Albans history mingle, and a series of lives of the abbots. Paris was a
scholar, who quoted from the texts of many state documents now lost;
he had an untiring zest for gathering and setting down facts about a
wider world, running from the Islamic lands to Scandinavia; and he
was a gossip recording priceless personal details about notabilities –
how King Henry III was pelted at St. Albans with sour apples by an
even sourer underpaid royal clerk, and received in London the gift of a
live elephant from King Louis IX of France. Paris drew the elephant, for
he illustrated his histories with vivacious, often sardonic drawings of
the people and events in his text – in which he gave full vent to his
prejudices against the pope, the friars, foreigners, and change of most
kinds. With some gaps, the fine series of St. Albans histories continued
until Thomas Walsingham covered in a majestic sequence the history of
his own times, from 1376 to 1420, wrote the life of one of the
outstanding abbots of St. Albans, Thomas de la Mare (1349–96), and
composed the best short history of England produced in the middle
ages. In a long life in the cloister, during which Walsingham was
precentor of St. Albans and, for a few years, prior of a daughter-house,
Wymondham, he could call on an impressive amount of time and
energy for his writings. A keen student of the classics, he wrote a book
about the pagan gods and another on the ancient world after the death
of Alexander the Great.

Canterbury and Westminster each produced a valuable series of

O felicia oscula Lactentis labiis impressa. cū
inter crebra iudicia reptantis inf... facie
vt pater ver? er te fili? nivi alludret... cū
nevus er patre dr̄ dī gentē imparet.

I... MATHIAS PARISIENSIS

chronicles, without altogether matching St. Albans. Leicester had its Henry Knighton and Chester its Ralph Higden in the reign of Edward III, and both were followed by 'continuators'. Unexpectedly, even inexplicably, monastic chronicle-writing was beginning to peter out by Walsingham's own lifetime. He was the last great historian of St. Albans, and monastic chroniclers, whether writing in Latin (as was normal) or English (in which an important chronicle was written at St. Mary's Abbey, York, in the late 14th century), failed after 1420 to supply a running narrative of national history anything like so copious and rich in detail as their predecessors had done for centuries – the one outstanding exception being the historians of Crowland in the fens.

European thought and the friars

It was soon after 1220 that the English religious orders began to make a profound and far-reaching contribution to European thought. This contribution was mainly Franciscan, Oxford was its starting-point, and it commenced with the work of a secular cleric neither friar nor monk. Robert Grosseteste taught in the Franciscan school at Oxford for six years before he was made Bishop of Lincoln in 1235. Grosseteste was the first English teacher to grasp the philosophical system of Aristotle, who was now coming to dominate academic thinking, and the first medieval European to say that the science and mathematics of the ancient world should be the foundation on which to build philosophy, theology and biblical explanation. Grosseteste and his colleagues and pupils played a significant part in adapting Aristotle's principles to Christian speculation. The Italian Dominican Thomas Aquinas perfected this process within a few years.

In England, the friars were now pushing forward the frontiers of knowledge and understanding at a dynamic pace, with schools in every friary and general schools in Oxford and Cambridge. Perhaps the most famous product of the Franciscan schools was Roger Bacon; but his reputation arises from his having been thought to be a powerful necromancer, and inventor of the telescope and gunpowder and – like Leonardo da Vinci – a prophet of the machine age. All that is chiefly myth; but Bacon, who, unlike Grosseteste, loved the humanism and classical style of antiquity, turned away from abstract thought to mathematics, natural science and a rudimentary sociology. Given enough pupils and less personal eccentricity, Bacon might have been the salvation of later medieval thought from its increasing isolation from the living world.

Duns Scotus and William Oakham

Intellectual tension between the two major mendicant orders built up after 1250. The Dominicans denied that only the Franciscans imitated Christ's poverty. The Franciscans claimed that they were at least as learned as the Dominicans. Beneath the surface of learned and specialised academic arguments on points of logic and doctrine – running year after year between Paris, Rome and Oxford – lay a fundamental disagreement. Aquinas believed that the elements of a true and complete philosophical system could be found in Aristotle. Leading Franciscans found gaps in Aristotle, denied his orthodoxy on the creation, the future of the soul, and the freedom of the will, and began to doubt whether human reason by itself could discover the truths of natural religion. These controversies involved major churchmen like John Pecham, the Franciscan Archbishop of Canterbury, who abused the followers of Aquinas for 'filling the whole world with a war of words', and they culminated with two revolutionary thinkers, both Franciscans, John Duns the Scot, from the border country, and William Ockham from near Guildford in Surrey.

They taught and wrote both at Oxford and in continental universities, and their influence spread wide. Scotus mounted a powerful and comprehensive attack on the system of Aquinas, claiming that only relative proofs could be reached by arguing back from effects to causes: hence there were no conclusive arguments for the existence of divine providence and the immortality of the soul. The complex prose of Scotus, weighed down with an armoury of difficult technical terms, was anything but lucid and, later, his humanist critics were keen to condemn him as too subtle, too clever by half, and to turn his surname into a noun, 'dunce'; but he was the first medieval man to create a metaphysical system of his own. The key to it was divine will, divine reason. Knowledge of God and the universe comes not from Aquinas's description of how the God of Reason should act, but from what faith tells us.

What Scotus, who died in 1308, taught about God's will deeply influenced Ockham in the next generation. Ockham struck at the roots of all medieval theories when he denied that there was any real contact between the speculative human mind and the world of being, and universal concepts were anything but words. Neither he nor Scotus would agree that divine illumination was needed for a man to attain to certainty or that his senses could receive true impressions on which they could found valid concepts. The human reason is autonomous, and its way to the truth is through the individual's intuitive perception and his faith. Ockham's 'Nominalism' did not destroy the 'Realism' of Aquinas; but he prepared the way for modern scepticism.

Scotus identified the divine will with the divine love; but when Ockham died in 1349 he left his followers with a God who seemed to them less like a father and a saviour than a supreme being of unfettered power whose will was arbitrary and inscrutable in its ways. Many of them sought God not through reasons, but through the emotions, through mystical experiences, or purely through the words of the scriptures. Meanwhile, the religious orders were drawn anew into public controversy. The friars, criticised by so great a thinker and preacher as Richard Fitz Ralph, Archbishop of Armagh, for their privileges, cupidity and failure as confessors, and their theories of poverty, struck back at the 'possessioners' – the monks, the bishops and other higher clergy – declaring that their enjoyment of their property had drawn them down into greed and luxury: only confiscation of its wealth could save the Church.

Poverty and possessions

Two Benedictines, Uhtred of Bolton and Adam Easton, ably defended the monks: gifts to monasteries were gifts to God, and God could not justly be deprived of what man had given him. Uhtred went on to develop the idea that monasticism was not a choice of path put before a man's feet, but instead a choice of a way of life implanted in his nature and put before him by his reason. He defended possessions, but he counselled his readers not to neglect the 'substance' – the mass, the vows of religion – for the 'accidents', whether study or the management of lands.

In the political life of England a group was emerging with a strong interest in heavier taxation and eventual confiscation of church property. They were encouraged by the friars' views and those of John Wyclif, who argued that those in mortal sin could not lawfully exercise lordship, while those in a state of grace should have lordship over all creation; and the possessioners had notoriously fallen from grace. Wyclif, undermining the possessioners with his theory of Lordship and Grace, and calling for church lands and goods, if no longer used for spiritual purposes, to be returned to the donors or their heirs, failed – if he ever intended – to inspire a powerful political or popular movement. His Oxford teaching on the nature of the mass, with its denial of transubstantiation, was condemned in 1382 by the Archbishop of Canterbury, with the advice of the Oxford and Cambridge friars and the support of the monks – and men fell away from Wyclif the heretic; but the tide of criticism of the monks as possessioners stayed high till about 1420.

What the English monks and friars taught and wrote has taken us into the mainstream of European philosophy, and the cantankerous politics of Richard II's reign. The volume of their work was too great to go on analysing here. Its range and variety deserve a final word. Not everyone was partisan. Those who tried to hold the balance could find encouragement in the preaching of the black monk Thomas Brunton. A monk of Norwich, an Oxford scholar and doctor, proctor at the Papal Curia for the English Benedictines, he became Bishop of Rochester in 1373. His published sermons, delivered in their day to Parliament and Convocation, at St. Paul's and in the wake of Richard II's coronation, castigated the rich, the usury of the money lenders, the harsh taxes and wasteful government of the Crown, but also the savagery of the rebels of 1381. From every pulpit, he called on the church to resist the encroachments of the lay powers. Brunton was preaching on behalf of men quieter than himself: men like Nicholas Trivet, chronicler, annotator of the classics, expositor of biblical texts, England's most learned Dominican; the Oxford Benedictines, Carmelites and Franciscans who devised the best astronomical clocks and calendars in all Europe; John Capgrave, Austin friar of King's Lynn, encyclopaedist of the lives of the saints; John Lydgate, black monk and serene English poet of the beauties of the liturgy, of love and of the life of London.

Monks and Friars: the World and the Flesh

John Wyclif's claim that the religious orders were not in a state of grace was implicitly supported by two contemporaries of his, famous poets commenting on the social scene. Langland's bitter anger was vented on the monks and friars for the evil uses he said they made of their endowments; but he wanted them reformed, not suppressed. Chaucer was a sharp observer, but amused. His monks are men of the world, not specially serious in their regard for their Rule. The hunting monk in Chaucer's *Prologue to the Canterbury Tales* may have been inspired by the hunting Abbot Clown of Leicester. Chaucer's friar is a small-time charlatan and a rapscallion, who will gladly give advice and settle disputes, but fleeces the widows, the poor and the sick who come to him, and is not above comforting a sorrowing mother by inventing a vision of her dead child on his way to heaven. Chaucer's era abounds with examples of monks and friars who pursued their vocations – as preachers, confessors, scholars, administrators, contemplatives – with the greatest sincerity and energy.

Vocation and visitation

What Langland and Chaucer describe are practices and personalities which were frequent – but not universal – in their occurrence. The common thread is close involvement with the secular world, the flesh and even the devil. Whatever the hopes of Bernard or Francis, no religious order could sever itself from the world, and it was much less wilful choice than binding duty which took their members into it. The monasteries paid taxes to the Crown; some of them administered justice of every kind, in the king's name, over substantial districts, as Ely did over its Isle; a friar of outstanding skill and saintliness might be made confessor to the king and eventually rewarded and burdened with a bishopric. On average, there were usually four monks or friars among the English and Welsh bishops.

Simon Langham (1317–76), who went from the farming community of Rutland to be a black monk at Westminster, and quickly rose to be abbot, reformed his house's finances, strengthened its liturgical observance and its discipline, and eventually left it much of the money to rebuild the nave. Perhaps he was ambitious: but, if not, he still had little choice but to accept the high offices pressed upon him in quick succession: king's Treasurer, Bishop of Ely, king's Chancellor, Archbishop of Canterbury, Cardinal at the papal see.

No monastic community could expect to be ruled by an unbroken line of strict reformers like Langham; but every house was under inspection and correction from outside. Benedictines and Austin Canons were subject to visitations by the bishop of their diocese. A number of the greater houses, such as Bury, Westminster, Battle, had since their early days been exempted from the authority of their bishops, but both the Benedictines and the Austin Canons established, in each province of the Church, regular General Chapters which sought to maintain a common standard of observance, discipline and efficiency, and arranged their own visitations. The Cistercians, the Gilbertines, the military orders and the friars had been exempt since the start from all but the pope's authority and their own collective system of inspection and control. A mass of evidence survives of visitations of religious houses and what evils and backslidings the visitors uncovered. What is recorded of visitations made to the numerous non-exempt houses of their big diocese by the Bishops of Lincoln in the earlier 15th century may be taken as fairly characteristic of the efficacy of the system and the quality of monastic life brought to light.

The bishops were expected to visit annually; in practice they managed to visit, on average, every four years. After an opening sermon, the bishop or the official who might come in his place, would interview every monk or nun separately, and would ask for complaints and accusations. Where there was no complaint put forward, little was recorded in writing save 'All is well': merit and godliness were more difficult to describe than failings and sins, and the full picture of a house where all was indeed well often eludes us. Grievances and denunciations were investigated on the spot, and after the visiting bishop had left, he sent his findings – the *comperta* – in writing to the abbot and convent, with his injunctions for action. A simple analysis of the *comperta* for the whole diocese is hard to make. A house like Dorchester-on-Thames, in the extreme south of the diocese, yields evidence of monasticism at its worst. The Austin Canons of Dorchester spent their evenings in a common-room relaxing with women friends, best Abingdon ale and games of chess. Meanwhile their abbot was being solaced by five mistresses. Outside the precincts, the canons were addicted to hawking, hunting and frequenting taverns. A younger group, led by Canon Ralph Carnell, went about armed and even in jackets of mail, and brawled, when in drink, with the local youths, while Oxford undergraduates made trips down the Thames to join in. Carnell, who had given the prior a deaf ear in a fight, applied for study leave at Oxford. Some of the canons assured the bishop that 'All is well'. There is no record of the effect of the measures enjoined on the convent by the bishop, but it is known that a weak spot in the visitation system was the difficulty of reforming the worst houses.

Was all well? The average house where the bishop found that all was not well was a place not of open vice, like Dorchester, but of moderate zeal and competence and often a falling income. To have a weak or wilful or stupid abbot was a key defect, opening the door to financial mismanagement, sloth in attendance in choir, self-indulgence in food and drink, sports and games, dress and the company of the opposite sex. Probably the most widespread shortcomings of all, throughout the monastic system, were the pursuit of private accommodation – a suite of rooms, work-rooms, bedroom and parlour, or at least a personal chamber – and the discovery of lawful reasons for eating more flesh-meat. One problem thrust on the monks was the excessive demand for hospitality to the laity, from the King and Queen down. Ample warmth and comfort, good food and drink were required of them. This brought luxury into the monastery, ate up the revenues and created such dilemmas as whether to allow high-ranking and influential ladies to stay overnight or persuade them to leave at sunset. Standards were probably highest in the large houses, especially the cathedral priories, and (leaving aside the blatantly scandalous minority) lowest in small, needy and remote nunneries or Augustinian priories. Meanwhile the different orders came increasingly to resemble each other. Little now distinguished Cistercians from Benedictines: the handful of new Carthusian houses alone contrasted strongly with the others.

The friars had decreased in number since 1350, but in following their vocations they possibly attained higher standards than the monks. The nature of their calling put them always in the public eye, and in an age when a more literate and educated laity had higher expectations of the clergy, the friars were excessively criticised and lampooned. Thousands of late medieval lay wills made bequests to the friars and testify to the regard in which they were held as counsellors, confessors and preachers. They were the regular and trusted advisers of the archbishops on doctrinal questions. The strongest and most effective arguments against the false doctrines of the heretical Lollard sect were those staunchly put forward by the friars. Innumerable men and women preferred to have their bodies buried in the friaries: however, it was the Benedictine monks of Worcester to whom Henry VII entrusted the body of his elder son Arthur, and whom he commissioned to say masses in perpetuity for the soul of the prince whose survival would have prevented Henry VIII from coming to the throne.

The Dissolution of the Monasteries

Monasticism in England came to a sudden end. The Dissolution of the Monasteries by King Henry VIII was a process spread over only half a decade and entirely completed in 1540. Historians have long debated whether the monks and friars and nuns had lapsed so comprehensively from the high standards of their founders and forerunners that the dispersal of their communities and the confiscation of their properties were bound to come about in the 16th century. Henry VIII (1509–1547) was a powerful king, efficiently served by the men who brought about the Dissolution – Thomas Cromwell, the King's Secretary; Thomas Howard, Duke of Norfolk; and Sir Thomas Audley – but they would have been unable to push it through in the face of determined and nation-wide opposition, rooted in loyalty and devotion to the religious orders. Lay society as a whole stolidly accepted the Dissolution and of those with strong views more favoured it than tried to protect and save the monasteries.

Henry VIII

The idea of taking away the lands and wealth of the religious orders was not new in Tudor times. It had been widely discussed in Europe

A time for change

109

since the 13th century. In the 14th century Englishmen ranging from university intellectuals like John Wyclif to royal princes like John of Gaunt, Duke of Lancaster, had shown an interest in it. It could be justified by claiming that only the truly poor monk could be a true monk, or that the religious orders had been made so lax and corrupt by material possessions and preoccupations that they should be totally reformed. In England, by 1520 or 1530, there was much in them which required severe reform. The extent to which monks, friars and nuns had fallen into carnality and debauchery is difficult to assess from the evidence, though their critics and the apologists for the Dissolution made much of the point. In any event, it was in much less sensational and more debilitating ways that the arterial blood of monasticism had become anaemic and sluggish.

By 1500 there were only some 10,000 monks and 2000 nuns in

Poor Clares
(Franciscan nuns)
following the service, c.
1430.

England, although the kingdom's population, which had declined heavily in the later 14th century – largely but not wholly because of the Black Death – had recovered its former numerical strength and was still growing. There were too few monks and nuns in too many convents; and, especially but not exclusively in the smaller houses, under-manning and inadequate recruitment went hand in hand with poor financial management and heavy debts, while several of the greater abbeys were richer than their serious needs required. A sophisticated appraisal would have been that the number of monasteries should be reduced and that more of their resources should be diverted to education and to pastoral work in the parishes. Monks and friars were no longer indispensable to the academic health of the universities and they played little part in the schooling of children and adolescents. Far from ministering to the spiritual needs of parish communities, monasteries could often be found positively neglecting them.

Monasteries had the right to the tithes of many parish churches. In the 14th and 15th centuries they successfully requested the bishops and the crown to 'appropriate' to them the tithes of many more, to ease their own financial straits. It was then possible to economise on the obligation to provide priests for such parishes. An abbot or prior who supplied a parish with no more than a visiting priest who came over only on Sundays to say mass, mattins and evensong in the forenoon before going back to his dinner, might become the target for understandable complaints about infants dying unbaptised, old folk with no priest at their deathbeds to hear the last confession and give the last sacraments, marriages and funerals delayed and services rushed. The monks came among the laity more as landlords and owners of town properties, with rights and duties and material problems to solve, than they worked as teachers or pastors; and they were prone to take their pleasures conspicuously, riding, hunting, hawking, pursuing hobbies such as breeding rabbits, rearing swans, or merely watching dancers, mummers and musicians perform in the parishioners' churchyard. Within the cloister, hospitality to the laity might be good and morality on the whole conventional; but discipline had weakened and laxity prevailed in too many houses, under abbots and priors of indifferent quality. The Office was in many places ceasing to be an assembly of the whole convent at intervals throughout the day, and groups of monks were taking turns to attend the Hours. The postponement of bedtime for a talk over a drink after Compline was common, as was failure to get up in the small hours for Vigils.

Conditions and standards varied widely from monastery to monastery, and were still austerely high among the Carthusians and the Bridgettines; but inside the abbey walls, English monasticism seemed caught in the old liturgical, contemplative and studious tradition, its performance within that tradition more complacent and slack than corrupt or cynical. Flirting, gossiping and quarrelling were endemic, where fornication and violence were probably exceptional. If at

Canterbury and Westminster and Bath the monks were still building finely and well, in a considerable number of other houses leaking naves or dormitory roofs, dilapidated infirmaries or barns and unrestored fire damage told of neglect or penury. The lively distinction of some great houses in scholarship, the new classical humanism and the arts did not infuse a fresh cultural vitality into the religious orders as a whole.

On the continent of Europe, in the lands where monks and nuns and friars survived the Reformation and developed a new vigour under the Counter-Reformation, the contemplative and mystical urge was great, but it was more the determined move into pastoral, educational, nursing and missionary work which saved the orders and made them flourish. In England, by Henry VIII's reign, monasticism needed spiritual and pastoral quickening to have the chance of resisting powerful pressure from outside. The weight of English lay opinion was not antagonistic to the monks. They had kinsfolk and friends, tenants and neighbours, guests and hosts outside the cloister. An abbot could hunt with the head of a local knightly family, sell him wool, buy his timber, sit with him on the bench, go to law against him, earn from him a mixture of criticism and respect, but probably neither enmity nor ardent admiration. No one was now an Ailred of Rievaulx. There was a feeling that the time had come for change. The case was made for radical reform; but without internal strength and with more indifference than enthusiasm and active support outside, there was to be no resisting dissolution.

The canons of Aldgate In 1532, the Austin Canons of Christ Church Priory, Aldgate, in London, voluntarily surrendered their priory and their properties – and their massive debts – to Henry VIII. In effect they dissolved their own house. The king had the surrender and transfer embodied in an Act of Parliament, which recognised the Crown as the founder of Christ Church, Aldgate, and prevented any Londoners from claiming any founder's rights by descent from the priory's benefactors centuries before. Henry, at this time, probably wanted not so much to acquire all the lands and properties of the monasteries as to 'resume' everything that he believed or claimed previous kings had given them in the past.

The Aldgate affair was probably the turning point which led to the Dissolution; but it is strongly significant of a belief within monastic society that some houses had no future and that rationalisation and the freeing of monastic resources for new purposes were necessary. However, it was not a precedent. For as long ago as 1312, the Templars had been dissolved by a general council of the church, under the presidency of the Pope, and their properties had been re-distributed.

The alien priories War with France, intermittent but serious from 1294, continuous, despite frequent truces, from 1336 to 1453, the time of the 'Hundred Years War', jeopardised the position in England of another group of monastic houses. They were the 'alien priories', cells of abbeys in France, which managed them from across the Channel and drew profits from their lands. Most of these cells consisted of a prosperous grange where a couple of monks dwelt; but they included all the Cluniac priories in England, because of the centralised nature of the Order, with all houses governed by the Abbey of Cluny. The transfer in wartime of cash resources from the alien priories to their mother houses in France impelled English kings, from Edward I in 1294 onwards, to intervene in their affairs. Before long they faced the alternative of royal control of their finances and buying from the king expensive charters making them 'denizens' of England and freeing them of all obligations to houses overseas. Many of the small alien priories could not afford such charters, and the king arranged for them to be absorbed by larger English houses. Later, others were added to the properties of the new schools and university colleges (themselves not monastic) which were being established, like Winchester College and the 'New College' at Oxford, founded by William of Wykeham, and Eton College and King's College, Cambridge, founded by King Henry VI – whose father, Henry V, had enriched his Carthusian foundation at Sheen with suppressed alien priories.

Other small houses were being suppressed. Like the alien priories, they were made over either to larger monasteries or to colleges. Their properties did not disappear into lay hands. Spinney Priory, poor and ill-governed, was absorbed by Ely Cathedral Priory. At Cambridge, a nunnery was converted into Jesus College and other small houses were given to Christ's College, founded by Lady Margaret Beaufort. Cardinal Thomas Wolsey, the ambitious chief minister of the young Henry VIII, planned to follow the example of Wykeham, and establish a school in his native Ipswich and a college at Oxford. Between 1524 and 1529 Wolsey persuaded the Pope to close down twenty-nine lesser English monasteries, and allow him to transfer their resources, totalling £1800 a year, equivalent to the income of a single manor abbey, to his school and college. The Pope made the condition that the patron or founder should give consent. In every instance Wolsey arranged for the king to be declared (by descent) the founder, and the king conveyed the lands of the monastery to him. Thus dissolution was under way, and the intervention or consent of the king was crucial; but, whether with the Templars, the alien priories or the scores of smaller 'native' houses, papal authority was required, and nearly all the properties were made over to bigger monasteries or to educational purposes under the aegis of the Church.

When Wolsey fell from power and died, in 1529, the monastic properties he had amassed were taken over by Henry VIII. Wolsey's Oxford college came into being, as Christ Church, his Ipswich school did not. Meanwhile, King Henry, baulked by the Papacy of the divorce he wanted from his first queen, Catherine of Aragon, broke England away from the jurisdiction of Rome through a series of Acts of Parliament, to which the heads of nearly all the religious houses were consenting – in Parliament and in the Convocation of the Clergy. An Act of 1534 forbade any monk to travel outside the country on official

Cardinal Wolsey

The break with Rome

business. This severed the connections of the English monks with the Papacy. The same year the climax was reached with the Act of Supremacy, which made King Henry the supreme Head of the Church of England, and from which the monks of the London Charterhouse were almost alone in their dissent. Henry had made every effort to secure the agreement of the English monks to the breach with Rome and its consequences. He could hardly now use the pretext that the monks were hostile to the Crown to dissolve their houses.

Another Act of Parliament in 1534 granted the king, annually, one-tenth of the income of the Church. To levy the Tenth, Henry had an enquiry made by local commissions into the extent of all church revenues and properties. The product of these investigations was the taxation assessment of 1535 known as the *Valor Ecclesiasticus* (the 'ecclesiastical valuation'). Nearly eighty per cent of the monasteries appear in the *Valor* as having somewhat notional incomes of under £300 a year; sixteen per cent had £300–£1000 a year; and only twenty-eight (the remaing four per cent), nearly all of them Benedictine, had over £1000, with Westminster Abbey and Glastonbury Abbey soaring high above £3000. The inequality of resources, as between one monastery and another, is made startlingly clear, in impressive detail. The figures for monastic incomes totalled £165,000 a year: the *Valor* did not, in practice, cover the friars. Of all this wealth, some two-thirds came from the lands of the monasteries, and only three per cent was spent on charity for the sick and poor in lay society.

Cromwell's Visitors　　Thomas Cromwell, meanwhile, had been made Henry's Vicar-General or deputy in spiritual affairs, and set about the duty imposed on the king by the Supremacy Act – to visit and reform the houses of the religious orders. The Visitors sent by Cromwell round the monasteries moved with great despatch. They were laymen, royal servants, at heart not unfair, but worldly and insensitive towards the monastic life. The questions they put were those asked by visiting bishops and inspecting abbots in the past; but their examination of witnesses, weighing of evidence and issuing of injunctions were hurried and peremptory by former standards. They alarmed the monasteries from the first, forbidding any monk 'to go forth of the precincts' and banning from every community guests or servants of the opposite sex. Nor did they complete their visitation, omitting many houses altogether. In their findings they were severe, and determined to lay emphasis on financial incompetence, superstitious practices and the sins of the flesh; but they were guilty more of haste than of prejudice. Cromwell was probably more anxious to assert the new royal supremacy than to create a case for dissolution, and had some interest in the reform of houses capable of mending their ways.

The Dissolution begins　　The *Valor Ecclesiasticus* had identified half the monasteries of England as having incomes of less than £200 a year. The findings reported by Cromwell's Visitors by 1536 could not be regarded as branding this as the group of monasteries fit to be suppressed, and only the larger houses as worthy to continue. The quality of monastic life did not rise or fall constantly with monastic income. But early in 1536 the government decided for financial reasons to 'resume' into Crown hands a quantity of monastic land, and the easy course was to use the *Valor* to earmark the smaller houses and the incoming Visitors' reports to offer a moral justification. Great pressure was now put on the Crown by importunate would-be purchasers of monastic lands and by those who claimed to represent, by descent, the original founders. Henry VIII was able to evade long disputes about founderships by putting a bill through Parliament in March 1536, enacting that all religious houses with fewer than twelve monks or nuns and less than £200 a year should be closed, and 'His Majesty should have and enjoy' all their possessions. The Act roundly condemned the smaller houses as centres of 'manifest sin, vicious, carnal and abominable living', and added that in 'the great and solemn monasteries of this realm . . . religion is right well kept and observed'. Neither generalisation was supported by the Visitors' reports, and the turn of the 'great and solemn' houses was soon to come.

The general dissolution of the monasteries began with the Act of 1536. The king set up the Court of Augmentations to take central control of all the property confiscated and to secure afresh an assessment of the income, the value of the gold and silver plate, the bells, the lead and other chattels, and the number of monks and nuns, servants, corrodians and dependents of each house taken over. Yet

A wry view of monastic life *c.* 1300, from Queen Mary's Psalter.

115

Henry took care to guarantee the continuation of grants, leases and annuities which the monasteries had given or sold to laymen in the past. The monks were either given cash gratuities and licences to become parish priests, or transferred to other houses of their orders. The Gilbertine Order was exempted entirely from the closure of the '£200' houses. Its Master, after all, was high in the service of the king as President of the Council of the North. Many monks and nuns wished to go on leading a cloistered life, and Henry and Cromwell were anxious not to provoke the animosity of their relations and friends. Over seventy of the houses to be suppressed were allowed to buy exemption, but at a cost which gravely impaired their already straitened finances.

The Pilgrimage of Grace   In the autumn of 1536, a rebellion against Henry's government broke out in Lincolnshire and rapidly spread across the Humber to the rest of northern England. Known as the Pilgrimage of Grace, and mustered under the banner of the Five Wounds of the crucified Christ, it was a movement of the common people, its leadership soon taken over by lawyers, gentry and noblemen. Its purpose was to protest against high prices, the ill effects of enclosures, the introduction of the Bible in English, the conduct and policies of Cromwell, Cranmer and Henry's other chief servants. The suppression of smaller monasteries was only one of its causes, among many; but Robert Aske, the Yorkshire lawyer who was its principal leader, published a powerful defence of 'the abbeys in the north parts', for their hospitality, the alms they gave, the masses they said for men's souls, the places they provided for the younger sons and the daughters of 'the gentlemen', their maintenance of roads and bridges and sea dykes. The monasteries, he added, were 'one of the beauties of this realm to all men and strangers passing through'. Henry VIII put down the northern rebellion in 1537, with ease and speed and cold ruthlessness. For the monasteries, the tragedy was that several of them had been involved in the rising and their abbots or priors were now arrested, attainted as traitors, and executed, and their houses were dissolved. In this way Bridlington, Hexham, Jervaulx, Whalley and others came to an end, their property forfeit to the Crown and some of their monks hanged and the rest dispersed.

'Voluntary' surrenders   When the Act suppressing the smaller houses was passed, neither Henry VIII nor Cromwell was likely to have had a clear vision or even perhaps a firm intention that all the monasteries of England would be dissolved within four years. The voluntary surrender of a monastery, as at Aldgate, the parliamentary dissolution of a group of houses, and the suppression of a house where the abbot and others had been caught up in the treason of rebellion did not provide a way of bringing the religious orders to an end; but a way was found, rather fortuitously, as the result of the northern rising.

The royal commissioners who had brought about the suppression of Whalley Abbey, Lancashire, and the execution of its abbot, investigated its neighbour, Furness Abbey. They found no evidence of treason; but they appear to have reduced to fear and despair Abbot

Roger Pyle and his monks, who signed documents admitting their 'misorder and evil lives' and transferring by gift to the Crown their abbey and all that it possessed. The monks were not found places in other monasteries nor given pensions or licences to become secular. On the surface voluntary, this was unquestionably an induced surrender, and when it was too late the monks of Furness said that they had been under irresistible compulsion. All that the royal agents had intended was to clear up a suspected local centre of treason in the north; in doing so they provided a method for future dissolutions, which could be applied quickly, on the spot, without recourse to Parliament and under the cloak of legality.

By 1538, the majority of English monasteries, and nearly all the greater abbeys, were still in being. Cromwell – probably not falsely – persisted in giving the impression that the king did not contemplate a general dissolution. Individual convents, while their sister-houses were picked off one by one, clung to the hope of their own survival, and so refrained from doing what Cromwell did not wish, and selling or leasing their lands in a hurry. But the final phase of the Dissolution, which was to affect all the survivors – the majority of England's medieval religious houses, and nearly all the greater abbeys – had already begun. The method of induced surrender was applied in almost every instance. The justification, that monastic possessions were being handed over to those better able and willing to use them for good ends, was steadfastly reiterated.

As late as 1538, Cromwell was not necessarily pressing forward a tacit policy of total confiscation: rather, his commissioners were probing for and ferreting out vulnerable spots, to bring down one house or another. The commissioners themselves were often under pressure from individual noblemen and gentry in the royal favour, who coveted the buildings and estates of particular houses. The monastic communities were steadily pushed and persuaded into the mood to surrender. On the one hand, for all to note, was the turning out of the monks of Furness on to the world with no compensation, no provision for their future; on the other, the monks of Abingdon and the nuns of Wilton departed with substantial pensions charged to the lords of their houses: the last Abbess of Wilton was given a house and a small estate along with an annuity of £100. Readiness to surrender could at least guarantee a secure personal future, which refusal would forfeit.

In the first nine months of 1538, thirty-eight monasteries made induced surrenders, or, in one or two instances, like Woburn Abbey, were the victims of attainder. The confessions of sinful conduct and incompetent management which were a standard part of the surrenders should not, however, be taken at their face value, as some historians have been prone to take them. In the autumn of the year, the Gilbertine priories began to be dissolved. Meanwhile, the rich and famous shrines of the English monasteries were being dismantled by the government: the shrine of St. Edmund at Bury; of Our Lady of Walsingham (the

Dismantled shrines: dispersing friars

offerings of the pilgrims at the shrine gave Walsingham Priory two-fifths of its annual income); of St. Thomas Becket at Canterbury, from which gold and silver treasures and jewellery were taken away in wagon-loads. The justification in law for pillaging these and other shrines was thin, resting on Henry VIII's expressed disapproval, as Supreme Head of the Church in England, that money and valuables should be offered up at centres of pilgrimage. The blow struck fell as heavily on the morale and standing of the monasteries as on their income.

In 1538 came also the turn of the friars. A former Dominican, Richard Ingworth, Bishop of Dover, conducted visitations of all the friaries in England. He found that many of the friars – the best minds, the most eloquent preachers, and those in high authority in their orders – had already left their convents for good, in the previous four years. Those who remained had little will to resist. Faced with serious demands for rigorous and sweeping reforms, they preferred to surrender and disperse. The friars had few possessions to bargain with. Their properties, including their convents, were not their own, but were held in trust for them by bodies of laymen, and their income from offerings and legacies had never been guaranteed from year to year. They were given no pensions and scattered in penury, prohibited from entering any parish church to hear confessions or say masses without special licence from the local bishop. The mendicant orders throughout the country were dissolved in this single operation of Ingworth's.

'The great abbeys go down'

In the last eighteen months of the Dissolution, Cromwell sent groups of commissioners on great tours or sweeps across whole regions of England – the south-west, the midlands, the north, the eastern counties – systematically procuring the surrender of all surviving houses, shire by shire. The commissions were spurred on by Henry VIII's pressing need for money to finance a threatened foreign war, and they seized and carted away for the king's use notoriously vast amounts of gold and silver plate and jewellery, and of lead from the roofs of the monasteries. A new Act of Parliament, in 1539, vested in the Crown all the properties of monasteries so far surrendered, and all which might be surrendered in the future. This Act neither compelled nor authorised the final dissolutions; but it safeguarded the royal title to all the spoils.

'The great abbeys go down as fast as they may', wrote one of King Henry's ministers; and those few which would not go down, like Colchester, Glastonbury and Reading, Hinton and Montacute, soon found themselves in hopeless isolation. Their brother-abbots and sister-houses were all gone. They were cut off from the Pope. The lay families living on their estates knew that the king had guaranteed their own tenancies. The future, which was to be brutally brief, held only attainder for their abbots, with heroic martyrdom on the gallows, and expulsion. The Abbot of Glastonbury, trying to hide the treasure of his house where the king's thieves could not steal it, was himself in consequence convicted of robbing of its plate the abbey church – the church which men believed had been first built by Joseph of Arimathaea, who buried Christ in the sepulchre. The Abbess of Amesbury and the Prioress of Godstow, refusing to surrender to the commissioners, were able to escape any royal vengeance and at least procured for their nuns a year's respite from suppression, which gave them time to prepare a comfortable return to secular life. Early in 1540, the last great abbeys went down, Benedictine Evesham, Augustinian Waltham; and the Order of the Knights Hospitallers of St. John was dissolved, by Act of Parliament, throughout the realm, and its properties were vested in the Crown. William Weston, last Prior of the English Knights of St. John, and member of a Surrey family very close in service and friendship to King Henry, was awarded a handsome pension. However, he died on the day the royal agents entered his Priory of Clerkenwell: 'gold', as an observer wrote, 'though it is a great cordial, being no cure for a broken heart'. The dissolution of the monasteries had been accomplished.

Henry VIII had broken with Rome and dissolved the monasteries in the same decade. Either action would have been possible without the other, though the breach with Rome – fundamentally unopposed by the monastic orders in England – made the Dissolution easier. The thousands of dispersed monks, nuns and friars were not regarded as loyal adherents to the Pope, still less as papal agents: and very few were. They had been dispossessed and scattered rather than legally liquidated as convents or communities, and there was nothing to stop a monk from rejoining other members of his order in an attempt to follow their Rule and lead a conventual life. There were some short-lived attempts to do so, though not one existing convent preserved its integrity or kept the majority of its brethren together after 1540; and the monks, nuns and friars were regarded in law as having, either willingly or in some instances compulsorily, returned to the world outside the cloister. Probably the most significant feature of the Dissolution was that it met so little hostility or obstruction. The risings of 1536–37 were backed by monastic tenants in Lincolnshire who were ready to rebel against a change of landlord: but in nearly every other English county, the tenants of the monasteries were, on this particular score, unexcited. It had been easier for the ninth-century monks of Lindisfarne, expelled by heathen fire and sword, to keep together and survive conventually, than for sixteenth-century monastic society, with its implicit belief that the comforts and pastimes of lay people (the more innocent of them, at least) should be available to those living under religious vows. The Pilgrimage of Grace had been a regional rebellion only, by no means wholly preoccupied with the plight of monasticism, and easily crushed. Laymen accepted the Dissolution.

The Dissolution accepted

The great majority of houses were dissolved on terms which gave monks and nuns pensions which varied in quantity from house to house but were assessed fairly and without meanness and were in practice paid by the Tudor government over the succeeding years.

Monks, nuns and friars – their fate

Most monks in priest's orders were licensed to become the incumbents of parish benefices or chaplaincies if selected and invited. These arrangements were at the mercy of the uncomfortable inflation of the 16th century, but were supported by the English bishops, who made relatively few new ordinations between 1540 and 1558, thereby helping ex-monks to acquire parish benefices in the face of diminished competition from the young. How many former monks and friars failed to acquire pensions or parish benefices or both or else find employment in lay society, is not known and never can be. It may be that as many as a quarter of all monks, nuns and friars were put out on the world unprovided for in 1536–40.

For the heads, men and women, of abbeys and priories, history paints a clearer picture. A few great abbots were destroyed by the Dissolution. Most of them were given a truly generous pension, with a house and land, for life. Many became bishops and cathedral deans in the reformed church of Henry VIII and Edward VI. Most members of the religious orders, men and women, were given a fair and quite generous deal at the Reformation. For every former monk, friar or nun who lapsed into poverty, went into exile or suffered a kind of martyrdom at the hands of the Tudor state, there were many who meekly accepted revolutionary change, drew their pensions, found new employment, not least among the parish flocks, or rejoined the secular society which they had earlier left. Ex-priors slid comfortably into the rôle of country gentlemen; ex-nuns quite often found husbands.

The monasteries plundered
Once a monastery had surrendered, it was ransacked and largely reduced to ruins by the royal agents. Behind the prevailing insensitivity to sacred and beautiful objects, the greed and the deliberate vandalism – which are not to be doubted – there was a clear, if unspoken purpose to ensure that no monastery should be reoccupied by monks bent on reviving its religious life. The altar vessels and other gold and silver plate and candelabra were sent, without delay, to London, for the king to turn into bullion. So were the bronze bells and the leads of roofs and gutters, which were first melted down and cast into pigs on the spot: the furnaces were often fuelled (there is direct evidence of this) with the carved woodwork from the altars, the choir, the rood-screen and the pulpit. Stained glass windows were smashed to recover the lead which bound their lights together. Here and there, an abbey bell or two or some stained glass would be acquired for use in a local church: Magdalen College, Oxford, has panelling from Reading Abbey, and St. Mary's Church, Lancaster, has choir stalls from Cockersand Priory. Hardly any of the thousands of chalices and other altar vessels in the monastery have survived into the twentieth century.

All other chattels and movables of a dissolved house were inventoried, usually in meticulous detail, and auctioned on the site: altar-pieces – paintings on wooden panels – of which a very few still exist, the finest being the Wilton diptych with its portrait of King Richard II; statues and reliefs of sculptured stone – some bought by local people, many exported to the continent for re-sale; tapestries, vestments, often embroidered in the English mode, altar hangings and altar linen; household goods and stores, horses and vehicles. We learn of monks selling their own habits. It is surprising to realise that the liturgical books, including illuminated psalters and missals, bibles, and the devotional, theological and historical works (chiefly manuscript but some of them printed) in the monastic libraries were usually sold – after the jewels had been gouged out of the splendid bindings of the altar books – for their value as scrap vellum, parchment or paper. More than one contemporary observer wrote of the rapid conversion of many thousands of monastic manuscripts into materials for cleaning, wrapping and book-binding. Some great abbey churches survived the Dissolution, either because they were already cathedrals, like Canterbury, Ely and Durham, or were transformed into cathedrals for new dioceses, like Bristol and Peterborough; and they preserved, in varying measure, their medieval libraries, archives and account rolls. Later in the 16th century, there developed a growing interest in the collection of manuscripts. The Archbishop of Canterbury's library at Lambeth and the Oxford and Cambridge colleges were among the chief repositories for what had survived and could be retrieved. Fewer than four thousand monastic manuscripts and a limited number of incomplete collections of archives have come down from the English monasteries to the 20th century: enough to indicate the nature of the losses inflicted in 1536–40.

The royal decision to destroy all the buildings of the monasteries was implicit in the stripping of the roofs of their lead. By 1539, the king was explicitly ordering that the churches of the monks and all their conventual buildings should be razed to the ground at newly surrendered houses. The Hospitallers' Priory at Clerkenwell, for instance, was to be entirely demolished, and its stone, timber and lead moved across London to the Strand for the building of Somerset House. The extent to which there was total demolition, itself not cheap to carry out, as against comprehensive ruination, varied from house to house, and may still be roughly gauged by the sight-seer, provided it is realised that, decade by decade through the Tudor period, abandoned monasteries were used by local builders as easily worked quarries for ashlar and rubble. The plundering of sites was more intensive in regions where building stone was less abundant, such as Norfolk and Suffolk; but the very loneliness of some – especially Cistercian sites – tended to keep stone-robbers away. In the towns, the churches and conventual buildings of the friars were sold off for secular purposes, and in many instances were, within a few years, knocked down for redevelopment.

Demolitions

However, a substantial number of monastic buildings was deliberately preserved for new uses after 1540. The King naturally kept

Survivals of monastic buildings

121

intact his own Abbey of Westminster, replacing the abbot and the Benedictine monks with a dean and secular canons. For a short time Westminster Abbey had been used as the cathedral of one of the new dioceses carved by Henry and the reformers from the ecclesiastical map. There was more than one such scheme for remodelling the dioceses. The new bishoprics which emerged permanently were Bristol, Chester, Gloucester, Oxford and Peterborough, with five major town monasteries surviving as their cathedrals, despite some losses of spiritual and cultural treasures. The twelve monastic cathedrals which had existed since Old English and Norman times were also cleared of their monks, but kept their diocesan status and function, under their deans and chapters, their lands, and – especially at Canterbury, Durham and Worcester – their rich collections of manuscripts. Elsewhere, hopes of saving a fine group of monastic buildings were raised for a time – should Wenlock be a cathedral? Walsingham, Burton-on-Trent and Thornton-on-Humber colleges of secular canons? Evesham a collegiate school? – only to be dashed.

At nearly a hundred places, a monastic church continued to be used for worship after the monks had gone and the conventual buildings had been pulled down. The naves of several had long been parish churches, and continued so. St. Alban's is the greatest example, and is a cathedral today. A number of monastic churches elsewhere was brought into the parochial system after the Dissolution. Either there was no other church for the people within miles, and the bishop had to intervene, or else a local community or a group of wealthy men would buy a monastic church and arrange for it to have parochial status. Local initiative saved the abbey church at Tewkesbury, a gothic masterpiece with the tombs and chantries of the baronial house of Despenser along its nave. There is no more vivid illustration of the medieval layman's belief in the efficacy of the prayers of monks for the souls of the departed and his readiness to pay for them – but a belief incapable in the 1530s of calling forth lay resistance to the Dissolution, south of the Humber at least.

The roll of former monastic churches providing dignified and beautiful settings for parish worship (though sometimes with the chancel shorn away since the Dissolution) includes Bolton in Wharfedale, Cartmel, Christchurch, Dorchester-on-Thames, Dunstable, Evesham, Malton, Pershore, Ripon, Selby and Waltham. A few churches were converted for their lay purchasers into dwelling-houses, as at Buckland, where the transepts were incorporated into the house as well the nave and chancel; but this took place usually where the church was small, without aisles or transepts. To make a kitchen in the vestry under the tower, a hall in the nave, and a private chamber in the chancel was probably never easy. More often, the abbot's house or sometimes the gatehouse was adapted as a rich family's residence, as at Beaulieu, Titchfield, Woburn and dozens of other places, and the monastery kitchen, cellars, stables, barn and dovecot would be preserved. The original monastic choice of a well-watered, sheltered and beautiful site was probably as strong an attraction for the thrusting Tudor gentleman or nobleman, the Grenville, Russell or Wriothesley, looking for a country seat, as the abbot's house itself.

The Act of Suppression, in 1536, had stated that the wealth of the smaller monasteries to be dissolved was being spent 'for the maintenance of sin', and had promised that it should be 'converted to better uses'. The total wealth of the religious orders was some £150,000 a year at the time. Once confiscated, only a minute fraction of it was given to education or charity. The purpose of Henry VIII and Cromwell, as the setting up of the Court of Augmentations suggested, was to sell a proportion of it, and to retain the great bulk of the monastic lands as a permanent income-producing Crown endowment. That purpose failed hopelessly under the pressure of the royal need for large sums of ready money. The sales of movables were completed by 1543; but they yielded only small sums compared with what urban sites and, above all, agrarian land would bring. From the outset, the king was importuned by intending purchasers, and within a few weeks of the opening of the Court of Augmentations, its chancellor, Richard Rich, had bought the Priory of Leghs in Essex, as a residence, and much monastic land. Henry VIII made few gifts and few sales at favourable rates; but, though the land market was brisk, those who wanted to buy were not numerous enough to allow the royal agents to exact inflationary prices. The going rate was 'twenty-years' purchase' – twenty times the assessed value of the lands, other properties, and tithes to be sold. When he died in 1547, Henry VIII had already sold half of the monastic land he had acquired a decade before. The purchase money was not consolidated by the Crown into another kind of permanent endowment: it went to finance current and urgent needs. Nor was the land which the Crown held on to for a time so exploited as to wring from it the greatest possible profit. When Queen Elizabeth, third in line of succession to her father King Henry, came to the throne in 1558, only one-quarter of the wealth of the monasteries was still in Crown hands. That residue steadily ebbed away under Elizabeth and her Stuart successors, except in Lancashire, where about a half of the monastic lands remained part of the Duchy of Lancaster (itself a crown estate), which had absorbed them in 1536–40.

The sale of monastic lands

Thus within a generation of the beginnings of Dissolution, by far the greater proportion of what the monks, nuns and friars had held was owned by noblemen, gentry, lawyers and merchants. Few, if any, of them had bought monastic property to speculate with on the land markets. Hardly any except the Russells, Sadlers and Wriothesleys put together for themselves truly great estates from monastic sources. Their achievement was to increase handsomely their original estates by buying from the Augmentations Office. Their initiative had kept pace with the royal needs for cash and their purchases had brought more firmly into country society, especially in the shires around London, royal ministers like Rich, though not Thomas Cromwell, who had fallen

The end of the story

from royal favour and gone to the scaffold on Tower Hill in 1542. A merchant like Roger Barlow of Bristol bought monastic lands as an investment as far away as Pembrokeshire; William Stumpe bought the buildings of Malmesbury Abbey to convert into a cloth-making factory. The sale of the monastic lands did not lead to the creation of a new social class; but it enabled 'new', ambitious and successful individuals, families and groups among the burgesses, gentry and nobility to extend their holdings of land and town property the more quickly. The change-over had been the smoother because the lands of the monasteries were organised mainly in manors where professional stewards or bailiffs collected rents from the tenants, and where there was no longer much direct or demesne farming by the abbots or convents themselves. The Dissolution dislodged neither the bailiffs nor the tenants. They, like the laity and the secular clergy as a whole, accepted the end of monasticism in England and Wales without resistance or criticism. The Pilgrimage of Grace, though it had rightly alarmed the government for a few months, had not struck the keynote of society's reaction to the Dissolution. The protestant cleric who wrote in 1549 that the destruction of the monastic libraries had given the English the name, abroad, of despisers of learning, was less typical of his countrymen than those who hastened to the abbeys coming under the hammer to buy up the treasures of the great orders as usable junk or mere curios.

Henry VIII's daughter, the Catholic Mary Tudor, brought the Benedictines back to Westminster, placed Edward the Confessor's body in a new shrine, and re-established a few houses of Carthusians and friars. The meagre extent of her success, with only one hundred monks, nuns and friars back in their convents when she died, proves her failure. Under her sister, the Protestant Elizabeth, they went quietly across to the continent, and the spark rekindled by Mary sputtered out. English men and women of the Elizabethan era knew of and often feared the Pope and the religious orders in allegiance to him overseas. Even those who remained in private allegiance to Rome were soon forgetting the monks, the nuns, the friars, and the hospitallers who had been as a numerous, well-endowed community, influential and significant, if increasingly otiose, in the Tudor world, with a thousand years of spiritual and intellectual achievement behind them. As a living reality, they were a dwindling number of great-uncles and great-aunts, living on their pensions. As a memory, they were cowled ghosts, haunting those 'bare, ruined choirs, where late the sweet birds sang'.

The Monks and Friars of Scotland

In the Kingdom of the Scots, from about 900 to 1070, the church was *St. Margaret* largely isolated from the influences of popes and continental and English reformers. Earlier monasticism was dimly reflected in the communities of clergy known as Culdees ('the Servants of God') at Iona, St. Andrews, Scone, Brechin, Dunkeld, Dunblane, and a few other places. Monks they were not. They took no monastic vows, and were free to marry and individually to own property. The reform and reorganisation of the church in Scotland, and the bringing in of the revived monasticism and the new Orders were initiated and directed by the ruling house in the century and a quarter which followed the wedding in 1071 of King Malcolm III of the Scots, the prince who overthrew the usurper Macbeth, to the English Margaret, niece of Edward the Confessor and a refugee from the conquering Normans. The names of St. Margaret (for she was to be canonised), her sixth son, David I, King of Scots from 1124 to 1153, and her grandson, King William the Lion (1165–1214), are the most illustrious in the story of what was a joint achievement of the royal family and the nobility. They received guidance, help and recruits from England (especially from Canterbury, York and Durham) and overseas (notably the French Abbey of Tiron, near Chartres). Reformed Benedictinism was established in Scotland when Margaret brought English monks to Dunfermline on the Forth, which received generous endowments from successive kings and became a principal royal abbey of the kingdom. The chief royal contribution to monastic development was however David I's.

The rebuilding of the Scottish diocesan system was a main concern of *King David I* David's. He left his kingdom with ten bishoprics; but no King of Scots could silence the English claim that the Scottish bishops were under the authority of the Archbishop of York. In 1192 Pope Celestine III rescued the Scots by making their church a special daughter of Rome, in subjection only to the pope. St. Andrews by then was in effect the prime see of the Scots, though not made an archbishopric until 1472, as was Glasgow in 1492. A great new cathedral, high on the old 'King's Mount' with the North Sea washing its cliffs, was built for St. Andrews during the 12th century, and – with David's full support – became monastic when Austin Canons were brought there. The St. Andrews Culdees were moved to the adjacent church of St. Mary on the Rock.

Scotland had one other monastic cathedral, for the Premonstratensians came to the See of Whithorn in Galloway, as well as to Dryburgh Abbey in the border country. The Austin Canons, who had first appeared at Scone in 1120, were as important to the Scottish church as they had been for the English, with major houses at Holyrood, Jedburgh, Lochleven and Cambuskenneth, initially colonised with English canons. Similarly, the well-spring for the Cistercian Order in Scotland was Rievaulx in Yorkshire, at Melrose and Newbattle, Dundrennan and Kinloss, founded in David's reign, and Culross, Balmerino, Coupar Angus, Glenluce, and Deer under his grandsons and successors. The Scottish Cistercians developed sheep-farming as did their English neighbours; yet several Cistercian abbeys were granted lands far too productive to be called 'wilderness': in Strathmore, along the Forth and Tweed, and in the south-west.

The Tironensians
The Cluniacs were late in reaching Scotland, mostly after David's time; with houses on the holy island of Moy, in the Firth of Forth, and at Paisley and Crossraguel, they were fairly few in number. David's own enthusiasm was strongest for the Cistercians and the Tironensian monks, who in Scotland – unlike England – were a significant and distinctive order. The French Benedictine Abbey of Tiron had been founded in 1109. Its monks adopted a simplified liturgy, followed an austere daily life, and practised skilled crafts within the cloister. As early as 1113, David, not yet king, brought some of them to Selkirk. Fifteen years later, he moved them to Kelso, where their abbey could stand in the protection of the neighbouring royal burgh of Roxburgh. The Tironensians multiplied and prospered among the Scots, in their richly endowed Abbey of Arbroath, at Lindores, at Kilwinning. For some decades they were effectively part of an order supervised from the mother house of Tiron, until sheer distance parted the links.

The friars
William the Lion founded and endowed Arbroath Abbey; but it owed its wealth in part to the generosity of the Scottish nobility. If the late 12th century had been largely an age of royal foundations, it was the king's earls and barons and knights who were the chief 13th-century founders and benefactors, up to 1273, when Devorguilla Balliol made the last important foundation, the Cistercian Sweetheart Abbey. Meanwhile, from 1230 onwards, the friars established houses in all the principal towns. In Scotland, the Dominicans had twice as many houses and brethren as the Franciscans, and four times as many as the Carmelites. The Augustinian Friars set up only one Scottish house, very late, in 1329, at Berwick-upon-Tweed, which was to be wrenched from the Scots by the English king only four years after. The Trinitarians, or Red Friars, also settled in Scotland; they were not mendicants but canons, dedicated to raising funds to ransom Christian pilgrims and crusaders held captive in Islamic lands.

Despite the preponderance of the Dominicans – the great teaching order – among the friars, the favours shown them by kings and by townspeople, and their undeniable energy, their arrival did not lead to the founding of a Scottish university. Their theology schools in Ayr and Perth did not survive the 14th century; and not until the 15th had Scottish monks and friars in search of higher education any alternative to Oxford, Paris, or other foreign universities. At the 15th-century universities founded at St. Andrews, Glasgow and Aberdeen the majority of teachers and students were members of the religious orders; but the bright luminaries among Scottish university men – from Laurence of Lindores through William Dunbar to Hector Boece – were never monks, canons or friars, though the poet Robert Henryson was master of the grammar school maintained by the Dunfermline Benedictines.

The golden era of Scottish monasticism ran from David I's reign to the year 1286, when the problems of the succession to the crown began to lead towards war with England. In this century and a half, the religious orders set new and high standards of worship, almsgiving, hospitality and the care of the sick (and scores of almshouses, infirmaries and leper-houses were created); and in architecture, both romanesque and gothic, and music. It has been argued that abbeys like Melrose, Jedburgh and Dundrennan were built too grandly and lavishly, and that improved sanitation went with too much concern with comfort in the cloister; economic enterprise and prosperity with too much amelioration of the monks' plain and frugal diet. In all this, Scottish monasteries were hardly different from their sisters across the border. Their abbots might serve the state well, but became too powerful and authoritarian in the convent. Perhaps the Melrose monk who in 1261 praised Abbot Matthew for the splendid private apartments he built for himself and his successors should have remembered St. Bernard and thought again. Lay benefactors, moreover, could be too keen for a return on their generosity – expecting to nominate a new abbot when a vacancy arose, to place children of their own or of their retainers as novices in the cloister, even to look for annual renders in cash or kind from those they had endowed. The Scottish nunneries, chiefly Cistercian, were permanent residences for daughters and widows of the well-to-do; yet they were also centres which fostered the developing cults of both the Virgin Mary and St. Margaret.

The quality of Scottish monastic life

Nevertheless, Scotland was unusual in that its monasteries had an exceptionally large share of the kingdom's material resources – a kingdom neither rich nor populous. The nature of that share was unusual too, for a remarkably high proportion of it consisted of the teinds (tithes), which were a tax of ten per cent a year on agricultural and other produce, normally owed by parishioners to their rector and his church. In every Christian country, the tithes of some parishes were 'appropriated' to monasteries as revenue for the monks, who would be required to devote a modest proportion of them for the upkeep of priest and church. In England, by 1500, about one-third of the parish churches had been appropriated in this way. In Scotland, the proportion was vast: four-fifths of Scottish teinds were appropriated to monasteries, cathedrals and collegiate churches. Probably half, sucked away from parish priests and their flocks, came to monastic coffers. For example, five major abbeys – Arbroath, Holyrood, Kelso, Melrose and Paisley – received the teinds of a total of 150 parishes. In hard times, monks were prepared almost to starve the religious life of the parish, to shore up their monastery's economy.

Scottish monastic history from 1286 to the mid-16th century is too

Decline and criticism

127

complicated to sum up succinctly, and its records are scanty and patchy; but there are salient features. Intermittent but fierce war with England, mostly waged north of the border, damaged in every way the life of the many monasteries situated in the vulnerable regions. Rebuilding was constant: there was money for more than subsistence. Accident – in the form of big fires – was a menace as grave as the English, as St. Andrews, Arbroath, Dryburgh, Melrose, Newbattle and Sweetheart came to know. Scotland's literature, not least its poetry, flowered remarkably in the 15th century; but monks and friars contributed little, save the historians Walter Bower, Abbot of Inchcolm, and Andrew Wyntoun, Prior of Lochleven. Needy, if lusty, kings debased the monastic image by persuading the popes to confer lucrative appointments on unsuitable people. James V (1513–42) arranged for his illegitimate infant sons to be made Abbots of Holyrood, Kelso and Melrose, and Priors of Pittenweem and St. Andrews. Yet even such evidence of gross abuse is not wholly conclusive. Widespread respect for the friars, and belief in their godliness, can be traced side by side with condemnation of their alleged practice of living on alms meant for pauper families. What was inexorable was a rising tide of lay interest in putting money less into monasteries and friaries, more and more – especially in the burghs – into chantries and collegiate churches of secular priests.

The end of Scottish monasticism England's monasteries were suppressed in a few short years, and their dissolution can be considered somewhat separately from the general course of the Reformation. In Scotland, it was different. The monasteries were not dissolved: rather, they petered out. The doctrines of the reformers were inimical to monasticism: the denial that the Mass could be a propitiation for the sins of the departed and the living; the trust, not in priesthood but in the unique atonement on Calvary and the unvarnished words of the Bible.

So was the mounting denunciation of the conduct of monks and friars, even by critics who put faith before works, good or evil. As preachers, theologians and confessors, embracing true poverty, many friars were exemplary. In monasteries like Kinloss and Cambuskenneth and the one Carthusian house, at Perth, there was intellectual and spiritual vitality. Yet the average Scottish monastic community had now lost the vigour to live up to the vows and carry out the work prescribed by its founders and first brethren; and the heads of houses were more and more often laymen appointed as 'commendators', managing and profiting from the monastic revenues. The individual monk lived a life increasingly apt for a corrodian, in his own chamber, on his own portion of the revenues. Much monastic property had been 'feued' (permanently leased) to lairds and minor landowners who paid what was due to the monks but would never wish to return their holdings to direct monastic control. The resolve to reinvigorate the Christian life of the parishes in town and country was the driving force of the Scottish reformation. All too many of the teinds needed for this purpose were in the grip of monks, and rented out by them to 'tacksmen'. Scottish monks, nuns and friars lacked their own leaders, exercised little power over their own resources, put comfort before spirituality, and obstructed the path to the reform of local kirks, their ministers and flocks.

The complex religious and political struggles of the reigns of Mary Stuart and her son James VI, in which England and France both intervened, produced some lasting results by the 1570s. The authority of the Pope was abolished; so was the Mass. The King was supreme governor of the realm in matters religious. The Protestant and Presbyterian Kirk was coming into being as the established church. For all that, the dissolution of the monasteries had been neither explicitly preached nor carried out. Lay commendators had replaced abbots and priors everywhere, and secured hereditary tenure of their monastic properties and revenues. Individual monks retained their portions for life, and often continued to reside in the cloister; but no novices were recruited, and the monastic communities steadily died in the later 16th century. The descendants of the commendators and the feuars kept their gains. Monastic churches and buildings were either adapted to new uses, or crumbled to ruin, their lead, timber and stone carted off for sale. It is perhaps strange to reflect that the English deliberately dissolved their monasteries, while the Scots let theirs wither away; but then, paradoxically, it was the Catholic Queen Mary Stuart, not the Protestant reformers, who granted hereditary possession of the great Hospitaller Preceptory of Torphichen to the Conventual Knight of St. John who governed it, and to his descendants for ever.

Gazetteer

by

Chris Given-Wilson

The following eighty sites have been chosen because they are, in the opinion of the authors, the sites at which the modern visitor can most easily appreciate the conditions in which medieval monks lived and worked. The gazetteer entries are arranged alphabetically, and generally consist of a brief history of the monastery, followed by a description of the surviving buildings: firstly the church, secondly the buildings around the cloister, and thirdly outlying buildings. Architectural descriptions are by reference to points of the compass, and in many cases ground-plans are provided to help the reader to find his way around. Where plans are not provided, the easiest way to follow a description is to remember that churches were almost invariably built along an east-west axis, with the high altar within the chancel at the east end. Once the east and west ends of the church have been ascertained, the rest should follow without difficulty.

The following figure (Dundrennan) shows the normal arrangement of the main buildings ranges at a monastery:

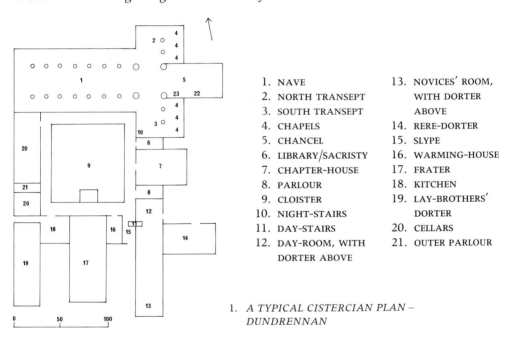

1. NAVE
2. NORTH TRANSEPT
3. SOUTH TRANSEPT
4. CHAPELS
5. CHANCEL
6. LIBRARY/SACRISTY
7. CHAPTER-HOUSE
8. PARLOUR
9. CLOISTER
10. NIGHT-STAIRS
11. DAY-STAIRS
12. DAY-ROOM, WITH DORTER ABOVE
13. NOVICES' ROOM, WITH DORTER ABOVE
14. RERE-DORTER
15. SLYPE
16. WARMING-HOUSE
17. FRATER
18. KITCHEN
19. LAY-BROTHERS' DORTER
20. CELLARS
21. OUTER PARLOUR

1. A TYPICAL CISTERCIAN PLAN –
DUNDRENNAN

Map references
The Ordnance Survey references given for the monasteries are based on the 1:50,000 (Second Series), available in many bookshops in red/purple covers. Each reference includes the sheet number, and the position, on that map, to within one square kilometre.

Glossary
Readers will find the following glossary useful when referring to the Gazetteer.

Glossary

Advowson – the right of nominating or presenting a clergyman to a vacant living

Aisle – lateral division of the nave or chancel of a church; see Fig. 2a

Almonry – place from which alms were dispensed to the poor

Ambulatory – aisle leading round an apse; see Fig. 2b

Apostate – one who renounces his faith

Apse – semicircular or polygonal end to a chancel, chapel or aisle; see Fig. 2b

Apsidal – apse-shaped

Arcade – row of arches, usually supported on columns;

> *blind or blank arcading* – arches attached to a wall, for decoration

Arch-brace – curved timber inserted to strengthen other timbers in a roof

Aumbrey – a recess or cupboard in a wall

Ballflower – decorative motif consisting of three petals enclosing a ball; common in the early fourteenth century

Barbican – fortification defending the gateway to a castle

Barrel-vault – see **Vault**

Bar-tracery – see **Tracery**

Bay – division of a building, usually by piers, buttresses, fenestration, or vaulting

Beakhead – Norman decorative motif consisting of a row of beast or birds heads pecking

Boss – decorative knob, usually covering the intersection of vaulting ribs

Buttress – projecting mass of masonry, giving additional support to a wall;

> *flying buttress* – arch carrying the thrust of a roof from the upper part of a wall to a free-standing support

Canted – inclined, or angled

Capitals – head of a column

2. *THE MONASTERY CHURCH*

(a) Cruciform church with square-ended chancel

(b) East end of cruciform church with apsidal chancel and radiating chapels.

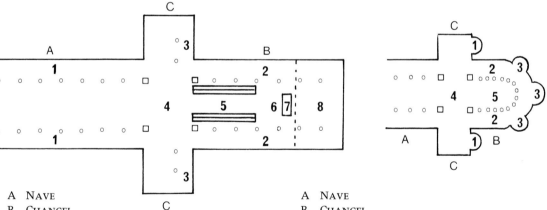

A	NAVE
B	CHANCEL
C	TRANSEPT
1	NAVE AISLES
2	CHANCEL AISLES
3	TRANSEPT AISLES
4	CROSSING
5	QUIRE, FLANKED BY CHOIR-STALLS
6	PRESBYTERY
7	HIGH ALTAR
8	RETRO-QUIRE

A	NAVE
B	CHANCEL
C	TRANSEPTS
1	APSIDAL TRANSEPT CHAPELS
2	AMBULATORY
3	RADIATING CHAPELS
4	CROSSING, USUALLY INCLUDING THE QUIRE
5	PRESBYTERY

NB: The French chevet type of east end is similar to Fig. 2b, but with larger radiating chapels set more closely together.

135

Carrels – divisions of a chamber or cloister walk into individual study areas

Cellarium – store-house of a monastery

Chancel – part of a church to the east of the crossing; see Fig. 2a

Chantry Chapel – chapel attached to a church, endowed for the saying of masses for the soul of the founder or another person (e.g., a wife, or husband) nominated by the founder

Chapter-house – room in which monks met daily, to discuss business and to hear a chapter of the monastic rule

Chevet – French type of east end of a church, comprising an apsidal chancel with ambulatory and radiating chapels; see Fig. 2b

Chevron – Norman zigzag decoration

Cinquefoil – see **Foil**

Claustral – pertaining to the cloister

Clerestory – upper stage of church elevation, above the aisle roofs, usually pierced by windows

Clustered-shaft – see **Pier**

Collar-beam – horizontal beam tying two rafters together above the level of the wall-top

Commendator – (with reference to Scottish monasteries in the fifteenth and sixteenth centuries) one to whom the rule of a monastery was granted, generally by royal favour, and who usually treated it as a sinecure

Compound – see **Pier**

Conduit – pipe or channel for conveying water

Consistory court – an ecclesiastical court, appointed by a bishop or archbishop, with jurisdiction extending to both clergy and laity

Corbel – stone projection from a wall, supporting a weight

Corrodian – lay person who had obtained the right to board and lodging in a monastery, usually by payment of a down payment at an earlier date

Corrody – agreement made by a corrodian with a religious house

Crenellation – embattled parapet

Crocket – leaf-shaped decoration added to pinnacles, gables, capitals, etc.

Crossing – part of a church between the transepts; see Fig. 2a

Crypt – chamber underneath a church, usually at the east end

Culdee – Celtic monks of Scotland and Ireland who flourished from the eighth to the fourteenth centuries, but who were mostly absorbed by the Augustinian canons from the twelfth century

Decorated – term applied to the style of Gothic architecture which flourished in England from about 1280 to about 1340

Denization, charter of – royal charter of naturalization

Dorter – monastic dormitory

Early English – term applied to the style of Gothic architecture which flourished in England from about 1220 to about 1280

Elevation – vertical stages by which the architecture of a wall is erected

Fan-vault – see **Vault**

Floriated – decorated with flowery patterns

Foil – leaf-like ornamentation in windows, etc;
  trefoil, quatrefoil, cinquefoil, sexfoil, etc., represent the number of leaves; see Fig. 3

3. *FOILS AND THE OGEE ARCH*

A   TREFOIL   B   QUATREFOIL   C   CINQUEFOIL

D   SEXFOIL   E   OGEE ARCH

Frater – monastic refectory

Gable – vertical triangular end of a building, from the eaves to the apex;
  gablet – small gable, often for decoration only

Galilee – chapel or vestibule, usually enclosing the porch at the west end of the church

Gallery – intermediate storey in the elevation of a church wall, between the arcade and the clerestory, opening in arches to the nave; see also **Triforium**

Garderobe – individual lavatory in a medieval building

Garth – central area of a cloister

Geometric – see **Tracery**

Gothic – general term used to describe the style of architecture which flourished in western Europe from the twelfth to the sixteenth centuries

Groin-vault – see **Vault**

Hammer-beam – horizontal beam projecting from the top of a wall to support arch-braces, struts and rafters

Hood-mould – projecting moulding over an arch or lintel, to throw off water

Interdict – papal ordinance debarring certain persons or the inhabitants of a certain place from participation in the sacraments, church offices and burial services

Jamb – straight side of a doorway or window

Knapped-flint – flint split for walling

Lancet – slender window with pointed arch
Lavatorium – trough with running water where monks washed their hands before meals
Leat – a channel conveying water, usually to a mill
Lierne-vault – see **Vault**
Lintel – horizontal beam or stone bridging a fireplace, doorway, etc.
Louvre – opening in the roof of a room to let the smoke escape
Lunette – semicircular opening

Misericord – decorated bracket placed on the underside of the hinged seat of a choir-stall, to provide the occupant with a support against which to lean while standing
Misericorde – additional monastic refectory, in which the eating of meat was permitted
Moulding – relief ornamentation
Mullion – vertical bar dividing a window into lights

Nave – part of a church to the west of the crossing; see Fig. 1a
Newel staircase – spiral staircase
Norman – term applied to the style of architecture which flourished in England from about 1050 to about 1200; see also **Romanesque**

Ogee – arch with a steep projection at the apex; see Fig. 3
Order – series of concentric stages (e.g. shafts) receding towards the opening of a window or doorway

Panel-tracery – see **Tracery**
Paterae – flat circular or oval ornamentation
Penstock – sluice for regulating the flow of water through a channel
Pentise – covered way, or small subsidiary building, with a sloping roof
Perpendicular – term applied to the style of Gothic architecture which flourished in England between about 1340 and about 1530
Pier – strong, upright support or pillar for arches, etc;
    compound pier – pier of composite section, not simply round or square;
    clustered-shaft pier – pier composed of several shafts or columns clustered together
Pilaster – shallow pier attached to a wall
Piscina – basin, usually set into the wall by an altar, for washing Mass or Communion vessels

Plate-tracery – see **Tracery**
Pound Scots – Scottish unit of currency, worth 1s.8d., used until the eighteenth century
Prebendary – one in receipt of the revenues attached to a canonry in a cathedral or collegiate church
Prelates – general term applied to the leading members of the ecclesiastical establishment
Presbytery – the part of a church around the high altar, to the east of the quire; see Fig. 2a
Pulpitum – pulpit projecting from a wall. Also, in large churches, a stone screen dividing the nave and quire
Purbeck marble – hard dark stone resembling marble, quarried from the Isle of Purbeck, Dorset

Quatrefoil – see **Foil**
Quire – the part of a church where services were sung, containing the choir-stalls; see Fig. 2a

Radiating chapels – series of chapels projecting radially from an ambulatory or apse; see Fig. 2b
Range – block of buildings
Reliquary – shrine or casket in which relics of saints were kept
Rere-dorter – building containing the monastic latrines
Reticulated – see **Tracery**
Retro-quire – chapel or part of a church east of the high altar; see Fig. 2a
Rib-vault, Ribbed-vault, Ribs – see **Vault**
Ridge rib – see **Vault**
Romanesque – term applied to the style of architecture which flourished in Europe from the early tenth to the late twelfth century; also called Norman in England
Rood-screen – screen below a crucifix, usually at the west end of the chancel
Rose window – see **Wheel Window**

Sacrist – monastic official responsible for the safekeeping of books, vestments and vessels, and for the maintenance of the monastery's buildings
Sacristy – a small building, usually attached to the chancel or transept of a church, in which vestments and sacred vessels were kept
Sanctuary – right of protection for fugitives within a church, or occasionally within the precinct of a monastery or cathedral. Also, sometimes used with the same meaning as **Presbytery**
Saw-tooth – decorated with serrations like a saw
Scallop – decoration consisting of a series of truncated semi-circular surfaces adjoining each other, usually applied to capitals
Scriptorium – room in a monastery set aside for the use of scribes copying manuscripts
Sedilia – seats for priests officiating at services,

usually built into the wall on the south side of the chancel

Segmental – in the form of a segment, or divided into segments

Seigneurial – lordly, pertaining to a feudal lord

Sexfoil – see **Foil**

Shaft – small or subordinate pillar;
  wall-shaft – vertical demi-shaft, bonded on to a wall

Simony – the offence of offering or receiving money to influence an appointment to ecclesiastical office

Skeleton-vault – see **Vault**

Slype – passage

Solar – upper living-room in a medieval house

Sole-piece – projecting base for roof trusses, etc., at the level of the wall-top

Spandrel – triangular surface area between the apexes of two arches

Springer – the point at which an arch unites with its pier, wall-shaft, etc.

Squint – the hole cut in a wall or through a pier to allow a view of the high altar from a place where it would not otherwise be seen; often used for those who had to be separated from the rest of the congregation, e.g., lepers

Star-vault, Stellar-vault – see **Vault**

Stepped – progressively staggered

Stiff-leaf – foliage ornamentation consisting of many lobed shapes, common in the thirteenth century

Strainer arch – arch inserted across the space between two walls, to stop them leaning

String-course – projecting horizontal band of masonry set along a wall

Super-arch – larger arch, often blank, enclosing two or more smaller arches

Temporalities – ecclesiastical revenues from secular sources, e.g., property

Tierceron-vault – see **Vault**

Tonsure – monastic hairstyle: shaving the top of the head and leaving a ring of hair around the side

Tracery – decorative openwork on the upper parts of a Gothic window (also used on blank arcading, vaults, etc.). *Bar-tracery* and *Geometric tracery* – both typical of the second half of the thirteenth century, consisting chiefly of foils within circles; see Fig. 4b. *Panel-tracery* – typical of the period 1340–1530, consisting of straight-edged vertical panels; see Fig. 4d. *Plate-tracery* – typical of the period 1180–1250, with simple decorative shapes cut through a solid stone window head; see Fig. 4a. *Reticulated tracery* – typical of the first half of the fourteenth century, consisting of foils drawn into ogee shapes at top and bottom to create a net-like appearance; see Fig. 4c

Transept – transverse portion of a cross-shaped church

4. *TRACERY PATTERNS*

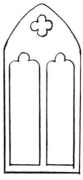

A PLATE-TRACERY

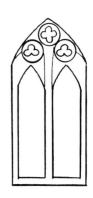

B BAR-TRACERY

C RETICULATED TRACERY

D PANEL-TRACERY

Transitional – term applied to the architecture of the late twelfth and early thirteenth centuries, during the transition from Norman or Romanesque to Gothic

Transom – horizontal bar across the lights of a window

Trefoil – see **Foil**

Triforium – intermediate stage in the elevation of a church wall, between the arcade and the clerestory, consisting of blank arcading or a wall-passage; see also **Gallery**

Truss – roof-timbers framed together to bridge a space

Tunnel-vault – see **Vault**

Tympanum – space between the lintel of a doorway and the arch above it

Undercroft – vaulted room (often a basement) below a more important building

Vault – an arched stone roof. *Barrel- or Tunnel-vault* – vault of semicircular section, usually Norman.

5. *Vaulting pattern, with liernes arranged to form a star-vaulting.*

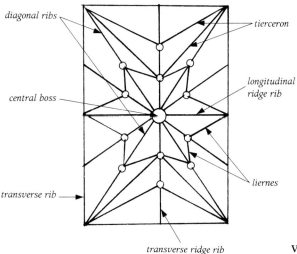

diagonal ribs

tierceron

longitudinal ridge rib

central boss

liernes

transverse rib

transverse ridge rib

Fan-vault – vault where all the ribs from the main springers are of the same length and curvature, spreading out to form a fan-shape; used from the late fourteenth century. *Groin-vault* – vault composed of two tunnel-vaults intersecting each other at right-angles, usually Norman. *Lierne-vault* – vault composed of liernes, i.e., tertiary ribs, springing from neither the central boss nor the main springers; common from the fourteenth century onwards; see Fig. 4. *Quadripartite,*

Sexpartite, Octopartite, etc., *Rib-vault* – vault in which the ribs divide each bay of vaulting into four, six, eight, etc., parts, by the addition or ommission of transverse or longitudinal ridge-ribs. *Rib* – thin band of masonry used either decoratively or structurally in a vault. *Ridge-rib (transverse, longitudinal)* – see Fig. 5. *Rib- or Ribbed-vaulting* – term which can be applied to any form of vaulting in which ribs are used (and thus almost any form of Gothic vaulting), but which is more commonly restricted to early vaulting forms of the twelfth and thirteenth centuries where only diagonal and ridge ribs are used. *Skeleton-vault* – vault where the cells between the ribs are not filled in, thus creating a false roof of ribs below the real roof; uncommon. *Star- or Stellar-vault* – vault with liernes arranged to form a star shape; common from fourteenth century onwards; see Fig. 5. *Tierceron-vault* – vault composed of tiercerons, i.e., secondary ribs issuing from the springers but not passing through the central boss; common from the thirteenth century onwards; see Fig. 4.

Vestry – small chamber attached to the chancel or transept of a church, in which the ecclesiastical vestments were kept and put on.

Waggon-roof – roof with arch-braces and rafters set closely together to give the appearance of a canvas roof over a waggon

Wainscot – wood-panelling lining for interior walls

Warming-house – the only room in a monastery (apart from the infirmary and kitchen) where a fire was allowed

Waterleaf – broad, leaf-shaped motif with a tied-ribbon effect at the top; commonly used to decorate capitals in the twelfth century

Wheel window (or **Rose window**) – circular window with radiating tracery resembling spokes

Arbroath Abbey

ORDER: Tironensian monks
COUNTY: Tayside
ROUTE: In town centre, on A92
OS REF: 54:6441

Arbroath Abbey was founded by King William the Lion in 1178, in part to serve as his contribution to the commemoration of the murdered Archbishop of Canterbury, St Thomas Becket, to whom the church was dedicated. It was colonised from Kelso and, being a royal foundation, was generously endowed. Throughout its history it was one of the wealthiest religious houses in Scotland. William the Lion was buried before the high altar in 1214. He had not lived to see the completion of his abbey, for it was not ready for consecration until 1233.

For the first century of its foundation the abbey prospered, but from about 1270 misfortunes befell it. In 1272 a fire destroyed the bell-tower and the bells, and from 1284 to 1303 the community was ruled by an abbot named Henry who, though useful to King John Balliol in the service of the state, was hated by his monks for the way in which he treated them and abused his office. He was followed by Abbot John, who was removed from office by the Archbishop of St Andrews in 1309, probably because of his pro-English sympathies. Eleven years later, on 5 April 1320, the chapter-house was the scene of one of the most famous events in Scottish history, the drafting and sealing of the Declaration of Arbroath, by which the assembled Scottish nobles declared their independence of England.

In 1350, and 1378–9, the abbey suffered at the hands of English raiders, and in 1380 a fire destroyed so much of the church that for a while the monks had to be sent to other religious houses. The extent to which the abbey was falling under the control of lay lords is shown by the celebrated Battle of Arbroath in 1446, when six hundred men are said to have died in a skirmish between the followers of Alexander Lindsay and those of James Ogilvie, each of whom claimed the highly profitable office of Bailie of the Regality. From the early 16th c. the abbey was held by a series of commendators, including three members of the Beaton family (1517–51), followed by James Hamilton (1551–1600). He granted the abbey to his son James, 2nd Marquis of Hamilton, for whom it was erected into a temporal lordship by Act of Parliament in 1606.

The church was built in the late 12th and early 13th cs. and never rebuilt, although its upper stages and roof had to be remodelled after the fire of 1380. It consisted of an aisled nave of nine bays with twin western towers, north and south transepts each with two eastern chapels, and a square-ended chancel of four bays, the western two aisled, the eastern two aisleless. In the 15th c. a sacristy was added to the south chancel aisle. The north transept and north walls of both nave and chancel have almost entirely disappeared, but the east and west ends and the south transept stand to a good height, the sacristy is well preserved, and the bases of the piers of the aisle arcade are still *in situ*. The style is Transitional, and characterised by the boldness of composition frequently found in Tironensian houses. The impression of the west front was marred by the addition of the gatehouse range in front of the south-west tower in the late 13th c., but it retains much of its original imposing nobility. The west doorway is deeply recessed and richly moulded; above it are three gablets and then the lower half of an enormous round window of which the upper half has broken off, leaving it looking much like the upper stage of the west front at Byland. The gablets and door were meant to be enclosed within a barrel-vaulted galilee which opened out from the wall on both sides; on the interior wall, the place of the gablets is taken by six narrow pointed arches. Between the central part of the west front and the north corner turret are two tall and narrow lancets; presumably there were two on the other side as well. As can be seen from the interior, the lower stage of the tower was incorporated into the arcading of the north aisle. To the east of the north tower was a porch of which the doorway still remains.

The south transept is one of the finest pieces of church architecture in Scotland, simple but powerful, and excellently proportioned in three stages. The lower stage contains three tiers of arcading: blank trefoil-headed, blank and sharply pointed, and then open round-headed. Above this is another pair of tall lancets, and then a round window in the gable. The east end does not stand to the same height as the west end of the transept; it contains a lower tier of blank arcading surmounted by three deep-set lancets, and was quite heavily

ARBROATH: *the west front, with gatehouse range on the right*

restored in the 19th c. The sacristy, entered through a door in the south chancel aisle, is a lofty square building with a simple quadripartite rib-vault. It was built during the rule of Abbot Walter Paniter (1411–49), whose arms can be seen on a shield over an aumbrey in the west wall. At its south-west corner is a small chamber used as a treasury for the abbey's plate and other valuables. Access to it was gained only by using a ladder, an intelligent precaution. During the 18th c. this chamber was used to house declared lunatics, and acquired the name 'Jenny Batter's Hole' after the last occupant.

The cloister was small and lay to the south of the nave; although the buildings around it are totally ruined, the foundations can be seen in several places and the plan is clear. To the south of the south transept came a slype, followed by the chapter-house of which the south-east corner remains. The rest of the east range was occupied by a long warming-house and the rere-dorter, with the dorter on the first floor. The south range contained, from east to west, a slype, the frater, kitchens, and abbot's house on an undercroft, while the west range presumably was used for cellarage. To the south of the frater was a courtyard with a parallel range of buildings along its south side, possibly the infirmary.

Of all these buildings, only the abbot's house, which adjoins and continues the south range to a considerable distance west of the west range, has survived. It dates from about 1500, but stands on an undercroft of about 1200. What the undercroft formerly supported is not known, but it is a fine example of early stone rib-vaulting, with simple quadripartite vaults dividing it into three double bays. The fireplace in the west wall is a later insertion, when it was incorporated into the abbot's house. The abbot's house, adapted as a dwelling-house after the Reformation, continued as such right into the 20th c. Architecturally it has been altered so much that it is difficult to recognise many medieval features. It is now a site museum, and includes the frontal of Abbot Paniter's tomb-chest and a headless effigy, probably Becket's.

Reaching west from the south-western tower of the nave is the gatehouse range, erected at the end of the 13th c. Through the middle runs the gateway itself, vaulted in four bays and formerly protected by gates and a portcullis operated from a chamber on the first floor. The building to the east of the gateway, between it and the church, is the better-preserved of the two flanking ranges. It contained two chambers, which have been restored since medieval times; fireplaces and garderobes show that it was intended as living accommodation. The range running to the west is more ruined, but the bulky tower with which it terminates at the west end still stands. It is of four storeys, the upper stages having been added about 1500. Here again, there are fireplaces showing that it was used for accommodation as well as defensive purposes. The projecting corbels around the top of the tower would once have carried an overhanging parapet walk. Presumably at least part of the gatehouse range was used as the abbey guest-house.

From the 17th to the 19th cs. the site was regularly used as a quarry for building materials; in 1773 Dr Samuel Johnson visited the abbey and came away lamenting 'these fragments of magnificence', and Sir Walter Scott wrote of it in *The Antiquary*, calling it the Priory of St Ruth. Between 1924 and 1930 the site was acquired by the Ministry of Works. Since then it has been gradually excavated and cleared. It was at Arbroath Abbey that the Stone of Destiny, on which the Kings of Scots took their seat to be crowned, removed from Westminster Abbey at Christmas 1950, was found abandoned on 11 April 1951.

Arbroath Abbey is now in the care of the Scottish Development Department.

Basingwerk Abbey

ORDER: Cistercian(S) monks
COUNTY: Clwyd
ROUTE: Off A548, 1¼ miles NE of Holywell.
OS REF: 116:1977

The plateau overlooking the Dee estuary on which stand the ruins of Basingwerk Abbey had been occupied for many centuries before the monastery was founded. Excavation has shown that it was inhabited during the Roman period, and the name of the abbey, which means the *weorc* (fort) of Bassa's people, suggests that it was a fortified site during the years when the kings of Mercia were supreme in England. Cenwulf, the son of the great Mercian king Offa, died at Basingwerk in 821, possibly while planning a new campaign against the Welsh.

The abbey was founded in 1131 by Ranulf, Earl of Chester, and was at first a house of the Savignac order. When all the Savignac houses were absorbed by the Cistercians in 1147, Basingwerk became Cistercian. Its position brought it into the mainstream of political events during the English conquest of Wales in the late 13th c. Edward I made it his headquarters while he was building Flint Castle in 1277, and in return for the abbey's loyalty, he granted various privileges to the monks. In the later middle ages less is heard of the abbey, although there is evidence to suggest a considerable relaxation of the monastic rule towards the end of its history. At the time of Abbot Thomas Pennant, towards the end of the 15th c., so many guests were staying at the abbey that they had to be fed at two sittings, where they had a choice of wines from Aragon, Castille and Brittany. Abbot Pennant himself married and resigned, only to be succeeded by his son Nicholas. Nicholas was the last abbot, surrendering the abbey to the crown in 1536.

Little remains of the church, although it has been fully excavated and its outlines are clearly visible on the turf. It was less than 200 ft. long and severely Cistercian in its simplicity, with an aisled nave of seven bays, north and south transepts each with two eastern chapels, and a narrow, square-ended chancel. There was no triforium. Only the west end, south wall of the nave, and south and west walls of the south transept stand above foundation level, and these date from the early

13th c. No trace of an earlier church has been found, and it is possible, though it would be unusual, that a temporary wooden structure was used during the first hundred years of the monastery's existence. Scattered through the church are a few remaining medieval floor-tiles. The monastic buildings show some interesting variations on the normal Cistercian plan. The cloister lay as usual to the south of the church (its lines are clearly marked), and the northern part of the east range is in accordance with standard Cistercian planning. To the south of the south transept comes the sacristy, followed by the chapter-house. The latter, originally built in the 12th c., was extended to the east in the 13th, and the arches leading through to the eastern bay can still be seen, together with the octagonal pillar which supports them. Around the walls are traces of the stone bench on which the monks sat to hear the daily reading of a chapter of the Rule. The small building to the south of this was the parlour, and then came the undercroft of the dorter, which was probably the room used by the novices. It was rebuilt in the 13th c. Its east wall still stands to first-floor level and contains three windows of the dorter, which as usual extended right along the east range.

The remaining buildings at Basingwerk deviate from the usual Cistercian arrangement. The large building which continues south from the under-croft of the dorter was the warming-house, more usually placed at the east end of the south range. During the 15th c. it was remodelled and a large projecting fireplace was inserted in the south wall. The line of buildings stretching east from the south end of the warming-house are not medieval, although they may be on the site of the monastic infirmary.

The south range continues the peculiarity of the Basingwerk plan, for the siting of the warming-house in the east range allowed for the frater to be placed at the east end of the range. It was rebuilt in the second half of the 13th c. to replace an earlier frater on an east–west axis, and is the most imposing structure on the site. The south wall was once filled with a remarkably large window. The west wall still contains the blocked arch which led to the pulpit at its south end, and the service hatch from the kitchen at its north end. Opposite the latter is a recessed cupboard, in which crockery and cutlery were kept. In the space between the frater and the undercroft of the dorter the day-stairs ascended to the dorter; the lower steps can still be seen.

Of the remaining buildings at Basingwerk very little is left. The western half of the south range was occupied by the kitchen, of which only foundations remain, although the position of the fireplace can still be detected against the south wall. The west range, which no doubt contained the lay-brothers' quarters as at other Cistercian abbeys, has almost entirely vanished.

After the Dissolution, the site was granted to Henry ap Harry of Llanasa and Peter Mutton of Meliden. When Henry ap Harry's daughter married a Mostyn of Talacre, it passed into the family in whose hands it remained until 1923 when the owner, Miss Clementina Mostyn, placed the ruins in the care of H.M. Commissioners of Works. They are now in the hands of Cadw: Welsh Historic Monuments.

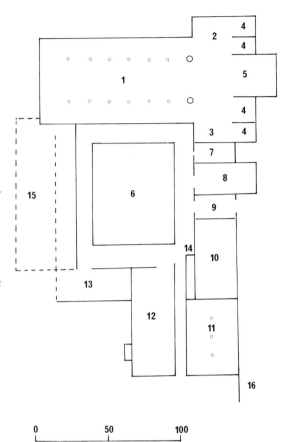

1. NAVE
2. NORTH TRANSEPT
3. SOUTH TRANSEPT
4. CHAPELS
5. CHANCEL
6. CLOISTERS
7. SACRISTY
8. CHAPTER-HOUSE
9. PARLOUR

10. NOVICES' LODGING
11. WARMING-HOUSE
12. FRATER
13. KITCHEN
14. DAY-STAIRS TO DORTER
15. SITE OF CELLARIUM
16. SITE OF INFIRMARY (probable)

Bayham Abbey

ORDER: Premonstratensian canons
COUNTY: East Sussex
ROUTE: Between A21 and B2169, 5 miles ESE of
Tunbridge Wells.
OS REF: 188:6536

Bayham Abbey stood on the very border of Kent
and Sussex, and had a gatehouse on each side
providing an entrance to the precinct from each
county. It was founded between 1199 and 1208 by
a merger of the ailing houses of Brockley and
Otham on a new and more hospitable site. The site
chosen, secluded in a level valley and with an
excellent water supply, was both picturesque and
ideally suited to the needs of a monastery. To avoid
any dispute between the mother-houses of Brockley and Otham, it was decided that Bayham should
be of abbatial status and directly dependent on the
mother-house of the whole order, Prémontré in
France. This was a distinction allowed to only one
other Premonstratensian foundation in England, St
Radegund's near Dover.

The founder was Robert Thornham, whose uncle
had been the co-founder of Brockley, and his house
was dedicated to the Blessed Virgin Mary. The
history of Bayham was uneventful, although the
second half of the 13th c. saw the canons engaged
in a long dispute with the canons of Michelham
over the advowson of the neighbouring church of
Hailsham; in the 15th c. the abbey seems to have
had more than its fair share of apostates. The
number of canons at Bayham was high for
a Premonstratensian house, reaching twenty in
1315. By 1472 it had dropped to eight and the
abbey was deeply in debt. Six years later, although
the debt had been reduced, the buildings were said
to be in a state of disrepair. It was suppressed in
1525, one of those supposedly unworkable monasteries dissolved by Cardinal Wolsey so that their
endowments could be used for his proposed
colleges at Oxford and Ipswich. Although the last
abbot was given another abbacy, the remaining
canons were apparently not provided for. They
joined with the discharged servants and some of
the local populace in rebellion against the suppression, occupying the buildings and electing a
new abbot. The rising was easily subdued, and the
ringleaders imprisoned. Eleven years later, treatment of those who resisted the suppression of

monasteries was to be far harsher.

The church, built in the early 13th c., was rebuilt
at its east end in a rather unusual manner towards
1300, and acquired a new nave in the 15th c. The
nave is narrow and aisleless; the 15th c. rebuilding
consisted of a new west end and north wall, while
the south wall was retained and into it were
inserted tall Perpendicular arches. Three of these
still stand to their full height. The buttresses
erected to support the new vault are so broad that
the north walk of the cloister passes through the
lower parts of them. The late 13th-c. reconstruction
of the east end commenced at the point where
the east claustral range reaches south from the
church. Here, as would be expected, were the
original transepts, each with two eastern chapels,
but when the east end was rebuilt it was decided to
build new transepts much further to the east.
Consequently, the old transepts were walled off on
a line level with the exterior walls of the nave to
form the quire. Another wall was built across the
middle of the north transept, and the northern part
of the space between the old and new south
transepts was also walled in, so that this part of the
church acquired what are in effect aisles. Most of
the old south transept was retained, since to pull
down its outer half, as was done to the north
transept, would have entailed a drastic restructuring of the east claustral range. Of the new transepts
at the east end, a fair amount still stands close to its
original height. They each had two eastern chapels,
and those of the north transept still retain their rib-
vault. The presbytery is relatively short and had an
unusual polygonal east end, forming three sides of
an octagon; only low masonry remains here, but
enough survives to include stepped sedilia in the
south wall. At the south-west corner of the new
south transept a sacristy was erected in the late
15th c.

The arrangement of the buildings in the east
range follows the Cistercian plan. The southern
half of the south transept was probably used as a
library after (if not before) the construction of the
eastern transepts, for in its walls are several
recesses of the kind used as book-cupboards. To its
south came the sacristy, with the base of the night-
stairs still visible in the western corner between it
and the south transept. Following this is the
chapter-house, rebuilt in the second half of the
13th c. It was vaulted in three by three bays, the
eastern bay projecting from the range. The

BAYHAM: *the church, looking west, with the Kentish gatehouse in the background*

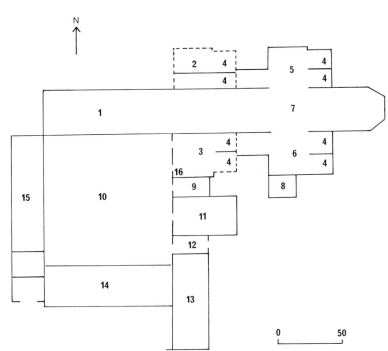

1. NAVE
2. OLD NORTH TRANSEPT
3. OLD SOUTH TRANSEPT
4. CHAPELS
5. NEW NORTH TRANSEPT
6. NEW SOUTH TRANSEPT
7. CHANCEL
8. NEW SACRISTY
9. OLD SACRISTY
10. CLOISTER
11. CHAPTER-HOUSE
12. SLYPE
13. UNDERCROFT OF DORTER
14. UNDERCROFT OF FRATER
15. UNDERCROFT OF ABBOT'S
    HALL OR GUEST-HOUSE
16. NIGHT-STAIRS

N

0   50

arcading between this and the central bay has survived, and shows that the whole room was rib-vaulted from four central piers. The rest of the range is taken up by a slype through to the infirmary, followed by the long undercroft of the dorter; only at its south end have some of the walls survived. As shown by the position of the night-stairs, the dorter extended over the whole east range south of the transept. The south range contained the frater, and probably the warming-house as well, on an undercroft. It is on an east–west axis, not north–south as in Cistercian plans. At its north-east corner can be seen the base of the day-stairs to the dorter, while towards the west end of its external north wall can be seen the lavatorium inserted in the early 14th c. The greater part of the range was built in the 13th c., but additions and alterations were made both in the 15th c. and after the Dissolution. Of the west range little survives apart from some masonry of the south and east walls. No doubt it contained the usual cellarage in the undercroft with either the abbot's hall or the guest hall, or both, on the first floor. The building at its south end, adjoining the west end of the frater, was built in the 18th c.

At some distance north-west of the church stands the picturesque Kentish gatehouse of the abbey (the Sussex gatehouse has not survived). It dates from the 14th c., although the façade wall was extended to the east later. The gable over the entrance arch contains a large window which has lost its tracery; there was a fair-sized chamber here, with small chambers on the ground floor on either side of the archway. The gatehouse has no pedestrian entrance, so possibly the Sussex gate was larger and contained one.

After the Dissolution, the site was leased for short periods to royal favourites until, in 1583, Elizabeth I sold it to two brothers called Adams, one of them a grocer and the other 'a gentleman'. After passing through the hands of several more owners, it was bought in 1714 by Sir John Pratt. Pratt's descendants became Earls of Camden, and the site remained in their hands until 1961, when 5th Marquess Camden placed the ruins in the care of the Ministry of Public Building and Works. The abbey ruins are now in the hands of English Heritage.

Beaulieu Abbey

ORDER: Cistercian monks
COUNTY: Hampshire
ROUTE: Off B3056, 6 miles E of Brockenhurst.
OS REF: 196:3802

Beaulieu Abbey lies in a position of great natural beauty on the left bank of the Beaulieu river, in the heart of the New Forest. Founded in 1204 by King John, it was the first of a small group of 13th-c. Cistercian foundations, and was colonised directly from Cîteaux via Faringdon, where in 1203 the king had originally proposed to site his new abbey. Since 1200, the king had been using questionable methods in an attempt to impose taxation on the Cistercians in England, and a legend grew up that, shortly before his foundation of Beaulieu, he dreamed that he was being flogged by Cistercian abbots, and as a result repented and decided to found Beaulieu as a penance.

It was a large abbey, built for thirty monks and a large number of lay-brothers. By 1329, the number of monks had reached thirty-six, but soon it began to decline, and at the Dissolution in April 1538 it was no more than twenty-one. Beaulieu had a right of sanctuary which extended through the outer court as well as in the church, and several famous people took advantage of this right. After the Battle of Barnet (1471), Queen Margaret and the Countess of Warwick (the widow of the 'Kingmaker') took refuge here, and although the Queen stayed only a short while, the Countess remained for fourteen years, until her honours and possessions were restored to her at the accession of Henry VII. In 1495 Perkin Warbeck, the pretender to the throne, also sought sanctuary at Beaulieu after the failure of the Cornish Rising. He was enticed out by promises of a pardon, but was promptly incarcerated in the Tower.

In total area, Beaulieu was the largest Cistercian church in England. This was due not only to its length—336 ft. overall—but also to its unusual width of 186 ft. across the transepts. It consisted of an aisled nave of nine bays, an aisled apsidal chancel surrounded by a ring of ten chapels, and north and south transepts each with an eastern chapel containing three more chapels. The north transept was broader and longer than the south, having a western as well as an eastern aisle, and a galilee north of its north wall. The only parts of the church remaining above ground are the south aisle wall of the nave and the west wall of the south transept, against which the monks' night-stairs to the dorter can still be seen. The monastic buildings were situated south of the church, and conformed to the standard second-stage Cistercian plan. From north to south, the eastern range contained a narrow library-cum-vestry (probably constructed as part of the south transept—note the thickness of its south wall), the chapter-house, parlour, and undercroft of the dorter, with the monks' dorter extending over the whole range and well into the present cemetery. The fine triple-arches of the chapter-house were restored early in the twentieth century. To the east of the eastern range is another complex of excavated foundations: the large building was the infirmary, the projecting building to the east of it the infirmary chapel, and the annexe to the north-west of it the misericorde. The south claustral range consisted of the monastic frater on a north–south axis flanked by an eastern warming-house and a western kitchen. The latter two buildings have been quite obliterated by the cemetery, but at the Dissolution, the frater was converted into the parish church.

This church although extensively restored and added to, is in an excellent state of preservation. The beautiful pulpit, formerly the monastic reader's pulpitum, is built into the thickness of the west wall and reached by a flight of eighteen stone steps. Although the arcading has been replaced by Purbeck marble columns and the vaulting has been partially restored, its basic design is still as originally built, and it is one of the finest examples of its kind. Also remarkable is the waggon roof of the church, a curious and unusual design but apparently dating from the late 14th c. and thus evidently part of the monastic frater.

The western claustral range originally contained, as usual, the lay-brothers' quarters, with cellarage to the north, frater to the south, and dorter on the first floor. It too is extremely well-preserved, although again much restored, and contains a restaurant and cafeteria in the northern part and the abbey museum in the southern part. The range also continued further to the south, as is evident from the remaining walls. The restaurant, on the first floor of the northern half of the range, has a fine 13th-c. wooden roof. The museum contains a model of the abbey as it was when completed, and a stone double-heart coffin. In

BEAULIEU: *aerial view from the south-east*

medieval times it was common practice to remove the hearts from corpses and find a separate resting-place for them. By tradition, this coffin was intended for the hearts of King John's son, Richard, and his third wife.

Apart from the frater and the western range, the third major survival is the gatehouse, converted after the Dissolution into Beaulieu Palace House. Although greatly restored and extended, it still has several excellent medieval features, notably the vaulting in the dining-room and inner hall. Carefully restored, it has sometimes been described as fan-vaulting, but is in fact an advanced form of rib-vaulting, and must date from about 1300. The vaulting system is very similar to that used in

Exeter Cathedral nave, begun about 1280. Several of the wall arches in the Palace House are also medieval, as is the excellently preserved tracery of some of the windows. In the corner of the ground-floor dining room and the first-floor drawing-room are entrances to the monks' 'Secret Staircase'. The smaller Outer Gatehouse of the abbey still performs its original function.

To the north of the abbey can be seen the ruins of the monks' wine-press, and to the east and south of it two monastic fishponds. The monks took their water from the stream which runs into these fishponds, draining it underneath the buildings and back into the river.

After the Dissolution, the abbey and manor of Beaulieu were acquired by Thomas Wriothesley, who had already acquired the surrendered

BEAULIEU: *the pulpitum in the frater*

Titchfield Abbey. During the next fifty years, under him and his successors, the church was pulled down and the Palace House built. In the mid-19th c. the property passed by marriage to the Duke of Buccleuch, and some twenty years later a cadet of this family inherited it and was ennobled with the title Montagu of Beaulieu. It is now the property of the 3rd Lord Montagu of Beaulieu.

Binham Priory

ORDER: Benedictine monks
COUNTY: Norfolk
ROUTE: Off B1388, 5 miles SW of Blakeney.
OS REF: 132:9839

The priory of the Blessed Virgin Mary at Binham was founded by Peter de Valognes around 1091, as a dependency of St Albans. Although the buildings were planned on a fairly generous scale, it never grew much in size or importance. In 1320 there were fourteen monks at Binham; by 1381 the number had dropped to eleven, and in 1539, when it was dissolved, there were only six.

The nave originally consisted of nine bays, the western seven of which still stand and form the parish church of St Mary. The west end is particularly interesting from an architectural point of view, for the St Albans chronicler Matthew Paris tells us that it was built under his contemporary Prior Richard Park, who died in 1244. Consequently, the bar-tracery in the large central window must be the first example of bar-tracery in England, a development normally connected with the building of Westminster Abbey. Indeed the west front as a whole, with its fine moulded doorway set in five orders of columns and the flanking pairs of slender and steeply-pointed arches, forms an imposing composition. Although the aisles on both sides of the nave have disappeared, their west ends remain standing on either side to add further breadth to the front. The interior of the nave is thoroughly Norman, with arcade, gallery and clerestory of firmly rounded arches set between double shafts rising right up across the levels. It dates from the first half, and probably the first quarter, of the 12th c. The present east end marks the point at which stood the pulpit in the original church; the two eastern bays were demolished with the transepts and chancel after the Dissolution. The plan of the eastern half of the church can be clearly deciphered from what remains, although little of it stands to a reasonable height, apart from the crossing piers and parts of the exterior transept walls. The original chancel, which presumably was built first, about 1100, had an apsidal east end following a presbytery of two bays, and aisles on each side which also ended in apses. Later, probably in the 15th c., the chancel was lengthened, with both its aisles, and all three were given square ends. The lines of both east ends are clearly marked.

The monastic buildings followed the standard Benedictine plan, and the plan of the entire complex is easily visible. South of the south transept came the square-ended chapter-house, strangely spacious for a dependent priory with so few monks, followed by the parlour, a narrow slype, and then the warming-house with its large fireplace in the east wall. Over the whole east range, and projecting considerably to the south of the cloister, ran the dorter, followed presumably by the rere-dorter, although the method for drainage of the rere-dorter is not obvious. The south range included the frater, probably on an undercroft, from the west end of which the kitchen projected at right angles. The west range contained cellarage on the ground floor and the prior's lodging above, and as at nearby Castle Acre, it projected beyond the west end of the church. The vaulted room adjoining its south-west corner was probably the guest house on two floors. North-west of the church stand the remains of the gatehouse, divided into a narrow pedestrian entrance and a wider arch for carts.

Apart from the nave, which as has already been mentioned is in use as the parish church, the surrounding priory ruins are in the care of English Heritage.

BINHAM: *the west front*

Bolton Priory

ORDER: Augustinian canons
COUNTY: North Yorkshire
ROUTE: On B6160, 6 miles ENE of Shipton.
OS REF: 104:0754

The Priory of the Blessed Virgin Mary and St Cuthbert at Bolton-in-Wharfedale is one of the most beautifully situated of British monasteries and its setting, in a narrow wooded valley on the south bank of the river Wharfe, has been memorably described by Wordsworth and Ruskin and is the subject of a famous water-colour by Turner.

It is traditionally called Bolton Abbey. This is incorrect, for Bolton was never granted abbatial status. In 1120–1 William Meschin and his wife Cecilia de Rumilly founded the priory at Embsay, 4 miles west of Bolton, as a daughter-house of Huntingdon Priory; but the land proved unproductive, and in 1154–5, with the consent of the new patroness Alice de Rumilly, it was moved to the present site. In 1194 it was freed from dependance on Huntingdon and became an independent priory. It was never a large or important house, the average number of canons being about fifteen. In the early 14th c., Bolton suffered so severely from Scottish raids that on one occasion, after the 'White Battle' of Myton-on-Swale in 1320. several of the canons had to find temporary accommodation in other Augustinian houses. It was probably as a result of this raid that the splendid Decorated chancel was built, the earlier one having been destroyed. At the Dissolution, on 29 January 1540, the priory was surrendered peacefully to the crown by a prior and fourteen canons.

The priory contains one or two noticeable irregularities of design. For a start, it is clear that the church in its final form was far too big for the cloister: the south transept extends almost the whole length of the east claustral walk, and the nave of the church, even without the base of the western tower begun in 1520, extends considerably west of the west claustral walk. Thus the original church, built in the late 12th and 13th cs., must have been on a much smaller scale. The nave of this church, now used as the parish church, dates from the mid-13th c. It has an excellent series of six broad twin-light lancets in the south wall, and an unusual feature, a north aisle but no south

aisle. It was at this time that the west front of the church, much of which is now obscured by the tower base, was built. The transepts are abnormally large in relation to the rest of the church; this is due to a 14th c. refashioning of the original structures. The original chancel was much smaller than the present one, which has Norman work at its west end—note the round-headed blank arcading on the walls—but most of it was built in the second quarter of the 14th c., after the Scottish raids which so devastated Bolton. With its five large windows on each wall and enormous east window, it is one of the masterpieces of mature Gothic architecture in England, creating an atmosphere of light and spaciousness remarkable in so modest a structure. The tracery has disappeared from almost all the windows, and only in the south-western one, which is partly bricked-in, can the pattern of three lights and flowing tracery be made out. The last addition made to the church was the west tower, the massive and ornate base of which stands immediately to the west of the west front. It was begun by the last prior, Richard Mone, in 1520, and would have been incorporated in the church by the removal of the west front, but before it could be completed, the Dissolution came.

Of the monastic buildings, little remains above ground, but the foundations of the claustral ranges are all there. Here we come to another of Bolton's little irregularities: the south transept is not at right-angles to the church, but veers slightly to the east, taking with it the whole eastern range. This consists of a narrow passage-cum-vestibule followed by the undercroft of the dorter, with the foundations of the rere-dorter stretching away to the east at its south end, and then the prior's lodging; this dates from the 14th c., and replaced the original prior's lodging in the west range. The passage south of the south transept leads through to the chapter-house, which unusually was not included in the east range but was situated to the east of it. It is an octagonal structure, similar to the chapter-houses at Thornton, Whalley and Westminster Abbey, and must have been a beautiful building. The south claustral range contained the frater, on an east–west axis; the west range had a parlour to the north and cellarage to the south, with the original prior's lodging on the first floor. Parts of the monastic infirmary are incorporated in the walls of the 16th c. rectory to the south of the frater.

BOLTON PRIORY: *watercolour by J. M. W. Turner*

To the west of the abbey is Bolton Hall, built around the medieval priory gatehouse; as usual, the archway is divided into a broad entrance for carriages and horses and a narrower one for pedestrians. It has four diagonally-set towers and an extremely complex vaulting system which creates the effect of panelling. The parts on either side of the gatehouse were added by the Cavendish family (Dukes of Devonshire from 1694) who acquired the property after the Dissolution. A wall was built at the east end of the nave so that it alone could be used as a parish church. It was restored in the late 19th c. Bolton Priory is scheduled as an Ancient Monument.

Bristol Cathedral

ORDER: Augustinian canons
COUNTY: Avon
ROUTE: On College Green near city centre.
OS REF: 172:5872

St Augustine's Abbey, Bristol, was one of the six monasteries designated cathedrals by Henry VIII after the Dissolution. Archaeological evidence suggests that there may have been a religious house on the site before the Norman Conquest, but the present abbey was not founded until 1140–42. The founder was Robert fitz Harding, a Bristol burgess who supported Queen Matilda and her son Henry II during the civil war of the time, and was consequently granted the nearby Lordship of Berkeley. He probably ended his life as a canon in the abbey which he had founded. The number of canons at Bristol may have never exceeded thirty-five, dropping after the Black Death to twenty in 1379, seventeen in 1491, and nineteen in 1534. The great builder at Bristol was Abbot Knowle, who ruled the monastery during the first third of the 14th c. and who was responsible for giving the church its present appearance, although there are interesting survivals from both earlier and later periods. The abbey was dissolved on 9 December 1539, and reconstituted as one of the new cathedrals in 1542.

It is the chancel which distinguishes Bristol. The nave (not built until the 19th c.) is only an imitation of it. The chancel dates from the early 14th c. It is Abbot Knowle's work, though the name of his master mason has not survived, which is a great pity, for this is one of the most original buildings in England. Pevsner writes that, 'from the point of view of spatial imagination—which is after all the architectural point of view *par excellence*—(it) is superior to anything else built in England and indeed in Europe at the same time. It proves incontrovertibly that English design surpassed that of all other countries during the first third of the fourteenth century.'*

Bristol Cathedral is basically a hall-church. The impression is of breadth rather than height, and although the low height of the vault (only about 50

*NIKOLAUS PEVSNER *The Buildings of England: North Somerset and Bristol* pp. 371–2 Harmondsworth

ft. to the apex) is partly responsible, the treatment of the aisles is far more important. They are not aisles in the conventional sense, for they reach up to the same height as the central bays of the chancel and every attempt is made to minimise their structural separation from the central area. The usual relatively low arcades surmounted by triforia are dispensed with entirely, their place being taken by a simple row of tall pointed arches. Thus the whole chancel area is opened out to form one visually coherent whole. So Bristol is one great big hall, not three separate rooms running parallel to each other. The spatial impression created is apparent immediately, but the problem for the 14th-c. master was how to support his central vault without any aisle roofs to help him. He did so by throwing what are, in effect, flying buttresses across the upper parts of the aisles between the 'arcade' piers and the exterior walls, in the form of horizontal 'bridges' across the top of the arches in the aisles. By this means, he transferred the weight of the chancel vault from the piers to the outside walls, and was thus able to dispense with the aisle arcades and triforia. Not content with creating space at a diagonally horizontal level, he built his aisle vaults so that openings could be left immediately above the 'bridges' of the aisles. This provided a clear line of vision from one bay to the next and created a diagonally vertical vista, impossible to achieve with a conventionally low-aisled church plan. The effect is startling and unique, and with the large fourlight windows in the aisles illuminating the whole chancel, Bristol is one of the brightest churches in England.

Four chapels project from the chancel: the Lady Chapel at the east end, the Elder Lady Chapel to the east of the north transept, the Newton Chapel to the east of the south transept, and the Berkeley Chapel to the south of the eastern bay of the chancel. The Berkeley Chapel—especially its ante-chapel—is the most interesting, for this was undoubtedly designed by the same master who built the chancel, and his use of space in the vault is again strikingly original. It is basically a simple rib-vault, with transverse as well as longitudinal ridge-ribs, but with one essential difference: there is no actual vault, but a flat stone ceiling below which are erected the flying arches and ribs which would normally run along the ridges of the vault. Again the effect is to create space, for the result of this maze of apparently intersecting lines in mid-air is

BRISTOL: *vaulting in the south quire aisle*

to make the ceiling of the ante-chapel appear taller than it is. Such a device, known as a skeleton-vault, was to become a favourite *motif* of German architects, as demonstrated in the south porch of Prague Cathedral, built by the Bohemian master Peter Parler in the years 1396–1420.

The present nave of Bristol Cathedral was built between 1868 and 1888, by G. E. Street, the Norman one having been demolished soon after the Dissolution. Street was commissioned to build 'such a nave as Knowle would have built had he lived'. He did so admirably, using the same system as his 14th-c. predecessor, and making his nave exactly the same length as the chancel. The one difference is in the vaulting, for whereas Abbot Knowle's master used liernes and dispensed with a transverse ridge, Street erected a simple tierceron-vault. The transepts and crossing are Norman in outline, but were entirely remodelled about 1500, and what is now visible is perpendicular; so is the two-storeyed crossing tower, with its parapet and pinnacles. In the south transept can be seen the monks' night-stairs to the dorter, which leads us on to the monastic buildings.

A fair amount survives of the ranges around the cloister, but often interwoven with buildings from later centuries. Of the cloister walks, only the east, and a short eastern section of the north, survive. They still contain Norman work, although they were largely rebuilt about 1500. The main survival from the east claustral buildings is the chapter-house, with its three-bayed vestibule, built in the third quarter of the twelfth century and unaltered in essential points since, although the east wall was rebuilt after the riots of 1831. The north and south walls are typical late Norman work, with a lower tier of plain recessed arches, a middle tier of intersecting blank arcading, and an upper lunette with a zigzag frieze. Both vestibule and chapter-house are rib-vaulted. To the south of the chapter-house comes the slype followed by the undercroft of the dorter, also dating from the 12th c. Along the top of this range ran the dorter, and although parts of this floor still contain medieval work, it has been very largely rebuilt since the Dissolution. The south range contained the frater, but the building is now used by the Cathedral School; its lower parts date from about 1200, its upper parts from the 15th c., but with much subsequent refashioning. To the east of this range stood the abbot's lodging, which later became the bishop's palace but was destroyed during the 1831 riots as was the chapter-house; although they destroyed many old books and manuscripts, and did enough damage to require the rebuilding of the east wall, further harm was prevented by the sub-sacrist William Phillips. A tablet in the south transept commemorates him.

The only other surviving building of importance is the great gateway to the west of the nave. It was a double entrance, for pedestrians and carriages, and was also built towards 1200; the upper parts, however, were rebuilt at the end of the 15th c. by Abbot Newland, whose effigy is in the eastern Lady Chapel, and who was also known as 'Nail-heart'.

BRISTOL: *skeleton vault in the ante-room of the Berkeley Chapel*

Buildwas Abbey

ORDER: Cistercian (S) monks
COUNTY: Shropshire
ROUTE: On B4380, 5 miles S of Wellington.
OS REF: 127:6404

The Abbey of Our Lady and St Chad at Buildwas stands on the right bank of the Severn, on open sloping ground which enhances the simple dignity of the ruins. Founded on 8 August 1135 by Roger Clinton, bishop of Lichfield, and colonised from Furness, it was originally a Savignac house but became Cistercian when the two orders were merged in 1147. Its endowment was not extensive (part of its income was tolls exacted for the use of the neighbouring bridge over the Severn), and it never became a house of wealth or importance. Moreover, it was near enough to the border to suffer from what was ruefully called the 'levity of the Welsh'; in 1350 the abbot was kidnapped and imprisoned by raiders from Powys, and in 1406 its estates were laid waste by the followers of Owain Glyndwr. The abbey had its internal problems as well: in 1342 the abbot was murdered by one of his own monks, Thomas Tong. Tong managed to evade arrest, and later had the effrontery to petition for reinstatement in the Cistercian order. In the late 14th c., the number of monks at Buildwas had dropped to four. By the early 16th c. it had risen to twelve, but by 1535, when the abbey, being classed as one of the smaller religious houses, was peacefully surrendered to the king, the number had again fallen to seven.

The church, which except for the roofs and the aisle walls is largely intact, is a model Cistercian construction. It is relatively small, no more than 180 ft. in overall length, and dates from the second half of the 12th c. Nearly all the remains at Buildwas are remarkably uniform in date, which is surprising when one considers the amount of rebuilding undertaken through the centuries by most monastic houses. The nave is of seven bays, with an arcade of stocky, rounded piers (apart from the easternmost pair, which are octagonal), and arches which are only just pointed. There is no gallery, only a clerestory with round-headed windows. The nave was never vaulted, but had a sloping roof, the line of which can clearly be seen against the west wall of the tower which still stands over the powerful crossing. On the east and west sides, the crossing arches stand on corbels so as to leave room for the choir stalls, while on the north and south sides, in the corners of the transepts, they stand on triple orders of columns. The transepts themselves are short and each has two groin-vaulted eastern chapels. The chancel is severely Cistercian, short, square-ended, and originally rib-vaulted on short shafts which are little more than extended corbels. It is here that we find work undertaken after the original construction, for the three slender eastern windows and the sedilia on the south wall belong to the early 13th c. The whole church has an aura of dignified restraint characteristic of the best in early Cistercian building.

Because of the slope of the land to the north and west, the monastic buildings at Buildwas were placed on the north (i.e., the lower) side of the church instead of the usual south side (this also accounts for the lack of a door in the west front of the church). The low foundations to the south of the south aisle belong to a chapel which was added in about 1400. Since it was not connected to the church by any doors, it may have been intended for use by the laity, who were not allowed to enter Cistercian churches. This is a somewhat unusual feature, but the cloister itself and its ranges seem to have conformed entirely to the standard Cistercian plan. The west range, which contained cellarage and the lay-brothers' quarters, and the north range, which contained the frater and (presumably) the kitchen and warming-house, are largely ruined. Moreover, most of the north range and the northern parts of the west and east ranges are in private ground and have not yet been excavated.

The east range, of which there is much to see, continued on from the north transept, and it will be noticed that its north bay is raised above the level of the rest, the reason being that there is a crypt underneath. Why this crypt was inserted is not certain; probably it was a method of overcoming the slope of the ground between cloister and church. The crypt, groin-vaulted in three bays, is still accessible from the cloister. To the east of it is the sacristy-cum-library, a narrow room originally of two bays, but later having a third bay added to it when the space between the north-eastern chapel of the north transept and the south-eastern bay of the chapter-house was filled in and roofed.

BUILDWAS: *view of the church across the cloister*

Many books from the Buildwas Abbey library have survived at Trinity College, Cambridge, and Lambeth Palace.

Next comes the fine chapter-house, entered from the cloister by a large doorway which originally had three orders of shafts; it still retains its roof, and is rib-vaulted in nine bays, the ribs resting on four slender central piers, two round and two octagonal. Further east is the small parlour, also rib-vaulted in two bays, and beyond this the undercroft of the dorter, which would have extended over the whole of the east range. North of the parlour, however, the ruin is in private hands. The five bays of arcade incorporated into the private house here probably belonged to the infirmary. The house also incorporates the remains of the abbot's lodging, including his private chapel.

After the Dissolution, the site was granted to Edward Grey, Lord Powys. It remained in private hands until 1925 when the owner, the late major H. R. Moseley, placed it in the guardianship of the Commissioners of Works. It is now in the care of English Heritage.

Bury St Edmunds Abbey

ORDER: Benedictine monks
COUNTY: Suffolk
ROUTE: In town centre, off Abbeygate St.
OS REF: 155:8564

The scanty remains of the Abbey of Bury St Edmunds do little justice to what was once one of the greatest abbeys in England. Strategically placed at the heart of wealthy and populous East Anglia, the abbey was constantly involved in the political life of the nation. It was among the six richest Benedictine houses in England, and one of only seven abbeys granted freedom from episcopal control. Although the remains now visible are fragmentary and difficult to decipher, Bury is included here because its history is well-documented and demonstrates both the power and influence of a great abbey and the precarious nature of relations between monks and towns-people, and also because it still boasts two splendid gatehouses.

The first religious house at Bury was founded about 633 by King Sigebert, the first Christian King of the East Angles. In those days, the place was known as Beodricsworth. In 903 the relics of King Edmund of the East Angles, slain by the Danes near Norwich in 870 and then canonised, were brought to Beodricsworth and enshrined. In 1020 Aelfwine, Bishop of Elmham, replaced the secular clergy with twenty monks from the abbey of St Benet of Hulme, and freed his newly-founded house from the bishop's control. King Cnut hastily granted a charter to the abbey; his father, Sven of Denmark, had died after making demands for ransom from the lands of St Edmund's, and it was rumoured that the saint's remains had caused Sven's death.

The history of the abbey was eventful and often stormy. The early period of building was in the late 11th and early 12th cs., but about 1150 there was an extensive fire in the east and south ranges which led to substantial restructuring. The church itself was not completed until the time of Abbot Samson (1182–1211). Samson has been called 'probably the single English abbot of the later Middle Ages of whom there is widespread knowledge among his countrymen', this being due to Jocelin of Brake-lond, the monk of Bury who wrote Samson's biography and produced a delightful masterpiece of monastic literature. Samson was more than a great builder; he was a friend to two successive English kings, Henry II and Richard Coeur-de-Lion. While Richard was imprisoned in Germany, Samson was active in helping to raise money for his ransom, and it is recorded that one of the king's first visits after his return to England in 1194 was to Bury St Edmunds.

In November 1214, the earls and prelates in opposition to King John met at Bury and all swore on the high altar of the church to make war on the king unless he was prepared to grant them a new charter of liberties; the following June, Magna Carta was sealed at Runnymede. Throughout the 13th c. the abbey continued to prosper, the number of monks in about 1260 being eighty, with twenty-one chaplains and 111 servants, and intermittent building operations continued; but the wealth and power of the community increasingly irked the townspeople, who longed for civic independence, free from the control of the abbey. In 1327 matters between the abbey and the town came to a head. The townspeople, desperate to see the abbot's seigneurial rights quashed, spent much of the summer rioting, sacking and burning parts of the monastery, killing several monks, and abducting the abbot himself to Brabant. Much damage was also done to property belonging to the monastery, and although in the end the rioters were heavily fined, the abbey lost very substantial revenues.

In the Peasants' Revolt of 1381, Bury was one of the worst sufferers. A combined force of peasants and townsmen led by John Wrawe first executed Sir John Cavendish, the King's chief justice, who lived in the town, and then advanced upon the abbey bearing his head on a pike. The prior, John Cambridge, took flight, but was found hiding in a wood near Newmarket and, after a mock trial before Wrawe, summarily beheaded. At the abbey itself, another monk was slain, £1,000 worth of treasure was seized by the rebels, and there was considerable destruction. The violence at Bury had been so great that it was the only town excepted from the royal amnesty of December 1381, after the collapse of the Revolt.

In 1433 Henry VI announced that he would spend Christmas at the abbey; he found it so congenial that he stayed on for four months. In 1447 Parliament was summoned to meet in the frater of the abbey to try Humphrey Duke of Gloucester but, on the day after his arrest, he was found dead at St Saviour's Hospital by the north

gate of the town. Although Humphrey suffered from palsy and had had several strokes, there were rumours of murder, and suspicion centred on the Queen, Margaret of Anjou, and the King's chief minister, William de la Pole, Duke of Suffolk.

In 1430 and 1431, the south and east sides of the west tower collapsed, and in 1465 repair work was still being carried out when some workmen away at dinner left a brazier burning in the tower; a wind arose, and the whole church and frater were rapidly burnt out. When the church was re-built, stone vaulting was inserted to make it more fire-resistant. Towards the end of its existence, the abbey's history was more peaceful. In 1533 Henry VIII's sister Mary, Queen of France, was buried in the abbey in great state, but soon her body was removed to the parish church of St Mary's, which stands in what used to be the south-west corner of the abbey precinct. Two years later, there were still sixty-two monks at Bury, but by 4 November 1539, when it was surrendered to the King, there were only forty-five left.

The abbey in all its glory must have been a magnificent sight. The church was 505 ft. long, with an aisled nave of twelve bays, north and south transepts each with two apsidal eastern Chapels, and an apsidal east end with three projecting chapels. The west end was formed by a second transept 246 ft. across with a soaring central tower and spire flanked at each end by an octagonal tower with a spire. Little of this has survived. Part of the west front is visible, but on to it several houses have been built in more modern times and no impression can be gained of the imposing medieval entrance to the church. At the east end, the foundations of the crypt beneath what was the presbytery have survived, as have parts of the north wall of the north transept and the piers of the crossing. From these, and from a few other scattered stones and broken arches, some idea of

the magnitude of the structure can be gleaned. The cloister lay to the north of the church, and the conventual buildings generally followed the usual conventions; traces of most of them can be picked out. The exceptionally large 'abbot's palace' occupied a range of buildings along the east side of the great court, which corresponded roughly to the modern oval-shaped pleasure gardens.

The best-preserved buildings of the abbey are the two gateways which front on to the main street. The taller, southern gateway, which faces Church-gate Street, is the Norman Tower of St James, built in the first half of the twelfth century to serve both as an entrance to the abbey church and as a belfry to the adjoining church of St James which it still is. The shorter Great Gate, facing Abbeygate Street, was built between 1327 and 1346 to give access to the great court and the abbot's palace. The lower storey bears the arms of Edward the Confessor, Edward III, his brother John of Eltham, his uncle Thomas Brotherton, and his cousin Henry of Lancaster. The upper storey was built later, between 1353 and 1384, and was originally capped by two octagonal turrets. In the statue-niches around the gateway are arrow-slits; the events of 1327 had not been forgotten.

After the Dissolution, the townspeople at least must have been satisfied, for they were at last accorded self-government; so must John Eyer, for he acquired the entire abbey precinct from the crown for £412. 19s. 4d. Apart from the abbot's palace, which was converted into a dwelling-house and remained so until 1720, the property was stripped of all its valuable building material and the ruins were allowed to become a quarry for the townspeople, a facility they must have relished. In more recent centuries several houses have been built on the site, some of which still survive. Bury St Edmunds Abbey is now in the care of English Heritage.

Byland Abbey

ORDER: Cistercian (S) monks
COUNTY: North Yorkshire
ROUTE: Off A170, 7 miles ESE of Thirsk.
OS REF: 100:5478

The Cistercian Abbey of Byland shared in its heyday, with Fountains and Rievaulx, the distinction of being called one of the 'three luminaries of the north'. It is only four miles across Scawton Moor from Rievaulx, and two miles west of the modern Benedictine Abbey of Ampleforth.

Its beginnings were inauspicious. In 1134 the Savignac Abbey of Furness sent twelve monks with an abbot, Gerold, to found a monastery at Calder, a few miles south of Egremont on the west coast of Cumberland. In 1138, however, the new foundation was plundered by Scottish raiders. The community decided to return to Furness, but a problem arose when Gerold refused to resign his abbacy. Accordingly, the little community once more left Furness, to seek help from Archbishop Thurstan of York, who had done so much to help the community at Fountains, but when they got to Thirsk they were welcomed by Gundreda Daubeny the mother of Roger Mowbray, who encouraged them to join her kinsman, Robert Alneto, who had been a monk at Whitby and was now a hermit at Hood, just east of Thirsk. In 1142 the community, joined by Robert, secured release from the jurisdiction of Furness, but the site at Hood was too small for their growing numbers and in 1143 they moved north to Old Byland, a site granted to them by Roger Mowbray. This was less than two miles west of Rievaulx, and the two communities could hear each other's bells at all hours 'which was not fitting and could by no means be endured', so in 1147 they moved south again to Stocking, also granted to them by Mowbray. Here they built a small monastery. That year, the Savignac order was absorbed by Cîteaux, and the community became Cistercian.

Mowbray's grant included a tract of swampy land a mile and a half east of Stocking, and after a while the community, thinking this would make a better site, set about clearing and draining it: 'they began manfully to root out the woods, and by long and wide ditches to draw off the abundance of water from the marshes'. The community had grown considerably, and when building began at the eventual site of Byland, it was probably intended to accommodate thirty-six monks and a hundred lay-brothers. The western range at Byland was one of the earliest parts of the complex to be built, and it seems likely that some of the lay-brothers were sent on ahead to supervise the building operations. By 1177 the new monastery was considered habitable, although little more than the western range and the south walls of the church had been completed, and the community moved in; presumably for the first few years the monks were accommodated in the western range. Thus, after forty-three years and four false starts, Byland

1. NAVE
2. NORTH TRANSEPT
3. SOUTH TRANSEPT
4. CHANCEL
5. CHAPELS
6. LIBRARY/SACRISTY
7. CLOISTER
8. CHAPTER-HOUSE
9. PARLOUR
10. SLYPE
11. DAY-STAIRS
12. DORTER
13. ABBOT'S LODGING
14. DAY-ROOM, WITH DORTER ABOVE
15. INFIRMARY HALL
16. CRYPT OF INFIRMARY CHAPEL
17. MEAT KITCHEN
18. WARMING-HOUSE
19. FRATER
20. KITCHEN
21. LAY-BROTHERS' RERE-DORTER
22. LAY-BROTHERS' RANGE
23. LAY-BROTHERS' LANE
24. GALILEE

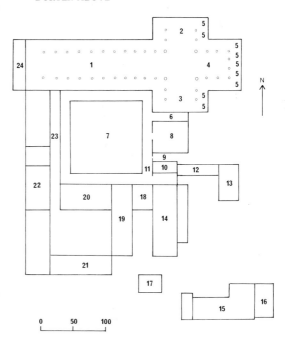

Abbey as we know it was founded. Doubtless the final move to Byland was planned and master-minded by the great Abbot Roger, who succeeded Gerold in 1142 and continued to rule the community for fifty-four years before retiring because of old age in 1196.

Byland prospered, acquiring a spiritual reputation comparable to that of the greatest Cistercian houses, and building went on apace. By 1200 most of the eastern and southern claustral ranges, the walks of the cloister itself, and the greater part of the church excluding the western end of the nave, had been completed. Another twenty-five years and the church was finished and the abbot's lodging had been added. Byland was still prosperous at the end of the 13th c., but in 1322 it was pillaged by the Scots. Edward II, who may have been dining here just before the raid, was almost captured. By 1381 numbers had dropped to twelve monks and only three lay-brothers, but by 1538 there were again twenty-five monks excluding the abbot. The abbey was surrendered on 30 November 1538.

Once the swamp had been drained, the site presented few problems to the builders of Byland, and consequently the monastic complex is an almost perfect example of the way in which a Cistercian monastery should be arranged. The church is large, 330 ft. long with an aisled nave of eleven bays, a square-ended presbytery with five eastern chapels, and north and south transepts each with two eastern chapels and a western aisle. In the south transept, this aisle enclosed the monks' night-stairs to the dorter. Much of the north, west and east walls of the church still stands, but of the south wall little remains. The west front, with its three lancets set in an arcade of very slender blind lancets beneath the remains of a great wheel window 26 ft in diameter, is the finest surviving feature of the abbey. Its central doorway is fully shafted and carried a trefoiled head set on capitals with waterleaf moulding, a motif that occurs again and again at Byland. The doorway to the south aisle is round-headed and so must have been built earlier than the central and northern doorways, which are both pointed. The whole church was originally tiled in green and yellow geometrical patterns, and in the south transept chapels and parts of the crossing some of this paving remains to show how the church must have looked, although in many places the glaze has worn away.

The cloister is exceptionally large, 145 feet square, and is set some feet below the level of the church, thus necessitating a flight of stone steps leading to the door in its north-east corner. Much of the cloister was rebuilt in the 15th c., but the remains of the buildings around it all date from 1150–1220. The east range follows the normal Cistercian plan, with a narrow library-cum-vestry adjoining the south wall of the south transept, followed by the chapter-house, which was rib-vaulted in three bays on pillars and corbels with the typically Byland waterleaf capitals, an open-ended parlour, and an irregular passage leading from the cloister to the abbot's lodging. In the south-eastern corner of the passage are the monks' day-stairs to the dorter. To the east of this passage are the undercroft of the rere-dorter, along the south side of which the great drain can still be seen, and the undercroft of the abbot's lodging, set at right-angles to the south, through the centre of which runs another branch of the drain. To the south of the passage was the day room, and over it, stretching all the way along the first floor of the eastern range for over 200 feet from the south wall of the south transept, was the dorter. In the fifteenth century five small rooms with fireplaces were added to the eastern side of the day room, probably for those who had been benefactors of the monastery and came to live there in their old age. A large flying buttress, the base of which can still be seen, had to support this extension.

The remains of two free-standing buildings stand to the south of the eastern range; the smaller of these was the meat-kitchen, dating from the 15th c., while the larger was the infirmary, built in the 14th c., and its chapel, the crypt of which dates from the late 13th c. Along the southern range of the cloister were, from east to west, the warming-house, of which the walls still stand to a considerable height, the cellar, over which was the frater, and the kitchen, with the remains of three fireplaces. The western range, extending 275 ft. to the south from the south-western corner of the nave, provided as usual living quarters for the lay-brothers and was supported by flying buttresses on the west side. Between the northern half of its east wall and the west walk of the cloister a lane ran, serving as the lay-brothers' cloister; in the east wall of this lane thirty-five recessed seats were set. Running at right angles from the south-eastern corner of the western range are the remains of the

BYLAND: *aerial view from the north-west*

lay-brothers' rere-dorter, the north-east corner of which joined with the south-west corner of the monks' frater to form a courtyard to the south of the kitchen. To the west of the nave runs the lane to Oldstead, and a little way along it an arch with some attached masonry spans it; this is all that remains of the original gateway to the abbey precinct.

After the Dissolution, the site was granted to Sir William Pickering, and part of the eastern range was converted into a dwelling-house. It passed successively to the Wotton, Stapylton and Wombwell families, and is now in the care of English Heritage.

Calder Abbey

ORDER: Cistercian (S) monks
COUNTY: Cumbria
ROUTE: Off A595 at Calder Bridge, four miles SSE of Egremont.
OS REF: 89:0506

Calder Abbey, on the north bank of the river Calder three miles from the coast, had a somewhat shaky start. The first monastic house here was founded in 1135 by Ranulf Meschin, lord of Cumberland, and colonised from the Savignac house of Furness, but the original community remained only a little over three years. The foundation was poorly endowed and suffered from Scottish raids, so that in 1138 the monks crossed the moors and eventually settled at Byland. In 1142, however, it was decided to make a second attempt to found a house at Calder, and a second colony under Abbot Hardred was sent to restore the ruins of the first house. Although this settlement was successful and Calder became Cistercian when the two orders were merged in 1147, it never became an important house, suffering throughout its history not only from the Scots but from the poverty of its endowment. The number of monks probably never increased above the original thirteen, and by 1381 it had dropped to four, with three lay-brothers. The abbey was suppressed as one of the lesser monasteries in 1536, at which time there were nine monks in residence.

The church dates from the second half of the 12th c., with parts possibly from the early 13th. It is a typically severe Cistercian construction, with an aisled nave of five bays, north and south transepts each with eastern aisles, and a short, square-ended chancel. The round moulded arch and waterleaf capitals of the west doorway, which is still well preserved, mark it out as the oldest part of the church. Since churches were nearly always begun at the east end, this must mean that the chancel here was rebuilt almost as soon as the nave had been completed. Apart from the west end, the only part of the nave which has survived to any height is the north aisle arcade, with its pointed arches on alternating quatrefoil and octagonal piers. Against the west wall of the south transept can be seen the eaves-line of the south aisle of the nave. The crossing and transepts still stand to a good height. Considering that they supported a central tower, the base of which can still be seen,

the piers of the crossing are in no way thick; the arches which they carry soar impressively and make an imposing sight. The south transept is considerably better preserved than the north one. It preserves its eastern aisle divided into two bays, with a lancet in each bay below and two blank arches per bay, with quatrefoils in the spandrels, above. In the south wall can be seen the doorway through which the monks' night-stairs from the dorter were connected with the church. The north transept was no doubt almost identical, but in modern times the aisle has been separated from the rest of the transept by a buttressing wall. In the north wall is a small doorway which may have led to the monks' cemetery. Only the western end of the chancel has survived, but this still stands to a good height. The lower parts of the walls contain several trefoiled sedilia, while the upper part has some blank arcading similar to that found on the east wall of the south transept. The line of the east end has been discovered only by excavation.

The cloister lay in its usual position to the south of the church. The west range has disappeared entirely. The east range has a small peculiarity: immediately to the south of the south transept there was the usual small book cupboard, but instead of being built as a separate unit it was structurally included in the chapter-house, of which it occupied the north-west corner. The whole of this range was rebuilt during the thirteenth century, with the chapter-house being rib-vaulted in three bays, of which the east bay and the north-west corner forming the book cupboard are entirely preserved. Above the vault of the book cupboard ran the night-stairs from the dorter, leading to the door in the south transept's south wall noticed earlier. The dorter, as usual, stretched along the first floor of the east range, and its east and west walls, with their rows of slender lancets, are well preserved. South of the chapter-house on the ground floor a narrow slype ran through the range, no doubt giving access to more buildings (the infirmary?) further east which have since disappeared. Both doors of the slype can still be seen. Further south was no doubt the undercroft of the dorter, but this has all been superseded by an imposing late Georgian mansion which was built in about 1770.

Although scheduled as an Ancient Monument, Calder remains in private hands, and the site has not been fully cleared.

Canterbury Cathedral Priory

ORDER: Benedictine monks
COUNTY: Kent
ROUTE: In town centre, off Burgate.
OS REF: 179:1557

Ever since the arrival of St Augustine's mission of 597, Canterbury has been the focal point of the church in England, the seat of the Archbishop, Primate of All England. When Augustine came here, Canterbury was a royal city, the home of Ethelbert, King of Kent, and it was because Ethelbert was so ready to welcome him that Augustine founded his first monastery here and established the city as the home of English Christianity. According to Bede, there had been a church here in Roman times which Augustine 'recovered' and dedicated to Christ; the discovery of a Roman brick pavement beneath the nave in 1737 suggests that he may have been right. Although initially a monastery, the cathedral reverted to being a house of secular canons in the 9th c., and was not re-founded as a Benedictine monastery until 997. This was a surprisingly late date considering that St Dunstan, the man who more than anyone was responsible for the revival of Benedictine monasticism in England, became Archbishop of Canterbury in 960. It was Archbishop Aelfric (995–1005) who replaced the canons with monks, at the papal command.

The church, which had received extensive additions and restorations through the centuries, was plundered by the Danes in 1011 and almost destroyed by a great fire in 1067. This coincided with the Norman Conquest and the appointment in 1070 of William I's great statesman-prelate, Lanfranc of Bec, as Archbishop. Lanfranc completely rebuilt the church and monastic buildings; although hardly anything now remains of what he built, the ground-plan of his cathedral was largely adhered to during subsequent rebuildings. At the time of the Conquest there were said to be 150 monks at Canterbury; this figure dropped to sixty in 1080, but by the mid-12th c., there were 100 monks.

Two events in the 1170s changed the history of the cathedral. The murder in 1170 of Archbishop Thomas Becket in the north-west transept, was committed by four of Henry II's knights; whether or not the King himself ordered the murder (which is unlikely), he had to face severe political consequences. For the cathedral, the consequences were great too: the shrine of the martyred Archbishop became the most celebrated place of pilgrimage in Britain, bringing tremendous financial benefits in the form of alms and other offerings. The money given by the pilgrims enabled the monks to overcome the financial consequences of another great fire of 1174, the second major event in the cathedral's history at this time. This fire left the chancel no more than a gutted shell, but within ten years a new and magnificent chancel and Trinity Chapel had been completed. In the late 14th and early 15th cs. the nave was rebuilt, and at the beginning of the 16th c. the central tower, known as Bell Harry, was added.

Apart from the erection of a north-west tower to replace the one built by Lanfranc, which collapsed in 1832, the cathedral remains to this day much as it was at the time of the Dissolution, and has suffered very little, as cathedrals go, at the hands of restorers. The monastery was dissolved in 1540, but Canterbury remained the metropolitan cathedral of Reformation England, with provision for a Dean and twelve prebendaries.

The total length of the church is 515 ft., the height of the central tower almost 250 ft. The church consists of an aisled nave of nine bays (including the two western towers), two sets of transepts divided by an aisled quire of five bays, and an east end which consists of a chancel of which the walls are canted inwards towards the east, followed by the apsidal Trinity Chapel and the Corona. The nave was built in 1378–1405 almost exactly on the ground-plan of the 11th-c. nave. It was designed by Henry Yevele, the royal master-mason employed by both Edward III and Richard II and possibly the greatest of medieval English architects. The south-west tower was added by Thomas Mapleton in 1424–35, and the north-west tower built by George Austin to match it in 1832. One of the notable features of the nave is the height of the arcade relative to the triforium panelling and the clerestory, a feature which will also be noticed in the quire. The cathedral is singularly bright, an effect which Yevele achieved by closely relating the positioning of the arcade openings to the windows and making the windows as large as he could. With its tall clustered shaft piers and lierne-vault at a height of 80 ft. above the floor, it is one of

CANTERBURY: *the church from the south-west,*
showing Bell Harry tower

the finest Perpendicular church interiors in England.

The western pair of transepts was rebuilt by Yevele at the same time as the nave; they contain very large eight-light windows with panel tracery, and although the Norman walling is retained in some places, the elevation and details are almost exactly the same as the nave. The north-west transept is known as the martyrdom, for it was here, in the late afternoon of Tuesday 29 December 1170, that Archbishop Becket was murdered. The fine trefoil-canopied tomb of Archbishop John Pecham (d. 1292) is also here. To the east of the transept is the Lady Chapel, fan-vaulted in two bays. This was added about 1460, forty years after St Michael's Chapel had been added in the same position on the south side of the church.

Over the crossing is Bell Harry, one of the finest cathedral towers in the country. It was built by John Wastell at the beginning of the sixteenth century, before he went on to complete King's College Chapel in Cambridge and, like King's Chapel, it has a high fan-vault. In order to support his tower Wastell had to throw strainer arches across between the piers of the crossing, but he took a risk and did not put one up on the north side; apparently this was so that the view into the

martyrdom should not be impeded.

Eastwards of the western transepts, the cathedral is essentially the work of two men: William of Sens, and William the Englishman. After the fire of 1174, the monks apparently hoped that the remaining shell of the quire could be patched up to look as it had before, but the architect they called in, the Frenchman William of Sens, insisted that, although the external walls could be retained, the arcades and clerestory must be demolished so that a completely fresh start could be made. For four years, from 1175, William of Sens worked continuously at his new building but in 1179, while preparing to bring the vault over the high altar, he fell some 50 ft. from the scaffolding and was so badly injured that he had to retire and return to France. Between 1178 and 1184 the work was

1. NAVE	10. ST ANDREW'S CHAPEL
2. QUIRE WITH STALLS	11. ST ANSELM'S CHAPEL
3. TRINITY CHAPEL	12. HENRY IV'S CHANTRY
4. CORONA	13. TREASURY
5. WESTERN TRANSEPTS	14. HIGH ALTAR
6. EASTERN TRANSEPTS	15. CHAPTER-HOUSE
7. THE MARTYRDOM	16. CLOISTER
8. LADY CHAPEL	17. SLYPE LEADING TO
9. ST MICHAEL'S CHAPEL	MONASTIC BUILDINGS

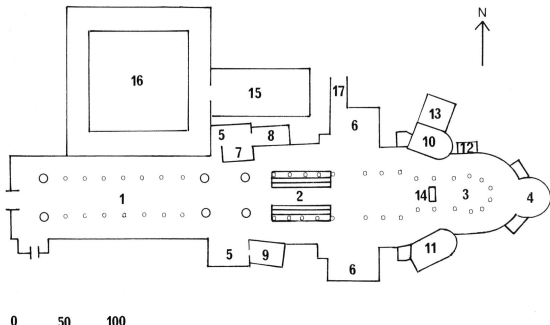

CANTERBURY: *the north nave aisle, looking west*

completed by William the Englishman, probably to a design drawn up by the Frenchman before his accident. Fundamentally, the quire and eastern transepts were the work of William of Sens, while the Trinity Chapel and Corona were the work of William the Englishman. The retention of the outer walls meant that the width of the structure was decided before William of Sens began, but the height and proportions of the elevation were his to determine, and like Yevele two hundred years later, he decided to build high arcades and place less emphasis on the triforium and clerestory.

Throughout the eastern half of the church Purbeck marble is used lavishly, which serves to emphasise verticality, and sexpartite rib-vaults are used for the ceilings. Canterbury is emphatically one of the first Gothic buildings of England, and because of the prestige and influence of the place itself, it must have done much to help the swift spread of the new style through the British Isles.

Originally the church ended in an apse around the present presbytery; two of the chapels which projected from this apse, those of St Andrew and St Anselm, were saved from the fire of 1174, so when the east end was rebuilt it was decided to cant inwards the walls at the east end of the presbytery in order to retain these chapels. In the Trinity Chapel, also known as St Thomas's Chapel, stood the shrine of the murdered Archbishop, the goal of innumerable medieval pilgrims; at the Dissolution it was dismantled by Henry VIII's agents, and its jewels were carried off to swell the royal treasury. On the south side of the Chapel is the tomb and excellent gilded effigy of Edward, Prince of Wales (1330–76), the 'Black Prince', the son of Edward III who defeated the French and captured their king at Poitiers in 1356. On the north side is the chantry of his nephew Henry IV (1366–1413), the first Lancastrian King of England. The chantry chapel is dedicated to Edward the Confessor. The eastern apse of the church is the Corona, only 27 ft. in diameter. During the middle ages a jewelled reliquary, said to contain Becket's tonsure, was kept here to be shown to pilgrims. The Corona now houses St Augustine's chair, constructed in three sections from Petworth marble and completed in 1205. On this chair, Archbishops of Canterbury sit to be enthroned.

The whole east end of the church is built over crypts, one under the quire built in the late eleventh century and extended in the early twelfth, and the other under the Trinity Chapel built probably by William the Englishman. Both are remarkably spacious, and sufficiently high above the ground to be well lit by windows. The capitals of the piers in the crypt beneath the quire are particularly fine examples of Norman carving.

The cloister at Canterbury has always stood to the north of the church, and to the west of the western transepts. The monastic buildings around it were built by Lanfranc after 1070, and although many of them have vanished or been replaced, several of the later buildings were built in the same positions, so that it is possible to gain an impression of what the monastery looked like, and of the scale on which it was built, in the eleventh century. The cloister walks were rebuilt by Prior Chillenden (1390–1411), and have fourlight openings to the garth and lierne-vaults. There are eight hundred and twenty-five heraldic bosses on the roofs, commemorating those who contributed to the rebuilding. To the north of the north transept, but completely detached from it, is the oblong chapter-house. Built by Lanfranc, it is a remarkably large building, extended by Prior Eastry in 1304. It is also very light, owing to some extensive restoration undertaken by Prior Chillenden. He inserted all the present windows, which like those of the cloister are mostly of four lights, and he erected the waggon-vaulted roof with its gilded ribs. The Prior's seat in the centre of the east wall, with its gabled canopy surmounted by pinnacles, was inserted in Prior Eastry's time. The most impressive feature of the Canterbury chapter-house is its unusual size, particularly its height.

North of the chapter-house comes the narrow passage known as the Dark Entry, which leads through the range to the infirmary buildings. The rest of the east claustral range is taken up by the great dorter built by Lanfranc. Built to accommodate up to one hundred and fifty monks, it measured 148 ft. by 78 ft., and not surprisingly it never had to be replaced. A library now occupies what was its south end, but north of this the piers of the dorter undercroft still stand, and in the west wall some of the masonry of the dorter itself can be seen. Two buildings ran east from the dorter, both near the north end: the southern was the second dorter, now almost totally vanished, while the northern was the rere-dorter. Several of the arches which supported the privy seats can still be seen here.

CANTERBURY: *the east end*

The north range of the cloister contained the frater, of which nothing remains except a fine doorway and part of the east wall. Opposite the doorway, in the cloister walk, are the remains of the lavatorium. The site of the frater is now the garden of the Archdeacon of Canterbury's house. In the west range was the cellarer's lodging, and to the west of this stands the Archbishop's Palace; this was rebuilt at the end of the nineteenth century, although it incorporates some thirteenth-century work, notably on the north side. The buildings to the north of the frater were the kitchen, cellarer's hall, and guest-house, the latter having been built by Prior Chillenden and also being known as Chillenden's chambers. The row of thirteenth century arches and the newel staircase belong to the cellarer's hall, while the kitchen is recognisable from a hearth in one of its angles. From this group of buildings a pentise runs north-east to the North Hall and Court Gatehouse. To the east of the cloister stood the infirmary. Passing through the Dark Entry, one comes first to the lavatory tower, a remarkable and almost unique survival added about 1150. The washing arrangements have disappeared, but the central stem through which the water flowed from the cistern is still there, as are the octagonal outer walls.

The passage continues past this tower and contained the prior's chapel on the first floor just west of the infirmary buildings themselves, built by Prior Ernulf at the beginning of the twelfth century, when St Anselm was Archbishop. The total length of the infirmary, with hall and chapel in a line from east to west, was 250 ft., and the rows of arcading give a clear indication of the remarkable scale on which the building was planned. The western part formed the hall, where the beds for the sick monks were ranged, while the eastern part formed the chapel, lengthened in the fourteenth century. To the north projects the fourteenth-century Table Hall, an additional frater which has been much restored and is now the Cathedral Choir School. The small building projecting from the south of the range was the Treasury, built in the mid-12th c. It is now used as a vestry leading into the north-east transept of the church. It has an octopartite rib-vault. To the east of the infirmary is the building known as 'Meister Omers', a Prior's guest-house erected by Prior Chillenden and now a boarding-house of the King's School.

To the north of the cloister was the Green court. Its east side is bounded by the Deanery, built over an unidentified medieval building. It's north side embraced the bakehouse, brewhouse and granary, converted in modern times into classrooms for the King's School. At the north-west angle of the court are the North Hall and Court Gatehouse, both erected in Norman times, although the north Hall has been heavily restored. Despite the restoration, the delightful twelfth-century external staircase to the Hall has been preserved. The Gate is large and well-preserved, with double entrance archways into which Perpendicular arches have been inserted, leading through to a tunnel-vault 36 ft. deep. Finally, on the other side of the church, and now providing the normal entrance for visitors, is the Christ Church Gate, built in 1517–21. The heraldic shields commemorate the visit to Canterbury in 1500 of Arthur, Prince of Wales (1486–1502), elder son of Henry VII and brother of Henry VIII. The archway is lierne-vaulted, and there are octagonal turrets at the angles. The stone pilasters which flank the entrance arches are decorated with Renaissance motifs, among the earliest in England; a timely reminder that this gate was completed only a few years before winds of change were to sweep away the whole way of life for which these fine buildings were constructed.

Carlisle Cathedral Priory

ORDER: Augustinian canons
COUNTY: Cumbria
ROUTE: In city centre.
OS REF: 85:3956

According to Bede, there was a religious house at Carlisle in the 7th c. If so, it was certainly destroyed by the Danes in the 9th c. During the 10th and 11th cs., Carlisle was in Scottish hands; King William Rufus recaptured it but the priory itself was not founded until 1122, by King Henry I following his visit to the city. In 1133 Henry, a particular patron of the Augustinian order, founded the diocese of Carlisle, and the priory became a cathedral as well. He chose as first bishop of the new diocese his confessor Athelwold, formerly Prior of Nostell. Within a few years Carlisle once again fell to the Scots, but at the beginning of his reign, Henry II (1154–89) restored it to England, and the building of the monastery went on apace. Originally it had been endowed for twenty-six canons. During the late thirteenth and fourteenth centuries it suffered repeatedly from Scottish raids, and from a serious fire in 1292 which necessitated much rebuilding in the chancel. In 1304 Edward I granted the canons licence to appropriate a church and a chapel 'in compensation for the burning of their houses and churches, and various depredations by the Scots'. By 1379 the number of canons had dropped to twelve. The priory was surrendered on 9 January 1540, at which time there were twenty-three canons and four chantry priests. It was reconstituted in May 1541 as one of only fourteen former monastic houses to attain or retain cathedral status in Reformation England, with provision for a dean, four prebendaries, and eight minor canons.

The church is probably the most extraordinary cathedral church in England. Built in the second quarter of the twelfth century, it had a nave of eight bays and a chancel of two. By the late fourteenth century, the chancel had been extended to eight bays as well, but in the 17th-c. civil war the six western bays of the nave were removed by the parliamentary forces, so that since then the situation has been completely reversed, with the nave shrinking to two bays while the chancel retained its eight. The chancel is also some 12 ft. broader than the nave, and while the south transept still survives from the 12th c., the north transept was rebuilt early in the 15th c. Apart from the grey stone of the surviving Norman parts, the cathedral is built in red sandstone.

The west front of the church, with its enormous stepped buttresses coming down to rest on two piers which originally formed part of the arcade of the Norman nave, was redesigned by Ewan Christian in the 1850s and contains a large and rather unconvincing five-light window. Inside, what remains of the nave was, in 1949, dedicated as the Border Regiment Chapel; but the masonry dates from the Norman building period and is solid though plain. The triforium openings, although large, admit no light, and neither the arches nor the capitals carry much decoration, although some of the capitals in the south transept and in the clerestory of the nave are scalloped. To the modern visitor, the most interesting feature is the depression of the arches, particularly the arch leading from the nave south aisle to the south transept. It is not certain when this depression occurred, but the likely time would appear to be during the century after the Reformation, when the whole nave was allowed to fall into a considerable state of disrepair and its six western bays were removed. In the south transept there is also a strange stone bearing the runic inscription *Dolfin wrote these runes*; it has been suggested that this Dolfin was the governor of Carlisle dispossessed by Rufus in 1092, and that, being proud of his Norse descent, he decided to inscribe the runes on a stone which was later used for the building of the church. The south wall of the south transept, with its three-light window and deeply moulded portal set in a sharply-pointed gable, was redesigned by Christian in the 1850s, but the rest of the south transept belongs to the original Norman building period.

The north transept provides a complete contrast. It dates from the early 15th c., but was heavily restored by G. E. Street, who followed Ewan Christian's work in the third quarter of the 19th c. The roof dates from this restoration, but the rest of the work is 15th-c. and unsatisfactory. The window, for instance, is set in a beautiful arch, but its tracery gives the impression of being too cluttered. Notable, however, is the Perpendicular strainer arch at the entrance from the crossing to the north transept; at one time, when the north transept roof was lower, it was used as a window. William Strickland, the early 15th-c. bishop who

CARLISLE: *choir-stall misericord of a dragon swallowing a man in a kilt*

rebuilt the north transept, was also responsible for the crossing tower as we now see it, with its unambitious but highly effective lierne vault.

The chancel, extended to seven bays in the mid-19th c. and then to eight in the 14th c., is the pride of Carlisle Cathedral. The decision to rebuild the Norman chancel was probably taken by Abbot Hugh of Beaulieu, who became bishop in 1219. More altars were needed and, in accordance with the new trends in architecture, it was thought that the old chancel was too dark and dismal. Abbot Hugh also decided to make the chancel broader; since the monastic buildings were on the south, the extra 12 ft. of breadth had to be added to the north side, which is why the nave and chancel are out of alignment. All that has survived of the 13th-c. chancel is in the aisles: the series of three-light windows above cinquefoiled blank arcading running the length of the aisle exterior walls, the rib-vaults, and the small chapel dedicated to St

Catherine immediately to the east of the south transept. The central part of the chancel, the aisle piers, the east window and the clerestory were all rebuilt after the disastrous fire of 1292 and rank with the finest Decorated architecture in England.

The east window in particular is magnificent. It dates from about 1340 and has nine tall lights surmounted by thirteen quatrefoils set in a design which, although highly elaborate, has an essential freedom and simplicity which creates an impression of complete harmony; particularly skilful is the use of thicker and thinner ribs of masonry to emphasise the most important features of the stained glass. The scene portrayed is the Last Judgement, with Christ sitting in judgement at the top. It will be noticed that the tracery running around the top of the central circle containing the quatrefoil is thicker than that at the bottom: the intention is to emphasise how the lower areas, the scenes of eternal punishment, are a place apart. Although most of the stained glass in the lower parts of the window has been replaced over the years, some glass in the upper parts of the window

CARLISLE: *depressed arches in the nave*

dates from about 1358. The sculptured capitals of the aisle piers form a full series of fourteen, in a state of perfect preservation. The two eastern capitals were originally behind the high altar before it was moved to the east bay of the chancel; the other twelve represent the months of the year. They contain some very fine sculpture of men, animals, monsters, and highly detailed foliage. It is interesting to see that one of the motifs portrayed, a fox killing a goose, is also carved on one of the misericords of the wooden choir-stalls. These forty-six stalls and their canopies were given in the first half of the 15th c. by Bishop Strickland and Prior Haythwaite, and again have some fascinating motifs, such as a dragon swallowing a man in a kilt.

Carlisle cathedral church has undergone much renovation and refurbishment down the centuries since the Reformation. For over a century after the priory was dissolved, it was allowed to fall into serious disrepair, and during the siege of 1644, the parliamentary army demolished the western six bays of the nave to use the stone for fortifications. A century later, in 1745, after the Duke of Cumberland had secured the surrender of the city, the Jacobite soldiers who had been occupying the city took refuge in the cathedral. Further alterations were made by Charles Lyttleton, Bishop of Carlisle from 1762 to 1768, before the major restorations carried out by Christian and Street in the mid-19th c. The vestry which stands immediately north of the nave was built in 1957. In 1967 the floor level of the sanctuary was lowered and a new marble floor inserted. Yet despite all these alterations, the essential design and fabric of the church, excluding the loss of most of the nave, has remained unaltered since the 14th c.; Carlisle cathedral is still a medieval building.

Of the monastic buildings by far the most important survival is the frater, in its usual position along the south range of the cloister, still in an almost perfect state of preservation and now used as the chapter-house and cathedral library. To the west and south, it has large Perpendicular windows, although all the tracery in them is mid-nineteenth century, and in the south-west corner is the pulpitum set in the wall; the tracery on both sides of it is original. The two hatches in the west wall probably led to the monastic kitchen. Although built in the fourteenth century, this building was extensively remodelled by Prior Thomas Gondiber about 1500. Beneath the frater its undercroft too is well preserved, with its rib-vaulting on extremely short and stumpy octagonal piers. The remains of a drain can be seen here, presumably leading to or from the kitchen. The west claustral range has entirely disappeared, but the outlines of the east range can be made out and a few walls here stand to a reasonable height. South of the transept came a vestibule, then the chapter-house, which was octagonal, and then the undercroft of the dorter, with the dorter extending along the first floor of the whole range.

The only other monastic building still standing is the gateway, built by Prior Christopher Slee in 1527 and still bearing his inscription on its arch. It is tunnel-vaulted in two parts, with a division in the middle between the pedestrian and carriage entrances. It is through this gateway that the modern visitor enters the precinct of Carlisle cathedral.

Castle Acre Priory

ORDER: Cluniac monks
COUNTY: Norfolk
ROUTE: Off A1065, 4 miles N of Swaffham.
OS REF: 132:8114

The priory of St Mary, St Peter and St Paul at Castle Acre was founded by William Warenne, 2nd Earl of Surrey, in 1089, his father the first earl having founded the first Cluniac house in England at Lewes twelve years earlier. The first site, which was within the outer defences of the castle a little to the east of the present ruins, proved unworkable, and within a year the monks moved and began to build on the present site. The earl's endowment was generous, and it included one of his serfs, Ulmar the stonemason, to give the monks some skilled help in building their church. (Although a serf himself, Ulmar no doubt had free men working under him for wages.) The original community consisted of twenty-six monks, and by the late 13th c. thirty-five, although numbers dropped to twenty-six again in 1349–50, and to twenty in 1450.

In common with the other 'alien priories' (those dependent on Cluny and other French houses), Castle Acre suffered from severe royal taxation and other restrictions during the French wars of the 14th c., and this may have contributed to the apparent relaxation of discipline at the priory. In 1351, a royal sergeant-at-arms was ordered to arrest some of the monks from Castle Acre who had 'spurned the habit of their order and were vagabonds in England in secular habit'. Eventually in 1373, on payment of a heavy fine, the priory secured royal letters patent of denization, ensuring that it would in future be treated as a native not an alien monastery and would thus be exempt from additional taxes. In 1401 Castle Acre obtained a special indulgence from Pope Boniface IX to encourage pilgrims to visit the priory and contribute towards its finances. Its most valuable relic was the arm of St Philip. It may have been the extra money obtained from the granting of this indulgence which allowed the monks to build a luxurious new prior's lodging at the end of the 15th c. The priory was dissolved on 22 November 1537, there being at that time ten monks in addition to the prior.

The remains of the church and other buildings at Castle Acre rank among the most noble monastic ruins in the south of England. They were built in the late 11th and 12th cs., and although there was extensive later remodelling, notably of the chancel and the west claustral range, the essential plan and most of the stonework dates from the original Norman construction. The church as built then had a nave of seven bays with aisles and two western towers, north and south transepts with apsidal eastern chapels, and an apsidal chancel with aisles which also ended in apses; so that the east end formed a group of five stepped apses. The nave remained unaltered throughout its history.

The west front still stands close to its original height and is a perfect example of Late Norman becoming Transitional architecture. The lower stages contain a richly-moulded doorway of four orders surrounded by much of that plain and intersecting blank arcading beloved by the Normans; but by the time the upper stages were reached new ideas were filtering through, there was less emphasis placed on the blank arcading, and the west window was given a pointed arch.

The north-western tower is ruined, but its southern counterpart is the best preserved part of the church, and on this must be based our assessment of how the elevation of the rest of the church was planned. The compound piers, wall-passage in the clerestory, and groin-vaults were no doubt continued along both aisles. The central part of the nave was, however, roofed with timber. The walls of the nave have mostly disappeared above the lower stages, and the piers are little more than stumps in the turf, but of the transepts more remains. To the north of the north transept is the outline of the sacristy added in the late twelfth century; in its north wall are the remains of a Tudor fireplace next to which is a small brick oven, which was used for baking the priory's sacramental wafers. The east end of the church was rebuilt in the 14th and 15th cs.; the chancel was extended and given a square end, the south quire aisle was squared off, and the north quire aisle both squared off and broadened, in the process of which the eastern apse of the north transept was demolished. The south transept retains its apse, and the outlines of the other eastern apses have been displayed on the turf. In the south-east corner of the south transept is a door leading to a spiral staircase which

CASTLE ACRE: *aerial view from the south-east*

went up to the wall-passages and the roof. The crossing originally carried a tower.

The cloister, exactly 100 ft. square, lay to the south of the nave, and the buildings around it are in their usual positions. Much of the exterior walling remains, but with the exception of the rebuilt west range little of the detail has survived. To the south of the south transept came the chapter-house, a rectangular building with an eastern apse. The apse has vanished, although its outline is marked on the turf, but the remaining walls stand to a good height. The room was barrel-vaulted and there is plenty of the usual Norman blank arcading. In its south-east corner is a door leading to the infirmary range. South of the chapter-house is a doorway which led to the monks' day-stairs to the dorter, and then the undercroft of the dorter itself. This was 110 ft. long and divided in two by a row of eight central piers, the bases of which remain. On the upper floor the windows of the dorter can still be seen, as can the outlines of the partition walls which separated off the various parts of the undercroft. There are two doors leading into the undercroft from the cloister. The northern one led to the parlour, the southern into a slype which went straight through the range to the infirmary.

At the south end of the east range is the remarkably large rere-dorter (91 ft. long), at near right-angles to it. It connects with the dorter by a bridge and runs over a stream; the arrangements for flushing and drainage have been excellently excavated and are clearly visible. The two oblong buildings to the east of the eastern range were the infirmary halls, the northern hall built in the twelfth century, and the southern in the early 14th c. They were connected to each other, to the east range, and to the south aisle of the chancel by a series of covered walks, the outlines of which remain.

In the south-east angle of the cloister is the pit of the dorter garderobe, and next to it the entrance to

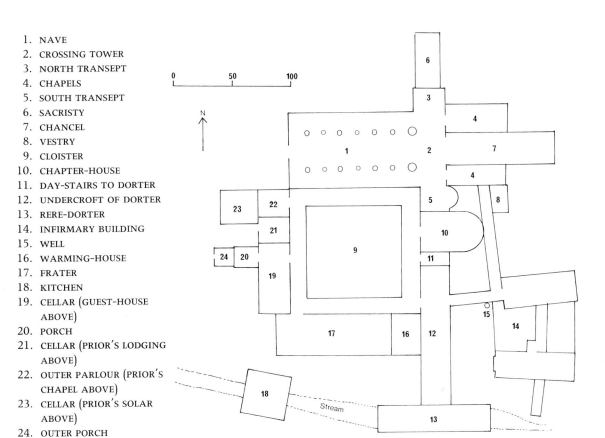

1. NAVE
2. CROSSING TOWER
3. NORTH TRANSEPT
4. CHAPELS
5. SOUTH TRANSEPT
6. SACRISTY
7. CHANCEL
8. VESTRY
9. CLOISTER
10. CHAPTER-HOUSE
11. DAY-STAIRS TO DORTER
12. UNDERCROFT OF DORTER
13. RERE-DORTER
14. INFIRMARY BUILDING
15. WELL
16. WARMING-HOUSE
17. FRATER
18. KITCHEN
19. CELLAR (GUEST-HOUSE ABOVE)
20. PORCH
21. CELLAR (PRIOR'S LODGING ABOVE)
22. OUTER PARLOUR (PRIOR'S CHAPEL ABOVE)
23. CELLAR (PRIOR'S SOLAR ABOVE)
24. OUTER PORCH

the warming-house, connected to the undercroft of the dorter by two doors. The long building stretching along the rest of the south range was the frater, with at its west end the original kitchen; the four large central bases in this kitchen probably supported a louvre. In the 15th c., a new kitchen was built just to the south of the old one, on a bridge over the stream (which was far more convenient for waste disposal). The bridge has since collapsed and only low masonry survives of the walls.

The west range, as built in the 12th c., was a simple oblong about 105 ft. long, divided into two by seven bays with a row of central piers supporting a groin-vault. In the late 12th c. a porch was added in the middle of the west wall, and the northern bay was sectioned off to form an outer parlour. In the 15th c. a far more drastic restructuring of the range was planned, which consisted of adding a second range of the same length and width along the west wall of the first range and a remodelling of parts of the original range to form a new lodging for the prior. Although foundations of the west wall of this second range can still be seen, it is doubtful if the plan was ever brought to completion, although extensive additions were made. The first floor of the west range already (since the 12th c.) contained the prior's lodging and his chapel over the northern three bays and the guest-house over the southern four. By about 1500 plans for a complete new range outside the old one had been abandoned, and instead two separate blocks were built, one with the prior's solar (or sun-parlour), to the west of his chapel in the northern two bays, and the other with his new lodging, built around the 12th-c. porch to the west of the range's central bay. Both these buildings were incorporated in a dwelling-house after the Dissolution and were considerably altered during the following centuries; but various medieval details such as fireplaces, circular staircases, new windows and a lavatorium basin testify to the high standard of living enjoyed by the last priors of Castle Acre. Even before its conversion to a

185

CASTLE ACRE: *west front, with prior's solar on the right*

dwelling-house, it must have borne a far closer similarity to a rich layman's house than to a monastic building.

The only other surviving building at Castle Acre is the gatehouse to the north of the church. It has the usual double entrance for pedestrians and carriages, and was built about 1500, at the same time as the prior's new lodging. The upper storey has vanished, apart from a few window openings, but just above the string-course on the north side can be seen four armorial shields with the arms of (from left to right) Fitzalan and Warenne quartered, the Royal Arms, Warenne again, and Maltravers. Over the doorway is another panel with the arms of the priory.

After the Dissolution, the whole site was granted to Thomas Howard, Duke of Norfolk. In Elizabeth I's reign it passed to Thomas Gresham, who sold it to Thomas Cecil, Earl of Exeter. His son William in turn sold it to Sir Edward Coke. In 1929 Coke's descendant, 4th Earl of Leicester, placed it in the hands of the Commissioners of Works, and it is now in the care of English Heritage.

Chester Cathedral

ORDER: Benedictine monks
COUNTY: Cheshire
ROUTE: In city centre, off Eastgate St.
OS REF: 117:4066

St Werburh's Abbey, Chester, only became a cathedral in 1541, when an enormous new diocese, including parts of Yorkshire and Westmorland as well as Lancashire, was placed under the jurisdiction of the former abbot. The first religious house here was founded about 907 by Aethelflaed, the Lady of the Mercians, the daughter of Alfred the Great, at the time when Chester was being re-fortified as a stronghold against the Danes. Soon after this, the relics of St Werburh, the 7th-c. Mercian princess and abbess, were brought to the church from Hanbury in Staffordshire, and the new foundation was dedicated to her. It was an establishment for secular clerks. The man responsible for re-founding the house as a Benedictine monastery was Hugh Lupus (Hugh the Wolf), the second Norman Earl of Chester, who, in 1092, invited Anselm, soon to become Archbishop of Canterbury, to Chester to help him to re-organise Chester along Benedictine lines. The first monks came from Bec, the renowned Norman monastery of which Anselm had formerly been prior.

Although an important house, Chester was never in the first rank of the English Benedictine abbeys, and the number of monks probably never exceeded forty. The most famous monk produced by Chester was Ranulf Higden, whose 14th-c. *Polychronicon* is one of the longest and most interesting of medieval monastic chronicles and was continued in the 15th c. by various successors. By 1382 the number of monks at Chester had dropped to twenty-five, and in 1538 it stood at twenty-six. Two years later the abbey was dissolved, only to be reconstituted in 1541 as the cathedral of Christ and the Blessed Virgin Mary, the last abbot becoming dean of the new establishment.

The church is 355 ft. in overall length, not long as cathedrals go, and although cruciform, the disparity in size between its north and south transepts gives its ground-plan an unbalanced look. Compared to many of England's other cathedrals, the quality of its architecture is not of the highest order; moreover, extensive 19th-c. restorations have made it look significantly different from the medieval version. It consists of a nave of seven bays (including the baptistery and consistory court in the western bays, which are screened off), a very small north transept with an eastern chapel, a very large south transept with an eastern as well as a western aisle and four eastern chapels, and a chancel of five bays ending in an eastern Lady Chapel. The west front dates from the early 16th c., but Barclays Bank now conceals the northern third of it and it is difficult to gain an impression of it as a whole. The west doorway and eight-light Perpendicular window above it are original (i.e., c. 1520), but the battlemented and turreted upper stages are the work of Sir Gilbert Scott between 1868 and 1876.

The nave dates from the 14th and 15th cs., the south side having been built about 1360–70 and the

1. TOWER	9. INNER PARLOUR
2. NAVE	10. WARMING-HOUSE
3. TRANSEPTS	11. FRATER
4. CHANCEL	12. KITCHEN
5. LADY CHAPEL	13. CELLARIUM
6. CLOISTER	14. OUTER PARLOUR,
7. VESTIBULE	WITH ST ANSELM'S
8. CHAPTER-HOUSE	CHAPEL OVER

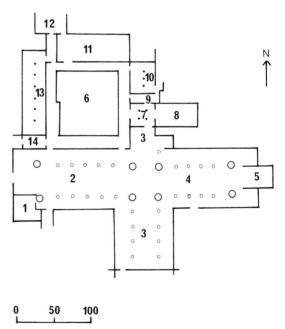

north side about 1490; what is interesting is the lack of stylistic difference between the two. Such conscious reversion to an outdated architectural style for the sake of symmetry is most un-medieval, only really occurring in England on any scale, and even here only in a few places (e.g., Westminster Abbey). The lierne-vault is of timber and is part of Scott's restoration; he also re-vaulted the aisles. The north-west corner of the nave now forms the baptistery. (It has a font which came from Venice in 1885 but is early Christian in style; the peacocks carved on it symbolise the everlasting life given by Christ at baptism.) The stonework here is mid-12th c., one of the few parts of the church where the masonry of the Norman church was retained.

The north transept is the other main area in which the original Norman work was retained and this dates from about 1100, making it the oldest part of the church. The great Norman arch and six-arched triforium above it have the typically rough stonework of the period; the two-bayed chapel to the east dates from the early 13th c., while the clerestory stage of the transept is Perpendicular. The window in the north wall is Scott's. The monastic buildings at Chester lie to the north of the church, so when, in the 14th c., the monks felt the need for more chapels, they were unable to extend the north transept, and consequently rebuilt the south transept on a disproportionate scale. The eastern aisle contains four chapels, and the southern chapel is roofed with the only genuinely medieval rib-vault in the cathedral.

The tower over the crossing is Perpendicular, although its upper stages were restored by Scott, who added the pinnacles. The lower stages of the chancel date from the early 14th c., while the clerestory and wooden vault were remodelled by Scott, who also erected the vaults in the quire aisles and remodelled their east ends. At the east end of the south quire aisle he demolished the ambulatory and constructed a polygonal apse with a roof rising right up to clerestory level. Although he claimed to have found evidence that this was how the roof had originally been constructed, most authorities have remained sceptical. In this aisle may be seen the tomb of Ranulf Higden. At the entrances to both the north and south quire aisles are some gates of excellent Spanish wrought-iron work, made for a chapel in Guadalajara in the mid-16th c. and brought to Chester in 1876. The north quire aisle extends further east than the south aisle (the

eastern part of the south aisle was knocked down by Scott) and ends in a Perpendicular chapel which in 1921 was dedicated to St Werburh. At the east end of the church, is the lovely little Lady Chapel, which was built in the third quarter of the 13th c. to re-house the relics of St Werburh; it has a fine roof with a ridge-rib and tierceron vault containing some large bosses, one of which depicts the murder of St Thomas of Canterbury.

The cloisters date mainly from 1525–30, replacing cloisters built at the time of the foundation. The south wall of the south walk, however, is Norman, for it also forms the north wall of the nave and would not have been pulled down when the cloisters were rebuilt, and the rest of the south walk was also rebuilt by Scott. The vaults have both diagonal and ridge ribs, and the windows are Perpendicular. The arrangement of the buildings around the cloister show slight variations from the norm, with the chapter-house and its vestibule coming immediately to the north of the north transept without the usual intervening passage, which at Chester is placed north of the chapter-house. The entrance to the chapter-house was rebuilt during the mid-19th c. restoration by R. C. Hussey, which preceded that of Scott; but the rest of it, and the vestibule, are original, and date from the mid-13th c. The slender lancets, the ridge-ribbed vaults, the triple vaulting-shafts, and above all the admirable proportions of the rooms place them firmly in the 'classic century', and fortunately they were by-passed by the 19th-c. restorers. The warming-room, or parlour, with a rib-vault and octagonal piers, comes to the north of the slype, entered through an archway in which start the monks' day-stairs to the dorter, which has vanished.

The north walk contains the 13th-c. frater, the windows of which were altered in the 15th c. to give it the appearance of a later building. The excellent hammer-beam roof was erected in 1939 by F. H. Crossley, a local architect and historian. A rare survival is the fine pulpitum, its stairs set into the thickness of the south wall from which the pulpitum itself projects on a triangular corbel. From here one of the monks read to the others while they ate their meals. Against the west wall hangs a tapestry of a scene from the Acts of the Apostles, a copy of one of the Raphael cartoons woven at Mortlake in the 1620s. Finally, along the west range, there is the groin-vaulted undercroft which

CHESTER: *interior of the church, looking east*

dates from the early 12th c. and would have been used for cellarage; above this was the abbot's lodging, and south of it what is still called the abbot's passage. Above this in turn is St Anselm's Chapel, built in the 12th c. but extensively remodelled and embellished in the 17th and given a plaster vault in the 19th. In its south wall is a window from which one can see down into the nave of the cathedral.

To the west of the cloisters is Abbey Square, formerly part of the monastic precinct, in the south-west corner of which is the 14th-c. abbey gateway; it is vaulted in three bays with a narrow entrance for pedestrians and a wider one for carriages. The remainder of the buildings in the square date from the 18th and 19th cs., none of the outlying monastic buildings having survived. In the south-east corner of the precinct, on the other side of the church, is the new Bell Tower, covered with Bethesda slates, where the cathedral bells are hung. Designed by George Pace and completed in 1974, it is a sombre but enjoyable structure, the first free-standing bell tower built for an English cathedral since the 15th c.

Cleeve Abbey

ORDER: Cistercian monks
COUNTY: Somerset
ROUTE: On the S fringe of Washford, off A39, 6 miles SE of Minehead.
OS REF: 181:0440

Cleeve Abbey was one of the last Cistercian foundations in England. Between 1186 and 1191 William de Roumare, whose grandfather the Earl of Lincoln had founded Revesby Abbey in 1143, granted to the abbot of Revesby all his lands at Cleeve for the purpose of founding a daughter-house, and in June 1198 the first abbot of the new house, Ralph, brought twelve monks to the site and began building. It took a hundred years before the first set of buildings was completed and during this century the community grew, until by about 1300 there were twenty-eight monks here. In the 14th c., however, there was a decline in the abbey's fortunes. The abbot's receiver was outlawed for failing to render his accounts, one of the monks apostatised in 1339, the number of monks dropped, and the abbey was heavily in debt to various London merchants. This state of affairs seems to have continued through to the mid-15th c., when the finances of the abbey improved, and in the late 15th and early 16th c. a new series of building operations began.

This period of rebuilding has left the magnificent south claustral range at Cleeve, containing one of the best-preserved monastic fraters in the country. Although attempts were made to save Cleeve from suppression (it was reported that there were seventeen monks left there in 1537, all 'priests of honest life who keep great hospitality'), the house was duly dissolved in the same year, the abbot, subprior and thirteen monks being granted pensions. One of the thirteen was John Hooper, later to be remembered as a Protestant martyr: in 1551 he became Bishop of Gloucester, but when Mary came to the throne he was deprived of his position, imprisoned, and burnt at the stake as a heretic in Gloucester on 9 February 1555, 'for the example and terror of others'.

Of the church practically nothing has survived at Cleeve, although its plan has been recovered by excavation and the outlines are marked on the turf. It was built in the 13th c. and never rebuilt. Thus it conforms to the usual model of Cistercian austerity, with an aisled nave of seven bays, north and south transepts each with two eastern chapels, and a short square-ended chancel. Only parts of the south transept and the south aisle wall of the nave, on the south side of which can be seen the recess for the abbot's Collation seat (where he sat to read from Cassian's *Collationes Patrum* before Compline), stand above ground. The cloister lay as usual to the south of the nave, and around it are the best survivals: the east and south ranges at Cleeve are among the finest in England.

With the exception of its roof, the east range dates almost entirely from the 13th c. It begins to the south of the south transept with the sacristy, a barrel-vaulted oblong room with recessed lockers in its walls, original wall-paintings, and an eastern wheel window next to a piscina in the south-east corner. It is entered from the south transept, so the first door along the east walk of the cloister leads to the library. Most Cistercian houses built only one room to serve as both sacristy and library, but the library at Cleeve is separate and has a barrel-vault and a lancet in the east wall. The books were probably kept in presses standing around the wall.

South of the library comes the chapter-house. Originally this was built in three bays, but only the foundations of the eastern bay have survived; the western two bays are still there, however, and retain their quadripartite rib-vault as well as traces of painted decoration from the 13th c. South of this come the day-stairs to the dorter. They were built in the 15th century, replacing earlier ones at the east end of the south range when that range was rebuilt, and they mark the only serious structural alteration made to the east range after the 13th c. Behind the stairs is the parlour, with twin lancets in the east wall, and then to the south comes the slype through to the infirmary range followed by the undercroft of the southern half of the dorter. This was used as a common room by the monks and had a large fireplace in the middle of the east wall, though this was much ruined by having a door knocked through it and then blocked up after the Dissolution. It was originally vaulted in three bays of quadripartite ribs, but the ceiling collapsed long ago, and only the bases of the piers from which the vault was carried remain. To the east of the range stood the infirmary complex, while the rere-dorter stretched east from its south-east angle, but neither of these has survived.

The first floor of the range contained as usual the dorter, running along the top of the whole range from the south wall of the south transept to the site of the rere-dorter. It is still reached by the monastic day-stairs, and retains its windows, walls and doors. The central partition was erected in the 18th c., no doubt after the collapse of the vault of the common room, so we must imagine the whole range as one large room in the middle ages, 137 ft. long and 25 ft. wide, with the beds ranged along the east and west walls. Later in the middle ages, the room was divided into individual cubicles, probably with wainscot, and some of the window-seats seem to have been remodelled. This increased emphasis on privacy is one of the features of monastic rebuilding or remodelling in the later middle ages. In the south-eastern corner of the dorter can be seen a squint passing through the wall with an iron ring in the lintel; from this hung the night-lantern, the squint being set so that it would light both dorter and rere-dorter simultaneously. The roof of the dorter was added in the 18th c., when the claustral ranges were used as farm buildings.

The south range as built in the mid-13th c. conformed to the normal second stage Cistercian plan with, from east to west, the day-stairs to the dorter, the warming-house, the frater on a north–south axis, and the kitchen. In the second half of the 15th c. the range was completely rebuilt in two storeys, with a third storey over the western part. This rebuilding has survived almost in its entirety, and is one of the finest surviving examples of a complete claustral range in England. The ground floor consists of a passage through the range at the east end, followed by a set of living rooms, two bedchambers and two studies. They now have cobbled floors, which were put in when they were used as stables after the Dissolution. In the south wall are two garderobes, one for each set of rooms, and an oven; in the space underneath the stairs leading up to the frater a cellar was constructed. In the north wall, the arch of the lavatorium can still be seen next to the stairs, and to the south of the western part of the range are the paving tiles of the 13th-c. frater, which from their heraldry can be dated to the last quarter of the century. Some of them bear the arms of Richard, Earl of Cornwall, the brother of Henry III and a known benefactor of the abbey, and two others show Richard I and Saladin riding to their celebrated combat. On the first floor is the frater

itself. It is interesting that the Cistercians, who had developed the plan of south ranges with fraters on a north–south axis in the mid-12th c., were reverting to the idea of building them on an east–west axis in the later middle ages. The walls are pierced by a series of three-light windows in two tiers with delightful panel tracery in the heads, and near the east end of the south wall can be seen the remains of the pulpitum and its stairs, largely destroyed when a 17th-c. fireplace was inserted in its place. The pride of the frater is its roof. It is of arch-braced collar construction, with five main and five subsidiary trusses enriched with fifty bosses at the junctions and resting on sole-pieces which are carved in the shape of crowned angels. The angels on the sole-pieces of the main trusses carry scrolls and rest on stone corbels in the shape of shields. It was the builders' intention that it should be a waggon-roof of the type so popular in Somerset, but this was never filled in. Nevertheless, it is among the finest of timber roofs of late medieval England, an age which produced such masterpieces as the hammer-beam roof of Westminster Great Hall.

The west end of the south range is partitioned off and contains an office known as the painted chamber, for the east wall is covered with a late 15th-c. wall-painting showing St Catherine with her wheel and St Margaret of Scotland on either side of a bridge on which stands an old man. A dragon and a lion as well as several varieties of fish and flowers also feature in the composition. Above this western chamber is a third storey with an upper chamber containing a fireplace and traces of further wall-painting. This was originally reached by an outside newel staircase in a turret at the north-west corner of the range, but this has broken away and access to the upper chamber is now through a trap-door in the roof of the gallery of the painted chamber. Of the west range, which contained cellarage and the lay-brothers' quarters, hardly anything remains, though the west walk of the cloister, which was rebuilt early in the 16th c., is more extensively preserved than any of the other walks. Abbot Dovell, the last abbot of Cleeve, was still rebuilding the west walk in 1534–5 and he also began work on an upper storey too.

To the north-west of the cloister and its attendant ranges stands the great gatehouse beside a double-arched stone bridge; attached to its west side is the almonry. Although built in the 13th c.,

CLEEVE: *the interior of the frater*

this has been extensively remodelled both in the later middle ages and in modern times. It is a two-storeyed building with a barrel-vault, and above the northern archway an inscription reads *porta patens esto, nulli claudaris honesto*, translated as 'Gate be open, be shut to no honest person'. Over the southern archway a floriated panel commemorates the abbot who remodelled the gate-house shortly before the Dissolution, with the simple inscription 'Dovell'. The upper chamber, which has lost its floor, was probably used as the courtroom from which the monks exercised their jurisdiction over the men who worked their estates. After the Dissolution a 21-year lease on the site was sold to Anthony Busterd, after which it passed into the hands of the Earl of Sussex, to whom the rest of the abbey's lands had been granted in 1538 as a reward for his services in helping to suppress the Pilgrimage of Grace. The site passed through several hands and eventually became part of the Dunster estate of the Luttrels. In 1951, the abbey was placed in the hands of the Minister of Works, and it is now in the care of English Heritage.

Crossraguel Abbey

ORDER: Cluniac monks
COUNTY: Strathclyde
ROUTE: On A77, 2 miles SW of Maybole.
OS REF: 76:2708

Crossraguel, one of only three Cluniac houses in Scotland, was founded early in the thirteenth century from Paisley, probably by Duncan, Earl of Carrick. The date of foundation is not known, but it seems that the foundation was originally only meant to comprise an oratory served by the monks of Paisley. In 1244, following a complaint from the monks that the Earl's intention had been the foundation of a monastery proper, the matter was brought before Bishop William of Glasgow, who decreed that this should be done. Despite continued protest from the convent at Paisley at the loss of valuable lands, Crossraguel was endowed with all the lands in Carrick included in Duncan's original grant, and the new house was declared to be independent of Paisley, with the right of electing its own abbot.

Building had not progressed far when the Scottish War of Independence intervened, and the 13th-c. buildings were almost totally destroyed. In the 14th c. however, Crossraguel prospered (due in large part to the patronage of Robert Bruce, Duncan's great-grandson), and in 1404 the monastery was granted a Charter of Regality, giving the abbot extensive jurisdiction over civil and criminal cases in the district. The effect of this grant was to make the abbot 'almost sovereign in Carrick and the greatest person in Ayrshire'. From 1520 the abbey was held by a series of commendators, notable among whom was William Kennedy (1520–47), responsible for the erection of the singularly un-monastic Tower House and gatehouse which still rise high above the ruins of the claustral ranges at opposite ends of the precinct. He was succeeded by his nephew Quintin Kennedy, a theologian and fierce opponent of the Reformation who is renowned chiefly for holding a disputation with John Knox on Maybole Green which lasted for three days. In 1561 the abbey buildings were sacked and partially destroyed by a band of Reformers led by the Earls of Argyll and Glencairn, but commendators continued to be appointed until 1617, when the abbey and its lands

were annexed to the Bishopric of Dunblane.

The church is remarkable only for its plainness. It is a long and narrow building without aisles or transepts, divided centrally by a 16th-c. screen wall to form a ritual nave and quire. The screen wall still rises to gable height, while the walls of the church stand for the most part to the height of the eaves, although the roof has gone. The south wall of the nave and the north-western angle are the only survivals from the destroyed 13th-c. church. The rest of the nave dates from the 14th c., while the quire, apart from the wall abutting the sacristy, was re-built in the 15th c. Only at the polygonal east end was any concession made to contemporary architectural development. To the north of the church can be seen the foundations of the transept of the 13th-c. church. On the south side, a well-preserved sacristy occupies the position of the south transept. It is reached by a narrow passage containing the monks' night-stairs to the dorter, and is rib-vaulted in two bays; the corbels on the north and south walls, of two lions and two bears respectively, are fine 15th-c. carvings, and in the east wall is a three-light window of trefoiled-head design.

The chapter-house to the south of the sacristy is again excellently preserved and dates from the 15th c. It is rib-vaulted in four bays from a central compound pier which is now somewhat mutilated, and from triple vaulting-shafts on the walls and corbels in the angles. In the east wall a corbel replaces a vaulting-shaft, for the latter would have interfered with the abbot's seat below, and there are two three-light windows with trefoiled heads surmounted by spherical quatrefoils. Around the walls runs the stone bench on which the monks sat. The layout of the cloister derives from the 14th c. and is notable for the absence of a west range. In the centre of the garth is a well, sunk between 1450 and 1550. The east range continues to the south of the chapter-house with a small treasury, with a recess for a safe in the north wall, then a slype-cum-parlour, and then the undercroft of the dorter. This originally comprised two equally-sized rooms, the northern a warming-house and the southern a novice's room, but in the 15th c. it was subdivided to make cellarage space. Over the range stretched the dorter, which originally reached right up to the church (cf. the night-stairs by the sacristy), but was curtailed by the high vaults of the sacristy and chapter-house in the 15th c., when the present wall

195

CROSSRAGUEL: *aerial view from the west*

with its protruding gable was built. At the south end of the range was the rere-dorter, with the stream which drained it still flowing through it.

To the east of the east range another group of buildings was ranged around the abbot's court. The south side of the court contained the abbot's lodging, erected in the 14th c. but modified in the 15th. The ground floor contained a series of cellars intersected by a passage, some of which are well preserved, while on the first floor were the abbot's private apartments. They are now ruined and the arrangement is impossible to recover, but it seems likely that the abbot's bedchamber was at the west end, so that it was connected to the monks' dorter by a door, thus enabling the abbot to claim that he complied with the rule that he slept in the same building with his monks. Along the east side of the court a kitchen block was inserted in the 16th c.; the stone base for the oven can still be seen in the

southmost room of the block. This kitchen was primarily to serve the needs of those dwelling in the Tower House which stands just outside the south-east angle of the court and is one of the most interesting survivals at Crossraguel.

The Tower House is a four-storeyed building of about 1530, of which the north-eastern corner has fallen. The original staircase to the second and third floors has also collapsed. The ground-floor was used as cellarage, the first as a hall, the second as an antechamber, and the third as the private chamber. Gun-loops and elaborate fireplaces betray the essentially secular nature of the building. It has been plausibly suggested that William Kennedy may have built it as accommodation for himself while he was commendator (and titular abbot) of the abbey, for his nephew Quintin was a minor in William's wardship for eleven years and may have been installed by his uncle in the abbot's house.

Returning to the cloister, the ruins of the frater

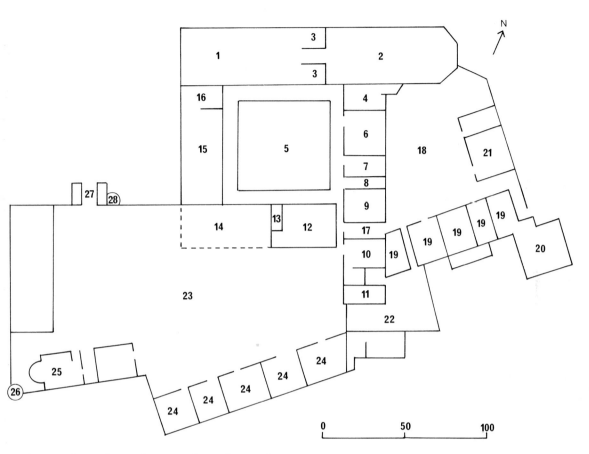

and its undercroft can be seen along the south range. At the east end is a narrow slype leading through the range to the south court. The undercroft of the frater was used as a common hall and has a service hatch in its west wall. The frater above was reached by a flight of stairs from the south walk, which can still be seen, a little to the west of centre in the range. The western half of the range included the kitchen, but is now very ruined. There was no west range except for a small outer parlour abutting the south wall of the church. Until the 16th c., the exterior wall of the west claustral walk formed the outer wall of the monastery, but a new outer wall was built to the west of this when the gatehouse was built. To the south of the south range is a large walled area with various buildings and known as the south court. Along its south side are a group of five corrodians' houses, built in the 15th century when corrodians were increasingly proving themselves a drain on monastic resources. They have fireplaces and

1. NAVE
2. CHANCEL
3. CHAPELS
4. SACRISTY
5. CLOISTER
6. CHAPTER-HOUSE
7. TREASURY
8. INNER PARLOUR
9. WARMING-HOUSE
10. NOVICES ROOM (probable)
11. RERE-DORTER
12. COMMON HALL, WITH FRATER ABOVE
13. STAIRS TO FRATER
14. SITE OF KITCHEN
15. WEST RANGE
16. OUTER PARLOUR
17. SLYPE
18. INNER COURT
19. CELLARS, WITH ABBOT'S LODGING ABOVE
20. TOWER HOUSE
21. KITCHEN
22. OUTER COURT
23. SOUTH COURT
24. CORRODIANS' HOUSES
25. BAKEHOUSE
26. DOVECOT
27. GATEHOUSE
28. STAIRCASE

CROSSRAGUEL: *view across the cloister towards the east range*

garderobes, and were no doubt divided internally into two chambers by wooden partition walls. In the south-west corner of the court is a dovecot in which the rows of nests can still be seen around the upper stages; the lower stage was used as a storeroom. There are remains of other buildings distributed around the court; that nearest to the dovecot was probably a bakehouse (cf. the rounded oven at its west end) while the others were no doubt granaries, brewhouses or small buildings in which a monastic industry such as tanning could be carried on.

The gatehouse is set in the north wall of the court, and dates from about 1530. It is a three-storeyed building with an imposing façade and an attached turret at the east side. On the ground floor is the gateway, with a porter's lodge set into the wall on the west side. Access to the upper floors is through a staircase in the turret. The first floor contains a single chamber with a garderobe closet, the second floor another chamber, from which there was access to the wall walk. The floors and roof are modern restorations. Like the Tower House, it is a singular example of the secularisation of monastic architecture in the late middle ages.

Crossraguel Abbey is now in the care of the Scottish Development Department.

Croxden Abbey

ORDER: Cistercian monks
COUNTY: Staffordshire
ROUTE: Off B5031, five miles NNW of Uttoxeter.
OS REF: 128:0639

Croxden Abbey was a late Cistercian foundation in England, its mother-house being Aunay-sur-Odon in Normandy. The first monks from Aunay arrived in 1176 and planned to build their monastery on land granted to them by Bertram de Verdun at Cotton, but they must have found the site inhospitable, and in 1179 they moved to Croxden. Although the original community was French, the first abbot, Thomas, was an Englishman. He ruled the abbey for over fifty years, dying in 1229, and during his rule most of the abbey buildings were completed, although not until about 1285 was the western range finished. The history of the house was uneventful, though there were regular lawsuits concerning property (one dispute with the nearby abbey of Dieulacres lasted over a century). Most of the abbey's wealth came from sheep-rearing. In the late 14th c. there were seven resident monks. In 1536 Croxden avoided suppression on payment of a £100 fine to the crown, but two years later, on 17 September 1538, the abbey was surrendered. There were at that time twelve monks and the abbot.

The buildings are ruined, but there is enough left to give a clear impression of the plan, and the surviving parts have mostly been excavated. The site, indeed the church itself, has been bisected by a modern road which passes within a few feet of the angle of the nave and the south transept. The church, which was built from east to west and finally consecrated about 1250, had an aisled nave of eight bays, north and south transepts with eastern aisles, and an apsidal chancel of the French *chevet* type, with an ambulatory from which five circular chapels radiated. Such an east end was more sumptuous than would have been permitted in a Cistercian church thirty years earlier, while St Bernard was alive. A fragment of the north-western of these five chapels can be seen on the northern side of the road, but the remaining ruins are all on its south side. The west wall stands to a good height; it has a fine four-ordered doorway of richly-moulded arches and three tall lancets, of

which the central one stops short to leave room for the doorway. The south aisle wall of the nave stands, and the south and west walls of the south transept reach close to their original height. Here again are those long lancets which feature prominently in north country churches, and in the south wall there are two doorways, the lower leading to the sacristy and the upper connecting the monks' night-stairs with the dorter.

The arrangement of the buildings around the cloister conformed to the normal late Cistercian plan. South of the south transept comes the usual sacristy-cum library, a groin-vaulted room in three

1. NAVE	11. RERE-DORTER
2. NORTH TRANSEPT	12. WARMING-HOUSE
3. CHAPELS	13. FRATER
4. CHANCEL	14. SITE OF KITCHEN
5. SOUTH TRANSEPT	15. SITE OF WEST
6. LIBRARY/SACRISTY	RANGE
7. CHAPTER-HOUSE	16. ABBOT'S NEW
8. PARLOUR	LODGING
9. SLYPE	17. SITE OF INFIRMARY
10. DORTER	
UNDERCROFT	

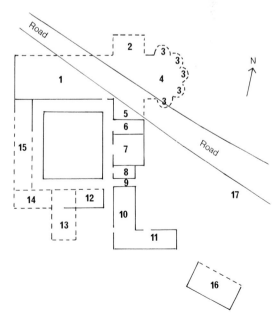

199

CROXDEN: *the west front*

bays, of which the western bay was used as a library and the eastern two as the sacristy. Next comes the square chapter-house, vaulted in nine equal bays from piers of which the bases can still be seen. The south and east walls have disappeared, but the west wall stands and contains a four-ordered entrance portal flanked by two two-light windows. The portal has undergone extensive restoration. South of the chapter-house came the parlour, followed by the slype and the undercroft of the dorter, with a round-headed doorway between them. The original dorter, which ran along the top of the east range, was extended further to the north in the 14th c. The area over the chapter-house was previously covered by a chamber which may have been used as a treasury. Earlier, in the late 13th c., it had also been extended further to the south, possibly to form a new lodging for the sixth abbot, William Howton. From the east wall of this southern extension the rere-dorter runs at right-angles to the range; the drain which flushed it has recently been excavated. To the south-east of the rere-dorter can be seen the remains of yet another new abbot's lodging, built for the thirteenth abbot, Richard Sheepshed, in 1335–6. To the north, immediately east of the farm buildings, was the infirmary; no traces of it remain,

and the road covers its northern part.

The south range followed the Cistercian plan of, from east to west, warming-house, frater and kitchen. In the south-east angle of the range there are traces of the monks' day-stairs to the dorter, and in the warming-house the fireplace can still be seen, although it was much altered after the Dissolution. The original frater was built on a north-south axis and stretched much further to the south than the line of the present wall, which was erected in the 15th c., no doubt because numbers had fallen and there was no longer any need for a large frater. The site of the kitchen has been superseded by the Georgian Abbey Farmhouse, the drive of which also cuts across the southern half of the west range. The walls of the northern part of the west range can still be seen, however; the range no doubt contained cellarage in the undercroft and the quarters of the lay-brothers above, with the northernmost bay separated off to form an outer parlour where business with the outside world could be transacted.

After the Dissolution parts of the monastic buildings were evidently converted into a dwelling house (note the restructuring of the fireplace in the warming-house). In 1936 the owner, W. G. Vickers, placed the ruins in the care of the Commissioners of Works. They are now in the hands of English Heritage.

Cymmer Abbey

ORDER: Cistercian monks
COUNTY: Gwynedd
ROUTE: Off A470, 2 miles NNW of Dolgellau.
OS REF: 124:7219

Cymmer Abbey stands at the head of the Mawddach estuary near the point where it meets the River Wnion (the word Cymmer means meeting), in surroundings of great natural beauty. Founded in 1198–9 by Maredudd ap Cynan and his brother Gruffyd, it was colonised from Abbey-Cwmhir in Powys, with which it has on occasions been confused. Thus it was one of the later Cistercian foundations in Britain. Throughout its history, although in the middle ages it was situated on an important thoroughfare (the lowest fording place of the estuary), it remained small, poor and unimportant. It was suppressed in 1536.

The ruins have been systematically excavated, but only in the church do the walls stand to any height above the ground. The church at Cymmer is one of the plainest among those of an Order which prided itself on the austerity of its architecture. It is a straight, aisled construction with no transepts and no division into nave and chancel. Some of the aisle arcading remains on each side; at the west end is the base of a small square tower added in the mid-14th c., and in the east wall are three stepped lancets. The east end of the church stops a little way short of the east walk of the cloister, and this may provide the clue to the excessive austerity of the architecture at Cymmer, for it suggests that the church when built may only have been intended as the nave of a far larger church, but that funds ran out and so it was decided to throw up the east wall and abandon the more grandiose scheme. If an eastward extension was planned, it was never built.

The lines of the square cloister are clearly marked, but of the buildings which surrounded it little remains. The east range, which presumably contained the chapter house and dorter, is covered by farm buildings. Along the south walk lie the remains of the frater, built on an east–west axis. This was how the earliest Cistercian fraters were built, but from the middle of the 12th c. the Cistercians had begun to build their fraters at right-angles to the south walk to allow room for the kitchen and warming-house to abut the cloister on either side of the frater. As at Valle Crucis, another late foundation in Wales, the monks of Cymmer reverted to the original plan. A drain runs under the frater from the west, but it is not medieval. The west range, which housed the lay-brothers, has completely vanished, but the farm-house to the west of the church includes medieval work, and was probably the monastic guest-house.

Cymmer Abbey is now in the care of Cadw: Welsh Historic Monuments.

Dryburgh Abbey

ORDER: Premonstratensian canons
COUNTY: Borders
ROUTE: Off A68, 4 miles SE of Melrose
OS REF: 74:5931

Dryburgh Abbey, founded in 1150 by Hugh Morville, Constable to King David I of Scots, and colonised from Alnwick, was the first and most important Premonstratensian house in Scotland. The rich, mellow freestone of the buildings, set in wooded surroundings, makes it one of the country's loveliest ruins. Of the early abbots, the best known was Adam (1184–90). Renowned as a preacher and writer of theological works, he attracted fame to his house before visiting Val St Pierre, where he was inspired by the Carthusians and decided to leave Dryburgh to join the Charterhouse at Witham. His loss was both lamented and resented by the Premonstratensian canons.

Like most Scottish monasteries, Dryburgh suffered severely at the hands of the English in the 14th c. In 1322 Edward II's retreating army set fire to the buildings (either because they heard the abbey bells ringing to rejoice at their retreat or, more likely, they were frustrated at their inability to secure provisions from the abbey). In 1385 Richard II's army sacked and destroyed the church to such effect that most of the nave had to be rebuilt. In 1461 further damage was caused by a fire, and in 1523 and again in 1545 English armies wreaked their vengeance on the miserable monks. From 1507 the abbey was held by a series of commendators, the position always going to the Erskine family after 1541, until in the Scottish parliament of 1604 its lands were joined with those of Cambuskenneth Abbey and Inchmahone Priory and erected into the temporal lordship of Cardross for John Erskine, Earl of Mar.

The ground slopes to the south at Dryburgh, and the buildings, set within a horse-shoe bend of the Tweed, were on three levels: the church occupies the highest level, with the cloister garth a dozen steps below, and the east and south claustral ranges five feet lower still. The main survivals are the transepts and the east range. The church consisted of an aisled nave of six bays, north and south transepts, each with two eastern chapels which were stepped to form what is in effect an aisle for the western bay of the chancel, and a narrow, square-ended chancel. Apart from its south wall, the nave dates from the 15th c. The transepts and chancel date from the late 12th and early 13th cs. The nave is mostly reduced to its foundations, but the west front stands to a reasonable height and is interesting for its use of the round arch in the doorway, a feature which was being redeveloped in late medieval Scottish architecture. The north transept is particularly well-preserved, probably because its two chapels were adopted as the burial vaults of the Haliburton and Haig families. The tombs of the most famous descendants of these families, Sir Walter Scott and Field-Marshal Haig, can be seen here. The transept is a notable piece of early 13th-c. architecture. Its verticality is emphasised by the compression of the triforium into decorative quatrefoil openings and the extension of the clerestory with a continuous row of lancets resting on clustered shafts. The bays are clearly marked off by vaulting-shafts which run from the capitals of the main arcade. Beneath the five-light window in the south transept are the remains of the canons' night-stairs to the dorter.

The east range is probably the finest in Scotland. South of the steps leading down through the east processional door to the cloister is an aumbrey which probably was used as a book cupboard, and then the range continues with a vestry-cum-library, inner parlour, chapter-house, warming-house, and novices' room, with the canons' dorter on the first floor of the range. The library, known as St Modan's chapel, and the parlour are barrel-vaulted; the parlour is not open to the public. The chapter-house is also barrel-vaulted and has a fine sculpted basin and fragmentary remains of 12th-c. mural paintings. The basin was found over a century ago near the entrance to the frater and probably formed part of the lavatorium. The doorway in the south wall of the chapter-house, leading to the warming-house, is a post-Reformation insertion. Beyond the chapter-house are the canons' day-stairs to the dorter. The fireplace in the warming-house was a 14th-c. addition; in the 18th c. this room was a cow byre. Between the warming-house and the novices' room ran a ground-floor passage above which was contrived a narrow chamber at the south end of the dorter. This chamber was probably the abbey's treasury. At the south end of the dorter, which ran

DRYBURGH: *the west doorway of the church; in the background, the north transept*

1. NAVE
2. CHANCEL
3. CHAPEL
4. NORTH TRANSEPT
5. SOUTH TRANSEPT
6. CHAPELS
7. NIGHT STAIRS
8. CLOISTER
9. LIBRARY/VESTRY
10. PARLOUR
11. CHAPTER-HOUSE
12. DAY-STAIRS
13. WARMING-HOUSE
14. SLYPE
15. NOVICES' DAY-ROOM
16. CANONS' DORTER
17. TREASURY
18. UNDERCROFT OF FRATER
19. SITE OF KITCHEN
20. CELLARS
21. LAVATORIUM

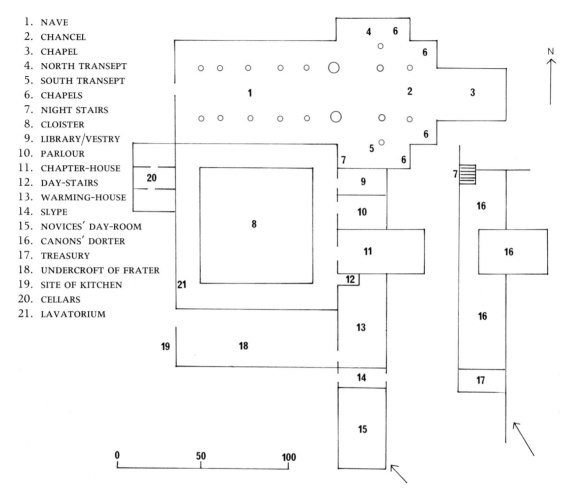

along the whole of the first floor of the range, was the canons' rere-dorter, conveniently situated close to the leat from the Tweed.

The south range contained the frater on an east-west angle, of which the two end-gables and the outlines of the undercroft can be seen. The west gable has a fine wheel window. The original position of the lavatorium can be seen in the enclosing wall which runs along the west side of the cloister. The monastery was never planned to include a west range, but in the 16th c. three vaulted cellars were added to the exterior of the north end of the enclosing wall. They now house a collection of sculptured stones from various parts of the abbey. Any buildings which stood to the east of the east range (the infirmary, presumably, and the abbot's lodging) have disappeared, but to the south-west of the frater, across a bridge over the

leat which was the abbey's main water channel, are the remains of the late 15th-c. gatehouse. The heraldic shields on the gable include the arms of the Greenlaw and Ker families.

An interesting anecdote survives concerning the abbey in modern times. In 1746, after the site had been acquired by Thomas Haliburton, grand-uncle of Sir Walter Scott, a woman who had lost her lover in the Jacobite rising retired to the vaults of the abbey to live the life of a recluse. Never again, it is said, did she look upon the light of day, but she communed with a spirit whom she named Fatlips, and who used to help her to clean her home.

Since the death of Sir Walter Scott, Dryburgh has become something of a place of pilgrimage for English-speaking people to pay homage to the memory of the 'Wizard of the North'; it is now in the care of the Scottish Development Department.

DRYBURGH: *the cloister, showing the entrance doorways to the east range and (left) the east processional doorway.*

Dundrennan Abbey

ORDER: Cistercian monks
COUNTY: Dumfries and Galloway
ROUTE: On A711, 6 miles ESE of Kirkcudbright.
OS REF: 84:7447

Dundrennan must have seemed an almost perfect site for a medieval Cistercian community. Lying in a secluded and wooded valley traversed by a burn which runs down to the Solway Firth only a mile and a half distant, it was remote, yet not too difficult of access by land and sea. It was founded by King David I, probably in collaboration with his friend Fergus, Lord of Galloway, in 1142, and colonised from Rievaulx. St Ailred of Rievaulx visited Dundrennan on more than one occasion, and in 1167 the daughter-house achieved distinction when its first abbot, Sylvanus, was elected to succeed Ailred as Abbot of Rievaulx. The monks prospered. They maintained their own ships at Abbey Burnfoot, a mile and a half to the south on the Solway Firth, and engaged from there in international trade. Despite its remote position, Dundrennan suffered from the Scottish War of Independence, for in 1299 the convent petitioned King Edward I of England for compensation of £8000 (Scots) because their lands had been burnt and destroyed. Again, in 1328, they asked Edward III to restore the revenues from their lands in Ireland from which they had been expelled.

The abbey church and buildings, however, do not seem to have suffered as did so many other Scottish monasteries. By 1529 nevertheless, the buildings were said to be in a state of decay, although there were still at least twelve monks at the Reformation. In 1567 Mary, Queen of Scots, spent her last night on Scottish soil in Dundrennan Abbey, before embarking for England the next morning from Abbey Burnfoot. From 1523 the abbey was held by a series of commendators. The last was John Murray, on whom it was conferred in 1599, and for whom it was erected into a temporal lordship by the Scottish parliament in 1606.

The abbey church, built in the second half of the twelfth century and unaltered, apart from the addition of a western porch, in later centuries, is one of the earliest surviving examples of Transitional architecture in Scotland. It consists of an aisled nave of eight bays, north and south transepts

each with three eastern chapels, and an aisleless, square-ended presbytery. The west porch has disappeared, although the corbels which supported its lean-to roof can be seen on the exterior of the west wall. The west wall itself stands to some height. It has a boldly decorated doorway of three borders, which has been considerably restored, as have other parts of this wall. Set into a recess of the wall is a fascinating effigy of an abbot which was

1. NAVE	13.	NOVICES' ROOM,
2. NORTH TRANSEPT		WITH DORTER
3. SOUTH TRANSEPT		ABOVE
4. CHAPELS	14.	RERE-DORTER
5. CHANCEL	15.	SLYPE
6. LIBRARY/SACRISTY	16.	WARMING-HOUSE
7. CHAPTER-HOUSE	17.	FRATER
8. PARLOUR	18.	KITCHEN
9. CLOISTER	19.	LAY-BROTHERS'
10. NIGHT-STAIRS		DORTER
11. DAY-STAIRS	20.	CELLARS
12. DAY-ROOM, WITH	21.	OUTER PARLOUR
DORTER ABOVE		

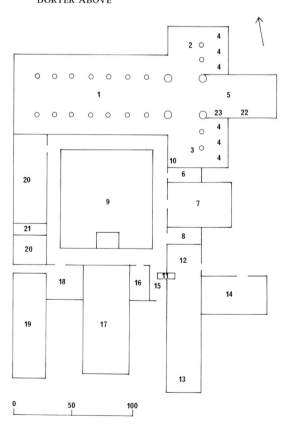

DUNDRENNAN: *view across the cloister, towards the transepts and entrance to the chapter-house*

clearly made for a tomb-chest. His right hand is laid on his heart, and below his neck, on the left side, his breast is pierced by a dagger. At his feet is another figure, partly-clothed, with a wound in the abdomen. It seems clear that the abbot was assassinated, while the figure at his feet probably represents the assassin. The rest of the nave is reduced to foundation masonry, with the bases of the piers *in situ*, but of the transepts and their chapels several of the walls stand to their full height.

The architecture is characteristic of the Transitional style, with pointed arches used for structural purposes and round-headed windows inserted above them. Clustered-shaft piers and rib-vaults point the way to more developed forms of Gothic, making Dundrennan's position in the development of Scottish ecclesiastical architecture comparable to, though less advanced than, that of Roche Abbey in English ecclesiastical architecture. The survival of the north wall of the north transept

shows the steep pitch of the roof. The east end has fallen, although the first two bays of the chancel stand, the corbels high on the wall showing that this part of the church was rib-vaulted too.

The monastic buildings are in their usual position to the south of the cloister, and conform to the standard Cistercian plan. To the south of the south transept came the narrow sacristy-cum-library, entered by doors from the transept and from the cloister. Then came the excellent, rather large chapter-house. It was re-built in the late 13th c. and shows the marked departure from initial severity which characterised so many later additions to early Cistercian houses. The triple arches of the entrance are richly sculptured, with twin-light windows against a background of foliage ornamentation in each of the flanking windows, and a cinquefoiled head to the arch of the central doorway, which is also enriched with foliage moulding. Above the north window a piece of the dorter wall displaying the jamb of a window reaches up. The building itself was vaulted in four triple bays from slender clustered shafts, the bases of which are still in place. It must have been a room of great beauty. The tomb-slabs of several abbots buried here can be seen on the floor.

Of the remaining buildings at Dundrennan little stands to any height, although much foundation masonry has survived to indicate their scope and lay-out. The east range continued with a narrow parlour followed by the undercroft of the dorter, probably used as a novices' room. The dorter was long, extending over the whole range, and the rere-dorter projected from it to the east, on a line roughly level with the south claustral range. This, the south range, was built from the first in accordance with the second stage Cistercian plan with, from east to west, the warming-house, frater on a north–south axis, and kitchen. The surviving doorway at the west end was the main entrance to

the kitchen. The west end was originally for the use of the lay-brothers, and contained their frater and warming-house on the ground floor and their dorter on the first floor. After the disappearance of lay-brothers in the 14th c., it was remodelled into cellars for storage. Several of these cellars can still be seen.

After the Reformation, the Lords of the Congregation ordered Lord Herries, General Justiciar of the district, to demolish the abbey buildings; this he refused to do, and part of the church continued in parochial use until 1742. For a hundred years it lay derelict and was plundered as a stone-quarry, until in 1842 it was taken over by the Commissioners of Woods and Forests. It is now in the care of the Scottish Development Department.

Dunfermline Abbey

ORDER: Benedictine monks
COUNTY: Fife
ROUTE: In town centre, off Canmore St.
OS REF: 65:0987

The earliest known church on this site was a small Culdee church in which King Malcolm Canmore of Scots married his second wife St Margaret, the Saxon princess who had fled from the Normans in 1068. When this was built is not known. Within a few years of her marriage, probably in 1072, Margaret had a second church built here, at the same time asking Lanfranc, Archbishop of Canterbury, to send some Benedictine monks to her. Lanfranc sent three, and they formed the nucleus of the Benedictine Priory established at Dunfermline. Under David I, the Scottish king responsible for the spread of Roman monasticism in Scotland, the priory became an abbey. The first abbot was Geoffrey of Canterbury, consecrated in 1129. David also built a new church here, dedicated in 1150; the western half still forms the nave of the present church. It grew to be one of the wealthiest abbeys in Scotland, the burial place of eight Scottish kings (including David I and Robert Bruce), four queens (including St Margaret), five princes, and two princesses; in 1245 Pope Innocent IV granted the abbot the use of the mitre.

Like so many other Scottish monasteries, however, Dunfermline suffered during the Scottish War of Independence. Edward I of England stayed here in 1290 and 1303, on the second occasion setting fire to the monastic buildings as he left. Grants from Robert Bruce helped to repair the damage, but in 1385 Richard II's army caused further damage to the monastery. The combination of monastery and royal palace on one site, paralleled at Westminster, meant that Dunfermline was constantly visited by kings; the chronicler Matthew Paris declared that Dunfermline had 'so many princely edifices that two distinguished sovereigns with their retinues might be accommodated with lodgings at the same time without inconvenience to each other'. The royal palace continued in regular use until the 17th-c. (Charles I was born here in 1600, and Charles II agreed to the 'Dunfermline Declaration' here in 1650), but by then the abbey had ceased to function. Held by a series of commendators for most of the 16th c., its lands were systematically apportioned to various lords between 1587 and 1589, and in 1605 Alexander Seton, the hereditary baillie, was created Earl of Dunfermline by Act of Parliament.

The church begun by David I was probably not completed until the mid-13th c. The nave was complete by 1160, at which time it was joined to the east end of the church built by St Margaret, but gradually during the next century this east end was demolished and a new, much longer chancel was built. In 1250 the church consisted of an aisled nave of eight bays, north and south transepts with eastern chapels, and an aisled chancel of six bays from which projected a narrow, square-ended sanctuary at the east end. A Lady Chapel was added to the north side of the chancel in the 14th c. In the 19th c. the transepts and chancel—that is, everything to the east of the eastern bay of the nave—were demolished and replaced by a new east end. The 12th-c. nave was spared, and remains probably the finest Norman church interior in Scotland. The west front with its twin towers is basically original, although the Early English windows are of course later insertions. At the end of the 16th c. the north tower was damaged and, when the king's master mason, William Schaw, repaired it, he added the present spire, which gives the composition an unbalanced look. The west door is deeply recessed in five orders with bold decorative motifs. The nave itself is immediately reminiscent of Durham, notably in the great cylindrical piers with incised markings. The arches of the aisle arcades are enriched with moulding, but the triforium and clerestory are plain. Some of the aisle windows are clearly recognisable as later additions, as are the large external buttresses. The north porch was added by Abbot Bothwell in about 1450.

Throughout the church can be seen the tombs and memorials of members of the Scottish royal families. Pride of place is given to the tomb of Robert Bruce, which is covered by a memorial brass set in porphyry. His remains were found wrapped in a cloth-of-gold shroud inside an oak coffin by workmen clearing the ground for the rebuilding of the east end of the church in February 1818. On examination, it was found that his breastbone had been sawn apart after death so that his heart could be removed and buried in Melrose Abbey, according to his own last wish. The body

was re-interred in its present position.

The cloister lay to the south of the nave. The east and west ranges have almost entirely disappeared, the only remaining fragments being at the south end of the east range, where the rere-dorter and the line of the drain to the south of it can still be seen. The south range was occupied by the frater, the shell of which has been fully excavated and still stands almost to roof level. It was built in the 13th c. on ground which slopes steeply downhill to the south. In its west wall is a large 15th-c. window which retains much of its tracery. At its east end a small scriptorium was screened off. A gateway tower at the south-west corner of the frater connected it with the kitchen (now on the other side of the road, which passes under the gateway arch), an arrangement which must have been inconvenient. The building on the other side of the road seems originally to have been the monastic guest-house, but later it was converted into the royal palace in which Charles I was born. To the north-east of the church was the abbot's house, parts of which have been incorporated into a later building which stands beyond the burial-ground. The abbey precinct covered twenty-eight acres, and part of the precinct wall can be seen in Canmore Street.

Services are still held in the abbey church; and the monastic buildings are in the care of the Scottish Development Department.

Durham Cathedral Priory

ORDER: Benedictine monks
COUNTY: Durham
ROUTE: In city centre
OS REF: 88:2742

Durham Cathedral is probably the most famous medieval religious house in England. It was an architectural watershed: a precursor of the Gothic style, but at the same time an emphatically Romanesque building, the major enduring statement in Britain of the majesty of early Norman architecture. It also housed the shrine of St Cuthbert, the greatest saint of the north country and the most charismatic figures of early Christianity in this country.

In his youth Cuthbert was a shepherd boy on the hills of Lammermoor. After seeing a vision of the soul of Aidan being carried to heaven by angels he was inspired to become a monk and, despite his own declared preference for the eremitic life, he was consecrated Bishop of Lindisfarne in 683 and buried in the church there following his death two years later. Before his death he had told his monks that, should they ever leave Lindisfarne, they were to take his body with them. So when, in 875, the Danish raids on the island of Lindisfarne became too frequent and fierce to allow the community to remain there, they opened his grave and, to their astonishment, found that the saint's body was entirely without signs of decay. Placing the body in a wooden coffin, they set out on their famous wanderings which were to last for 120 years, settling first at Chester-le-Street and then, under the leadership of Bishop Aldhun, moving in 995 to the steep outcrop almost encircled by the River Wear which was to become the site of Durham Cathedral and Castle. The 'White Church' of the Saxon monastic community here was dedicated on 4 September 998.

After the Conquest, however, the new Norman Bishop, Walcher of Lorraine, decided that the rule followed by the English secular priests at Durham was not strict enough (the bones of women and children dating from this period have been found in the graveyard, suggesting that some at least of the priests were married). Although Walcher was murdered by a mob at Gateshead before he could reform the house, his intentions were carried out when his successor William of St Calais refounded the monastery for twenty-three Benedictine monks from Jarrow and Monkwearmouth in 1083. Throughout the middle ages it was one of the most celebrated and wealthy monasteries in Britain, with the shrine of St Cuthbert to attract countless pilgrims from all ranks of society and the enormous wealth which they brought with them, and the castle at the neck of the peninsula to protect it from the ever-present danger of Scottish raids. It was the only major town near the border never to be taken by the Scots.

Among the many famous medieval churchmen who resided at Durham one in particular deserves mention: John of Wessington (or Washington), appointed prior in 1416, who spent the enormous sum of £7,881. 8. 3d on repairs to the church and monastic buildings during the thirty years of his rule, and whose family, over three hundred years later, was to provide America with its first president.

The monastery also provided us with a book known as the *Rites of Durham*, a unique and fascinating account of day-to-day life in the monastery on the eve of the Dissolution, written in 1593 by an aged Elizabethan who had been a monk of Durham in his youth. Just before the Dissolution, there were forty monks at Durham; during the 13th c. the number had reached seventy. The end came on 31 December 1540, when the priory and all its riches were surrendered to the king, to be reconstituted in the following May as one of the cathedrals of Reformation England, with provision for a dean and twelve prebendaries.

When Bishop William of St Calais of Durham was accused in 1088 of plotting against King William Rufus, he was sent into exile in Normandy for three years. This may have been one of the most fortuitous banishments in the history of English architecture, for during these three years Bishop William had ample opportunity to examine the splendid new churches being built in Normandy, and no doubt he determined that, when he returned to England, he would replace the old Saxon 'White Church' at Durham with something equally splendid. In 1092, a year after his return, the 'White Church' was demolished. On 11 August 1093, the foundations of the new cathedral were laid, and by 1133 the church was complete. Only two major alterations have been made since then: the addition of a galilee at the west end about 1175,

DURHAM: *aerial view from the south showing cathedral and castle*

and the replacement of the east end by the chapel of the nine altars during the 13th c. Neither of these really changes the impression created by the church. Everything that makes Durham what it is dates from 1093–1133.

To many Durham is an architectural landmark because it has the first high rib-vault ever built in Europe, and since rib-vaulting is considered to be one of the hallmarks of Gothic, it is argued that Durham heralded Gothic architecture in Europe. There is considerable justification for this argument. Rib-vaulting not only looks, but is, much lighter than barrel- or groin-vaulting. The thrust of the roof's weight is carried outwards and made to rest on the four corners of the vault rather than being supported by the whole wall, and instead of being confronted by solid masses of masonry the eye is led along slender ribs which emphasise the upward sweep of the elevation rather than the oppressive weight of the roof. Durham was rib-vaulted throughout, the vaulting of the chancel having been completed by 1104. This is thirty years before the first real Gothic buildings in Europe, which are to be found in France, were built. Hence the master-mason who designed Durham (whose name has not survived) was both an architect of vision and a technical innovator of brilliance. Indeed he may be said to have invented the vaulting system which was to revolutionise European architecture. Yet Durham is still a Romanesque building. It is not just the rounded arches of all three stages of the elevation, but the sheer size of everything. The incised patterns on the cylindrical piers, which alternate with compound piers along the nave and chancel, carry the most striking series of designs, the intention of which is clearly to give them the greatest possible prominence. And they are enormous: 27 ft. high and 7 ft. in diameter. To wish to emphasise such solid and massive pieces of masonry was quite alien to the bent of mind of the Gothic architect. So without wishing to detract from the extraordinary achievement of the mason who invented the rib-vault, it cannot be denied that he hardly understood the implications of his invention: the French master-masons of the 1130s and 1140s may have looked to England for the rib-vault, but they were the first men to realize what could be done with it.

The cathedral church consists of a western galilee or Lady Chapel, an aisled nave of eight bays with two western towers, north and south transepts flanking a central crossing tower, and an aisled chancel which was reduced to four bays when the chapel of the nine altars replaced the original apsidal east end during the thirteenth century. From a distance, the towers and the east end give the cathedral a late-medieval look, for although the lower stages of all three towers are Norman, the two western towers were re-modelled in the 13th and 14th cs. (the pierced and battlemented parapets were only added in 1801), and the crossing tower was completely rebuilt in the third quarter of the 15th c. The excellent slender-shafted galilee is in a strange position, since it was more common to add such chapels at the east end. It was the chief contribution of Bishop Hugh de Puiset (1151–95), and was originally begun at the east end. There are two stories told as to why it was moved. The first is that Bishop Hugh was so disgusted at the idea of allowing women to enter the eastern parts of the church that he decided to move his new chapel as far west as possible; the second is that the building was not far advanced when cracks began to appear in the walls; this was interpreted by the monks as a sign that St Cuthbert did not want such a chapel built so close to his shrine, so they promptly abandoned this site and began again at the west end.

Of the main parts of the church enough has been said already; what is important about Durham is the overall impression it creates, not its architectural detail. The north and south windows in the transepts are much later than the masonry of the transepts, which dates from the original building period; the north transept window of six lights in two stages was put in by Bishop Hatfield about 1360, while the south transept's south wall has in its upper stages another six-light window, dating from the second quarter of the 15th c. At the east end of the chancel, immediately behind the high altar, is the Neville screen, given by John, Lord Neville of Raby, about 1380. Made of Caen stone, it was constructed in London and brought by sea to Sunderland. It originally contained 107 alabaster figures, but even without them it is a marvellously delicate and spiky example of late Decorated sculpture in England. Behind the screen is the tomb of St Cuthbert, still on the site of his ancient shrine. Until 1370 it also contained the remains of the Venerable Bede, but in that year they were moved to their present site in the galilee, where they can still be seen.

DURHAM: *interior of the church, from the west*

DURHAM: *St Cuthbert's tomb and the Neville screen, from the east*

Around the tomb of Cuthbert, a white line marks the position of the apse which originally formed the east end of the cathedral. It was to replace this that the chapel of the nine altars, designed by the master mason Richard of Farnham, was erected during the second and third quarters of the 13th c. The idea of an 'eastern transept' containing extra altars for the monks to celebrate mass was all but unique; the only other example, at Fountains Abbey, pre-dates the Durham chapel, so it may be assumed that Fountains is where the monks of Durham got their idea from. It is a beautiful chapel, Durham's contribution to the 'classic century' of Gothic architecture in England, and could hardly provide a more telling contrast to the rest of the cathedral. Here it is all slender grace and height (the floor of the chapel was lowered to provide an effect of greater height). The thinness of the shafts which make up the piers is emphasised by the use of Frosterley marble, while the use of double ribs for the vaulting of the centre bay is another device, first used here at Durham, to emphasise elegant verticals rather than weighty horizontals. The boss in the middle of this vault contains some excellent figure sculpture of the four evangelists. This 13th-c. reconstruction of the east end was also carried into the eastern bay of the chancel, on either side of the high altar; although the stages of the Norman elevation were maintained with admirable fidelity here, the difference is immediately noticeable.

The monastic buildings around the cloister to the south of the church are in general excellently preserved. The cloister arcades were rebuilt in the late 14th and early 15th centuries, although the tracery and the timber ceilings were heavily restored in the late 18th and early 19th cs. respectively. To the south of the transept is a parlour followed by the chapter-house. The latter dates from about 1140 and was rib-vaulted, but in 1796 its east end was pulled down and not re-erected until 1895; the reconstruction is said to be a faithful copy of the original. The next room in the east range was used as a prison for monks who had committed minor offences. Turning east from the south end of the east range is the modern Deanery. Originally built during the 1070s to serve as the monks' dorter, it incorporates, along with the undercroft of the south range, the earliest surviving work at Durham. Its upper stages were extensively remodelled in 1476, by which time it was already being used as the Prior's Lodging. Attached to its south-east corner is a beautiful little chapel dating from the early 13th century.

On the first floor of the south range is the Cathedral Library, formerly the monastic frater, in

DURHAM: *St Cuthbert's coffin*

its usual position. The west end of this building, known as the 'Covey', connects with the kitchen to the south of it, a remarkable example of 14th c. domestic architecture. It was designed by John Lewyn and built between 1366 and 1370, and is basically square but made octagonal by the insertion of a large fireplace in each corner. The shape of the building is reflected in the octagonal central area of the vault which carries the louvre, an effect obtained by a remarkable and original vaulting system involving eight intersecting ribs. On the first floor of the west claustral range is the Cathedral Museum, which houses a fine collection of manuscripts and other objects, including St Cuthbert's coffin. Originally it was the dorter, built around 1400 in a most unusual position; its original timber roof is still *in situ*. The north end of this building was once a small monastic treasury, while the monks' rere-dorter runs west from a position close to its south end. The undercroft of the west range is earlier than its first floor, dating probably from the 13th c.

During the centuries, Durham has suffered the same vicissitudes of fortune as most of our medieval cathedrals. After the Battle of Dunbar in 1650, for instance, ten thousand Scottish prisoners were herded down to Durham and four thousand of them were shut up by Cromwell's victorious forces in the cathedral. Being allowed no coal, they broke up the choir stalls and any other woodwork which they could find and used them to make a huge fire to warm themselves; only the clock case was preserved because it had a Scottish thistle carved on it. During the 18th and 19th cs., the cathedral underwent alterations at the hands of well-intentioned Gothic revivalists which have done little to enhance its appearance. The screen between the crossing and the quire, for instance, was erected in the 1870s, by Sir Gilbert Scott, and although Scott is deservedly famous for some of his restorations, it is hard to imagine a screen less in sympathy with the rest of the church. Yet so much that is original has survived at Durham that it continues to be one of the essential stopping-points for anyone interested in medieval churches or monasteries. The cathedral priory was one of the largest and richest monasteries of England; so if the monastic buildings have been remodelled and re-used to the extent that it is difficult for the modern visitor to imagine monastic life here, they still have the grandeur appropriate to one of the greatest of medieval religious houses. As for the church itself, it is one of the truly great products of medieval architecture, a building which revolutionised construction methods not only in England, but throughout Europe.

217

Easby Abbey

ORDER: Premonstratensian canons
COUNTY: North Yorkshire
ROUTE: Off B6271, 1 mile ESE of Richmond.
OS REF: 92:1800

The Premonstratensian Abbey of St Agatha juxta Richmond, or Easby Abbey, was founded in 1151 by Roald, Constable of Richmond, and its history was singularly uneventful. In the 14th c. it suffered considerably, not only from Scottish raiding parties, but from English soldiers too. In 1346 the English army, billeted on the abbey on their way north to the Battle of Neville's Cross against the Scots, caused severe damage at Easby. Soon after this, the patronage of the abbey was acquired by the Scroope family of Bolton, and it was Richard Lord Scroope who, in 1392–3, increased the abbey's endowments to allow it to accommodate ten more canons and founded a hospital attached to the abbey to support twenty-two poor men. Easby had originally been founded for thirteen canons, which by 1380 had increased to nineteen, so with the addition of ten in 1392 the number was close to thirty. By 1488 it had dropped to twenty-two, and by 1535 to seventeen and the abbot. Easby was said to have resisted suppression in 1536, which is probably why none of the canons apart from the Abbot, Robert Bampton, received a pension when the house was eventually dissolved in 1537.

If the abbey's history lacks interest, its position on the left bank of the river Swale makes it one of the most picturesque of monastic ruins, and its architecture is full of interest. The siting of the buildings at Easby is unorthodox. Instead of being in its usual place to the north of the monastic complex, the church is set in the middle of the conventual buildings, with the infirmary range and later abbots' rooms to its north (usually they were east of the east claustral range), and the other buildings to the south of the nave. Moreover, the dorter, usually forming the upper storey of the east range, is here situated along the west range, in a similar position to the dorter at Durham.

Of the church itself little remains. It was built soon after the foundation of the abbey, in the second half of the twelfth century, with a broad aisled nave, north and south transepts each with three eastern chapels, and a short, square-ended

1. NAVE
2. CHANCEL
3. NORTH TRANSEPT
4. SOUTH TRANSEPT
5. CHAPELS
6. SACRISTY
7. CHAPTER-HOUSE
8. CLOISTER
9. EARLY PARLOUR
10. STAIRCASE
11. FRATER
12. KITCHEN
13. BUTTERY, WITH LOFT ABOVE
14. GUEST-HOUSE WITH PRIOR'S SOLAR ABOVE
15. WARMING-HOUSE, WITH DORTER ABOVE
16. UNDERCROFT OF DORTER
17. GUEST'S SOLAR
18. RERE-DORTER
19. GARDEROBE
20. INFIRMARY PASSAGE, WITH ABBOT'S GALLERY ABOVE
21. MISERICORDE, WITH ABBOT'S SOLAR ABOVE
22. INFIRMARY HALL
23. CELLAR, WITH ABBOT'S HALL ABOVE
24. PANTRY, WITH ABBOT'S CHAPEL ABOVE
25. BUTTERY, WITH ABBOT'S CHAPEL ABOVE
26. INFIRMARY KITCHEN
27. INFIRMARER'S LODGING ABOVE
28. EARLY INFIRMARY CHAPEL
29. LATER INFIRMARY CHAPEL

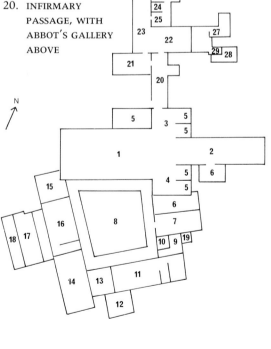

EASBY: *aerial view from the north*

presbytery. Early in the 14th c. the presbytery was lengthened by three bays, a sacristy was added to the south side of the presbytery and quire, and a chapel to the north side of the nave. By tradition this was the chantry-chapel of the Scroopes of Bolton, but in fact it was built before the Scroopes acquired the patronage of the abbey. As completed, the internal length of the church was about 220 ft. Access to the buildings to the north of the church was through a door in the north transept leading to the infirmary passage. On the east side of the passage the remains of a garderobe and, further north, another small room, both 14th c. additions, can be seen. At the north-west end of the passage a door opens into the misericorde, which was built about 1300. At the northern end of the passage is the infirmary hall, originally built as one room in the early 13th c. with a garderobe in its north-eastern corner and the infirmary chapel in its south-eastern corner. In the 15th c. the hall was partitioned and the chapel was rebuilt on a much smaller scale; its altar can still be seen. North of the infirmary hall the walls of the buttery, pantry, and infirmary kitchen still stand, and to its west some of the walls of the cellar. Above all these buildings were the abbot's apartments. His chapel was over the buttery, his hall over the cellar, his solar over the misericorde, and over the infirmary passage was his gallery, partitioned into a bedroom to the south and a private chamber with projecting oratory to the north.

The cloister, which lies to the south of the nave, is irregular in shape, its west walk being 100 feet long, its north walk 98 ft., its south walk 82½ ft., and its east walk 63 ft. The buildings around it date almost exclusively from the early 13th c., although several of them have 15th-c. additions. The east range is not set axially with the south transept of the church, but diverts about five degrees to the east. It consists of a sacristy immediately south of the south transept, into the south wall of which a staircase to an added upper floor was built in the 15th c., the chapter-house, originally vaulted in four bays, and a small parlour. The parlour was considerably altered in the 15th c. when a spiral staircase was added just inside the west wall and a garderobe tower built on to the outside of the east wall. The use of the rooms of the upper storey added in the 15th c. is not certain; those over the south transept and the eastern part of the sacristy were probably the sacrist's lodging and the monastic treasury, while those over the southern rooms may have served as a new abbot's lodging or as a range of small private rooms such as were built in other monasteries at this period.

The most visually impressive building at Easby is the frater, which extended most of the length of the south range of the cloister. The undercroft, dating from the early 13th c., was partitioned into three areas. The three eastern bays gave access through the range between the cloister and the outer court, the three central bays were used for cellarage, and the two western bays provided access from the cloister to the kitchen. The whole area was vaulted in eight double bays from a row of central octagonal piers. The upper half of the building, the frater itself, was rebuilt about 1300. It was entered from the cloister through a staircase in the second bay from the west, and contains a beautiful range of six three-light windows in the south wall, all fully-shafted with trefoiled heads

and geometric tracery. Even more delicate is the lovely east window of five lights, with its two broad twin-lights flanking a slender lancet, and the whole crowned with a circle filled with five trefoils. Only the five eastern bays were used as the frater, the western bays being used as vestibule and cellarer's office, with a loft above it.

To the south of the western end of the frater was the kitchen, of which only the barest remains are visible. The west wall of the frater also formed the east wall of the guest-house, which occupied the southern half of the west claustral range. Little remains of the guest-house apart from some foundation walls and a row of blank arcading along the exterior of the frater wall. It was built on two storeys, the lower storey being the guest's hall, and the upper the prior's solar.

The west claustral range is the most complex and original piece of architecture at Easby. It has an inner and an outer range. The inner range consists of the dorter with undercroft beneath, lying along the west walk of the cloister. The outer range, lying west of the inner range, contains the guests' solar and the rere-dorter. The position of these buildings was determined by the drainage facilities, for the Swale runs alongside the west range and it was easier to cut a drain from it to pass underneath the rere-dorter if the latter was sited at the western edge of the monastic complex. The subvault of the dorter was vaulted in six bays and divided by screen-walls into four rooms. The southern room, by far the narrowest, provided access from the cloister to the lower storey of the guests' solar, the two central rooms were used for cellarage, and the northern room of two bays was the canons' warming-house. Between the guests' hall and the dorter were the day-stairs providing access to the upper storeys of all the buildings in the western range. The doorway from the cloisters to these stairs has a rounded arch and beakhead decoration (i.e., it is pure Romanesque), but it has probably been moved from another part of the monastery buildings.

What makes the planning of this whole range particularly skilful is the different levels on which it was built. Thus the guests' hall, the lowest part of the whole monastic complex, has above it the prior's solar, which is on the same level as the subvault of the dorter, i.e., on ground level relative to the cloister, making the guests' hall effectively a basement. Moreover, the outer half of the west

EASBY: *interior of the frater*

range, that is, the guests' solar and canons' rere-dorter, was built on three storeys, while the dorter range had but two. The lowest storey of the guests' solar was again in effect a basement, being on the same level as the guests' hall, with its two upper storeys corresponding to the two levels of the dorter range. The two lower storeys of the guests' solar were vaulted, the corbels still being visible between rows of blank arcading along the walls. This room was partitioned into a narrow eastern part and a broader west part with a large fireplace in the east wall and a passage from the north-west corner into the lowest storey of the rere-dorter. The second storey of the rere-dorter was reached from the guests' solar, while its top storey was reached from the north end of the dorter. The purpose behind the complexities of the west range was to be able to accommodate the canons and their guests within the same range of buildings while at the same time keeping them separate and giving them access on different storeys to the rere-dorter and through different doorways to the cloister. Although lacking in symmetry and beauty, the west range of Easby was an ingeniously planned and highly functional building.

The abbey precinct was originally reached by a gatehouse which now lies on the other side of the road beyond the parish church, about 100 yards to the south-east of the frater. The gatehouse was rebuilt in the 14th c. and much of it still stands. Besides an outer and inner portal, both round-arched, it has a central doorway divided for pedestrians and horses or carriages. It also had an upper storey, reached by stairs on the exterior of the west wall.

The parish church of St Agatha, set in its churchyard between the gatehouse and the monastic buildings, dates mostly from the 13th c. and is well worth a visit. It contains in particular some fine sculpture, including a cast of the famous Easby Cross, dating from bout 800, the original of which is in the Victoria and Albert Museum in London.

After the Dissolution no attempt seems to have been made to convert any part of the monastic buildings into a private dwelling-house, but the fine series of canopied choir-stalls now in Richmond parish church, with their carved inscription enumerating the ten characteristic breaches of monastic discipline, were removed from Easby Abbey at about this time. The site was excavated in the late 19th c., and is now in the care of English Heritage.

Egglestone Abbey

ORDER: Premonstratensian canons
COUNTY: Durham
ROUTE: Off A66, 1 mile SSE of Barnard Castle.
OS REF: 92:0615

The Premonstratensian Abbey of St Mary and St John the Baptist at Egglestone was founded in the last decade of the 12th c. by Ralph Moulton and colonised from nearby Easby Abbey, the original community probably consisting only of an abbot and three canons. In about 1205, a further grant from Gilbert de Leya enabled another nine canons to join the community, but it is doubtful if there were ever more than 15 canons at Egglestone, and throughout its history its endowment remained inadequate. Indeed, in the early 13th c., there was a move to reduce it to the status of a priory, although it remained an abbey. In the reign of Edward I the canons refused to pay the dues demanded by the mother house of Prémontré in France and thus escaped being taxed as an 'alien priory' during the Hundred Years War. Nevertheless the abbey's financial picture remained grim. In 1323 it was so severely plundered by the Scots that the canons were sent to other houses of the order until the abbey could be repaired, and in 1346 it again suffered considerably when the English army passed through on their way to the Battle of Neville's Cross. There were eleven canons at Egglestone in 1381, and fifteen in 1491, eight of whom were serving churches or chapels outside. It was dissolved on 5 January 1540.

As at several other houses of the Premonstratensian canons, who were neither careful nor systematic builders, the architecture at Egglestone has various irregularities. The monastic buildings are all on the north rather than the south side of the church. The north side of the nave reaches only about two thirds of the way along the south walk of the cloister, the cloister itself is an irregular shape, and the south transept of the church is broader than the north. Some of these peculiarities are, however, explained either by the drainage facilities afforded by the site or as the result of rebuilding.

The church, built soon after the foundation, was considerably smaller than it is now, with a narrower nave and south transept, and a shorter and narrower presbytery. The north and west walls of the nave and the west wall of the north transept are all that remain of this first church. Rebuilding of most of the church began in about 1250 and continued for fifty years. The presbytery, much of which stands close to its original height, was rebuilt first, with twin lancets in the north and south walls and aumbreys in either side wall of the eastern bay, which was used as a sacristy, the high altar being positioned in the second bay. The east window is very strange, five straightforward lights simply separated by mullions which bear no tracery. Possibly this is the result of careful repairs in the 17th c.; otherwise it is mid-13th c. and most unorthodox for its time. The south transept was rebuilt and greatly enlarged about 1275. Most of its west wall, with bar-traceried lancets and picturesque crocketed gables on the buttress at the south-west angle, still stands. The stair-turret in the angle of the transept and the nave's south wall dates from the 15th c.

Finally, about 1300, the nave was broadened by rebuilding its south wall further to the south and adding what now forms its angle with the west wall. The south wall contains a fine range of contemporary windows, four fully-shafted arches each containing three slender stepped lancets which are created by a simple bifurcation of the mullions near the top. Between each window is a buttress, and at ground level in the western bay is a finely-moulded, shafted doorway. This now became the main entrance to the nave, the original doorway in the west front being blocked with masonry, probably as soon as the new one was built. The crossing of the church originally supported a central tower, but it is suggested that this was pulled down after the Dissolution because it spoiled the view from the monastic buildings, some of which were converted into a dwelling-house. In the centre of the crossing can be seen the large table-tomb of Sir Ralph Bowes of Streatlam, missing its top but still bearing some fine ornamental sculpture. Immediately to the west of it are the inscribed tomb of Thomas Rokeby and seven other tombs the occupants of which have not been identified.

Of the claustral buildings little remains except in the east range. The western range was divided into two parts, with the northern, smaller part containing the kitchen, and the southern part probably providing accommodation for guests, and cel-

EGGLESTONE: *aerial view from the west*

larage. Its foundations are clearly laid out, as are those of the north range. This contained the frater on the first floor, while the undercroft was divided into four rooms. The eastern room was the warming-house, while the next three rooms were used for storage. The whole range dates from the earliest period of building at the turn of the 12th and 13th centuries, but the piece of standing masonry adjoining the north wall near to its western end is part of a post-Dissolution structure and not connected with the monastic buildings.

The east range was converted into a dwelling-house by Robert Strelly in the second half of the 16th c., but something of the monastic remains can still be seen. North of the north transept came the chapter-house, which dated from the earliest building period but of which little survives above the foundations, and over the rest of the range came the canons' dorter. The latter was very largely rebuilt by Strelly and now resembles an Elizabethan house more than a medieval monastery. At the end of the east range, stretching beyond the north wall of the frater, the remains of the rere-dorter can still be seen, with its undercroft of three bays. This building again dates from the beginning of the 13th c. although, strangely, the vaulting was inserted later, about 1275, at the same time as the east wall was rebuilt. Within this undercroft are collected several fragments of masonry gathered from around the site and from Rokeby, where pieces of the masonry had been taken at the beginning of the present century when the monastery was partially demolished to provide building materials. Pieces of the cloister arcade and the arcade of the crossing and transepts are here. The first floor of this building was the rere-dorter, although there are also two privy seats on the ground floor. The drain can still be seen running along the north wall of the rere-dorter; it was flushed by a channel cut from Thorsgill Beck, which runs along the foot of the slope on which the abbey was built.

The site of Egglestone Abbey was granted to Robert Strelly in 1548, and the mansion he built passed through various hands until in 1770 it was sold by Sir Thomas Robinson to John Morritt of Rokeby. For a time, the buildings were converted into labourers' cottages until the materials were wanted for building at the beginning of the 20th c. After he had placed the site in the guardianship of the Commissioners of Works in 1925, Major Henry Morritt managed to secure the return of some of the pieces of masonry earlier taken from the site, as well as the tomb of Sir Ralph Bowes, which had been removed to Mortham Wood. The site is now in the care of English Heritage.

EGGLESTONE: *drainage channel*

Ely Cathedral Priory

ORDER: Benedictine monks
COUNTY: Cambridgeshire
ROUTE: In city centre, off the High St.
OS REF: 143:5480

The first religious house at Ely was founded by Etheldred, daughter of a king of the East Angles, in 673. Her first husband, Tonbert, a Gyrvian from the fens of Cambridgeshire, gave her the isle of Ely as her jointure. When he died, she made an illustrious marriage to King Ecgfrith of Northumbria, who gave her Hexham as a jointure. Etheldred now lived, with her husband's consent, under a vow of chastity. She gave St Wilfred the lands for him to found Hexham Abbey. In 672, she became a nun at Coldingham, but when her husband regretted having allowed her to take the vow, and prepared to abduct her, she fled from the nunnery to her native East Anglia. Here she did what Ecgfrith had feared and gave her fenland isle, with its abundant fish, to found an abbey for monks and nuns. She was the first abbess, and after her death in 679, her sister (Sexburga), niece and great-niece were successive abbesses of Ely. The only survival of her church is the base of a stone cross in the south aisle of the nave inscribed *Lucem Tuam Ovino da Deus et Requiem Amen* (God, grant thy light and rest to Ovin. Amen). Ovin, the East Anglian who had been Etheldred's household steward in Northumbria and later became a monk at Lichfield, had come to join Etheldred's community at Ely.

The church built by Etheldred was destroyed by the Danes in 870, although eight priests returned and established a secular college soon afterwards. In 970 this was converted into a Benedictine abbey when Edgar, King of the English, confirmed the whole Isle of Ely to the monks. The relics of St Etheldred, said to be uncorrupted, were placed in a shrine in the church and were reported to possess great powers of healing. This monastery became the headquarters of Hereward the Wake during his legendary resistance to William the Conqueror's Normans in 1070. After Hereward's defeat, William placed a Norman abbot, Simeon, to rule the monastery, and about ten years later began the building programme which created the nucleus of the cathedral we have today. In 1109 Abbot Herve

was made bishop of the new diocese of Ely. With the consequent division of the monastery's estates between bishop and community, Ely was changed from an abbey to a cathedral priory, the bishop ruling the diocese and the prior the monastic community. This meant that Ely, formerly the richest monastery in England after Glastonbury, now became much less wealthy. Yet it remained a large and important house, with seventy-two monks in the early 12th c. Just before the Black Death of 1349 the number stood at fifty-three, but after the plague it dropped to twenty-eight. It rose again to forty-eight in 1379, and then gradually declined to forty-four in 1427, thirty-seven in 1532, and twenty-five on the eve of the Dissolution in 1539. Although the priory was dissolved in that year, Ely was reconstituted in 1541 as one of the cathedrals of Reformation England, with provision for a dean and eight prebendaries.

Although the interior of the nave is still much the same as when built in the 12th c. (it was not completed until 1189), the west front is much altered. The galilee porch to the nave is Early English work, superimposed on the Norman west

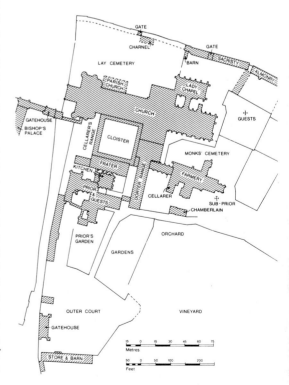

ELY: *the west front*

front by Bishop Eustace in the first quarter of the 13th c., and the northern of the two western transepts has disappeared completely. This happened as early as the 14th c., and has left the west end of Ely looking sadly asymmetrical ever since. If the western transept to the north were as beautiful as that to the south, with its delightful slender octagonal towers, then the original west front must have been an imposing structure. The western tower is Norman, although the topmost stage was not added until the 15th c. The interior of the nave is in twelve bays, and nearly 250 ft. in length. The bays are divided by alternating round and square piers with attached shafts running from ground level to the ceiling, creating an impression similar to that at Norwich. The roof was never vaulted (the present paintings only date from the mid-19th c.), although the aisles are groin-vaulted in the usual Norman way.

Over the crossing is the masterpiece of Ely, the octagon and lantern tower. Both in conception and execution, this is one of the great architectural feats of the middle ages. The need for a new central tower was caused by the collapse in 1322 of the Norman crossing tower, and responsibility for the erection of a new tower was put in the hands of the priory's Sacrist, Alan Walsingham. It was Alan who, in conjunction with his master-mason and with advice from Edward III's carpenter William Hurley, designed and supervised the building of the octagon and lantern. First the crossing area was opened out to form an octagonal space 74 ft. across. Then the area was roofed with timber (it was too broad to make a stone vault feasible), and into the centre of this roof a second octagon was placed— the Lantern. The Lantern itself is formed around eight enormous uprights of oak each a yard thick, which rise straight upwards for 63 ft., supported at two levels by a complicated series of timber struts which reach out to the pillars and walls of the lower octagon. These struts had to support no less than 400 tons of wood and lead, and yet so brilliantly was the whole structure designed that it seems as if these 400 tons simply rest suspended in mid-air, 94 ft. above the crossing floor. At the base of the hood-mould of the north-west arch of the octagon are two portraits carved in stone, of Alan Walsingham and his anonymous master mason. In the same position on the south-east arch are the portraits of their contemporaries, Bishop Hotham and Prior Crauden. These were the men who provided Ely

with one of the most superb examples of engineering genius which have come down to us from the days of Gothic architecture.

The transepts on either side of the octagon have aisles on both the west and east and excellent hammer-beam roofs, brightly painted and with statues of angels forming the hammer-beams, dating from the 15th c. To the north-east of the north transept is the Lady Chapel, almost exactly contemporary with the octagon and lantern and displaying another example of the unsurpassed skill of the architects of Ely at this time. It is a lovely and spacious building, with tall and broad windows, and once contained some excellent sculpture, most of which was destroyed during the Puritan revolution; but the most remarkable feature of it is the lierne star-vault, the widest vault erected in medieval England. It is 46 ft. across and only eighteen inches higher in the centre than at the sides, an extraordinary achievement with stone. The first stone of this chapel was laid by Alan Walsingham in 1321, but a year later he was diverted from this task to the construction of the octagon, and the building was completed by a monk called John Wisbech. It is difficult to believe, however, that the guiding spirit behind this chapel was not in fact Alan himself, who must go down as one of the most visionary English architects of the middle ages. His tomb is at the east end of the nave.

The other major alteration to the church built in the 12th century was the lengthening and re-structuring of the chancel, which occurred during the episcopacy of Hugh Northwold in the second quarter of the 13th c. As originally built, Ely had a relatively short chancel ending in an eastern apse, but by Bishop Hugh's time the number of visitors to the church's shrines had increased so much that access to the tombs in the chancel became difficult, and so it was decided to build a new and more spacious one. The first three bays of the Norman chancel were retained (although they were later to be largely rebuilt by Alan Walsingham when the crossing tower collapsed on them in 1322) and here the choir stalls were placed. A further six bays of classic Early English Gothic were added to the east of them, culminating in a straight east end of three tall lancets surmounted by five stepped lancets at clerestory level. The transformation from nave to chancel is immediately apparent in the latter's multi-ordered arches, slender piers with detached shafts, and ridge-ribbed vault. The aisles have

ELY: *interior of the church, looking west*

ELY: *the octagon and lantern*

simpler quadripartite rib-vaults. The three western bays of the chancel, which form the quire, are, as we see them now, largely the work of Alan Walsingham, for he it was who designed the stalls (which were meant to be placed under the octagon, and were moved to their present position in 1850); he too was responsible for the rebuilding of these three bays in the Decorated style and the erection of the lierne vault above them. Since the 15th c. no major structural alterations have been made, although much of the cathedral's statuary was destroyed after the Dissolution, and in the mid-19th c. Sir Gilbert Scott supervised a general restoration of the structure, which included extensive repairs to the lantern. In 1951 death-watch beetle was discovered to have been at work in the timbers of the roofs (including the struts of the lantern), but prompt action was taken, and the damage repaired.

The outline of the cloister garth, the north walk of which only occupied the eastern two-thirds of the nave's length, is still clear to the south of the nave, but the usual buildings which surrounded it, the chapter-house, dorter, frater and west range, have almost totally vanished. The sumptuous Norman doorway in the cloister's north-west angle is original and is known as the prior's door since it connected the church and the prior's buildings. In the north-east angle is the monks' door, which led from the church to the main monastic buildings. Several of the other monastic buildings survived, although nearly all incorporated in more modern structures.

To the south of the cloister stands the guest-house, from the west end of which runs the Queen's Hall (so-called following a visit by Queen Philippa to Prior Grauden in the 1330s). From its east end runs the prior's lodging, with its excellent Norman undercroft. At the south of the Prior's lodging is the delightful little chapel built by Alan Walsingham for Prior Crauden in 1324. It is still in use and has some of the finest medieval floor tiles in England. West of this is the great gateway, known as the Ely Porta, a structure of remarkable breadth, while to the east, beyond the road known as Oyster Lane, which cuts through the precinct, stand the great infirmary (190 ft. in length) with its ancillary buildings, the cellarer's range, and the house built by Alan Walsingham for himself (presumably after he became prior). Many of these buildings have medieval undercrofts in good preservation, and many other original features such as doors and windows. Most of them are now connected with either the modern administration of the diocese or the King's School (founded by Henry VIII, although there had been a school attached to the monastery since at least the 11th c.; it is known that Edward the Confessor received some of his education here).

Unusually, some of the monastic offices also lay to the north of the church, along the line of the present High Street, notably the almonry, with its excellent undercroft dating from about 1200, and the sacristy adjoining it, built by Alan Walsingham, again for his own use. The remains of two towers to the west of the cathedral are all that is left of the grandiose palace which Bishop Alcock (1486–1501) built for himself and his successors.

Ewenny Priory

ORDER: Benedictine monks
COUNTY: Mid Glamorgan
ROUTE: On B4524, $1\frac{1}{2}$ miles S of Bridgend
OS REF: 170:9177

The early history of Ewenny is shrouded in obscurity. There was clearly a religious foundation of some kind here by the 11th c. at the latest, but it was probably no more than a church, dedicated to St Michael. After the Norman Conquest of Glamorgan, William de Londres, a Norman lord who had established himself at Ogmore, re-built the church at the beginning of the 12th c. and granted it to the Abbey of Gloucester. However, it was not until about 1141 that his son Maurice founded a monastic community to be attached to the church, at the same time confirming the grant to Gloucester Abbey and making his foundation a cell dependent on the Abbey. Originally intended for a prior and twelve monks, it remained throughout its history a small and unimportant house, and after the patronage of the de Londres family dried up with the death of William's last male descendant in the early 13th c., there was little further building at the priory. Although only three monks remained in 1534, Ewenny was surprisingly not suppressed until 1540.

The priory lay in an area studded with early medieval castles, and it is included here not because its church and monastic buildings are well-preserved or of particular interest, but because it is one of the finest examples of a monastery which was almost a fortress in its own right. Of the medieval walls, towers and gatehouses which enclosed the monastic precinct, much still stands; until the 19th c., they were almost complete.

The church consists of a nave of five bays with a north aisle along its four eastern bays, north and south transepts each with two stepped chapels to the east, and a short, square-ended chancel. The nave is the earliest part of the church, built at the beginning of the 12th c., but it has been much altered since the Dissolution and little of the original masonry can be seen. The north aisle and porch were also rebuilt, both in the 16th c. and in more modern times. The nave and aisle still constitute the parish church, as they have since at

EWENNY: *eighteenth-century engraving*

least the 13th c., when the screen wall at the east end of the nave was built to separate the two halves of the church. The transepts and chancel date from the mid-12th c., although the crossing-tower was a later addition which was again re-built after the Dissolution. The north transept and its chapels are totally ruined, although in the north wall of the chancel can be seen a squint, used probably by lepers, giving a view from the inner chapel east of the transept on to the high altar. The chapels of the south transept are also ruined, but the transept itself still stands. The arches which led to the chapels are now blocked, and between them is a pier into which a niche was inserted in the 13th c. The tomb in the south wall also dates from the 13th c. In the south-west corner of the transept is a turret containing the night-stairs which led to the monks' dorter; on the exterior wall of the turret can be seen the blocked doorway through which this passage led. The chancel is of three bays, of which the western two are barrel-vaulted with

central ribs, while the eastern is groin-vaulted with ribs attached to the joints. The piscina and altar, the latter having been reconstructed using the original slab, can still be seen. The eastern part of the church also contains many monuments and other masonry fragments found on the site, some of which date from before the Conquest and several relating to the de Londres family.

The cloister was small, and the buildings around it have almost entirely disappeared. The east range contained the chapter-house and dorter, the south range the frater, and the west range the prior's lodging. Parts of the south and west ranges are incorporated in the modern dwelling-house. The precinct enclosed by the walls measures 570 ft. by 390 ft. Although the walls are battlemented and liberally punctuated with towers and gatehouses, the stretch of wall along the east side must have been highly vulnerable, and it is possible that the fortifications were in fact built to impress rather than to serve a genuinely defensive purpose. Both north and south gatehouses are well-preserved, though the southern one has been considerably

rebuilt in modern times; the low wall which connects them is a modern addition. To the west, the medieval battlemented wall stands to its original height, with the remains of a round tower at its north-western corner. The bases of two rectangular towers can also be seen in the middle of the north wall and at the south-east corner of the precinct, clearly demarcating the lines which the precinct walls followed. A stretch of the east wall also remains, but the eastern parts of both the south and north walls have vanished. The south-east tower, which dates from the mid-12th c., is the earliest of these structures; the north tower of about 1300 is the latest. The gatehouses, built in the late 12th c., were remodelled about 1300.

After the Dissolution, the nave continued in use as the parish church, while the rest of the site was granted to Sir Edward Carne. From the Carnes it passed to Edward Turberville, and it was a descendant of the Turbervilles, Mrs E. M. Edmondes, who in 1949 placed the ruins in the hands of the Ministry of Works. Most of the site is now in the care of Cadw: Welsh Historic Monuments.

Finchale Priory

ORDER: Benedictine monks
COUNTY: Durham
ROUTE: Off A1, four miles NNE of Durham
OS REF: 88:2947

Finchale Priory, the picturesque ruins of which lie a few miles downstream from Durham in a crook of the River Wear, had one of the most bizarre beginnings in monastic history. Its life as a religious house began when St Godric settled there in 1115. Godric, a native of Norfolk, went to sea in 1085 at the age of twenty and soon became a merchant-adventurer with trading interests in countries as far apart as Denmark, Scotland, Italy and the Holy Land. He was probably the 'Guderic, a pirate from the Kingdom of England' (there was often little difference between merchants and pirates at this time) who gave King Baldwin I of Jerusalem a lift from Arsuf to Jaffa in the Holy Land in his boat in 1102. Returning to England via Spain, where he landed and made a pilgrimage to the shrine of St James at Compostela, he made two further journeys to Rome. On the second he took his mother with him. Despite, or perhaps because of, the adventures of his youth, he seems to have had a desire to leave the world and live the life of a hermit. Between 1104 and 1106 he joined a hermit at Walsingham, but began his travels again when the hermit died. While at Walsingham he had been told in a vision that St Cuthbert would find a place for him at Finchale. Ignorant of where Finchale was, but knowing that the body of St Cuthbert was at Durham, he moved there and soon discovered the location of his promised place of retreat. In 1110 Ranulf Flambard, Bishop of Durham, gave him permission to settle at Finchale. For the first five years he seems to have lived on a site about a mile north of the present ruins, but in 1115 he moved south, and in a short time had built his first dwelling-place, a little hut with a roof of sods, with a chapel of St Mary attached to it.

He continued to live here until 1170, when he died at the good age of 105 and his hermitage came into the hands of Durham Cathedral. It continued to be used as a hermitage by two monks sent from Durham until 1196, when it was finally decided to make Finchale into a priory dependent on Durham. At first only temporary buildings were provided, but in 1237 work was begun on the permanent buildings the ruins of which are now visible. Yet Finchale was not destined to be a normal monastic house for long. Some time during the 14th c., it was decided to convert it into a rest-house for the monks of Durham, with a prior and four monks in permanent residence, and further groups of four monks taking it in turns on a rota system to spend three weeks there each year resting. This unusual arrangement continued until the Dissolution which, although the priory's annual income was below £200, did not come to Finchale Priory until 1538.

The church dates from the mid-13th c. and, as originally built, consisted of an aisled nave of five bays; north and south transepts with a Lady Chapel in the south transept and a Chapel of St Godric adjoining the east wall of the north transept; and an aisled, square-ended chancel which was slightly longer than the nave. In the 14th c., however, the aisles on both sides of the

1. NAVE	13. KITCHEN
2. NORTH AISLE	14. RERE-DORTER
3. SOUTH AISLE	15. WARMING-HOUSE
4. NORTH TRANSEPT	16. FRATER
5. SOUTH TRANSEPT	17. HALL (PLAYER
6. CHAPEL OF ST	CHAMBER)
GODRIC	18. PRIOR'S CHAMBER
7. CHANCEL	19. STUDY
8. NIGHT-STAIRS	20. CHAPEL
9. CLOISTER	21. GUEST-HOUSE
10. CHAPTER-HOUSE	22. SITE OF EARLY
11. PARLOUR	MONASTIC
12. LARDER	BUILDINGS

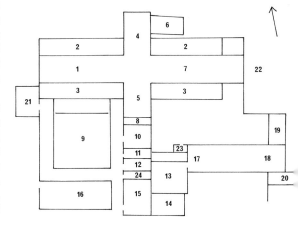

FINCHALE: *aerial view from the north-west*

nave and chancel were removed along with St Godric's chapel, no doubt because the church was far too large for the purposes of the monks residing there and money could thus be saved on repairs. The wall which formed the south aisle of the nave was retained, since it was now converted into the north walk of the cloister. The other three exterior aisle walls were demolished, the arches of the nave and chancel arcades being filled in with masonry below and given tracery above. Throughout the church, more or less, the walls still stand to a uniform height: roughly the height of the aisle arcade. Only the narrow east end and the north wall of the north transept have almost completely disappeared, although the south wall of the nave is rather lower than the other walls. The west door of the church, set in three orders of colonettes, is well preserved; so are some of the capitals of the original arcade piers of the chancel, which exhibit some fine stiff-leaf and fir cone carving.

The central part of the chancel was made into a chapel dedicated to St John the Baptist—it is supposed to be on the spot where Godric erected his own chapel to the Baptist—and on its north side can still be seen Godric's tomb, hewn out of a single piece of rock. It is only just over five feet long, an interesting piece of circumstantial evidence as his contemporary Reginald of Durham relates that Godric was a man of exceptionally small stature. At the south-west corner of the church a two-storeyed building was erected in the 14th c., the ground floor of which was vaulted; probably this was the monastic guest house.

The monastic buildings around the cloister were subject to considerable alterations during the later middle ages, but even when originally built they had differed from the standard monastic plan. No west range was ever built. The south range, which contained the frater on a vaulted undercroft, still stands to a good height. It was built in the early 14th c., but its western half was soon divided into two storeys of chambers over which yet another

235

storey was added in the 15th c., while from the latter part of the century it does not seem that the frater was used as a dining-hall at all, for by then there were so few monks that they all apparently dined in the prior's lodging. There is always this problem with Finchale: the buildings look as if they were meant to accommodate at least twenty monks, but most of the time there was less than half that number there, and to what uses the redundant buildings were put remains a mystery. Possibly they were used to accommodate pilgrims, for Godric's tomb acquired fame as a shrine soon after his death. It is the same with the east range: to the south of the south transept is the chapter-house, with its roof missing but still with its entrance arch with flanking windows and the ring of stone seats around the walls (the prior's seat was under the east window, which was filled in in the 15th c.). South of this there are three narrow rooms and then a larger one with the rere-dorter running off to the east of it at right-angles. In the early days these were presumably the parlour, then perhaps a larder, a passage to the kitchen, and the monks' warming-house, but what happened to them later is impossible to say. Above this whole range came the dorter, but the extent to which it was used is suggested by the fact that the day-stairs to it, originally built in its south-west corner, were blocked in from an early date.

To the north of the rere-dorter, in the angle between it and the east wall of the dorter, was the kitchen, in a most unusual position. Its walls date from the 15th c., so presumably it replaced an earlier kitchen and was built here because by this time the monks had begun to dine in the prior's lodging. Where the earlier kitchen was is not known; there are no foundations to the west of the frater, which was the usual position. Perhaps the

chamber which forms the west end of the south range, and is structurally a part of the same building as the frater, was used.

To the east of the east range comes a long range of two-storeyed buildings known as the prior's lodging. The lower storey is vaulted and was probably used for cellarage, while the upper storey was divided into two roughly equal halves, with the western (slightly smaller) half serving as the hall, and the eastern half as the prior's chamber. From its eastern end two buildings branch off, a chapel to the south and a study to the north. In these buildings was the 'holiday home' for the monks from Durham. The lower part of the western half probably served as a dining-room, for a service hatch leads to it from the adjoining kitchen. The upper half was probably the room known as the 'Player Chamber'—the room reserved for those who were on leave. The whole range was extensively remodelled in the 15th c., and equipped with several fireplaces. Further east are the foundations of the brewhouse and bakehouse, while to the north of the prior's lodging are the low remains of the temporary buildings erected between 1196 and 1237, before the priory's more permanent buildings were laid out. Little can be made out for certain, but they seem to have consisted of a central hall with a solar at its north end and a kitchen and garderobe to the south. Only in a very few monasteries have remains of temporary early buildings survived subsequent rebuilding, and their survival here is a happy accident. It would be interesting to know what St Godric and the other early hermits of Finchale would have thought of their secluded house being used as a retreat hostel for the late medieval monks of Durham.

The site has been fully excavated, and is now in the care of English Heritage.

Fountains Abbey

ORDER: Cistercian monks
COUNTY: North Yorkshire
ROUTE: Off B6265, 4 miles SW of Ripon.
OS REF: 99:2768

The Cistercian Abbey of St Mary *ad fontes* is one of the most famous and beautiful of all monastic ruins. Its fame derives not only from the splendour of its ruins, but also from the fact that it was one of the earliest, largest, and most celebrated of Cistercian foundations in Britain; its foundation, however, was unorthodox and surrounded by controversy.

The history of Fountains Abbey begins at the Benedictine Abbey of St Mary's at York where, in 1132, thirteen of the monks including the prior and the sacrist, both called Richard, reacted against the laxity of monastic life under their aged and ineffective Abbot Geoffrey and asked to be placed under a stricter rule. Archbishop Thurstan of York, a friend of Prior Richard's, was invited to inspect the Abbey, but on his arrival at York on 9 October he was met at the door of the chapter-house and refused entry by Abbot Geoffrey. When the Archbishop countered by laying an interdict on the abbey, there followed a violent scene in which Thurstan, along with Prior Richard and the other rebellious monks, blockaded themselves in the church, eventually making their escape to the Archbishop's palace. After a while one of the original thirteen monks returned to St Mary's, but others joined the little band under Thurstan's protection, and when the Archbishop moved to his estates at Ripon to celebrate Christmas he took them all with him and granted them the piece of land in Skeldale on which they were to build their abbey. There was a large elm tree between the Skell and the steep slopes of the valley, under which the first wooden huts were erected, and there was fresh water in abundance from the springs (*fontes*) on the slopes from which the abbey took its name.

The land was entirely uncultivated and during the first winter the monks suffered considerable hardship and were dependent on what Thurstan continued to give them. They elected ex-prior Richard as their abbot, however, and early in 1133 wrote to St Bernard, Abbot of Clairvaux, asking for permission to join the Cistercian order. This was granted readily, and back with the reply came one of the elder monks of Clairvaux, Geoffrey, to teach the monks of Fountains the Cistercian way of life. Life was hard for the community, and by 1135 the monks were on the point of despair when Hugh, Dean of York, a wealthy and cultured man who had accompanied Thurstan on his visit to St Mary's in October 1132, resigned his deanship and joined the community at Fountains, bringing with him money, lands, and the nucleus of a library. This turned the tide. Further benefactors came forward and the fame of the community soon spread, attracting a flood of new recruits. In 1135–6 work was begun on more permanent buildings, using stone from a local quarry, and despite the early deaths of the first two abbots (Richard died at Rome in 1139, and his successor, the ex-sacrist Richard, died at Clairvaux in 1143), by 1150 Fountains had sent out no less than ninety-one professed monks to colonise six new abbeys in England and one in Norway, Lysa.

It was during the rule of the third abbot, Henry Murdac, an energetic northerner who had followed the call to Clairvaux and become one of Bernard's most trusted disciples, that a grave setback occurred. In 1140 Archbishop Thurstan of York had died, and when in the following year William Fitzherbert, former treasurer of York, was elected in his place, there were strong grounds to suspect irregularity in the election. Although he had powerful political support in the person of Henry of Blois, Bishop of Winchester and younger brother of King Stephen, Fitzherbert was a man of dubious morals. For the next six years considerable pressure was put on the Papacy by the Cistercians—particularly St Bernard and, after 1144, Abbot Henry Murdac—to remove Fitzherbert. When, in early 1147 Pope Eugenius III, himself a Cistercian, finally deposed the Archbishop, Fitzherbert's followers laid the responsibility for the Pope's action on Murdac and raided Fountains, burning what they could and inflicting great damage. It was said that the object of the raid had been the death of the abbot, but Murdac, lying prostrate before the altar, was overlooked, 'for the hand of the Lord protected him'. When a new election was held in July, it was Murdac who became Archbishop of York; by a strange twist of fate, after Murdac's death in 1153, Fitzherbert was re-elected to the see, only to die a year later while celebrating mass, amid rumours of poisoning.

Probably only timber structures and scaffolding were destroyed in the fire, and re-building began at once. The abbey soon expanded, growing in fame as a centre of spiritual zeal, and by the end of the 12th c. there were probably more than fifty monks and at least two hundred lay-brothers. The first half of the 13th century saw much re-building under three abbots: John of York (1203–11), John of Ely (1211–19), and John of Kent (1220–47). During the rule of John of Kent, the famous Chapel of Nine Altars, forming a second transept at the east end of the presbytery, was built. By 1291 the abbey's total revenue was over £356, but in the 14th c. Fountains suffered considerably from Scottish raiding parties who plundered the granges and other outbuildings, and from the Black Death of 1348–9, which brought a sharp drop in the number of lay-brothers. By 1380, there were thirty-four monks and only ten lay-brothers. In the 15th c. Fountains became a mitred abbey, and from 1475 to 1528 there was a last great period of re-building.

1. GALILEE
2. NAVE
3. HUBY'S TOWER
4. NORTH TRANSEPT
5. SOUTH TRANSEPT
6. CHAPELS
7. SACRISTY
8. CHANCEL
9. CHAPEL OF THE NINE ALTARS
10. CLOISTER
11. SLYPE
12. CHAPTER-HOUSE
13. INNER PARLOUR
14. UNDERCROFT OF DORTER
15. DAY-STAIRS
16. FUEL STORE, WITH CHAMBER ABOVE
17. WARMING-HOUSE, WITH MUNIMENT ROOM ABOVE
18. FRATER
19. PULPITUM
20. KITCHEN, WITH ROOM FOR MASTER OF LAY-BROTHERS ABOVE (probable)
21. CELLARS BELOW, WITH LAY-BROTHERS' DORTER ABOVE
22. OUTER PARLOUR
23. LAY-BROTHERS' FRATER BELOW, WITH LAY-BROTHERS' DORTER ABOVE
24. LAY-BROTHERS' RERE-DORTER
25. CELLARER'S OFFICE
26. MONKS' RERE-DORTER
27. ABBOT'S CHAMBER ABOVE
28. PRISON, WITH ABBOT'S HALL ABOVE
29. INFIRMARY PASSAGE
30. CHURCH CHAMBER
31. CHURCH PASSAGE, WITH ABBOT'S GALLERY ABOVE
32. MISERICORDE
33. INFIRMARY HALL
34. INFIRMARY CHAMBERS
35. INFIRMARY CHAPEL
36. INFIRMARY KITCHEN
37. CONDUIT HOUSE

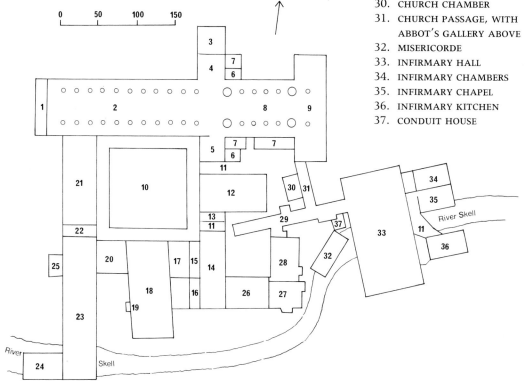

FOUNTAINS: *aerial view from the west*

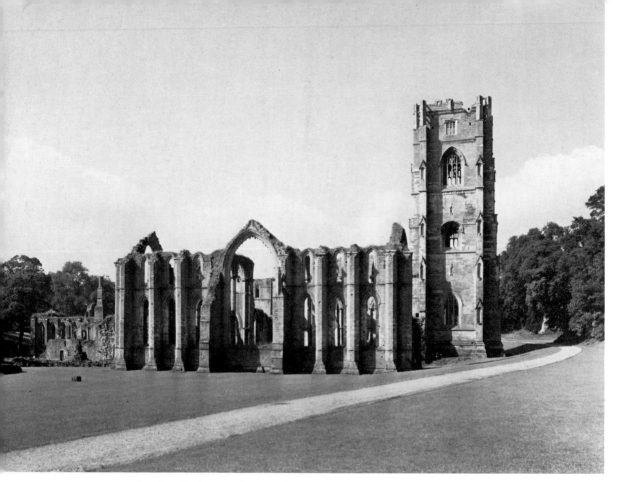

FOUNTAINS: *the Chapel of Nine Altars and Huby's Tower*

It was under Abbot Marmaduke Huby (1494–1526) that the four-storey tower over the northern transept was built. Huby's successor, William Thirsk, was forced to resign the abbacy by Henry VIII's commissioners in 1536 after being accused, spuriously in all probability, of immorality, sacrilege and theft. In the following year, he was declared a traitor and hanged at Tyburn for his part in the Pilgrimage of Grace. He was replaced by Marmaduke Bradley, who, along with the remaining thirty-one monks, peacefully surrendered Fountains Abbey to the King on 26 November 1539. At the Dissolution, the commissioners seized plate, ornaments and vestments to the value of £700, as well as 1,976 horned cattle, 1,146 sheep, 86 horses, 79 swine, and 221 quarters of various grains.

There is so much of architectural beauty at Fountains, the ruins are so noble and in many ways so complete, that it is necessary to be selective. Four features are particularly impressive: the Chapel of Nine Altars at the east end of the presbytery; the tower over the northern transept of the church; the cellarium which extends the whole length of the western range; and the way in which the course of the river Skell was ingeniously incorporated into the southernmost parts of the monastic complex.

The church was long and narrow, extending to over 350 ft. in its final form, with an aisled nave of eleven bays, and north and south transepts with eastern chapels. The chancel originally consisted of only three bays, but was lengthened and beautified by the three Abbots John in the early 13th c. It now has on each side a row of twenty-two trefoiled arches set within five bays and topped by lancet windows, and its eastern end is the Chapel of Nine Altars. The arrangement by which a second transept was built on to the eastern end of a church presbytery is unusual, and finds an English parallel only at Durham. The eastern transept at Durham was almost exactly contemporary with that at Fountains, but it was probably at Fountains that the idea originated. The great east window, surrounded by delicate lancets, the lofty, slender octagonal pillars which were originally embraced by marble shafts, the decorated doorways, and the

FOUNTAINS: *the cellarium*

rows of trefoiled arcading behind the altars at ground level, combine to form one of the architectural splendours of northern England.

Huby's Tower, which rises 170 ft. above the north transept of the church, was built about 1500. Such a construction was forbidden by the original Cistercian statutes, which aimed at simplicity and restraint in building as in all things, and is a most unusual feature in a Cistercian church. Abbot John Darnton (1478–94) had tried to heighten the original, considerably shorter, tower over the crossing of the north and south transepts, but in doing so he strained the foundations on the south side, to which a crack in the wall of the south transept and hastily-constructed buttress against the south-east pier of the crossing bear witness. Huby's tower over the north transept, supported by twin buttresses at every corner and topped by battlements, was a more successful attempt, and does much to enhance the view of Fountains from the east.

The conventual buildings followed the normal Cistercian plan, with the cloister, 125 ft. square, to the south of the nave, and beyond that, reaching almost to the present-day bank of the Skell, the kitchen, warming-house, and well preserved frater, 110 ft. in length. To the east of the cloister are the narrow sacristy-library adjoining the south transept, the chapter-house, where many of the abbots' tombstones can be seen, the basements of the dorter, rere-dorter, and abbot's rooms, and further east still the foundations of the infirmary with its own chapel, kitchen and cellar.

The cellarium in the west range was erected late in the 12th c. It is over 300 ft. long and is double-aisled in twenty-two bays, with nineteen columns supporting ribbed-vaulting; technically and aesthetically it is a masterpiece, and in beautiful condition. The northern end of the vault contained cellarage, while the southern end formed the lay-brothers' frater. The arches in the northern half of the vaults are round-headed, while those in the southern half are pointed, and it is possible that some of the northern end had been built before the fire of 1147.

To the west of the southern half of the cellarium are the remains of the lay-brothers' infirmary and the two guest-houses; here, as in the construction of the monks' infirmary, the frater, and the rere-dorters, it can be seen how skilfully the waters of the Skell were incorporated in the plan of the abbey. In medieval times the river was con-siderably broader than today, and passed under the south end of the frater and of the monks' rere-dorter. It still passes directly under the southern end of the cellarium, and under the middle of both infirmaries, the monks' infirmary being built on four tunnels to channel it. Particularly enterprising is the way in which water from the river was carried through an arch in the west end of the monks' rere-dorter and through a series of four arches to flush the drain, which ran along the south side of the rere-dorter. The incorporation of the river into the site achieved maximum use of the water supply with minimal alteration to the normal Cistercian plan.

After the Dissolution, Fountains was sold by the King to Sir Richard Gresham, who within a year had stripped the church and the cloister of their lead, glass, woodwork, and furniture. In 1597 the abbey and its lands were sold to Sir Stephen Proctor who, in the early 17th c., used much of the stone from the infirmary and its surrounding buildings to build neighbouring Fountains Hall. In 1768 the site was acquired by the Aislabie family, who united it to their adjoining estate of Studley Royal and did much to clean up the site, as did Earl de Grey in the middle of the 19th c. Soon after the Second World War there was a suggestion that the site was to be acquired for a Benedictine com-munity who would rebuild as much as practicable of the ruins, but nothing came of the scheme, and in 1966 the abbey was acquired by the West Riding County Council and placed in the care of the Ministry of Public Buildings and Works. In 1983, the abbey was bought by the National Trust.

Furness Abbey

ORDER: Cistercian (S) monks
COUNTY: Cumbria
ROUTE: Off A590, $1\frac{1}{2}$ miles NNE of Barrow-in-Furness
OS REF: 96:2171

The noble ruins of the Abbey of St Mary at Furness lie barely a mile from the outskirts of Barrow, in a situation which, in medieval times, was far from easy of access. To the north were the undrained swamps and the hills of Lakeland, while the only access from the 'mainland' was over the treacherous sands of Morecambe Bay. Thus Furness conformed admirably to the Cistercian ideal of remoteness.

The house was founded in 1123 by Stephen Count of Blois and later King of England (1135–54), at Tulketh near Preston, but after four years was moved to its present site. Originally a Savignac house, it protested strongly when that order was absorbed by the Cistercians in 1147; the monks' protests were of no avail, however, and Furness duly became Cistercian. Its endowments and privileges were substantial; it owned lands as far away as Ireland and Yorkshire, had the right to elect the Bishop of the Isle of Man, and exploited the iron deposits of the Furness peninsula as well as breeding sheep. Thus throughout the middle ages it remained wealthy and influential.

Being close to the Scottish border, however, it inevitably suffered like so many other northern monasteries at the hands of Scottish raiders. Once, towards the end of its history, the abbey became involved in national affairs: it was at Furness that the pretender Lambert Simnel landed with an army in 1487 in an attempt to depose King Henry VII. His men apparently left the abbey undisturbed before marching south to their own annihilation. At the Dissolution Furness was, after Fountains, the second richest Cistercian house in England. As such it should not have been suppressed in 1537 but some of the monks became involved in the Pilgrimage of Grace during the winter of 1536–7, and this hastened the abbey's end. It was surrendered, under pressure, to the king on 9 April 1537. There were at that time thirty monks at Furness and another two in Lancaster gaol awaiting trial for their part in the Pilgrimage of Grace.

The steep slopes of the ravine in which the abbey was built presented some constructional problems, and the church had to be built on what is almost a north-east to south-west axis. The description which follows will however conform to the practice of earlier writers on the abbey, in treating the orientation of the church as if it were liturgically correct, that is, with the chancel at the east end.

The exterior length of the church including its western tower is some 320 ft. The tower protrudes into the western bay of the nave, following which there are a further nine bays with north and south aisles, transepts with eastern chapels, and a short, square-ended chancel. Only the exterior wall of the nave's south aisle dates from the early 12th c., the time preceding absorption into the Cistercian Order. The Cistercians greatly enlarged the church, and what remains of the nave as well as the western halves of the transepts date from this extension in the second half of the 12th c. These remains rarely rise above the level of low foundation walls. The main surviving parts of the church are the western tower, transepts and chancel. The western tower stands to a good height. It was built immediately after the reconstruction of the east end of the church in the late 15th c. and was directly connected with it, for it was an attempt to build a tower over the crossing which had led to the rebuilding of the chancel after the central tower had collapsed and smashed down into the old chancel. The proximity of the west end to the hillside compelled the intrusion of the tower into the nave, and made access to the church from the west end most inconvenient. Accordingly a staircase was constructed in the second bay of the north aisle, to serve as an entrance to that end of the church.

Before the late 15th-c. reconstruction, the transepts were much narrower, but when they were rebuilt it was decided to add eastern aisles to them. In the north transept the eastern aisle contained three chapels; the eastern aisle of the south transept had one chapel on its south side, while the northern part was converted into a sacristy which connected with a vestry still further east flanking the chancel. The south transept's western wall shows signs of hasty 15th-c. repair work following the collapse of the central tower; the doorway in its south wall was originally reached by a flight of steps which have now

FURNESS: *aerial view from the south-west*

disappeared, and formed the monks' night-stairs to the dorter. The east wall of the chancel contained a great east window which has lost both its head and its tracery, but on the outside its hood moulding, which culminates in the carved heads of a king and queen, can still be seen. The chancel north wall contains two large windows, the south wall two much smaller ones, because of the existence of the vestry behind the lower part of the wall. The sedilia here are among the finest in the country: four seats with a piscina flanked by towel recesses to the east, the whole row surmounted by beautifully carved canopied heads and then a moulded cornice with Tudor flower cresting.

The monastic buildings reflect the wealth of Furness Abbey, and when complete must have been among the finest series of claustral ranges in Britain. The east range was the longest in England. It begins immediately to the south of the south

transept with a row of five superb arches, three larger followed by two smaller, all of four moulded orders, all round-headed, and all excellently preserved. The first and third arches lead into square barrel-vaulted chambers which were used as book cupboards. The central arch of the three leads through a delightful little vestibule, which is vaulted with diagonal as well as ridge ribs and with trefoil-headed blank arcading around the walls, into the chapter-house, one of the glories of Furness. Originally vaulted in twelve bays (four by three) it has now lost its vault but still retains the bases of the slender eight-shafted piers which carried it. The trio of windows in the east wall and the window adjoining them in the north wall are all formed by twin lancets with elaborate paterae in the spandrels. It dates from the second quarter of the 13th c., having been built to replace a much smaller 12th-c. chapter-house. The rest of the east range dates from the same period as the surviving chapter-house. It consists of a narrow parlour, a

244

1. TOWER
2. NAVE
3. NORTH TRANSEPT
4. SOUTH TRANSEPT
5. CHANCEL
6. SEDILIA
7. VESTRY
8. CHAPTER-HOUSE
9. CLOISTER
10. PARLOUR
11. SLYPE
12. UNDERCROFT OF DORTER
13. RERE-DORTER
14. GUEST-HOUSE (LATER)
15. EARLY INFIRMARY, LATER ABBOT'S LODGING

16. LATER INFIRMARY HALL
17. INFIRMARY CHAPEL
18. INFIRMARY KITCHEN
19. WARMING-HOUSE
20. SITE OF FRATER
21. LAY-BROTHERS' FRATER
22. KITCHEN
23. VESTIBULE
24. CELLARS
25. OUTER PARLOUR
26. LAY-BROTHERS' RERE-DORTER
27. PORCH
28. CEMETERY GATE
29. EARLY GUEST-HOUSE (probable)

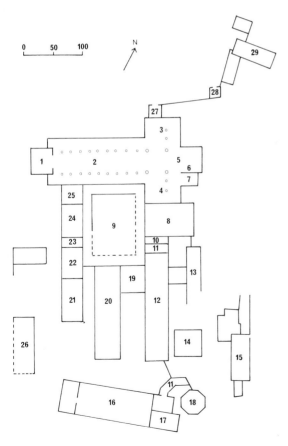

slype leading to the buildings to the east of the range, and then the extraordinarily long undercroft of the dorter, originally rib-vaulted in twelve double bays. Over the whole of this east range ran the monks' dorter; the lancet windows of its east and west walls can be seen towards the north end, but the further south the building goes, the less has survived.

The south range is nowadays no more than building outlines in the turf, but during the centuries of Furness's existence it saw no fewer than four fraters. The first, built by the Savignac monks between 1127 and 1147, was on an east–west axis in the space which now forms the southern part of the cloister, for the cloister was originally square. When a new frater was built in the late 12th c., it was switched to a north–south axis in accordance with the new Cistercian trend. It was not built over the first frater, however; that was simply demolished and left to become part of the cloister, which now became oblong. The new frater was started further to the south and a warming-house was inserted in the space between its east wall and the east range. The third frater, built in the mid-13th c., was an enlargement of the second, making it much longer and a little broader, while the fourth and last, built about 1500 (by which time the number of monks had fallen considerably), was a contraction to a frater of even shorter length than the second. The last frater was built in two storeys, the lower floor being used as a misericorde. One can just make out the lines of parts of the walls of all four buildings in the turf. Of the west range a little more survives, but still not much more than low foundation walls. As usual in Cistercian houses, it was given over largely to the lay-brothers. It is of exceptional length, being vaulted in fifteen double bays. The northern part contained cellarage and an outer parlour, where monks could converse with tradesmen from the world outside. The southern part contained the lay-brothers' dorter on the first floor, with the monastic kitchen and the lay-brothers' frater below. To the south-east of the range are the scanty remains of the lay-brothers' rere-dorter.

The remaining buildings scattered around the site are the monks' rere-dorter, the guest house, the abbot's lodging, and the monks' infirmary. The monks' rere-dorter is to the east of the central part of their dorter, with the stream running through it; little remains of either it or the squarish guest

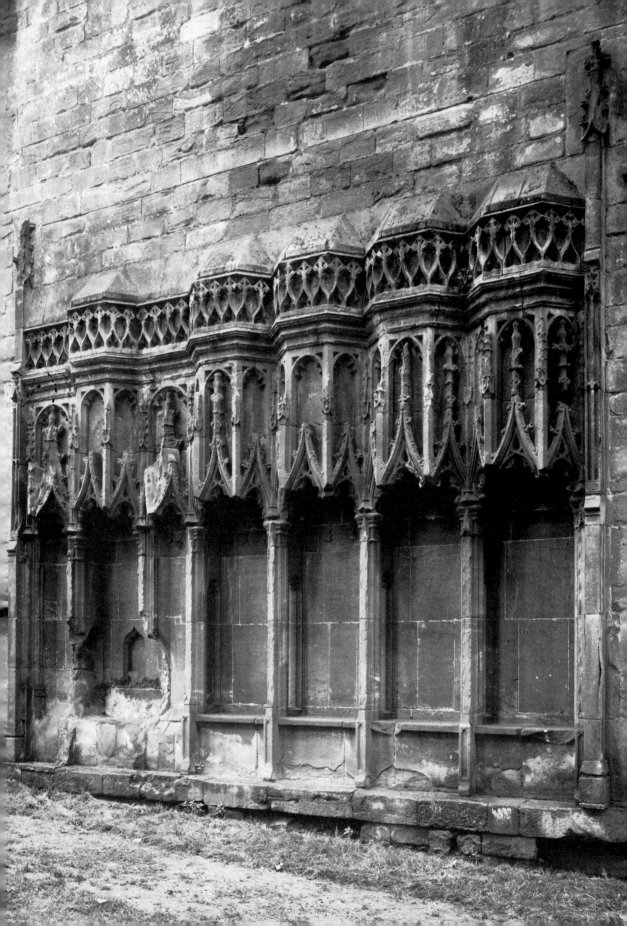

house immediately to the south of it. Further east is the ruin of the abbot's lodging. This was initially built in the mid-13th c. as the monastic infirmary, but after the new infirmary was built in the early 14th c., the old one was adapted to form an abbot's lodging and a second storey was added, the eastern wall of which was built into the solid rock of the hillside. Further buildings, in one of which can be seen a fragment of the abbey's complex drainage system, were added later.

The more substantial remains at the southern end of the site belong to the fourteenth century infirmary. Nothing demonstrates the wealth of Furness Abbey better than this magnificent building, built moreover at a time when the monastery was suffering severely at the hands of the Scots. It consisted mainly of a great hall 126 ft. by 47 ft., with recesses around the walls into which fitted the heads of the beds, a rere-dorter at the west end and, a remarkable luxury, a long covered passageway leading north from a point close to its north-eastern corner to the warming-house, so that the warming-house could continue to be used by the sick or aged monks. In the south wall there is also a large double fireplace, and at the south-east corner of the hall is a doorway leading to the infirmary chapel. This is excellently preserved, vaulted in three bays with diagonal and ridge ribs, and is now a museum. The windows have triangular heads, a most unusual feature, and in the north wall is a fine piscina. The exhibits include 13th- and 14th-c. effigies brought from the church. To the north of the chapel, accessible from the hall, is the buttery of the infirmary, which also retains its double-bayed rib-vault and was connected by a short covered passage to the octagonal kitchen of the infirmary further east. Of this only low walls remain, but part of the refuse disposal system can be distinguished, a chute to the stream running below. The scale on which the whole infirmary complex was planned is impressive; but then everything at Furness was on a grand scale, and the warm reddish tones of the local sandstone in which the monastery was built have left it a beautiful and dignified ruin.

In 1539 the site and some of the abbey's lands were granted to Henry VIII's chief minister Thomas Cromwell, but two years later, after Cromwell's fall, they passed to a local landowner, Sir Thomas Curwen, and from him to his son-in-law John Preston. From the Prestons, the site passed to the Lowthers in the 18th c., and then to the Cavendish family. In 1923 Lord Richard Cavendish placed the abbey in the hands of the Office of Works. It is now in the care of English Heritage.

Glastonbury Abbey

ORDER: Benedictine monks
COUNTY: Somerset
ROUTE: In town centre.
OS REF: 183:5038

Glastonbury is probably the oldest religious house in England. Whether or not Joseph of Arimathea came here a few years after the time of Christ, or King Arthur and Queen Guinivere were buried here, or there was an episcopal see founded here in the 5th c., the ground on which the present ruins stand is one of the most sacred and historic sites in Britain. The earliest definite date relating to a monastery here is 601, in which year a charter is said to have been granted to the house. In 705 it was apparently re-founded by King Ine of Wessex after his conquest of Somerset. Regarding the earlier legends, archaeology has recently established that there was a settlement on this spot as early as the 1st c. A.D., but whether the settlement was connected with a religious foundation is impossible to tell. King Ine (689–728) built a new church here, but it was not until the second quarter of the 10th c. that Glastonbury decisively established itself as one of the greatest of English monasteries. This was due to the appointment in 940 of St Dunstan as abbot. Dunstan ruled the monastery for 16 years before the vicissitudes of ecclesiastical politics drove him into exile. During this time, he introduced the reformed Benedictine rule to Glastonbury and, with the help of his monks and disciples, carried reform to many of the other monastic houses in the south and west of England. Generally regarded as the greatest figure behind the 10th-c. monastic revival, he returned from exile in 957 and three years later was consecrated Archbishop of Canterbury, where he remained until his death in 988.

From now on Glastonbury flourished. Throughout the middle ages it remained the wealthiest monastery in England (although at times its annual income was overtaken by that of Westminster Abbey), and its buildings were commensurate with its wealth: in its final form, the church was over 550 ft. long. There were disasters as well, however: on 26 May 1184 a great fire started and soon spread with devastating effect, until the entire church and monastic buildings were almost totally destroyed.

Rebuilding began at once (Henry II donated large sums towards the reconstruction), and everything that is now visible dates from the late 12th to the 14th cs. Numbers of monks at Glastonbury were not so large as might be expected, considering its wealth: in 1172 there were seventy-two monks, but after the fire the number dropped to forty-nine in 1199, forty-five in 1377, and forty-seven in 1525. Despite its history, the abbey was suppressed in 1539, after the last abbot, Richard Whyting, and two of his monks had been executed on the summit of Glastonbury Tor on 15 November for alleged treason, an act which was, and still is, generally considered to have been one of the most ruthless and unwarranted of the deeds of Henry VIII and Cromwell at this time.

The ruins at Glastonbury are not extensive. For the most part they belong to the church, but the lines of some of the monastic buildings are visible, among them one notable survival, the abbot's kitchen. At the west end of the church stands the shell of the chapel of St Mary, built immediately after the great fire of 1184. It is a delicate and excellently proportioned building of seven bays, in the Transitional style, with the four western bays separated from the three eastern by a fine crossing arch which still stands. Further east, three bays of the south aisle wall stand to a good height, as do two of the piers of the crossing, parts of the north transept, and the south wall of the chancel. The extraordinary length of the church can be ascertained from markings in the turf. The site of the high altar is marked in the turf too, as are the outlines of the Edgar Chapel, an eastern addition erected by Abbot Bere (1493–1524).

The cloister lay to the south of the nave. Only low masonry and the stumps of a few piers survive, but the arrangement seems to have followed the normal plan, with chapter-house and dorter occupying the east range, and the frater along the south range. At the south end of the east range, the lines of the rere-dorter are marked in the ground. The west range has disappeared completely, but to its south-west, beyond the site of the abbot's lodging, stands his kitchen. It is a highly attractive building, with a square outline on top of which an octagonal sloping roof reaches up to a central octagon with two trefoil-headed lights on each face; above this is yet another octagon, much smaller still, with a pointed roof. These octagons form the louvre through which the smoke escaped

GLASTONBURY: *the abbot's kitchen*

after being carried from the four corner fireplaces by a system of flues. The last survival at Glastonbury is the only one which pre-dates the Conquest: just to the west of St Mary's Chapel the outlines of a small rectangular building are marked on the turf: this was the chapel of St John the Baptist, built by St Dunstan in the 950s, soon after he had refounded the Glastonbury community.

Glastonbury Abbey is now owned by English Heritage.

Glenluce Abbey

ORDER: Cistercian monks
COUNTY: Dumfries and Galloway
ROUTE: Off A75, 1½ miles NW of Glenluce.
OS REF: 82:1858

Glenluce Abbey, the seventh of twelve Cistercian foundations in Scotland, was founded by Roland, Lord of Galloway and Constable of Scotland, on 21 January 1192. It was probably a daughter-house of Dundrennan, although it may have been colonised from Melrose. Little is known of its history before the 16th c., although it is said to have been severely damaged during a local rebellion in 1235. In 1329 Robert Bruce visited the abbey, a few months before his death. During the 16th c. the buildings were subjected to considerable destruction by a series of disputes between lords who each claimed the position of commendator. In 1545–6 it was twice invaded, first by the followers of the Earl of Cassilis, and then by those of John Gordon of Lochinvar, both of whom were trying to enforce their claims to the post. In 1560 a protégé of the Earl of Cassilis, Thomas Hay, had to be installed as commendator in the parish church because James Gordon, brother of John, had occupied the abbey and expelled the monks. The struggle for the abbey's lands between the two factions continued after the Reformation, being finally resolved when in 1602 the abbey was erected into a temporal lordship for Laurence Gordon by charter. His victory was modified, however, for most of the abbey's lands had already been alienated to the Earl. In 1619, the abbey was bestowed on the Bishop of Galloway.

The church consisted of an aisled nave, transepts with eastern chapels, and a square-ended chancel. The nave is largely ruined, apart from the lower stages of the west front and the south wall, but parts of the south transept and chancel still stand to a good height. The west front has three doors, which is particularly unusual for a Cistercian church, where the nave was reserved for the lay-brothers and the laity were not allowed to enter.

The south door was bricked up after a fire, probably in the early 16th c. Apart from the chapels of the transepts, which were rib-vaulted in stone, the church was roofed with timber. The south transept has survived in more detail than the other parts of the church, and still has the remains of the monks' night-stair in its south-west corner and the doorway to the sacristy at ground level. Some of the incised tiles with which the floor was covered have been re-set in the chancel. The line of the roof of the east range can be seen against the exterior wall of the south transept.

The monastic buildings lay in their usual position to the south of the church. The best survivals are in the eastern range, which contained the sacristy, then an inner parlour, on the floor of which can be seen more medieval tiles, and then the chapter-house. The chapter-house, which was re-built towards the end of the 15th c., is a well preserved and beautiful building, square and rib-vaulted in four bays from a central pier. It contains some fine late medieval stone-carving and two three-light traceried windows in the east wall; on the floor more medieval tiles have been re-set. To the south of the chapter-house are two barrel-vaulted rooms, one of which was presumably the novices' room. The dorter ran over the east range, and at its south end was the rere-dorter. The water supply system has been partially recovered here and exposed to view, with jointed earthenware pipes and inspection chambers. At the south-east corner of the building is a staircase and garderobe chute, which may have been connected with a vanished abbot's lodging. The remaining monastic buildings at Glenluce were much interfered with at later dates, and only the outlines of the buildings erected by the monks can now be ascertained. These seem to have followed the normal plan, with frater and kitchen in the south range and the lay-brothers' quarters in the west range.

Excavation of the site has revealed a considerable amount of medieval pottery, including high quality French ware suggesting that, as at nearby Dundrennan, the monks of Glenluce bought on an international market. The site is now in the care of the Scottish Development Department.

Gloucester Cathedral

ORDER: Benedictine monks
COUNTY: Gloucestershire
ROUTE: In town centre, between Northgate St and Westage St.
OS REF: 162:8318

Gloucester Cathedral only became a cathedral after the Dissolution. According to legend it was the seat of a bishopric in the 5th and 6th cs., but given the state of Christianity in England before the mission of St Augustine in 597 this is unlikely. A monastery for monks and nuns was founded here between 674 and 681 with the consent of Ethelred, King of Mercia. The founder was the local chieftain Osric, whose sister Cyneburh became the first abbess. Although deserted in the late 8th c., Gloucester was re-founded as a college of secular canons in 823, and then established as a Benedictine monastery by King Cnut in 1022. The monastery was soon burnt down, but a new abbey church was built by Aldred, Bishop of Worcester, in about 1058. At this time the abbey was small and unimportant, but William the Conqueror, recognising the importance of the town because it commanded a ford of the Severn, determined to revive the monastery, and in 1072 he made his chaplain Serlo abbot of Gloucester. For thirty-three years Serlo ruled the monastery, and by the time of his death in 1104 there were one hundred monks at Gloucester, and most of the outline of the church which remains to this day had been built.

Throughout the middle ages, Gloucester was one of the most important and wealthy Benedictine houses in England, retaining around fifty monks until the 15th c. when numbers began to decline, dropping to thirty-six on the eve of the Dissolution. An extensive building programme during the 13th c. led to severe financial difficulties for the abbey, and in 1272 Abbot Reginald Hume had to appeal to the Crown for help. Two factors contributed towards the improvement of the situation in the 14th c. The first was the election in 1284 of John Gamages as abbot, a hard-headed, sheep-rearer who revived the abbey's finances and presided over an intellectual revival at Gloucester (it was during his rule that a Gloucester monk, William Brook, became the first Benedictine to obtain the degree of doctor of theology at Oxford).

The second was the murder of King Edward II at neighbouring Berkeley Castle in 1327. John Gamages' successor, Abbot Thoky, was asked to bury the unfortunate king in his abbey, and after a magnificent funeral attended by a none-too-distressed Queen Isabella (Edward II's wife, the 'she-wolf' of France), and the fourteen-year-old new king Edward III, the murdered king's tomb began to attract pilgrims from all over the country, so that at the end of the 14th c. there was even a move to canonise him. (Ironically, one of the chief advocates of the movement to canonise Edward II was Richard II, who of course was also to suffer deposition and murder in 1399.) It was largely the offerings of these pilgrims which provided the money to finance the great 14th-c. rebuilding programme which has led to Gloucester being called the home of Perpendicular. The abbey was dissolved on 2 January 1540, and was reconstituted as the cathedral of a new diocese (carved out of the diocese of Worcester) in the following year.

The church consists of a nave of nine bays with north and south aisles and a south porch in the second bay from the west; north and south transepts each with eastern chapels; a central

1. NAVE	8. SITE OF DORTER
2. TRANSEPTS	9. INFIRMARY
3. CHANCEL	10. DARK ENTRY
4. LADY CHAPEL	11. SITE OF FRATER
5. CLOISTER	12. SITE OF KITCHEN
6. SLYPE	13. LAVATORIUM
7. CHAPTER-HOUSE	14. PRIOR'S LODGING

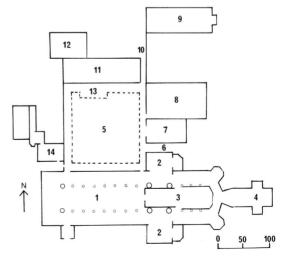

251

crossing tower; and an apsidal chancel with radiating chapels to north and south and an eastern Lady Chapel which is the same length as the rest of the chancel. As we see it now, it is of two periods: Norman and Perpendicular. Apart from the vault of the nave, the 13th-c. restoration was largely superseded by that of the 14th. The two western bays of the nave, with their clustered-shaft piers and lierne-vault, and the west front with its fine perpendicular window, are 15th-c. work, rebuilt after the collapse of the western towers, but the seven eastern bays are clearly Norman and date from the early years of the 12th c. The massive cylindrical piers are reminiscent of Durham as well as nearby Tewkesbury, and create a similar impression of solid weightiness. The triforium is narrow, and must have seemed narrower still before the addition of the Purbeck marble columns beneath the corbels supporting the vault. This vault, which does much to mitigate the solid impression created by the piers, is a 13th-c. addition replacing the timber roof of the Norman church. Its pattern changes after the two eastern bays, with more emphasis being placed on the transverse ridge ribs. According to the abbey chronicler, the monks built this vault themselves, without the help of craftsmen. It has been plausibly suggested that craftsmen called in by the monks may have begun the vault (from the east), but after the completion of two bays there was a disagreement between monks and masons, whereupon the monks decided to finish the work themselves, thus accounting for the variation in style.

The thirteenth century also gave Gloucester a new central tower and Lady Chapel, although both were replaced in the 15th c. The so-called Reliquary in the north transept, which is not *in situ*, is a beautiful piece of early 13th-c. work and may originally have been the porch of the Lady Chapel. The present crossing tower was built in the second half of the 15th c., during the rule of Abbot Seabrook, and probably designed by a monk named Robert Tully, who in 1460 became bishop of St David's. It is 225 ft. high, and one of the finest Perpendicular towers in England, although Tully felt constrained to support it with flying buttresses, since the original Norman crossing piers could not be expected to take its weight. The crypt, entered from the south transept, has short drum-like piers some of which may have been re-used from Bishop Aldred's church of 1058. It is

surrounded by an ambulatory so that it corresponds almost exactly to the plan of the choir above it. It was also in the south transept that the mason who re-structured the presbytery in the 14th c. began to work, and presumably the monks were so delighted with his work there that they then commissioned him to proceed with the presbytery. He was probably Master William Ramsey, who had recently built the new chapter-house at old St Paul's (burnt down in 1666).

The chancel at Gloucester, which was re-structured during the second quarter of the 14th c., marks a turning point in English architectural history. It is the true beginning of that peculiarly English style of Gothic, known as Perpendicular, which came to dominate the architecture of England from the mid 14th c. to the early 16th c. What makes Perpendicular so distinctive are its straight lines, particularly its verticals, but also its horizontals. What makes Gloucester so interesting is that its Perpendicular qualities are transplanted on to a basically Norman ground-plan, for the chancel was never rebuilt. What Ramsey did was to construct a series of stone screens around the inside of the Norman arcade. By pulling down the eastern apse and taking off the roof of the former presbytery he could raise these screens to a height of 92 ft. and cover them with a superb lierne vault, while in place of the apse he designed the great east window, known as the Crécy window, which measures 72 ft. by 38 ft. and contains in its lower tier the coats of arms of local lords who had fought at the Battle of Crécy in 1346. Higher up, the glass depicts the coronation of the Virgin surrounded by the apostles, pairs of male and female saints, abbots of Gloucester and bishops of Worcester. The screen behind the high altar was designed by Sir Gilbert Scott in the mid-nineteenth century, with figure sculpture by Redfern. The aisles, which form an ambulatory around the presbytery are still Norman, although larger windows have been inserted into their outer walls. Note how short and stocky are the Norman arcade piers here as compared to those in the nave. It is not easy to believe that the same architect was responsible for both.

Among the decorations and monuments in the chancel, the most notable are the sedilia on the south side of the high altar, built in the early 16th c., posssibly by Thomas Osborne, mayor of Gloucester; the bosses of angels playing musical instruments, known as the heavenly orchestra,

sculpted on the roof above the high altar; the 13th-c. cross-legged effigy of Robert Curthose, Duke of Normandy, the eldest son of William the Conqueror, who was an early benefactor of the abbey; and the tomb of Edward II in the north aisle of the chancel, with its delicate spiky canopy and excellent alabaster figure. To the east of the presbytery stands the long and narrow Lady Chapel, completed in 1499. Here one can see the culmination of the style begun a few yards to the west some 150 years earlier; the lierne-vaulted roof is the only really solid piece of masonry in the Lady Chapel, the walls being made up of great outline arches almost entirely filled with tall painted windows, rather like King's College Chapel, Cambridge. At its west end a bridge was built to connect the triforia on the north and south of the chancel; the passage and chapel above the bridge are known as the whispering gallery.

As the town cemetery lay to the south of the church, the monastic buildings were built on its north side, and here one comes to another great Gloucester innovation: the fan-vault in the cloisters. The cloisters, which were built in the years 1375–1410, have survived perfectly, although the same cannot be said of many of the surrounding monastic buildings. The fan-vault, the shape of which is self-explanatory, was an exclusively English device, probably invented at Gloucester (the earlier chapter-house at Hereford may have been fan-vaulted, but it is now ruined). Along the south walk of the cloister there are twenty recessed carrels, each of which could be fitted with a wooden desk to allow the monks to read and write; along the western half of the north walk is the exquisite little lavatorium with its own miniature fan-vault and the trough where the monks came to wash their hands before eating in the adjoining frater, the towels being kept in the aumbrey opposite. The arrangement of the buildings around the cloister seems to have followed the normal plan.

To the north of the north transept comes the slype, which was also used as an inner parlour and contains a stove for use in winter, followed by the chapter-house. This dates from the 12th c., and its entrance was not disturbed when the cloisters were rebuilt in the 14th. In its south-west corner, entered from the cloister, is a staircase which apparently led to a library. The western three bays of the chapter-house retain their Norman barrel-vault and blank arcading along the walls, but in the 15th c. the eastern bay was pulled down and replaced with contemporary work; the fine east window, consisting of a series of trefoil-headed lights surmounted by another series of stepped ones, dates from this time. In this room William the Conqueror is supposed to have decreed the compilation of the Domesday book in 1085. The monthly meeting of the Dean and Chapter of the cathedral is still held here.

Of the remaining monastic buildings little need be said. The dorter, frater and west range have almost entirely vanished. Beyond the north end of the east walk is a passageway known as the 'dark cloister' which leads to the infirmary, of which a noble 13th-c. arcade still stands. To the west of this are the Parliament Room, a fine half-timbered building on a 13th-c. undercroft, in which Richard II held a parliament in 1378, and St Mary's Gateway, which was the main gate through which the monastic precinct was entered. Here too is Church House, which was the medieval abbot's lodging, then the prior's lodging, and, after the Dissolution, the house of the dean.

Guisborough Priory

ORDER: Augustinian canons
COUNTY: Cleveland
ROUTE: In town centre.
OS REF: 94:6116

The Augustinian Priory of the Blessed Virgin Mary was founded in the early 12th c. by an ancestor of King Robert Bruce. Some doubt exists about the priory's date of foundation. The chronicler Walter of Hemmingburgh, himself a canon at Guisborough, gave 1129 as the year of foundation, but Pope Calixtus (1119–24) granted the priory a charter confirming its foundation, and thus there can be no doubt that the priory was already in existence by 1124. The accepted date for the foundation is 1119.

The founder of Guisborough was Robert de Brus, a local baron of wealth and influence, and his endowment was generous, ensuring the priory's freedom from financial problems. His brother William became the first Prior of Guisborough, and several of his descendants were buried in the church. They included Robert de Brus VI of Annandale, a claimant for the Scottish throne in 1291–2 and father of a son who went one better and gained the throne, the renowned King Robert Bruce. The priory became rich and was noted for its strict observance of the religious life. The first church was built soon after the foundation, but early in the 13th c. the community decided to rebuild the monastery completely, a task which continued to occupy them throughout the century. On 16 May 1289, however, disaster struck. A plumber, descending from the roof where he had been soldering cracks in the lead over the south transept, placed his iron pans with their burning coals on the dry beams, leaving his assistants to put out the coals. This they neglected to do, and within a few hours molten lead had engulfed the church, burning it to the foundations with the exception of the south aisle wall of the nave and the west end. The west end still shows traces of the fire. The rest of the church was completely rebuilt from the foundations upwards, and to judge from what remains it must have been a masterpiece of the Decorated style.

In the 14th c., owing partly to the massive rebuilding operation necessitated by the fire and partly to the devastating effect of the Scottish raids, Guisborough's financial situation deteriorated. In 1328 it begged to be exempted from the clerical tenth (i.e., a tax of one-tenth on clerical property) voted to the king, and in 1344 it was granted permission to fortify its buildings. In 1380 there were twenty-six canons and two lay-brothers at Guisborough. A few years before the Dissolution Prior James Cockerell, who was later to be executed for his part in the Pilgrimage of Grace, was replaced by Robert Pursglove, reputed to be a king's man, and thus the Dissolution came peacefully to Guisborough. Prior Pursglove and his twenty-four canons signed the deed of surrender on Christmas Eve 1539 and the house was formally dissolved on 3 April 1540.

The ruins of Guisborough Priory are dominated by the east end of the church, built immediately after the fire of 1289. It is backed by large, square, gabled buttresses and stands to its full original height of 97 ft., with broad lancets on either side and an enormous central window measuring 56 ft. by 23 ft. Today the window seems even taller than it was, for in the 19th c. the wall beneath it was knocked out, probably deliberately, to create a vista. Both the triforium and clerestory of the church were combined within a single arch at Guisborough to form a two-storeyed composition with the main arcade. The shafts of the window are slender and well-preserved, with an ornate gable and quadruple turrets. Of the rest of the church little remains except a portion of the south aisle of the nave, a few pier-bases, and fragments of the west end. Originally, the church was over 350 ft. in length.

The ruins to the south of the west end of the nave are all that remain of the conventual buildings, representing the foundations of the outer parlour and the west range, and a short service passage. Further south and to the west is the old monastic dovecot, which is not open to the public, and to the west of the church on the northern side part of the structure of the gateway can be seen, the only visible ruins dating from the first period of building in the 12th c.

After the Dissolution, the site was leased to Dr. Thomas Legh, one of the royal commissioners, and in 1550 it was sold to Sir Thomas Chaloner. In 1932 it was placed in the hands of the Commissioners of Works, and is now in the care of English Heritage.

Hailes Abbey

ORDER: Cistercian monks
COUNTY: Gloucestershire
ROUTE: Off A46, 3 miles NE of Winchcombe.
OS REF: 150:0530

Hailes Abbey was a late Cistercian foundation, and its beginnings were most auspicious. In 1242 Richard, Earl of Cornwall, brother of King Henry III and later to be crowned King of the Romans, narrowly escaped shipwreck at sea, and vowed that in thanksgiving he would found a monastery. Four years later his brother the king granted him the manor of Hailes, and on 17 July 1246 Richard fulfilled his vow by bringing ten monks and twenty lay-brothers from the abbey of Beaulieu, which had been founded by his father King John. The consecration, attended by the king and queen, thirteen bishops, and many of the greatest nobles of the realm, took place in 1251 and was one of the great English social occasions of the time.

In 1270 Richard's son, Edmund, presented to the abbey a phial containing some drops of the Holy Blood, which were guaranteed as genuine by the Patriarch of Jerusalem, later to be Pope Urban IV. A new east end and shrine were built to accommodate the relic, and the fame of Hailes soon spread far, attracting pilgrims from Europe as well as England and providing much-needed money in the way of offerings at the shrine. The number of monks may have exceeded thirty before the Black Death; in 1412 it was twenty-two, and in 1535 it was twenty-five. The abbey was surrendered on Christmas Eve 1539, and disillusionment followed hard on the heels of Dissolution, for the phial of Holy Blood was promptly removed to London and subjected to examination, following which the Bishop of Rochester publicly declared that in fact the drops were 'honey clarified and coloured with saffron, as has been evidently proved before His Majesty the King and His Council'. It must be remembered, however, that it was politically important for Henry VIII to do all he could to discredit Roman Catholicism, monasticism and holy relics.

The surroundings and setting at Hailes are beautiful; it lies on the western fringe of the Cotswolds and is surrounded by rows of cypress, yew and chestnut trees forming an outer 'casing' for the lines of the abbey buildings. Of these buildings themselves, though, little survives apart from outlines. The church was more elaborate than earlier Cistercian custom permitted, with an aisled nave of eight bays, north and south transepts each with three eastern chapels, and a chancel of four bays ending in an apse from which projected five radiating chapels. Trees now mark the position of the piers of nave and chancel, and the site of the high altar and shrine behind it are marked. The cloister lay to the south of the church, and around it several arches are set into the low masonry of the walls. To the south of the south transept came the narrow sacristy-cum-library, followed by the chapter-house and then a slype through to the infirmary range. Beyond this was the undercroft of the dorter, with the dorter itself extending over the whole range. The entrance arches to all these survive, standing in a row along the east walk. The chapter house was an oblong building vaulted in nine bays with a rib-vault from four central piers the bases of which can still be seen. Six of the nine bosses from the roof are preserved in the museum. The cinquefoiled head of the arch forming the entrance to the slype has clearly been interfered with at a later date, probably in the 16th c. In the south-east angle of the cloister are the remains of the day-stairs to the dorter.

The south range followed the second stage Cistercian plan, with warming-house, frater on a north-south axis, and kitchen. The entrance arch of the warming-house remains, and in its west wall can be seen the ruined fireplace which gave it its name. On the north side of its north wall, in the cloister walk, can also be seen the arch and trough of the lavatorium, to the west of which is the entrance to the frater; the old arch of this remains, but with a post-Dissolution doorway inserted. From here the frater extended 126 ft. to the south, beyond the present line of trees. On each side of the doorway in the interior wall are recessed cupboards in which the table services were probably kept. The west range contained cellarage and the lay-brothers' quarters, but of this little has survived apart from three bays of the cloister arcade.

To the north of the church, at the point where the modern visitor enters the site, is the museum, containing pieces of masonry and other objects, some of them found during excavations at the abbey. They include life-size models of a Cistercian monk and lay-brother clothed in their habits, an

HAILES: *view across the cloister, looking east*

impression of the abbey's seal, some glazed armorial tiles, roof-bosses from the vault of the cloister as well as that of the chapter-house, as already mentioned, and various plans and engraved views of the buildings before they were so ruined. In 1543 the site was granted to Henry VIII's sixth and last wife, Katherine Parr; after her death in 1548 it passed to her second husband, Thomas Lord Seymour, but when he was executed in the following year for high treason, it reverted to Katherine's brother, William Parr. It passed through the hands of the Hodgkins, Hoby and Tracy families, and is now in the care of English Heritage.

Haughmond Abbey

ORDER: Augustinian canons
COUNTY: Shropshire
ROUTE: Off B5062, four miles NE of Shrewsbury.
OS REF: 126:5415

The abbey of St John the Evangelist stands against the wooded escarpment known as Haughmond Hill and, largely because of the limit the hill placed on the extension of the buildings to the east, it has one of the most interesting of English monastic plans. The early history of the house is, however, sketchy. It was probably founded in the 1130s, or possibly a little earlier, by William Fitzalan of Clun, and does not seem to have acquired abbatial status until 1155. This fits the archaeological evidence, for the first church built on the site in about 1140 was considerably smaller than the second, built only about thirty or forty years later. So it seems probable that at first Haughmond was only intended to be a small priory, but when it expanded and became an abbey a new and larger church had to be built. Few Augustinian houses could claim abbatial rank, and throughout its history Haughmond was one of its Order's larger and more influential foundations. In the late 12th c. it probably housed twenty-four canons. By 1377 the number had dropped to thirteen, and the same number surrendered the house peacefully to the king on 9 September 1539.

The particular interest of the plan lies in the use of a double-cloister system, the buildings which would normally have been erected to the east of the east range being grouped instead around a second cloister to the south of the first.

At the north end of the site stood the church built in the late 12th c. Little remains of it but low foundation walls, but its plan is clear: it consisted of a long aisleless nave, square-ended chancel, and north and south transepts, each with two eastern chapels which are staggered, a device more often employed with apsidal chapels. Fragments of the foundation walls of the earlier church can be seen running across the south transept. Early in the 14th c. a north aisle and porch were added to the nave, of which the bases of three piers can still be distinguished, but the cloister naturally precluded the possibility of a south aisle. At the south-west corner of the nave a fine late Norman arched doorway leading into the cloister has survived, with foliage moulding and two almost life-size sculptured figures of St Peter and St Paul.

Of the walks of the first cloister, which lies in its usual position to the south of the nave, nothing has survived, but the inner wall of the west range with its strangely large lavatorium is still near-perfect. The range originally had cellarage space, the crenellation at the top of the wall having been

1. NAVE
2. CHANCEL
3. CLOISTER I
4. CELLARIUM
5. LAVATORIUM
6. SLYPE
7. CHAPTER-HOUSE
8. WARMING-HOUSE, WITH DORTER OVER
9. CLOISTER II
10. RERE-DORTER
11. FRATER
12. KITCHENS
13. INFIRMARY
14. ABBOT'S LODGING
15. PANTRY

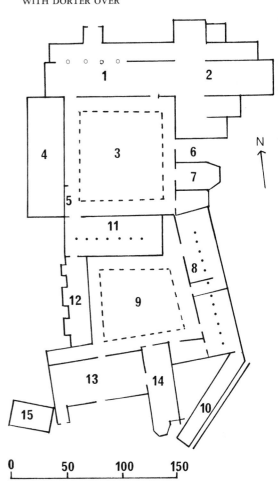

HAUGHMOND: *entrance to the chapter-house*

added in the 16th c. The east range contained a slype immediately to the south of the south transept, and then the chapter-house. The excellent entrance to this chapter-house consists of three arches, stepped and set on three orders of shafts. The outer two arches had twin windows each set on smaller shafts, while the central arch formed the doorway and has a decorated hood-mould. The sculptured figures between the shafts were added in the 14th c. The inside of the chapter-house was converted to form part of a mansion in the 16th c., its east wall being knocked down (it was originally oblong) and replaced with a bay window. It now embodies some architectural fragments dating from the 13th c. and a fine Tudor beamed ceiling. South of the chapter-house the east range continues at an angle slightly to the east, with the warming-house and, above, the dorter. The west wall of this building forms the east range of the second cloister. At its southernmost end the line of the rere-dorter,

the drain of which is clearly visible, returns at an angle towards the south end of the abbot's lodging.

The south range of the first, and north range of the second cloister contained the frater on an undercroft, the latter compensating for the fall of the land to the north. Of this the west and part of the south wall stand close to their original height. In the west range of the second cloister were the kitchens, their massive chimneys buttressing the outer wall. Forming the south range of the second cloister are the two best preserved buildings at Haughmond, the infirmary and abbot's lodging. It is the incorporation of these buildings, normally placed to the south and east of the dorter, into the second cloister, to form its southern range, which makes the Haughmond plan so unusual. The larger of the two buildings, which lies on an east–west axis, was the monastic infirmary, constructed early in the 13th c. It has a fine row of twin-light windows with unusual tracery along the south wall, and an excellent great window, flanked by twin turrets, in the west wall. The doors beneath

HAUGHMOND: *infirmary hall and (right) abbot's lodging*

this window led to the monastic buttery and pantry. It is a far finer infirmary than most monasteries could boast. To the east of it, jutting out from the south-eastern corner of the second cloister on a north–south axis, is the abbot's lodging. It was built in the 13th c. and had a flat south wall with a great window, but later (probably in the late 15th c.), the masonry below this window was knocked out and an oriel window was formed. From the southern end of the site this gives a most unmonastic impression, but there can be little doubt that the alteration was made before the Dissolution. The outer walls of the site are modern, for the precinct walls of the abbey have never been discovered. On the hill to the east of the site,

however, there is a small stone building which was used to protect the sources of the abbey's water supply.

After the Dissolution, Henry VIII granted the site to Sir Edward Lyttelton, from whom it passed into the hands of the Lord Mayor of London, Sir Rowland Hill, and then, through Hill's sister, to the Barker family. This family undertook the conversion of the east range and the buildings around the second cloister into a mansion—which was in turn destroyed during the Civil War of the 1640s. In the 18th c. the site passed to the Corbet family. In 1907 it was first excavated (at which time there were still inhabited cottages within the walls of the old frater), and then between 1931 and 1949 it was placed in the guardianship of the Commissioners of Works. The abbey is now in the care of English Heritage.

Inchcolm Abbey

ORDER: Augustinian canons
COUNTY: Fife
ROUTE: By ferry-boat from Aberdour.*
OS REF: 66:1882

The island of Inchcolm was formerly called Emonia. Its name was changed to Inchcholm in accordance with an old tradition that St Columba had stayed on the island during his mission to the Picts; thus it became known as St Columba's Inch (or Island), then Inch Columba, and finally Inchcolm. In the early 12th c. the island was occupied by a solitary hermit, who is said to have entertained King Alexander I and his followers for three days on one occasion when their ship was driven on to his island by a storm. They shared his diet of shellfish and the milk of one cow, and in gratitude the king founded a monastery for Augustinian canons here. This occurred in 1123, although it seems that the foundation of the monastery was protracted, and not completed until about 1150. At first a priory, the house was raised to the status of an abbey in 1235. The most memorable abbot of Inchcolm was Walter Bower, who ruled the monastery in the early 15th c. and continued Fordun's Chronicle of Scottish history from the year 1153 to 1437.

Although its isolated position offered some protection in time of war, Inchcolm did not entirely escape the depredations of the English, being sacked in 1335 and 1385, and deserted by the canons in 1421 'for fear of the English'. In 1547 it was occupied by English forces, and in 1548 by French. In the next year James Stewart became commendator, and within another fifteen years, conventual life on the island seems to have ceased. In the Scottish parliament of 1609, it was erected into a temporal lordship for James's son Henry Stewart, who thus became Lord St Colme.

Building at Inchcolm continued in a slow but almost ceaseless progression from the 12th to the 15th cs., entailing several alterations of plan and purpose. The final church is now largely ruined, but the claustral ranges are well preserved and retain their roofs. The original church was small

*Details of ferry times can be obtained from the Custodian (031-221-1332)

and occupied the north walk of the cloister. In the 15th c. a new church was built, to the north-east of the cloister and detached from it, consisting of a western vestibule leading directly into the monastic quire. There were north and south transepts, the south transept being now the only part of the church which stands to any real height, and a short square-ended presbytery. The chancel of the old church was beneath the tower, which was built in the 13th c. and still stands, while the nave of the old church was at first converted into the north walk of the cloister, and then into a cellarium. One of the peculiarities of Incholm is that the cloister walks were not under lean-to roofs abutting the surrounding ranges, but were the ground-floors of the actual ranges themselves. The first floor of the old nave was converted into an abbot's lodging early in the 14th c., and it was here, no doubt, that Abbot Bower wrote his continuation of Fordun's Chronicle. In the 15th c., when the nave of the old church was converted into a cellarium, a new cloister walk was erected along the north side of the garth, with a lean-to roof. The line of the roof can still be seen against the inner wall of the east range.

The claustral ranges are small and, on the whole, austerely built; they give an impression, perhaps better than at any other monastery, of how dark and claustrophobic monastic life could be. The one exception to the architectural simplicity is the chapter-house, built in the 13th c., before the main ranges of the cloister. Over it, in the 14th c., was built the warming-house, in a highly unusual position. The chapter-house is octagonal, with ribs springing from slender wall-shafts and meeting in the middle, where a carved boss is pierced by a circular hole through which a lantern could be raised or lowered between it and the warming-house. The only other octagonal chapter-house in Scotland is at Elgin Cathedral, which was not monastic. The warming-house was reached from a flight of steps from the dorter; it has a fireplace in the north wall. Allowing for the peculiarity of having the cloister walks along the ground floor of the ranges, the remaining monastic buildings at Inchcolm were arranged in accordance with the usual practice. The east range contained the dorter, the south range contained the frater with the kitchen at its west end, and the west range contained the guest house. All these buildings are still roofed, and many details such as the frater pulpitum, the service door from frater to kitchen,

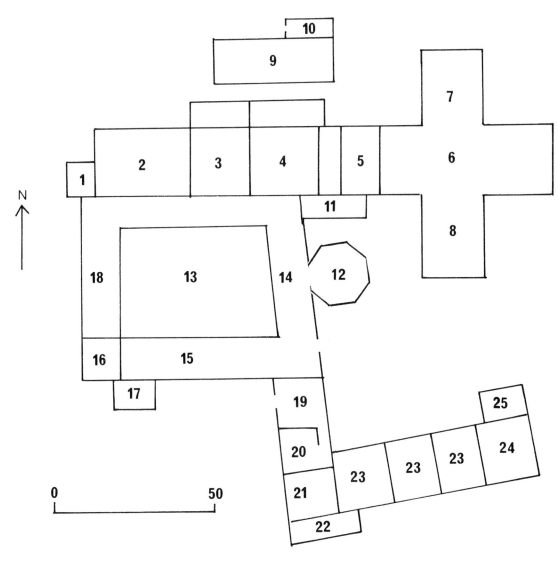

1. LOBBY
2. NAVE OF OLD CHURCH, WITH ABBOT'S CHAMBER ABOVE
3. CHANCEL OF OLD CHURCH, WITH TOWER ABOVE
4. COURTYARD
5. VESTIBULE
6. LATER CHURCH
7. NORTH TRANSEPT
8. SOUTH TRANSEPT
9. CHAMBERS
10. SLYPE
11. NIGHT-STAIRS
12. CHAPTER-HOUSE, WITH WARMING-HOUSE ABOVE
13. CLOISTER GARTH
14. EAST CLOISTER WALK, WITH DORTER ABOVE
15. SOUTH CLOISTER WALK, WITH FRATER AND KITCHEN (16) ABOVE
16. KITCHEN (ABOVE CLOISTER WALK)
17. STAIRCASE
18. WEST CLOISTER WALK, WITH GUEST-HOUSE ABOVE
19. VESTIBULE
20. CELLAR, WITH EXTENSION OF DORTER ABOVE
21. SLYPE, WITH RERE-DORTER ABOVE
22. DRAIN
23. CELLARS, WITH INFIRMARY CHAMBERS ABOVE
24. INFIRMARY KITCHEN, WITH INFIRMARY CHAPEL ABOVE
25. OVEN, WITH INFIRMARY CHAMBER ABOVE

INCHCOLM: *general view from the east, showing the octagonal chapter-house and warming-house*

the smoke-hole in the vault of the kitchen, aumbreys, staircases and fireplaces can be seen. These main claustral ranges date from the 14th c. There was an outside staircase to the guest house, so that strangers should not penetrate the seclusion of the cloister.

In the later 14th c. the east range was extended to the south, to provide more dorter space for the canons and a larger rere-dorter (its isolated position probably saved Inchcolm from the worst effects of the Black Death, for it did not suffer the usual drastic fall in numbers in the second half of the 14th century). The extension also brought the rere-dorter closer to the sea, by which its drain was flushed. The sea inshore had probably been silting up so that high tides no longer regularly reached the drain. The sea has continued to recede since then, and only freak tides now enter the later drain. The ground floor of this extension contained cellarage and a passage below the dorter and rere-dorter. The southern part of the east range is ruined, as is the range of buildings reaching east from the rere-dorter. This range was added in the 15th c., and

INCHCOLM: *view of the dorter, across the cloister*

contained the infirmary (with four small chambers and a chapel) on the first floor, and the infirmary kitchen and cellarage space on the ground floor.

In 1581 the abbey was apparently derelict, but soon afterwards it was adapted as a dwelling-house. Alterations were made to the rere-dorter and infirmary wings, and to this period too must be ascribed the ruins to the north of the church. Inchcolm Abbey is now in the care of the Scottish Development Department.

Jedburgh Abbey

ORDER: Augustinian canons
COUNTY: Borders
ROUTE: In town centre, on A68.
OS REF: 74:6520

Jedburgh Abbey was founded in 1138 by King David I of Scots, with the encouragement and probably the help of John, Bishop of Glasgow. Colonised from Beauvais, it was originally a priory, but was raised to the rank of an abbey some time between 1152 and 1154. The church was built during the following century, and must have been complete in all its essentials by 1250. Although never in the first rank of Scottish abbeys, it grew to be a sizeable and relatively wealthy house, and in 1285 was chosen by King Alexander III for his marriage to Jolande de Dreux. It was said that during the marriage ceremony a grisly spectre appeared to foretell disaster; whether the story is true or not, in the following year Alexander died when he rode over a cliff in the dark. He left no son, and Scotland was plunged into a succession crisis which was only eventually resolved after many bloody and destructive years of war with the English.

Standing within a few miles of the border, Jedburgh could not escape involvement in the troubles. In 1296 Edward I stayed at the abbey long enough to secure the appointment of a pro-English abbot, and in 1305 some of the lead was stripped from the roof of the church, by which side is not known. In 1313 several of the canons, fearing retribution for their English sympathies, fled southwards after the Scots had recaptured Rox-burgh Castle, and twelve years later they were still refused permission to return. Some of the other abbots of Jedburgh were less partisan, it seems: it is said that Abbot Kennock 'kept the peace between England and Scotland for ten years by unceasing prayer'. Sadly, Jedburgh was to suffer further. In 1523, and again in 1544, the abbey was burned by English armies, and it is surprising that so much has survived of the church. As late as 1545 there were still eight canons in residence, but conventual life must have been difficult during these upheavals. From the early 16th c. the commendatorship of the abbey was held by the Home family, and in 1606 its lands were combined with those of Coldingham

Priory and erected into a temporal lordship for Alexander, Lord Home, by Act of Parliament.

The church consisted of an aisled nave of nine bays, north and south transepts with apsidal eastern chapels, and a chancel which was aisled for two bays before terminating in an aisleless and square-ended presbytery. The nave is roofless, but stands to its full height from the west gable to the central tower. The west end is Transitional and one of the finest in Scotland. It has an entrance doorway deeply set in a projecting porch, with five orders of shafts and boldly ornamented arches, surmounted by a row of three gablets. Above this is a tier of blank arcading flanking a round-headed window, and above this again the gable itself, clearly re-built at a later date, with a rose window. The nave elevation rests on compound piers, and nowhere is the Transitional nature of the architecture more clearly seen than in the triforium, with its round-headed super-arches enclosing lancets with plate tracery and flanked by slender clustered shafts. The intricacy of the triforium (noticeable particularly from the exterior) makes the clerestory a little disappointing; one might have expected something more ingenious than the simple rhythm of four lancets per bay, two open flanked by two blank. The line of the nave's roof can be seen against the west wall of the central tower, which has lost its spire but otherwise stands to parapet height. It was re-built between 1504 and 1508. The transepts were originally small, projecting only a little way on either side of the nave and chancel. The south transept is now ruined, while the north transept has been re-built and extended in modern times to form a mausoleum and private chapel for the Catholic Ker family, whose head is the Marquess of Lothian.

From the 17th to 19th cs. the nave of the church had been used as a parish church. It was the then Marquis of Lothian, in 1875, who built a new parish church for the people of Jedburgh and did much to clear up and maintain the abbey church when it fell out of parochial use. The east end of the church is considerably ruined, but what survives of the chancel arcade in the two western bays is of extreme interest. The piers are cylindrical and not related in a structural way to the arches of the arcade, being instead carried up to support the arches of the triforium. The floor of the triforium and the arches of the lower arcade are simply bonded into the sides of the piers on corbels and

JEDBURGH: *the west front*

left as if suspended in mid-air. It is an unusual and imaginative variation on the normal three stages of the elevation; although the spirit is still Norman, it anticipates an unquestionably Gothic theme.

The monastic buildings stood to the south of the nave, and although they are all ruined, much foundation masonry remains to show the lay-out of the buildings. The ground falls steeply away to the south to give the site a terraced look, sloping down to the River Jed. The east range contained a slype-cum-parlour, followed by the chapter-house and the warming-house in the dorter undercroft, with the dorter stretching over the range. The square chapter-house was vaulted from a central pier, the base of which remains. The rere-dorter was at the south end of the range. It is along the south range that the ruins are best preserved. Here two undercrofts, parallel to each other, can clearly be seen. The northern, abutting the cloister walk, was the frater, while the southern was probably the infirmary, in an unusual position. At the west end of the range was a group of buildings difficult to identify, but it probably included the kitchen.

There are only scanty remains of the west range, which probably contained cellarage on the ground floor and perhaps the guest-house and abbot's lodging on the first floor. The length of wall reaching south from the west wall of the church represents the exterior wall of the second west range, built when the cloister was enlarged, probably in the 14th c.

The size of the old cloister garth is indicated in an imaginative and pretty way by the lay-out of the flower-beds. The central square of beds shows the first cloister, while the oblong flower-bed to the west shows the line of the west walk of the cloister after it had been extended to the west, when the later west range was built. That the south range was also re-built in the 14th c. suggests that these buildings were seriously damaged during the Scottish War of Independence. The whole site is now cramped by modern development, and outlying buildings which may have survived from the monastery have been buried beneath roads, factories and houses.

At the west end of the church is a small museum displaying fragments of stonework found during excavation. This site is now in the care of the Scottish Development Department.

Jervaulx Abbey

ORDER: Cistercian (S) monks
COUNTY: North Yorkshire
ROUTE: Off A6108 5 miles NW of Masham.
OS REF: 99:1785

The Cistercian Abbey of Jervaulx lies in Wensleydale, in the broad valley of the river Ure, from which it gets its name. The original community began its life in 1145 some fifteen miles up the valley, at Fors near Aysgarth, where Peter de Quinciaco and a small group of Savignac monks, who had been living under the protection of Alan, Earl of Richmond (Quinciaco was a physician of high repute, having saved Alan's life on one occasion), were granted some land by Acarius Fitz-Bardolf, Lord of Ravensworth. In 1146 the community was put under the Abbot of Byland, which in 1147, along with the other Savignac houses, was incorporated into the Cistercian order. Although joined in 1150 by nine monks from Byland, they found the site at Fors unattractive and the land unproductive, and in 1156, after several years of hardship during which the community had been partly dispersed, they were granted the new site at Jervaulx by Conan, son of Earl Alan, who had succeeded his father in 1146. Building began immediately and seems to have continued throughout the second half of the 12th c. Although there were later additions, most of the present remains date from the original building programme. In 1380 there were sixteen monks and two lay-brothers. In 1409 it became a mitred abbey.

Jervaulx escaped suppression in 1536, but unfortunately the last abbot, Adam Sedbergh, became implicated in the Pilgrimage of Grace, and as a result the abbey was forfeited. It seems that Abbot Sedbergh was unlucky. A group of rebels came to the abbey demanding that he should lead them, but he fled into hiding on Witton Fell for four days, declaring that rebellion was not a seemly occupation for monks. Eventually he took refuge with Lord Scrope at Barnard Castle, but after the suppression of the revolt Henry VIII and his agents removed him to the Tower of London and, deciding that he had been implicated in the rising, accorded him a traitor's death at Tyburn. The main witness against Sedbergh was one of his own former monks, Ninian Staveley, who had taken an active part in the revolt. When captured, Staveley turned informer in an attempt to save his own skin. In one of the rooms of the Beauchamp Tower, in the Tower of London, is the scribbled inscription *Adam Sedbar Abbas Jorvall 1537*, a sad reminder of one of many undeserved fates in those stormy years. As a result of its abbot's 'treason', Jervaulx was suppressed in the summer of 1537, the monks turned out without pensions, and the buildings were dismantled and blown up. From the sale of effects in 1537–8, the crown received about £1,300.

The outlines of the monastic plan at Jervaulx are still clearly visible, and several walls stand to a considerable height. The church was 264 ft. long, with aisled nave, north and south transepts with eastern chapels, and a relatively short, square-ended presbytery with aisles and five chapels against the east wall. Under the crossing is a mutilated effigy dating from the late 13th c., probably of Ralph Fitz-Henry. The cloister is in its usual position south of the nave, and along its eastern range came a narrow vestry followed by the chapter-house, with the shafted Romanesque windows on either side of its main doorway and several of the central octagonal pillars from which it was vaulted still intact. Next came the parlour and a doorway which led to the monks' day-stairs to the dorter. Over all this range, extending 180 ft. south from the south transept, is the dorter. Its western wall stands almost to its full height, with a fine range of early lancets along the upper (dorter) floor of its southern half. The undercroft of the dorter was used originally as the novices' rooms, and was later partitioned to form a series of private rooms. Towards the southern end of the dorter, the walls of the rere-dorter run to the east, with the great drain on its south side still visible.

At right-angles to the south of the rere-dorter is the 15th-c. abbot's lodging, with kitchen and cellarage space below. Further to the east the walls of the monks' infirmary stand quite high; it was vaulted in six bays, with bar tracery dating from the late thirteenth century in the upper windows and the remains of a large fireplace in the lower chamber. To the south of the abbot's lodging is a 14th-c. chapel, and connecting with it to the west, at the south end of the dorter, was the later abbots' dwelling-house.

Of the south range little remains, but it followed the normal later Cistercian plan with, from east to west, warming-house, frater at right-angles to the

JERVAULX: *aerial view from the west*

cloister walk, and monks' kitchen. Connecting the frater and later abbots' dwelling-house at the southern end of the dorter the walls of another 15th-c. addition, the misericorde, still stand. The western range, here, as in most Cistercian houses, given over to the lay-brothers, was large, some 200 ft. long, with the undercroft divided into cellarage in its northern half and the lay-brothers' frater in its southern half, and their dorter stretching along the whole of the upper floor. It is the earliest building surviving at Jervaulx, and was presumably put up first to accommodate the lay-brothers who were building the rest of the abbey. Its north wall, unusually, is detached from the south wall of the nave, the space between being filled with the stairs from the lay-brothers' dorter to the nave. At right-angles to the western range,

about two thirds of the way along it towards the south, the remains of the lay-brothers' rere-dorter project to the west. Through its centre ran the drain, the line of which, if prolonged to the east beneath the western and southern ranges and the monks' dorter, connects with the drain in the monks' rere-dorter. This is the line of the abbey's great drain. North of the lay-brothers' rere-dorter, the barest remains of the guest-house can be discerned, and to the south of it, the remains, again scarcely visible, of the lay-brothers' infirmary.

After the Dissolution, the site was leased to Lancelot Harrison for a term of twenty-one years and then granted to the Earl of Lennox. Early in the 17th c. it passed to Edward Bruce, first Lord Kinloss, but no attempt was made to convert the ruins into a dwelling-house. Early in the 20th c. the site was excavated. It is now scheduled as an Ancient Monument, but remains in private hands.

Kirkham Priory

ORDER: Augustinian canons
COUNTY: North Yorkshire
ROUTE: Off A64, 5 miles SW of Malton.
OS REF: 100:7365

Founded in about 1122 by Walter l'Espec, who was soon to achieve fame as the founder of Rievaulx Abbey, Kirkham Priory was dedicated to the Holy Trinity. Legend has it that l'Espec founded it in memory of his only son, who had died after falling from his horse near this spot. Certainly when the founder died at Rievaulx in 1154, having taken the habit in his later years, he had no direct heir to carry on his name.

Within twenty years of its foundation, Kirkham's life as an Augustinian Priory nearly came to an end. Inspired by the quality of religious life in the newly-founded Cistercian houses of Yorkshire, several of the canons drew up a charter agreeing to allow those who wished to remain Augustinian to leave and found a new monastery at Linton-on-Ouse, taking with them all the chalices, vestments, stained glass and other sumptuous ornaments spurned by the Cistercians, while Kirkham itself would offer its allegiance to Cîteaux, and those canons who wished to remain would join the Cistercian order. Waldef, stepson of the Scottish King David I, friend of St Ailred, and former Prior of Kirkham, had already left the priory to join the community at Rievaulx. What followed is not known, but in the event Kirkham continued to be an Augustinian Priory.

The first church was built in the 12th c., but during the first half of the 13th c. an extensive programme of re-building was undertaken. By about 1300 there were at least twenty-six canons and several lay-brothers. As with so many religious houses, however, the 14th c. was a time of severe financial embarrassment. Building had strained the priory's resources to their limit; the sale of corrodies, which had produced ready cash at the time, now took its toll, and it is said that in 1321 there were no fewer than twenty-two corrodians, while Kirkham's debts stood at over £1,000. By 1380 the number of canons including the prior had fallen to seventeen, and when the Dissolution came to Kirkham on 8 December 1539, there were eighteen canons.

Although the standing remains at Kirkham are scanty, the survival of practically all the foundation walls makes the plan of the priory easily decipherable, and of the more substantial remains there are two gems of 13th-c. architecture. One is the gate-house to the north-west of the church, through which the modern visitor still enters the site. It dates from the late 13th c. and is a splendid example of the Decorated style, with a wide arch set in a crocketed gable reaching up to the second stage. On the left and right of the gable are sculptures of St George and the Dragon, and David and Goliath, and immediately above its apex, a figure of Christ flanked by St Bartholomew and St Philip in trefoiled niches. Six shields can be seen along the centre of the outer façade, two outer at the bottom of the second stage and four inner at the top of the first stage; from left to right, they display the arms of l'Espec, Scroope, Roos, Roos again, Fors, and Fitz-Ralph. Between the five upper gables are four more shields with the arms of Clare, England, Roos and Vaux. Above these, the gate-house is topped by a leaf frieze and a frieze of quatrefoils, and the one buttress which stands to the right of the arch is topped by a pinnacle with gablets. To the left and right of the gateway were buildings, but of these little remains apart from the external walls running into the wall encircling the priory's precinct.

The church as completed in the 13th c. was about 300 ft. long, but the original church, built in the first half of the 12th c., had been much smaller than this. It consisted simply of a nave and square-ended chancel both aisleless, and narrow transepts, about 180 ft. in overall length. In about 1180 this church was rebuilt, with a consequent lengthening of nave and chancel and the addition of western towers, bringing the overall length of the church to 200 ft. or more. The present foundations of the south wall of the nave and part of the south transept date from the early twelfth century, while the north wall, north transept, and remains of the south-western tower date from the 1180 reconstruction. The rebuilding of the early 13th c. started from the eastern end; a quire and presbytery of eight bays, 125 ft. long and aisled, a new east wall with five chapels, and piers at the eastern side of the crossing which were intended for a central tower, were all added. The tower was never built, but in anticipation of it the chapter-house was rebuilt with its west wall 8 ft. to the east of the

KIRKHAM: *the gatehouse, from the west*

line of the cloister, for if the tower had been built the south transept and the east wall of the cloister would have had to be moved eastwards. What remains of the quire and presbytery dates from this 13th-c. reconstruction, apart from the two chapels to the north of the quire and the south of the presbytery, which were 14th-c. additions.

The monastic buildings contain several slight irregularities, notably the angles of the buildings in relation to each other. The cloister was not square, the south walk inclining further to the south at its western end. The chapter-house was set back from the line of the cloister, and the late 13th-c. dorter did not run south at right-angles to the chapter-house but at an angle of about $80°$; moreover, it did not adjoin the south transept, which was unusual, but was reached from the south-east corner of the cloister. At its south end the undercroft of the rere-dorter can be seen, with the drain running along its south side; it was probably used as the novices' infirmary. Again, it is not set exactly at right-angles to the dorter. Stretching in an arc to the east of it were the prior's hall, kitchen and solar, with a misericorde jutting back towards the chapter-house, and beyond them the infirmary and infirmary hall; of these little more than the foundations remains.

The south range of the cloister was entirely taken up with the frater, standing on a vaulted undercroft. It dates from the 13th c., but the doorway from the cloister at the west end is 12th-c., with a fine moulded Romanesque arch set on three orders of shafts with scalloped capitals. This doorway may have been built in a different position and moved when the frater was rebuilt.

Close to it, built into the southern end of the cloister's west wall, is the second of Kirkham's 13th-c. gems, the twin-bayed lavatorium. The lead-lined troughs in which the monks washed their hands before eating have long since disappeared, but the arches still include two beautiful arcades, each consisting of three blank arches and three spheres, the left and right spheres of each bay being cinquefoiled and the centre sphere quatre-foiled. Nothing remains of the cloister's west range, and possibly it was never built. To the south of where it would have stood are the foundations of the kitchen, a 14th-c. building, and the 13th-c. guest-house.

In 1927 the site was placed in the care of H.M. Commissioners of Works, and is now in the care of English Heritage.

273

Kirkstall Abbey

ORDER: Cistercian monks
COUNTY: West Yorkshire
ROUTE: Off A65, 3 miles NW of Leeds city centre.
OS REF: 104:2536

At Kirkstall, a greater proportion of the walls remain standing than at any other Cistercian Abbey in England, and it is probably easier here than at any other ruined monastery to visualise what the abbey must have looked like when it was completed and in use.

Like many other Cistercian abbeys, Kirkstall had a false start before the community settled down on its eventual site. The thirteen monks and ten lay-brothers sent out from Fountains first established themselves under Abbot Alexander at Barnolds-wick, about five miles north of Colne on the Lancashire–Yorkshire border, on land given to them by Henry Lacy, Earl of Lincoln. The land was unproductive, however, and the community was plagued by robbers, so after five years a new site was found at Kirkstall, on land given to the monks by William of Poitou, one of Lacy's vassals. The site had previously been a place of retreat for a group of hermits, some of whom now joined the monastic community.

The monastic buildings, which were erected in the second half of the 12th c. and remained substantially unaltered throughout the abbey's history, were probably built to accommodate about thirty-six monks, as well as a much larger number of lay-brothers. Initially the monks grew rich, largely through skilful management of their flocks of sheep for the expanding wool trade, but by the late thirteenth century the abbey had debts of £5,000 and had to appeal to the King for protection from creditors. He duly appointed Henry of Lincoln as their protector and financial advisor, and by 1301 the abbey was solvent once more and the flocks of sheep had been increased. The Black Death and the changed labour conditions of the 14th c. brought new difficulties, however, and by 1380 there were only seventeen monks and six lay-brothers. Kirkstall was surrendered to the crown on 22 November 1540, at which time there were thirty-one monks.

The church at Kirkstall, unlike some of the earlier Cistercian foundations in England, was not rebuilt in the 13th c., and thus retains the severe simplicity characteristic of the 12th-c. architectural creations of its Order. It was, however, built at a time when new architectural ideas were coming to the fore. While no one would call Kirkstall a Gothic building, it has, on a superficial level, some features which were later to become more closely associated with Gothic than with Anglo-Norman churches. Thus all the constructional arches are pointed, while the windows and doorways retain round-headed arches; the nave piers, while still circular, have convex members and slim shafts attached to them, which visually, if not constructionally, anticipate the clustered-shaft piers of 13th-c. buildings; moreover, the chancel and the aisles of the nave were rib-vaulted, although the nave itself was never vaulted and the transepts were barrel-vaulted.

The internal length of the church is about 220 ft., with a broad aisled nave of eight bays, north and south transepts each with three eastern chapels, and a short, square-ended chancel, the eastern part of the eastern bay of which was used as a vestry. In the centre of the west front is a fine porch, consisting of a round-headed doorway set in five orders of shafts with scalloped capitals. Above the arch is a row of four small blank lancets between five columns with capitals, the whole set in a gable which rests on wall-shafts flanking the porch. The ornamental turrets on each side of the gable are 15th- or early 16th-c. additions, as are the turrets on top of the east front and on the exterior walls of the north and south transepts. The crossing tower, which dominates the view of Kirkstall from afar, is also an early 16th-c. addition, the original crossing tower having reached only as high as the string-course below the large window. The steeple supported by this tower collapsed in 1779, and in 1891 the arcading in the east bay of the south aisle had to be filled in to support what remained of the tower. In the western bay of the north aisle is a curiously-positioned doorway which probably led to a galilee running to the north, a highly unusual feature. The east window of the chancel is a 15th-c. alteration. Its tracery has disappeared, but it originally contained nine lights in two rows.

The monastic buildings conform to the standard Cistercian plan, and with the exception of a few alterations the claustral ranges all date from the original building period in the second half of the 12th c. The east range is remarkably well pre-

KIRKSTALL: *view across the cloisters, with church and (right) entrance to the chapter-house*

served. A few paces to the south of the door from the church into the north-east corner of the cloister is a recess in the wall in which were kept the books which the monks read in the cloister. Behind this, but reached naturally from the south transept rather than the cloister, are the monks' night-stairs from the dorter. After the book-recess comes a small room which was used as a library, and then the chapter-house. This was originally a square room reaching no further to the east than the large pier which now stands in the centre of the room, but in about 1230 it was evidently found that it was too small for the community's needs and the eastern part, rib-vaulted in three narrow bays, was added. The western part of the room is also rib-vaulted, but in four square bays with the ribs springing from a central circular pier. The cloister façade of the chapter-house consists of six round-headed arches, two large central ones of three orders forming the double doorway, and two smaller ones on each side, the inner pair forming windows and the outer pair being left blank. The whole is elaborate and impressive.

South of the chapter-house is the parlour, again rib-vaulted in two bays and with an entrance arch similar to those of the chapter-house, but filled in during the 15th c. to leave only a small doorway with window over. To the south again were the original day-stairs to the dorter, replaced in the 13th-c. by a new flight at the east end of the south range, and beyond them a passage through the range to the buildings further east. Over all these buildings, extending some 170 ft. to the south from the south transept, was the monks' dorter; several of its windows can still be seen in the northern part, but towards the south it becomes pro-gressively more ruined. The undercroft of the southern half of the dorter was originally groin-vaulted in two rows of five bays, with the central bay serving as a passage through it, but what its purpose was is not clear. At its south end is another passage and then the remains of the drain-channel, over which was the rere-dorter.

To the east of the rere-dorter are the remarkably substantial remains of the three-storied abbot's lodging. It dates from the 13th c., and is unusually early for a building of its kind; it was not until the 14th or 15th c. that most Cistercian abbots moved out of the dorter into their private apartments. The staircase to the first floor can still be seen; to its east were the kitchen and cellar, and to the west the living rooms, as can be seen from the remains of the fireplaces. The building running north from the east end of the abbot's lodging was the lodging for visiting abbots, and at its north end was the infirmary complex, connected to the cloister by a passage which passed through the south end of the east claustral range. Neither of these buildings are nearly as well preserved as the abbot's lodging.

Originally the frater was built along the south walk of the cloister on an east–west axis, but it did not remain standing long and was pulled down in the last years of the 12th c. so that the south range could be built according to what had by then become the standard Cistercian plan. The amended south range consisted of, from east to west, the warming-house, the frater on a north–south axis, and the kitchen. The rebuilding led to one or two slight structural inconsistencies: thus the door from the cloister into the frater is not quite in the centre of the frater's north wall. In the 15th c. several additions were made to the south range: a second storey, used as a misericorde, was built over the frater, and a meat kitchen to serve the misericorde was built in between its south end and the rere-dorter. The fireplaces in both the frater and the warming-house are also 15th c. During recent excavation at Kirkstall, a small stone chamber with steps leading down to it and both inlet and outlet pipes was discovered just to the south of the warming-house. This may have been a monastic bath.

The west range, like that at Tintern, was built with its eastern rather than its western wall flush with the west end of the church, and thus projects further to the west than at most Cistercian houses. As usual, it was given over to the lay-brothers; their dorter was on the first floor, with the ground floor containing cellarage in its northern half and the lay-brothers' frater in its southern half. From its south end their rere-dorter projects further to the west; it is the best-preserved part of the range and is now used as the Abbey café. The remains further to the west are those of the former guest house, originally a one-storey building, with the first floor added in the late 13th c. when the existing accommodation was evidently found to be inadequate. The Abbey museum to the north-west of the church incorporates the old monastic gatehouse; it was divided internally into the usual wide arch for horses and carriages and a narrower arch for pedestrians. The museum exhibits much material from recent excavations at Kirkstall.

After the Dissolution the lead was stripped from the roof, the bells were removed to the royal foundry to be recast as cannons, and the site was granted to Thomas Cranmer, Archbishop of Canterbury. He was burnt as a heretic in 1555, during Mary Tudor's reign, and in 1584, after lengthy legal proceedings, the property came into the hands of the Savile family. In 1671 it passed to the Brudenells, Earls of Cardigan. In 1890 the abbey was bought by Colonel J. T. North, who presented it to the Corporation of Leeds. It is now scheduled as an Ancient Monument.

Lanercost Priory

ORDER: Augustinian canons
COUNTY: Cumbria
ROUTE: Off A69, 2 miles NE of Brampton.
OS REF: 86:5563

The priory of St Mary Magdalene at Lanercost was founded in about 1166 by Robert de Vaux, and probably colonised from Pentney. For the first 130 years of its existence the history of the house was uneventful, but the site is only a few hundred yards south of Hadrian's Wall, and during the Scottish wars of the late 13th and 14th cs. Lanercost suffered dreadfully at the hands of raiding parties. The first raid came in 1280, shortly after Edward I and Queen Eleanor had been staying there; this was followed by a more severe raid in 1296, when the cloister was burnt out. In 1306, Edward I lay six months at Lanercost, mortally ill, moving to Burgh on Sands only to die. This was followed by another raid. The worst attack came in 1346, when an armed force under King David II of Scotland wasted the monastery's lands, ransacked the buildings for spoil, and inflicted considerable damage on the church itself. After each raid the priory was re-occupied, and the community was vigorous enough to produce its own chronicle history of England.

In 1409 the canons claimed that they were impoverished, and it may be that they had suffered again from the disturbed state of the northern counties in the reign of Henry IV. Nor was this the end of Lanercost's troubles: after the suppression of the smaller houses (including this priory) in 1536, it seems that some of the canons became involved in the Pilgrimage of Grace, and Henry VIII sent the Duke of Norfolk to Lanercost 'without pitie or circumstance to cause all the canons that be in anywise faultie to be hanged without further delaye'. How many of the canons suffered in this way is not known, but Lanercost was finally suppressed in 1537.

The church is extremely well preserved, for although it was allowed to stand empty for two centuries after the Dissolution, in 1740 the nave was sealed off from the rest of the church at its east end, re-roofed, and once more used as a church; it remains in use to this day, although no attempt has ever been made to restore the crossing, transepts and east end, which still stand roofless. The whole structure consists of a nave of eight bays with a northern aisle, transepts on each side from which projected short aisles to the east, and a four-bayed chancel with a square end. Over the crossing a tower was built and still stands. Of the first church built in the last quarter of the 12th century little remains except a certain amount of the masonry around the south transept. In the 13th c. the entire church was rebuilt, starting from the east end about 1220 and ending with the west front about 1260. It is this church which the visitor to Lanercost sees today.

The west front, the latest part of the church, is the point of entry for the 20th-c. congregation. It consists of a deep and noble archway of four moulded orders below an arcade of trefoil-pointed openings; above the arcade are three tall stepped lancets and in a niche in the gable at the top, an excellent statue of St Mary Magdalene. The north and south sides of the nave are very different: on the south side there is no aisle, and the lower part of the wall is completely bare and windowless; higher up there are four tall lancets, and then at the

1. NAVE	7. WARMING-HOUSE
2. CHANCEL	8. FRATER
3. CLOISTER	9. OUTER PARLOUR
4. SACRISTY	10. CELLARIUM
5. VESTIBULE	11. SLYPES
6. CHAPTER-HOUSE	12. KITCHEN

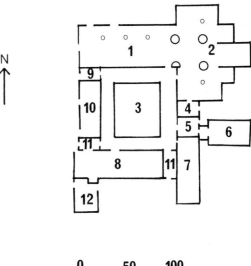

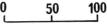

clerestory level eight short lancets. The same row of lancets at clerestory level is repeated on the north side of the nave, but below there is an aisle arcade supported by octagonal piers; towards the east end of the nave, there is a break in the arcade where a length of wall has been inserted, no doubt in the place of the medieval pulpitum. The wall across the east end of the nave dates from the mid-eighteenth century.

The roofless crossing and chancel make a noble ruin. With the exception of a chunk of masonry missing from its west wall, the tower is almost perfect. The pointed crossing arches, of which the arches on the ground level arcade are exact replicas in miniature, soar impressively. The arrangement along the transept walls and the two western bays of the chancel remains almost identical: a lower arcade supported by semi-octagonal and round piers, then a gallery of rounded arches divided into two lights by slender central shafts, then a clerestory with wall-passage (which continues right round the building), with four lancets on each side of the chancel set behind quadruple shafts. The two eastern bays of the chancel are different, with two tall and simple lancets on each side replacing the arcade and gallery. The eastern aisles projecting from the transept each contain two rib-vaulted chapels. In the south wall of the south transept can be seen the doorway which led to the canons' night-stairs from the dorter. The arrangement of the two eastern bays of the chancel is continued into the excellent east end at the lower stages, with three simple lancets, but it changes at the upper stages where there are another three lancets, stepped now, and taller than the lancets in the clerestory around the rest of the building. Even at the east end, however, the wall-passage in the clerestory continues.

Of the monastic buildings, which stood in their usual position south of the church, little remains above ground of the east range, although the layout of the buildings can be made out easily. South of the south transept came a narrow slype or sacristy, then the original chapter-house followed by the undercroft of the dorter; in the 13th c., however, a much larger chapter-house was built just east of the original chapter-house, the foundations of which are still visible. The south range contained the canons' frater, the undercroft of which is excellently preserved. It is nine bays long and rib-vaulted on octagonal piers. The west range stands to a greater height than any of the other buildings except the church, but only because it was converted into a dwelling-house after the Dissolution. The ground floor probably contained cellarage, while on the first floor was the prior's lodging, at the southern end. If the buildings are original, however, the detail is not: the windows and roof are 16th c. The tower which projects from the south end of the range was also a 16th-c. addition. The other monastic buildings have all perished with the exception of the gateway some way to the west of the church, of which the inner arch still stands. On its west side can be seen the springers for the ribs of the vault which once covered the gatehouse ceiling.

After the Dissolution, the site was granted to Sir Thomas Dacre of Naworth, who converted the west claustral range into Dacre Hall. Among the farm buildings around the site can be seen several stones filched from the derelict monastic buildings and re-used. This was a practice apparently indulged in by the canons themselves when they built Lanercost, for in the south-west corner of the cloister there is a stone inscribed: C CASSI PRISCI, which presumably was stolen from the ruin of Hadrian's Wall.

In the mid-20th c. the site passed into the hands of the Ministry of Works, and is now in the care of English Heritage.

Leiston Abbey

ORDER: Premonstratensian canons
COUNTY: Suffolk
ROUTE: On B1122, 4 miles E of Saxmundham.
OS REF: 156:4464

The abbey of the Blessed Virgin Mary at Leiston was founded in 1183 by Ranulf Glanvill, the renowned Chief Justiciar of England in whose name the most famous medieval treatise on the laws of England was written. The original site chosen was about two miles closer to the sea; it was colonised from Welbeck, and was for twenty-six canons. The house's history was uneventful except that the inroads of the sea on the Suffolk coast made the buildings increasingly liable to flooding, and in 1365 the canons obtained a papal licence to rebuild their monastery on a new site further inland. Thus the present ruins date from the late 14th c., although considerable amounts of stone from the old site were used for the new buildings. In 1380 a fire destroyed much of the new abbey, and rebuilding began again.

The buildings are now quite ruined, but many of the walls stand to a considerable height, and the plan of the monastery is clearly recognisable. The church was 168 ft. long, consisting of an aisled nave of five bays, north and south transepts without chapels, and a square-ended chancel flanked by aisles which stopped short of its east end. The remains of the nave have mostly been incorporated into a more modern house, but the transepts and chancel can still be seen. The north chancel aisle was used as a Lady Chapel and has also been incorporated into a post-Dissolution building. There is a large window in the north wall of the north transept, and an even larger one at the east end, but both have now lost their tracery, and the arch of the east window has been broken. In several places, notably on the east crossing piers and the arch into the north chancel aisle, re-used masonry from the first site can be seen.

The cloister lay to the south of the church, with the buildings around it arranged in the usual fashion. The east range included a sacristy-cum-library, followed by the chapter-house, slype, and undercroft of the dorter (used here as a warming-house), with the dorter running over the whole range on the first floor. The west wall of the range

still stands, though not to first-floor height, but of the buildings themselves little can be distinguished. The chapter-house was an oblong building of three bays. At the south end of the range a small building projected to the east, but its purpose is difficult to ascertain; it is too far south of the dorter to be the rere-dorter. The south range was occupied by the frater, apart from a small area in its south-east angle, which contained the monks' day-stairs to the dorter and a narrow slype leading to unidentified buildings, now almost totally vanished, further south. The walls of the frater, especially the west one, which had a large window, still stand at ground-floor level. In the north wall, facing the cloister, the recess for the lavatorium can be seen; at the east end of the south wall another recess marks the position of the pulpitum and its staircase. The west range was used for cellarage on the ground floor, possibly with the abbot's lodging or guest house above.

The site has recently passed into the hands of English Heritage.

1. NAVE
2. CHANCEL
3. SACRISTY
4. VESTRY
5. CLOISTER
6. LIBRARY
7. CHAPTER-HOUSE
8. DAY-STAIRS
9. SLYPES
10. WARMING-HOUSE, WITH DORTER OVER
11. FRATER
12. LAVATORIUM
13. PULPITUM
14. CELLARIUM
15. PORCH

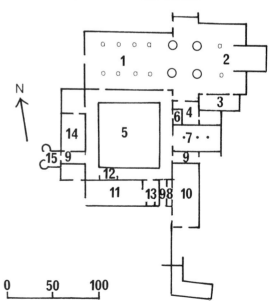

Lilleshall Abbey

ORDER: Augustinian canons
COUNTY: Shropshire
ROUTE: Off A518, 3 miles SSW of Newport.
OS REF: 127:7314

The Augustinian Abbey of Lilleshall was founded in the mid-12th c. for canons of the Arrouasian order (later absorbed by the Augustinians) brought from Dorchester-on-Thames by Philip de Belmeis to Lizard Grange, some three and a half miles south-east of the present site, in about 1143. The community soon moved to Donnington Wood, about a mile from Lilleshall, and by 1148, Philip's brother Richard, dean of St Alkmund's at Shrewsbury, had granted the revenues of St Alkmund's to the canons and provided them with a new house, probably timber-framed, at Lilleshall. Building in stone began at once. There were probably twelve canons and an abbot originally, but the house prospered and this number must have increased and come to include lay-brothers in the 13th c. About 1240 King Henry III was twice entertained at the abbey while on hunting expeditions. After the Black Death numbers dropped, and towards 1400 there were only ten or eleven canons, one of whom, John Mirk, wrote several religious works, and gained the distinction of having one of them printed by William Caxton in 1483 as part of *The Golden Legend*. In 1538 the house was surrendered peacefully, the abbot receiving a pension of £50 and a house, and the other remaining canons being also generously treated.

The church was large by Augustinian standards, measuring 228 ft. in length. The aisleless nave is long and narrow and probably had a western rather than a crossing tower; although not completed until the 13th c., several decades after the building of the chancel, transepts and quire, it was designed to fit in with the original plan, the head of the arch which forms the west door being deliberately semicircular in a fashion by then outdated. More in keeping with 13th-c. architectural trends is the fine Gothic-arched window which can be seen in the eastern bay of the nave's north wall. The transepts each had two eastern chapels, the inner chapel on each side originally reaching along the presbytery walls to almost twice the length of the outer chapel; the north transept has largely disappeared, but the walls of the southern one are substantially complete, as are those of the presbytery. This consists of four bays and has a fine late Geometric window in the east end, dating from the early fourteenth century. On each side of the presbytery is a tomb-recess.

Most remarkable is the processional doorway from the south-eastern corner of the nave into the cloister. The shafts of two orders are ornately decorated, the outer order with a spiral motif, and the Romanesque arch and tympanum are zigzagged, the latter resting on a plain segmental lintel. There are other similar doorways at Lilleshall, notably the two leading from the cloister into the rooms of the south range, but they are not nearly so elaborately decorated. A little to the south of the doorway, a twin-compartmented recess which used to be used as a book-locker is set in the east wall. Along the cloister east range beyond the transept are the sacristy, slype, and chapter-house in that order, with their walls still standing. In the chapter-house are the tombstones of several of Lilleshall's abbots. Stretching south beyond the chapter-house was the unusually long dorter, now completely vanished. The eastern end of the south range contains a narrow passage leading to what was presumably a court beyond. The rest of the south range was originally one large chamber containing the frater, which in the 14th c. was divided into two almost equal halves, the west end retained as a frater and the east used as a warming-house. Of the west range, which included the lay-brothers' and other servants' quarters, very little remains.

At the Dissolution the site passed into the hands of the Cavendish family, and it is said that the carved stalls now in Wolverhampton parish church were removed there from Lilleshall at that time. In 1540 the abbey was sold to James Leveson of Wolverhampton, whose descendants kept possession of it until the 20th c. One of them, Sir Richard Leveson, was a royalist during the Civil War, and in 1645 he fortified the abbey against the parliamentary troops and defended it staunchly for several weeks before an entry was forced through the north transept. No doubt this is why so little of that transept remains, and probably much damage was inflicted on the rest of the buildings at the same time. In 1950 the site was placed in the care of the Ministry of Public Buildings and Works. It is now in the care of English Heritage.

Lindisfarne Priory

ORDER: Benedictine monks
COUNTY: Northumberland
ROUTE: Turn east of A1 $1\frac{1}{2}$ miles S of Haggerston; the causeway to Holy Island is only accessible at low tide.
OS REF: 75:1241

Its remote and vulnerable situation and its deep-rooted religious associations have always added an aura of romanticism to Lindisfarne Priory. In 634, less than forty years after St Augustine landed in Kent to undertake the conversion of the English people, the Christian King Oswald of Northumbria settled a community of Celtic monks from Iona on the island of Lindisfarne. Under their bishop and abbot, St Aidan, they set out to convert the pagans of northern Northumbria. The first monastery at Lindisfarne, which was on the Irish pattern, was ruled by St Cuthbert in the late 7th c. and probably produced the magnificent Lindisfarne gospels now in the British Museum. Not surprisingly, it suffered repeatedly from Danish raids (the first raid on Lindisfarne, on 7 June 793, was also the first Danish raid on the English coast), and after eighty years of such marauding the monks abandoned the island in 875 and made their way first to Chester-le-Street and finally to Durham, carrying with them the sacred relics of St Cuthbert.

In 1083 the Norman bishop of Durham, William of St Calais, decided to refound the house at Lindisfarne as a priory dependent on Durham, and it was at about this time that the name Holy Island began to come into general use. Throughout the rest of its history the priory remained dependent on Durham cathedral, the priors being appointed and controlled by the mother house, and the numbers of monks on the island probably never reaching double figures. During the Scottish wars of the 14th c., Holy Island was regularly used as a stopping-place by the king's purveyors responsible for the collection of stores for the use of the English armies, and was in danger of Scottish attack. Consequently, both the island and the priory itself had to be fortified. The basalt ridge to the south of the priory, called the Heugh, formed a protective shield, and here a fort was built in medieval times. The fortress on the Beblowe, a second basalt outcrop at the south-east end of the

island, was not built until the 16th c., but there may have been a look-out tower there during the period of the monastery's existence. Such precautions were successful, and Lindisfarne Priory survived until it was dissolved in 1537.

The church, originally built in dark red stone, has weathered and lost much of its colour, but occasional glimpses (for example, the interior of the north wall of the nave) remind the visitor of how this noble ruin must have appeared in the middle ages. What can be seen now dates mostly from the first half of the 12th c. (building began in 1093, as at Durham) with the exception of the east end. Originally the church was only 142 ft. long, with an apsidal chancel the line of which can still be seen within the present chancel, but about 1150 it was decided to lengthen the chancel and square off the end of it; thus the church in its final form was close to 160 ft. long. It has a nave of six bays with north and south aisles, transepts with eastern apses, and an aisleless chancel. The west end is particularly well preserved, especially in its detail. The west doorway is typically Norman, three orders of columns supporting round arches with chevron moulding. There is blank arcading to the side and more round-headed windows further up, but on the top storey only two crossbow-loops—hardly a monastic feature but an indication of the order of priorities at Lindisfarne. The south-west corner of the church is filled by a massive turret with an internal spiral staircase which gave access to the crossbow-loops above the west door. There was originally a second turret on the north side of the door, but this has been almost totally destroyed.

The interior of the west front has a gallery above the door set behind four roughly-cut columns with block capitals forming narrow arches, two on each side, and a broader central arch. Only low foundations remain of the south aisle wall of the nave, but the north wall stands close to the height of the original triforium, and the two eastern bays of the north aisle arcade are intact; it is here that the original colour of the stone used at Lindisfarne can best be appreciated. From what remains of the circular piers of the north aisle arcade, it can be seen that they were decorated with the same zigzag motif as at Durham.

The massive crossing piers at one time supported a tower, but now support nothing more than one of the moulded ribs crossing diagonally from the north-west to the south-east pier; the preservation

LINDISFARNE: *aerial view from the west*

of this rib is a fortunate survival, adding another dimension to our view of the ruin. The transepts are roughly square (but with eastern apsidal chapels) and were rib-vaulted. The west wall of the north transept, with its arches through into the nave arcade and triforium, and the east wall of the south transept, with its attached eastern chapel, still stand to a good height. Much of the mid-12th-c. chancel also stands close to its original height. It was rib-vaulted and lit by four round-headed windows, two in each of the south and north walls, three of which can still be seen. The great window in the east wall was inserted in the 14th c. and probably contained five lights, but although the arch has remained intact, the tracery has disappeared. The piscina with a trefoiled head in the south wall, and the aumbrey in the north wall, are both 13th-c. additions. In the 15th c. the roof of the chancel was raised and probably flattened out; there are hardly any traces of the clerestory left to see.

The monastic buildings date amost entirely from the 13th and 14th c., and are really most unmonastic. Originally the cloister seems to have been square and in its usual position to the south of the nave, but later, as more buildings were added to the south end of the east and west ranges, it was extended to an oblong shape. The east range contained the chapter-house which, unusually, had its longer axis parallel to the east cloister walk rather than at right-angles to it. The northern bay of this building was partitioned off to form a vestry, access to which was through the door in the south transept which can still be seen. Immediately south of it is the small parlour, followed by a two-storeyed building which contained the warming-house on the ground floor and the prior's lodging on the first floor. These rooms were constructed in the 14th c. The large open fireplace of the warming-house, with its fine chimney stack almost perfectly preserved, can be seen against the north wall. Originally the rooms to the east of the warming-house seem to have been used as the monastic infirmary, but in 1341–2 these rooms were re-modelled and enclosed by a fortified wall which still stands to a considerable height, running round to a half-octagonal tower at its north-eastern corner and then returning to the south end of the chapter-house. No doubt these precautions were taken against the possibility of Scottish raids. What the old infirmary rooms were later used for is not

1. NAVE
2. NORTH TRANSEPT
3. SOUTH TRANSEPT
4. CHANCEL
5. CLOISTER
6. CHAPTER-HOUSE
7. PARLOUR
8. DAY-STAIRS
9. WARMING-HOUSE, WITH PRIOR'S LODGING ABOVE
10. OUTER COURT
11. SITE OF LOWER GATEHOUSE
12. BAKEHOUSE
13. BREWHOUSE
14. KITCHEN
15. LARDER
16. SITE OF FRATER
17. PANTRY
18. CELLARS

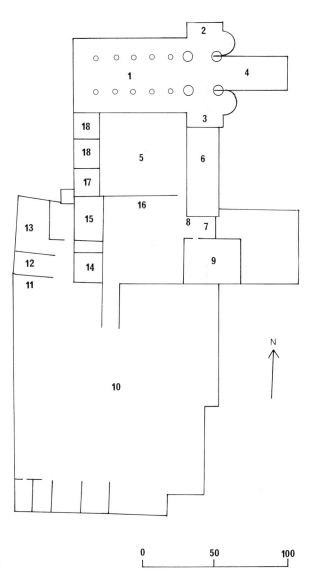

certain, but after this time the monks seem to have dispensed with an infirmary. When there were seldom more than five or six monks in the priory, it can hardly have been deemed necessary.

The dorter was placed above the chapter-house, while the frater occupied its usual position in the south range. Very little of it is left, but what evidence there is suggests that the frater was originally built further to the north and was later moved south (where the line of its south wall, with a window-sill embedded in it, can be seen) when extra buildings were added to the south ends of the east and west ranges. At the west end of the frater's south wall are the remains of a barbican reaching into the outer court—another sign of the double difficulties which faced the builders of Lindisfarne Priory. The west range of the cloister is its earliest part, dating from about 1200. It consisted of two cellars next to the church, then a pantry or buttery, and then a larder. Further south, next to the barbican, a kitchen was added in the 13th c., and then in the 14th c., to the west of these buildings, a unit containing a bakehouse and brewhouse was added. The walls of these buildings are exceptionally thick, no doubt for defensive reasons.

About 1300 an outer court was added to the south of the cloister. Although its surrounding walls are reasonably well-preserved, nothing more than low foundations remain of the buildings grouped around it, and it is not certain what they were used for. The large building in the south-east corner was probably a guest house, while those along the south wall may have been used for the storage or preparation of food. One must remember that the monks of Lindisfarne, isolated as they were, would have had to acquire a certain degree of self-sufficiency. The gap in the north-west corner of the outer court marks the position of the priory's lower gatehouse.

After the Dissolution the last prior, Thomas Sparke, who had received a life-lease of the site from the prior and convent of Durham, sub-let it to the king's surveyor of victuals at Berwick, and for a while the church was turned into a storehouse. As a result of this lease there was a lengthy legal dispute over the ownership of the site early in the 17th c., when Lord Walden, to whom the rights had passed, stripped the lead from the roofs of the priory buildings. Although he won his claim to the site against the dean and chapter of Durham cathedral, all the lead was sunk by a storm while being shipped southwards. In 1643 the priory was occupied by a royalist force, and in 1715 by supporters of the Old Pretender. Excavation of the site was begun in 1888. It was then placed in the hands of the Office of Works, and is now in the care of English Heritage.

Immediately to the west of the ruins of the priory church is St Mary's, a fine 13th-c. parish church, and at the south-east end of the island is Lindisfarne Castle, a remarkable early 20th-c. adaption of a 16th-c. fortress. Both are worth visiting.

Llanthony Priory

ORDER: Augustinian canons
COUNTY: Gwent
ROUTE: On B4423, 9 miles N of Abergavenny.
OS REF. 161:2827

Llanthony Priory had a romantic beginning. Some time during the last decade of the 11th c., a knight named William de Lacy took shelter in an old ruined chapel on this spot during a storm which broke while he was out hunting. This proved to be his conversion, and he decided that he must immediately abandon his worldly life-style and devote his life to study and religion, so he set up house in the chapel and began to lead a hermit's life. By 1103, his fame had spread and he was joined by a priest named Ersinius, who had been chaplain to Matilda, Queen of England. More disciples followed, a church was built, and in 1108 a priory of canons came into existence when the church was consecrated by the Bishops of Llandaff and Hereford and dedicated to St John the Baptist. William's kinsman Hugh de Lacy, Lord of Ewias, granted various endowments so that the priory should be placed on a proper financial footing, and it was decided to adopt the Augustinian rule. Ersinius became the first prior, and by about 1125 there were some forty canons at Llanthony. In 1129 the second prior, the saintly Robert of Béthune, was elected to be Bishop of Hereford, although he was reluctant to leave his community and did not take up his post until 1131. Soon after this came disaster. Shortly after the death of Henry I in 1135, there was a major Welsh national rising, aimed at expelling from South Wales the newly-arrived Norman conquerors. The priory was raided, the canons' food supply was cut off, and eventually they were forced to abandon Llanthony and take refuge with Robert of Béthune in his bishop's palace at Hereford. A new site on the outskirts of Gloucester was found for the refugees, which came to be known as 'Llanthony secunda'.

For about fifty years, the mother-house was abandoned, but eventually, towards the end of the 12th c., the canons returned and began to build their church and domestic buildings anew. After a short period during which the mother-house became paradoxically dependent on the daughter-house at Gloucester, an agreement was made in

1205 whereby the two priories would again elect their own priors and become independent. During Edward I's conquest of Wales, and again during the revolt of Owain Glyndwr in the early 15th c., the priory suffered serious damage. In 1448, more than thirty years after the suppression of Glyndwr's revolt, the abbot was exempted from appointment as a tax-collector because his lands had been so severely wasted by Owain's men. From this time onwards Llanthony was declining, and in 1481 it was finally decided to restore the priory's dependence on Llanthony secunda, so that for the last half-century of its existence Llanthony had only four canons in addition to the prior. On 10 March 1538, mother-house and daughter-house were simultaneously suppressed.

Everything that remains dates from the period 1180–1230, a telling reminder both of the severity of the damage inflicted on the priory during the 12th c., and of Llanthony's decline in the later middle ages. In the 15th c. two buttresses were added to the chapels east of the south transept; in many monasteries, the late 15th and early 16th cs. witnessed an 'Indian summer' of rebuilding before the Dissolution, but at Llanthony there was no such activity. Considerable portions of the church still stand to a good height, forming a very picturesque ruin.

It was a reasonably simple structure, consisting of an aisled nave of eight bays with two western towers, a crossing tower between transepts which both had projecting chapels to the east, and a narrow, square-ended chancel of three bays. The west front has lost its central window, and the towers on either side of it each had a fourth stage on top of the three which remain; but otherwise it is well preserved. The south-west tower has been incorporated into the Abbey Hotel, which also occupies the west range of the cloister. Architecturally, the west front is Transitional; the round-headed arches of the second stage and the blank arcading take us back to Norman, while the slender blank lancets of the third stage and the pointed recesses and door of the lowest stage are reminiscent of 13th-c. Gothic. Without its topmost stage, it looks much more squat than it would have when complete.

The north aisle arcade is almost complete, although parts of it are mutilated, and in the second bay from the west some of the vaulting remains. It is a simple quadripartite rib-vault, and no doubt

LLANTHONY: *the church from the north-west*

gives the clue as to how the rest of the church was vaulted. At the east and west ends the south aisle arcade also remains, but the arcade of the central bays has disappeared. The line of the nave roof can clearly be seen against the west wall of the crossing tower. Of this tower the north and east walls have fallen, but the south and west walls, supported by massive crossing piers, still stand above the level of the string-course which divided their first and second stages. A group of three round-headed windows, centrally placed in each wall, mark the level of the wall-passage which ran round the tower. There was a second wall-passage just above the string-course. An eighteenth-century sketch shows that there were three stages to the tower, so it was considerably taller than it now appears. Of the north transept little remains except a portion of the north wall, but the south transept retains its south wall to a good height; it contains two large lancets and an upper window in the gable. The

large round arch in the transept's east wall was inserted to replace two smaller arches in the early 13th c., when it was decided to extend the eastern chapels. Originally the chancel and transepts had been built around 1180–90. The arrangement of the eastern chapels of the transepts is on an unusually grand scale; indeed they are so long that they reach almost as far east as the chancel itself. Fragments of all three walls of the chancel remain, rising at the east end to a little above the height of the nave arcades. The opening for the east window— probably a group of three tall lancets—is clearly visible, and in the eastmost bay of the north wall a further lancet survives.

Less remains of the claustral ranges than of the church, but what does remain shows that the arrangement of the monastic buildings at Llanthony differed surprisingly from the normal plan. The east range began with a slype leading through to the cemetery. It has a fine broad archway of three orders with foliated capitals, and the ceiling retains its quadripartite rib-vault complete with bosses.

To the south of the slype are the remains of the chapter-house, a building of unusual but attractive shape which dates, like the rest of the claustral buildings, from the first quarter of the 13th c. It was vaulted in four bays, of which the three western bays formed an oblong, while the north and south walls of the eastern bay were canted inwards to form a semi-hexagon. The west wall has disappeared, but along the side walls blank arcading and a lancet can be seen, and against the east wall remains the stone bench on which the canons sat during their daily meeting.

There were buildings to the south of the chapter-house, but what purpose they served is not known, for they have vanished. What does seem clear, however, is that the dorter was not in the east range at Llanthony, as it was in almost all other monasteries, for the ceiling of the chapter-house is too high to allow for any first-floor above it. Instead the dorter was probably on the first floor of the west range, and the newel staircase in the south-western corner of the south tower was used by the canons as their night-stairs to the church. Nothing now remains of the first floor of this range,

for it has all been superseded by the buildings of the hotel. On the ground floor at the north end of the range is the outer parlour, which still retains its vault, and to the south of it are three stone-vaulted basements, one of which is used as the hotel bar. The walls dividing these rooms are modern, and in the middle ages they probably formed one large cellar. The south range contained the frater, but only low masonry of its north wall has survived. To the south of the cloister is the church of St Mary, a 13th-c. building which may have been the monastic infirmary, although it has been altered so much that it is impossible to be certain of its original use. To the west of the church, the priory gate house is concealed among farm buildings.

After the Dissolution the site was sold to a royal servant, Nicholas Arnold, for £160. In the 18th c. it came into the hands of Colonel Wood of Brecon, who converted the south-west tower of the church into a shooting box and built a house for his steward out of the west range. In 1951 the ruins were placed in the guardianship of the Ministry of Works, and they are now in the care of Cadw: Welsh Historic Monuments.

Melrose Abbey

ORDER: Cistercian monks
COUNTY: Borders
ROUTE: In town centre, on A6091
OS REF: 73:5434

The first religious house at Melrose was said to have been founded by St Aidan, who brought monks from Iona to Old Melrose, a site about two miles up the river Tweed, in the middle of the 7th c. Although this house was destroyed by Kenneth, King of Scots, in 839, there was still a church there in the 12th c. It was to that site that the Cistercian monks from Rievaulx came to found the new monastery of Melrose, at the request of King David I, in 1136–7, moving to the present site a few years later. The fame and prosperity of the abbey were due to two men: one was King David, the founder, whose generous endowment ensured that it was always one of the wealthiest houses in Scotland. The other was St Waldef, stepson of King David. He had been Prior of Kirkham, and only the opposition of King Stephen prevented him from becoming Archbishop of York. A friend of Ailred of Rievaulx, he became a Cistercian, was abbot of Melrose from 1148 to 1159, and endowed Melrose with a reputation for sanctity and learning which placed it on a par with houses such as Fountains and Rievaulx and made it second to none in Scotland. Successive abbots of the house were earmarked for early preferment, moving on to various Scottish bishoprics, and successive kings added to David I's original endowment, so that for the first 150 years of its existence, the story was one of almost continual growth.

The position of the abbey on one of the main roads from Edinburgh to the south was highly advantageous in time of peace; in time of war, however, it was to prove disastrous. The monastic buildings were badly burned during Edward I's campaigns of 1300–07, and then in 1322 Edward II's retreating army subjected it to a more serious sack and slaughtered several of the monks. Worse was to come: in 1385 Richard II led an expedition to Scotland, and the abbey church at Melrose was burned to the ground. A new church was built early in the 15th c., but this again was damaged in the Earl of Hertford's barbarous raid of 1545, along with many of the monastic buildings. The abbey

never recovered from this blow. From the late 15th c. it had, in any case, fallen under the control of lay lords who engaged in protracted litigation over its revenues and cared little or nothing for the fate of the religious. From 1541 it was held by a series of commendators (notably by James Stuart, eldest

1. NAVE
2. SOUTH TRANSEPT
3. NORTH TRANSEPT
4. CHANCEL
5. CHAPELS
6. CLOISTER
7. WAX CELLAR
8. CHAPTER-HOUSE
9. PARLOUR
10. DORTER UNDERCROFT
11. RERE-DORTER
12. SLYPE
13. SITE OF ABBOT'S HALL
14. COMMENDATOR'S HOUSE
15. WARMING-HOUSE
16. LATER FRATER
17. SITE OF EARLY FRATER
18. KITCHEN
19. EARLY LAY-BROTHERS' FRATER
20. PARLOUR
21. LAY-BROTHERS' CLOISTER
22. CELLARS AND LAY-BROTHERS' FRATER, WITH LAY-BROTHERS' DORTER ABOVE
23. SITE OF LAY-BROTHERS' RERE-DORTER

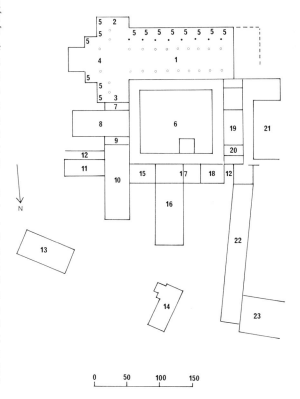

290

MELROSE: *the abbey as it might have appeared in the fifteenth century, assuming that earlier work had survived. From a drawing by Alan Sorrell*

bastard son of King James V, from 1541 to 1557), and in 1609 it was erected into a temporal lordship for John Ramsay, Viscount Haddington, who by Act of Parliament became Lord Melrose.

The ruins of Melrose are the most spectacular in Scotland, and among the finest in Britain. Although the church is ruined, much of it still stands to roof-height at the east end, and the foundations of the monastic buildings are extensive. The first, 12th-c., church at Melrose had a shorter chancel than its successor and only one aisle to the south, but it was of similar proportions. The church as rebuilt in the 15th c., from which nearly all the present ruins date, consisted of an aisled nave of nine bays with a second aisle containing eight chapels added to the south side, north and south transepts each with two eastern chapels, and a narrow, square-ended chancel with two projecting chapels, one on each

side of its western bay, giving the east end a stepped appearance. A further two bays were planned at the west end of the nave, but these were never completed, and the low ruins which now mark the west end date from the late 12th c.; sufficient remains to show that it was a typically severe and simple Cistercian west end, providing a striking contrast to the very un-Scottish flamboyance of the rest of the building.

The surviving parts of the 15th-c. church are a row of chapels along the exterior south aisle of the nave, the eastern three bays of the nave, the shells of both transepts, part of the west wall of the crossing tower, and the east end. The eastern three bays of the nave, which formed the medieval monks' quire, were converted into a parish church early in the 17th c., at which time the original rib-vaulting was taken down and a dreary barrel-vault erected. Although parochial use of the church was abandoned at the beginning of the 19th c., the barrel-vault has remained to mar the architecture of this part of the building. What remains of the

15th-c. church is unrivalled by any other church in Scotland. It is heavily influenced by both French and northern English designs (the east end was probably built by masons from York) of the late Decorated and early Perpendicular period, with large and elaborately-traceried windows, crocketed and pinnacled gables, and a profusion of sculpture set in exquisitely canopied and otherwise decorated niches. The gables of the south transept and east end are particularly sumptuous, although the south transept has lost all of its statuary and the east end about half of it. The flamboyance and ingenuity of the masons of Melrose are also demonstrated by the corbels, gargoyles and other wall-carvings, which range from delicately carved religious subjects, through representations of the mundane, such as a cook with his ladle and a mason with his mallet, to the grotesque, typified by two gargoyles on the south side of the church depicting a calf with wings and a pig playing the bagpipes. Flying buttresses, a rare sight in Scotland, were used to support the vault.

Presumably for reasons of drainage, the cloister was laid out on the north side of the church. Its foundations, and those of the ranges which surrounded it, are preserved on all sides, and show clearly the arrangement and extent of the monastic buildings. They all date from the 12th and 13th cs. The east range contained a small sacristy or wax cellar, followed by the large oblong chapter-house; this was re-built in the 13th c. and vaulted from a double row of piers along its central axis. Workmen digging here in 1921 uncovered a leaden casket containing a mummified human heart. It may well be the heart of King Robert Bruce, for it is known that this king, the most famous of Scottish monarchs, had asked that his heart should be buried here, and this was duly done. After examination, the casket, with the heart still inside it, was re-interred and is still beneath the floor of the chapter-house. The remainder of the east range was occupied by the undercroft of the dorter, probably used by the monks as a dayroom, with the rere-dorter running to the east at right-angles to it and the dorter stretching over the range on the first floor. The north range originally contained the frater on an east-west axis but, like so many Cistercian fraters, this was rebuilt about 1200 on a north–south axis, leaving room for the warming-house and kitchen to be placed on the east and west sides of it respectively. The west range at Melrose

is immensely long, and not surprisingly, for it was as usual given over to the lay-brothers, and there were two hundred lay-brothers at Melrose in its heyday. The southern part of the range, abutting the cloister, was originally the lay-brothers' frater with a small outer parlour at the north end, but later, when the extension to the west range was completed, it was divided into two rooms, which were probably used for one of the monastic industries such as tanning.

To the west of this range was the lesser cloister used by the lay-brothers, over which the road now runs. It was built at the same time as the northern extension of the range, the lay-brothers formerly having had a separate lane running parallel and adjacent to the west walk of the main cloister. When the lesser cloister was built, the lane was incorporated into the main cloister. The great northern extension to the west range, built at a slightly inclined angle to the east, contained the lay-brothers' frater and warming-house as well as cellarage space on the ground floor, and their dorter on the first floor; the rere-dorter projects to the west from its northern end, and from here the line of the great drain can be picked up. It is 4 ft. wide, 5 ft. deep, and was originally 1500 ft. long; it can be seen running back from the lay-brothers' rere-dorter, past the northern end of the monks' frater and dorter, through their rere-dorter, and then on towards the site of the vanished monastic infirmary. The monks obtained their water supply by damming the Tweed at a point 500 yds. to the west of the monastery and constructing a mill lade around the northern side of the cloister buildings. The leat can still be seen. It was a task requiring considerable skill, but it must be remembered that the first monks at Melrose came from Rievaulx, where the monastic water-supply had been obtained by diverting an entire river-bed.

To the north-east of the east range, just south of the mill leat, are the scanty ruins of the abbot's hall built for Abbot Matthew in 1246. To the north of it a bridge projected over the leat. To the west of it is the commendator's house, now the abbey museum. Built in the 15th c., it was altered in the 16th and again in modern times, when it was also extended. Originally it contained three ground-floor chambers with fireplaces and more rooms on the first floor reached by an outside staircase at the north end. Preserved in the museum are the remains of St Waldef's shrine.

MELROSE: *gargoyle of a pig playing the bagpipes*

The Lordship of Melrose remained with the Hamilton family until the late 17th c., when it was bought by Anne, Duchess of Buccleuch, widow of James, Duke of Monmouth. The property remained with her descendants, and in March 1919 the Duke of Buccleuch placed the ruins in the hands of H.M. Commissioners of Works; they are now in the care of the Scottish Development Department.

Monk Bretton Priory

ORDER: Cluniac (later Benedictine) monks
COUNTY: South Yorkshire
ROUTE: Off A628, 2 miles ENE of Barnsley.
OS REF: 111:3706

The Priory of St Mary Magdalene of Monk Bretton was founded in about 1154 by Adam Fitzswane and colonised from Pontefract, but Fitzswane's two charters of foundation were ambiguous on the question of how the prior was to be chosen, and for the next century and a quarter there were continual disputes between Monk Bretton and Pontefract, with each community claiming the right to choose Monk Bretton's prior. More than once, the prior of Pontefract sent an armed force to Monk Bretton, and both sides even appealed to the Pope and, in 1269, to Henry Lacy, Lord of Pontefract. In 1279, after an official Cluniac delegation had been refused entry at Monk Bretton, an appeal was made to King Edward I, and two years later the friction ended when the community of Monk Bretton broke its ties with Cluny and became an independent Benedictine house.

Apart from a disastrous fire in 1386, the later history of the priory is largely uneventful. The number of monks remained constant, between eleven and thirteen, and the house was surrendered on 21 November 1538. Although this brought the community's life to an end, the monks were among the more zealous of their kind in the 16th c., and after the Dissolution a group of them banded together, bought 148 books from the auctioned monastic library, and went to continue their communal life at the house of one of their number at Worsborough. They were still there in 1558.

The first, late 12th-c., church was only about 170 ft. in length, with a broad aisled nave of four bays, north and south transepts each with two eastern chapels, and a narrow, square-ended chancel. Within a few years, the chancel had been extended to five bays, however, and in the 15th c. a new east end with adjoining sacristy to the south was added. Only low walls remain, mostly of the transepts and chancel. In the central bay of the chancel's north wall are two small cylindrical holes in the stone which may have been put in to contain saints'

relics. Of the east range, too, little remains above the foundations. It was built early in the 13th c., and consists of a rectangular chapter-house immediately south of the south transept, with the base of the monks' night-stairs to the dorter still visible in the western corner of the two buildings, followed by a parlour which, surprisingly, was not reached from the cloister but from a door in its south wall which led into a passage through the

1. GATEHOUSE
2. ADMINISTRATIVE BUILDING
3. NAVE
4. NORTH TRANSEPT
5. SOUTH TRANSEPT
6. CHANCEL
7. CHAPELS
8. SACRISTY
9. CLOISTER
10. CHAPTER-HOUSE
11. INNER PARLOUR
12. SLYPE
13. EARLY WARMING-HOUSE
14. LATER WARMING-HOUSE
15. FRATER
16. RERE-DORTER
17. GUEST-HOUSE
18. INFIRMARY HALL
19. INFIRMARY KITCHEN
20. KITCHEN
21. SCULLERY
22. SERVICE HATCH
23. CELLARS, WITH PRIOR'S LODGING ABOVE
24. OUTER PARLOUR

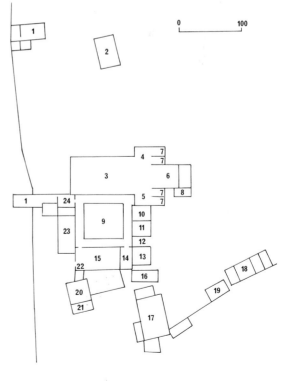

MONK BRETTON: *south and west ranges, across the cloister*

range. In the 15th c., an oven was inserted in the north-eastern corner of the parlour. The passage has another door in its south wall, leading to the first monastic warming-house, later abandoned in favour of a smaller warming-house immediately to the west of it. Over the whole east range stretched the dorter, but nothing remains of it. To the south of it is the free-standing monks' rere-dorter, with its main drain still visible. Further south again is a series of foundation walls showing the layout of the 14th-c. guest-house, from which a low wall runs north-eastwards to another group of foundation walls. This was the site of the monastic infirmary.

Apart from the later warming-house in its south-eastern corner, the south range consists entirely of the frater, built on an east-west axis. Its south wall stands to a considerable height and includes a fine central window and a narrower western one, both of which had Geometrical tracery. South of this are the remains of the kitchen and scullery, with a small service lobby connecting them at the west end. In the south-east corner of the kitchen yard is an inspection trap over the main drain, which is

grooved for a penstock; this allowed the flow of water to be held back in dry periods so that, when released, it would give a better flush to the rere-dorter. To the west of the kitchen are the remains of the prior's lodging, which consisted of a large hall flanked by a service area to the south and the prior's chamber to the north. The west wall of the chamber is well preserved, and contains a perfect recessed two-light window and a handsome fireplace with tapered stone hood. The lintel and lamp-brackets at each end of it are carved from the same piece of stone, a fine piece of workmanship.

The west claustral range also stands to a considerable height, and consisted of a cellar in the middle, with outer parlour to the north and a service lobby to the south. Originally built in the 13th c., it was much altered in the 14th and then, after the Dissolution, altered again to form part of the residence of Henry Talbot, fourth son of the Earl of Shrewsbury. Running west from the north end of the range are the remains of the 12th-c. inner gatehouse. The outer gatehouse is 230 ft. further to the north, at the far end of the monastic precinct. It included an almonry, lobby and porter's lodge, and was built in the 12th c., but in the 15th it was much altered, and a newel staircase was added in the

MONK BRETTON: *the prior's chamber*

south-west corner to lead to the first floor. This may have been used as living quarters for corrodians or lay officials at the priory, for to the north two garderobe shafts were added at the same time. The simple rectangular building of two storeys which stands to the east of the gatehouse was probably used as an administrative centre for the priory's estates, and may have included a manorial courtroom on the first floor.

After the Dissolution, William Blithman, one of the commissioners for the surrender, obtained a 21-year lease of the site, which in the following year was converted into a grant outright. In 1589 he sold Monk Bretton to the Earl of Shrewsbury, who gave it to Henry Talbot as a wedding present. Talbot converted the prior's lodging and part of the south and west ranges into a residence for himself and his wife, and from there it passed to the Armyne, Pierrepont, Wombwell, and Horne families. John Horne and his son excavated the ruins between 1923 and 1926. The site was later purchased by the Borough of Barnsley which, in 1932, placed it in the hands of the Ministry of Works. It is now in the care of English Heritage.

Mount Grace Priory

ORDER: Carthusian monks
COUNTY: North Yorkshire
ROUTE: Off A19, 6 miles NE of Northallerton.
OS REF: 99:4598

The Carthusian House of the Assumption of the Most Blessed Virgin and St Nicholas of Mount Grace in Ingleby, or Mount Grace Priory as it is more generally called, was founded in 1398, towards the end of the period of Carthusian expansion in England, and is by a considerable margin the best-preserved Charterhouse in the country, allowing the visitor to see clearly how the arrangements of these monasteries differed from those of the other orders.

The founder of Mount Grace was Thomas Holland, the nephew and court favourite of Richard II, created Duke of Surrey in 1397 and, unfortunately for the monks of Mount Grace, executed at Cirencester in January 1400 for his part in a conspiracy against the new king Henry IV. The consequent forfeiture of his lands led to lengthy legal wrangles over the endowment of Mount Grace, which were not settled until Henry VI confirmed a charter favourable to the monks in about 1445. Nevertheless, most of the building was accomplished during the first years of the house's existence, although a few additions continued to be made throughout the century. Early in the 15th c., the Prior, Nicholas Love, published important tracts against the Lollards. In 1534 five of the monks at Mount Grace were imprisoned, four of them having refused to take the Oath of Supremacy and the Prior, John Wilson, only having agreed to do so after the intervention of the Archbishop of York. In late 1539, when it was peacefully surrendered to the king by Prior Wilson, there were sixteen monks besides the prior, three novices, and six lay-brothers; this was the number of monks for which Mount Grace had originally been built, although the construction of five extra cells early in the 15th c. had at that time raised the number to twenty-one.

The architecture at Mount Grace is restrained and almost mean in appearance, in common with other Carthusian foundations. The priory's precinct enclosed two courts of roughly equal size, with the church and the other communal buildings

dividing them. The church was only 88 ft. long when originally built, with a nave and quire, but no transepts; in other words, a simple oblong. The chapels to the north and south of the nave, which give the church the appearance of having transepts, were later additions, as were the cross walls with their moulded arches at the east end of the nave, the central tower supported by these walls,

1. NAVE	12. SACRIST'S CELL
2. CHAPELS	13. FRATER
3. TOWER	14. SLYPE
4. CHANCEL	15. INNER PARLOUR
5. SACRISTY	16. KITCHEN
6. CHAPTER-HOUSE	17. BAKEHOUSE
7. LITTLE CLOISTER	18. BREWHOUSE
8. GREAT CLOISTER	19. GUEST-HOUSE
AND CEMETERY	20. GATEHOUSE
9. MONK'S CELL	21. GRANARY
10. GARDEN	22. STABLES
11. PRIOR'S CELL	23. OUTER COURT

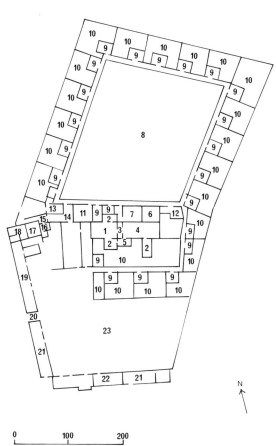

MOUNT GRACE: *aerial view from the west*

and the chancel: the latter brought the total length of the church to 118 ft. The little Perpendicular tower has a transomed bell-opening in each face and battlements around the parapet with a pinnacle at each corner. The foundations of the high altar can be seen against the east wall of the chancel, but little else of it remains. The remains of two tombs can also be seen, one between the stone plinths of the choir stalls, and one in the southern chapel. One of these may mark the spot to which the remains of Thomas Holland, the founder, were brought in 1412.

The buildings immediately to the north of the church, between it and the south wall of the cloister, are, from east to west, the sacrist's cell, the chapter-house, which had a door linking it with the chancel, then a small courtyard with a door to the quire and a flight of steps up to the cloister, followed by two monks' cells, the prior's lodging, and the small frater. Only on Sundays and feast days did the monks eat in the frater, receiving all their meals in their cells on normal days. The doorway from the cloister to the frater had a hood-mould ending in shields bearing the quartered arms of Redman and Aldeburgh. The prior's lodging was divided into two rooms on the ground floor, with a place in the north wall of the western room, but on the first floor there was only one room, with a fine oriel window overlooking the cloister, the heavy moulded corbel of which remains.

The great cloister, an irregular quadrangle of which the north, south, and east sides measure 231 ft. in length, and the west side 272 ft., lies to the north of the church. It was around the cloister that the cells of the monks were placed, each with its own garden and garderobe. From the cloister walk to the outer precinct wall was a distance of some 50 ft. all the way round the north, east and west walls of the cloister, with the cell almost invariably placed in one of the angles of the garden adjoining the cloister. Most of the doorways to the cells can still be seen, with the small food hatches next to them through which the monks were given their meals. Each hatch turned a right angle in the thickness of the wall so that the monk could not see the person who brought his food, any opportunity for speech thus being avoided. The foundations of most, and the standing walls of a few, of the cells can be seen, but the layout of the cells can best be learned from the cell in the middle of the north wall, which was cleverly reconstructed early in the 20th c.

The cells were on two floors, with a lobby, living-room with fireplace, study, and oratory-cum-bedroom on the first floor. From the back of the living-room a pentise led to the garderobe placed against the outer precinct wall in a corner of the garden. Stairs led to the upper floor, which seems to have been used as a workshop. The amount of space allowed to each monk was remarkably generous, and one can but think that the hardship imposed by the Carthusian vow of silence must have been adequately compensated for by the privacy enjoyed by each monk; privacy was a rare luxury in the Middle Ages. Each cell had a piped supply of water from a tap in an arched wall-recess in the lobby or the garden pentise. Indeed the water-supply arrangements are well-preserved at Mount Grace. The community drew its water from three springs to the east and south-east of the precinct, two of which were channelled into the drains along the back of the garderobes to flush them, while the third was channelled into the main conduit in the centre of the cloister and piped from there to the individual cells and other buildings such as the kitchen.

To the south-east of the church was a lesser cloister around which a further six cells were grouped; little remains of them now apart from the foundations. Of the outer court, which occupied a roughly equal area of land to the south of the church as the great cloister occupied to the north of it, the foundations of the walls can be seen as well as the external walls of the buildings along the south range, a later addition dating from the 15th c. The buildings constructed here were stables and granaries. There were no buildings along the eastern wall, but along the western wall were two guest-houses flanking the gatehouse. The gateway was vaulted in two bays, the vaulting arches still being visible, and the doorway in it led to stairs to the upper storey. To the south of the gatehouse the walls of the guest-house have largely disappeared apart from the western wall. It was originally a two-storey building with the top floor being used as another granary. The northern guest-house was converted into a dwelling-house in the mid-17th c. and extended further north at the beginning of the 20th c.; it is still in private occupation. At the north end of this old guest-house are the remains of the monastic brewhouse and bakehouse, the former a pyramidal building with a castellated flue. The space between the bakehouse and the frater was the site of the kitchen.

After the Dissolution the priory was granted to Sir James Strangways. It passed through various hands until in 1653 it was sold to Sir Thomas Lascelles, who immediately began work on converting the old northern guest-house. About 1900 the site was partly excavated and restored by the ironmaster Sir Lowthian Bell, and in 1918 it was accepted by the Treasury in lieu of death duties after the death of Sir Maurice Bell. In 1953 the Treasury gave the priory to the National Trust which, two years later, placed it in the care of the Ministry of Public Buildings and Works. It is now in the care of English Heritage.

Muchelney Abbey

ORDER: Benedictine monks
COUNTY: Somerset
ROUTE: Off A372, 1½ miles SSE of Langport.
OS REF: 193:4224

The first religious house at Muchelney was probably founded in 693, by King Ine of Wessex. Until recent times the village has been virtually an island, isolated and surrounded by marshes (Mucheln-ey means the 'big island'), and often inaccessible for long periods. Although a causeway now connects the village with Langport, severe flooding can still cut it off. The monastery founded by Ine was probably destroyed by the Danes in the 870s, and re-founded, first as a house of secular canons, but rapidly converted into a Benedictine monastery dedicated to St. Peter and St. Paul, in the mid-10th c. Although it tended to be over-shadowed by the fame of nearby Glastonbury, the abbey prospered and by the 12th c. there were about twenty-four monks. The history of the house was uneventful. During the later middle ages the number of monks fluctuated between thirteen and seventeen, but by the time the house was dissolved on 3 January 1538, there were only eleven.

For a long time, the site remained overgrown and ruined, but in the middle of the 20th c. it passed into the hands of the Ministry of Works, and systematic excavations undertaken since then have revealed clearly the plan of the church and claustral buildings. The Saxon church, the outlines of which have been recovered within the outlines of the later church, was small and apsidal; it was replaced after the Conquest by a church of typical French plan, with an aisled nave of six bays, north and south transepts with eastern chapels, and an apsidal chancel around which ran an ambulatory with three radiating chapels. A Lady Chapel with a square end was later added to the chancel, bringing the total length of the church to 260 ft. The outlines of the church are clearly marked on the turf.

The cloister was to the south of the church and had an upper storey, as can clearly be seen on the south side. The buildings of the east and west ranges followed the usual pattern, and although they have been excavated, and their outlines exposed, they are almost entirely ruined. The east range consisted of the chapter-house and warming-house on the ground floor with the dorter above and the rere-dorter at the south end. The original apse of the chapter-house and some of the windows of the rere-dorter can still be seen. To the east of the warming-house are the foundations of the in-firmary buildings around another small cloister. The west range no doubt contained cellarage.

The south range contained the frater and abbot's lodging, by far the most interesting group of buildings at Muchelney. The abbot's lodging was rebuilt at the beginning of the 16th c., as was the south cloister walk; the latter was given a fan-vault (following the example of Gloucester, no doubt) and four-light openings on to the garth. The south wall of the frater no longer stands, but at its west end is an anteroom with a staircase leading to the three small rooms on the first floor of the cloister walk. A wall-painting and a waggon-roof can be seen in the eastern two rooms, and in the western room, above the anteroom, is an excellent fireplace with a richly carved overmantel. The frieze is carved with quatrefoils and foliage patterns, and from each end shafts rise up to support two sculptured lions. In the south wall are two windows on each floor, straight-headed and clearly Renaissance rather than Gothic in conception. As at many other monasteries, the abbots of Muchelney at the end of the middle ages provided themselves with new lodgings which were strikingly un-monastic in their luxuriousness.

Immediately north of the church stands the parish church of St Peter and St Paul. Its south chapel is only 3 ft. from the north transept of the abbey church, a fascinating example of how close to each other monastic and parish churches were sometimes built in the middle ages. On the far side of the road is another delightful medieval survival, the little stone cottage that housed the parish priest.

The abbey site is now in the care of English Heritage.

See illustration overleaf

Much Wenlock Priory

ORDER: Cluniac monks
COUNTY: Shropshire
ROUTE: In Much Wenlock, on A458
OS REF: 127:6200

The first religious house on this site was a nunnery founded by Merewald, King of Mercia, about 680, for his daughter St Mildburg the first abbess. She was a saintly lady to whom miracles were attributed; it was said that when she was living at Stoke the geese did considerable damage to her crops, so she bade them go home and never return again. This they did, and in future years when flying over her land they always refused to alight, or if they did so out of fatigue, refused to feed there despite their hunger. The same story, unfortunately, is also told of Mildburg's cousin St. Werburga.

The nunnery lasted less than two hundred years, being destroyed by the Danes in about 874, but traces of what may have been part of the church were found in 1901 in the space between the transepts of the present ruins, when the site was excavated by the late Dr. D. H. S. Cranage, Dean of Norwich. In 1101 the Cluniac monks also discovered the burial-place of St. Mildburg and, with the permission of Anselm, Archbishop of Canterbury, removed and washed the bones and placed them in a new shrine; again it is said that miracles followed this discovery.

The second foundation at Wenlock was made in about 1050 by Leofric, Earl of Mercia and friend of King Edward the Confessor, who built a minster on the site, possibly for secular canons, and in 1080 Roger Montgomery, one of the most powerful of the Conqueror's followers from Normandy, who had been created Earl of Shrewsbury in 1070, asked Abbot Hugh of Cluny to send monks to serve the church. A few monks were sent from La Charité, on the Loire, Cluny's 'eldest daughter', and the Cluniac Priory was established.

The priory grew rapidly, and around it, as so often happened with important monasteries, grew the town of Much Wenlock. In 1163 the monks were faced with a rebellion of the peasants who tilled their land in the neighbourhood of the priory, but they weathered the storm. By 1169–70, when the number of monks in the priory had probably reached fifty, they were able to send thirteen of their number to Scotland to found a Cluniac priory at Paisley. After the middle of the 12th c., the number of monks at Wenlock declined a little, but it remained at around forty until the sixteenth century. Throughout the 14th c. the priory faced severe financial difficulties, largely caused by the heavy impositions laid on all alien priories during the French wars, but a charter of denization obtained in 1395, although only granted in return for a down payment of £400 in the exchequer, relieved the priory's financial situation in the 15th c. and effectively released it from its dependence on Cluny and La Charité. A Papal Bull of 1494 confirmed this release from French dependence. On 26 January 1540, it was dissolved peacefully, and the prior and twelve of the monks were granted pensions.

1. CHAPEL OF ST MICHAEL (probable)
2. NAVE
3. NORTH TRANSEPT
4. SOUTH TRANSEPT
5. LIBRARY ABOVE
6. CHANCEL
7. SACRISTY
8. LADY CHAPEL
9. CHAPTER-HOUSE
10. CLOISTER
11. LAVATORIUM
12. FRATER
13. WEST RANGE
14. UNDERCROFT OF DORTER
15. INFIRMARY HALL
16. INFIRMARY CHAPEL
17. PRIOR'S LODGE

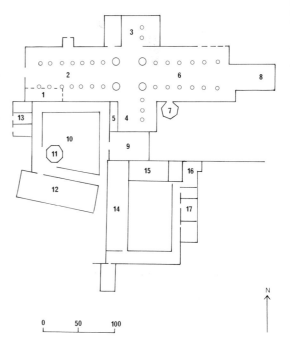

MUCHELNEY: *the fireplace in the prior's lodging*

MUCH WENLOCK: *infirmary and prior's lodging*

Of the church, which was built within the first forty or fifty years of the 13th c. out of money granted to the priory by Hugh Foliot, Bishop of Hereford, and Isabella de Say, daughter and sole heir of the Welsh border baron Hélias de Say, three separate fragments remain. The church was a noble and elongated structure, some 350 ft. in length, with a nave of eight bays and a chancel of seven bays, both aisled, north and south transepts each with three eastern chapels, and a projecting lady chapel at the eastern end. The most interesting surviving fragment, which may have been unique in England, is the small oblong chamber which occupies the three westernmost bays of the triforium on the southern side of the nave. Its purpose cannot be stated with certainty, but most probably it was a chapel of St Michael; the church was jointly dedicated to the archangel, and such chapels were not uncommon in French and Italian churches. The west wall of the north transept, to which a chapel with crypt was formerly attached,

still stands, as do three walls of the south transept. Between the west wall of the latter and the east walk of the cloister is another unusual feature, the long first-floor room which was used as a library. The existence of such a space between the transept and the cloister was almost certainly caused by the re-building of the church in the 13th c., when the Norman cloister-walk and chapter-house were retained.

Both the north and south walls of the roofless chapter-house contain fine examples of Norman stone-carving, with a triple-tiered motif of intersecting arches, the lowest row standing on shafts with decorated capitals. There is some fine figure sculpture, dating from the late 12th c., on the remains of the well of the octagonal lavatorium in the south-west corner of the cloister. For some reason the south walk of the cloister was not exactly parallel to the south wall of the nave.

Fifteenth-century additions included the small heptagonal sacristy adjoining the southern wall of the presbytery just to the east of the south transept, and, some time towards the end of the century, the

MUCH WENLOCK: *blind arcading on the north wall
of the chapter-house*

magnificent L-shaped infirmary and prior's lodge
to the south and east of the south transept. The
lodge is faced with a two-storeyed gallery which
forms a continuous grid of windows, probably
replacing an earlier cloister walk. With its steeply-
pitched, stone-slated roof, it is one of the finest
examples of late medieval domestic architecture in
England. After the Dissolution, these buildings
were converted into a private dwelling-house as
they remain to this day. Henry VIII thought of
using the church as a cathedral for a new diocese,
either Chester-cum-Wenlock or Shrewsbury-cum-
Wenlock, but nothing came of this.

Much Wenlock Priory is now in the care of
English Heritage.

Netley Abbey

ORDER: Cistercian monks
COUNTY: Hampshire
ROUTE: Off A3025, 3 miles SE of Southampton city centre.
OS REF: 196:4508

Planned by Peter des Roches, Bishop of Winchester, before his death in 1238, Netley was not founded until the following year, when a colony of monks arrived from Beaulieu. After some early difficulties, King Henry III became patron and co-founder of the abbey in 1251, and from this time onwards the abbey was jointly dedicated to the Virgin Mary (to whom all Cistercian churches were dedicated) and to Edward the Confessor, to whom Henry III bore particular devotion. Building continued throughout the second half of the 13th c., but in the 14th c. Netley encountered severe financial difficulties, and in 1328, when there were fifteen monks, it was forced to sell some property. In 1341, the monks claimed that their impoverishment was due largely to the continual coming and going of mariners who made repeated demands on their hospitality, and to royal sailors who, having

been set to guard the coast following the French sack of Southampton in 1338, had stolen great numbers of the abbey's sheep and lambs. For the last two centuries of its existence Netley remained a poor and undistinguished Cistercian house. Despite the fact that the royal commissioners reported favourably on the standard of religious life there, it was dissolved in 1536. At the Dissolution there were only seven monks remaining at Netley, but there were also thirty-three other inmates of the abbey, most of them officials and servants.

By the time Netley Abbey was founded, the strict rules of architectural austerity which had governed the construction of the earlier Cistercian foundations had largely been abandoned, and from the start the church was planned on a grander scale than any 12th-c. Cistercian church. It is 215 ft. in length, with an aisled nave and chancel of eight and four bays respectively and north and south transepts each with two eastern chapels. Originally there was also a short tower over the crossing. The north transept has disappeared, as has the arcading of both nave and chancel (apart from one plinth of a pier between the fourth and fifth bays of the nave's south aisle); but the rest of the church's outer walls stand to triforium level, and the massive plinths of the crossing piers can still be seen. The high altar

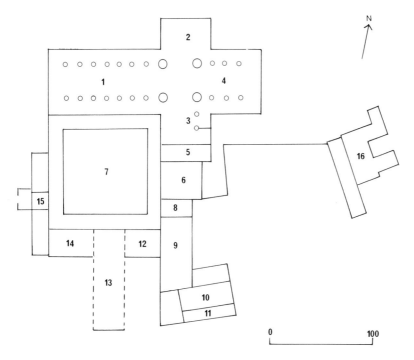

N

1. NAVE
2. NORTH TRANSEPT
3. SOUTH TRANSEPT
4. CHANCEL
5. SACRISTY/LIBRARY
6. CHAPTER-HOUSE
7. CLOISTER
8. PARLOUR
9. UNDERCROFT OF DORTER
10. RERE-DORTER, WITH INFIRMARY BELOW
11. DRAIN
12. WARMING HOUSE
13. SITE OF FRATER
14. KITCHEN
15. WEST RANGE
16. ABBOT'S LODGING

0   100

NETLEY: *aerial view from the north-west*

was placed against the east wall and had one altar on each side of it and a fine east window above it; the latter consists of two broad lancets which were originally subdivided further to form four lights. In both the eastern bays of the chancel are remains of the rib-vaulting which extended the length of the aisles. In the chapels of the south transept the vaulting has survived, and in the angle between it and the chancel a spiral staircase built into the thickness of the wall can still be seen, which presumably gave access to the gallery. The door immediately to the south of this was knocked out after the Dissolution. On the plinths of the crossing piers can be seen inscriptions relating to Henry III's part in the foundation of the abbey, one with a crown and cross, another with a pennon and cross above a shield, and another with a shield and cross and the legend H. DI. GRA. REX ANGL. (Henry, by the grace of God, King of England). Along with the presbytery and transepts, the south wall of the nave was completed in the latter half of the 13th c. In its eastern bay it contained the usual processional doorway to the cloister, but the doorway in the fourth bay from the crossing is a 16th-c. addition, put in after the nave of the church was converted into the great hall of a Tudor mansion.

The west front of the church and its north nave wall were not completed until the early 14th c., and the remaining three-light windows contain considerably more elaboration in the way of tracery than those of the south wall. The support system is different too: the designers of the south wall had to make do with relatively small, internal buttresses, in order not to impinge on the north walk of the cloister, whereas with the north wall there was no such problem and the larger buttresses could be placed externally. The west front of the church has a large central doorway and two small lateral ones, the southern of which led at an oblique angle into the west range of the cloister, thus dispensing with

NETLEY: *the east end of the church, with rere-dorter/infirmary in the background*

the need for a doorway leading directly from the western bay of the church to the cloister's north-west corner. To the north of the church are the foundations of two small buildings; the western one is undoubtedly post-Dissolution, while the date and purpose of the eastern one are uncertain.

The eastern claustral range contains a beautiful little sacristy-cum-library immediately to the south of the south transept. Its western bay was originally divided from the two eastern bays by a partition wall, and formed the library. It is reached by a doorway which is monastic, but the two doorways to the north of it, leading from the south transept to the cloister, are post-Dissolution insertions. The two eastern bays formed the sacristy and are reached by a doorway from the south transept. Beneath the twin-lancet window of the east wall some fine original tiling has been re-set, on which stood an altar; in the south wall are a piscina and aumbrey for the altar. The whole room

retains its original rib-vaulting. South of it is the chapter-house, the three eastern windows of which have twin lancets with a sexfoil in the head. The central western arch is the original doorway, while the flanking western arches originally had windows, the lower masonry of which has been knocked out on the north side. The doors leading through the range immediately to the east of the cloister are all post-Dissolution additions, there being no access to these rooms except from the cloister in monastic times. Next to the chapter-house is the parlour, which had a barrel-vault and an eastern door so that it also served as an east-west passage through the whole range.

The undercroft of the dorter was originally divided into two aisles of five bays each, and the two northern bays were further screened off from the three southern bays by a stone wall of which only the foundations remain. For what purpose the two northern bays were used is not certain, but the three southern bays were probably used as accommodation for the novices in the abbey's early days, and then, as monastic discipline relaxed, as a misericorde. Over the whole eastern range, from the south wall of the south transept to the south wall of the later misericorde, stretched the monks' dorter. From the markings on the exterior of the south transept's south wall, it can be seen that it originally had a high-pitched sloping roof. It was reached by both night and day stairs, both of which have disappeared; the former were in the south-west corner of the south transept, while the latter were in the south-east angle of the cloister.

Running east and returning slightly north from the south end of the east range is the monks' rere-dorter block. Although the ground-floor ceiling largely remains, the ribs with which it was vaulted have disappeared. There is some uncertainty as to the original purpose of this ground-floor chamber, but probably it was the monks' or novices' infirmary; there is a monastic fireplace in the north wall, and an infirmary would certainly have had a fireplace. Along the south wall the well preserved great drain can be seen; it was the line of this drain which no doubt determined the curious angle of this block in relation to the rest of the east range. The first-floor chamber was the rere-dorter itself, while the small irregular chamber to the west of the infirmary on the ground floor was probably a buttery, later used as a meat-kitchen to serve the misericorde. It may originally have extended further to the west, as its present west wall is a post-Dissolution erection. The foundations of another small irregular chamber to the north of the rere-dorter block, between it and the misericorde, represent another post-Dissolution addition.

The south claustral range was more radically altered after the Dissolution than any other part of the monastery. Originally it conformed to the typical secondary Cistercian plan, with warming-house to the east, kitchen to the west, and in the middle the monastic frater stretching about 100 ft to the south of the south cloister walk on a north–south axis. After the Dissolution, the frater was entirely demolished to make room for the gateway to the new Tudor mansion, which was entered from the south in the middle of the south range. All that now remains of the frater is a few feet of foundation wall projecting from the cloister wall, which would originally have formed its north-eastern angle. The south walls of both the kitchen and the warming-house were also rebuilt after the Dissolution, but their north walls are original. The entrance to the frater from the cloister was originally slightly to the east of the present gatehouse doorway into the cloister. Towards the eastern end of the cloister's south wall can be seen the surviving arcading of the monastic lavatorium. The valuable lead-lined troughs below the arches were of course removed at the Dissolution. Of the west claustral range little has remained; it was, as usual in Cistercian monasteries, occupied mostly by lay-brothers, but Netley was a late foundation with an unusually small number of lay-brothers, and the range was smaller than at most Cistercian abbeys.

To the east of the claustral complex are the detached remains of the abbot's lodging, dating from the 13th c.; this marks an early relaxation of the Cistercian rule that the abbot should be accommodated in the dorter along with the rest of the monks. It is a low-storeyed building, with hall, bedroom, and chapel on the first floor, and kitchen, cellarage space, and possibly the abbot's guest room on the ground floor. In the north-east corner is a garderobe. The foundations visible between the east claustral range and the abbot's lodging are the remains of the terraced gardens of the Tudor mansion.

After the Dissolution the site and buildings were granted to Sir William Paulet, later Marquess of Winchester, who converted the abbey into what must have been a superb mansion; the nave became his hall, the eastern range his living-rooms, and the southern range his gatehouse with flanking apartments. The cloister was used as a courtyard. The abbey continued to be used as a dwelling-house until in the 18th c. the site passed into the hands of a Southampton builder called Taylor. He intended to demolish the entire church, but while supervising the demolition of the west end, he was crushed to death by the falling tracery of the west window; this was taken as a sign that the building should not be demolished. Later, it passed into the hands of the Chamberlayne family of Winchester, and in 1922 Tankerville Chamberlayne placed the ruins in the hands of the Ministry of Works. Netley Abbey is now in the care of English Heritage.

Norwich Cathedral Priory

ORDER: Benedictine monks
COUNTY: Norfolk
ROUTE: In city centre, off Wensum St.
OS REF: 134:2308

The cathedral priory of the holy and undivided Trinity at Norwich was founded in 1095–6 by Bishop Herbert Losinga. The East Anglian see had been fixed at Dunwich in 670, only to be divided between Dunwich and North Elmham three years later. After the Conquest, the Norman policy was to move sees to large towns, and accordingly, in 1075, it was moved to Thetford. Thetford, however, proved to be too close to the large and powerful abbey of Bury St Edmunds, over which the bishops found themselves unable to exert control. So when Bishop Losinga returned from a visit to Rome in 1095 he decided to move his see once more and, no doubt because of the increasing economic importance of the town, he chose Norwich. Two large stones from the original bishop's throne at North Elmham can still be seen incorporated in the modern bishop's throne behind the high altar in the cathedral; they date from the 8th c. and possibly earlier. Although building at Norwich only began in 1096, the work went ahead so fast that within five years the monks were able to move in, and the church received its first consecration on 24 September 1101. Although Bishop Losinga has been accused of simony because he was said to have purchased his bishopric from the king, it must be remembered that this charge was first levelled at him by the secular canons who serviced the cathedral at Thetford before he became bishop. Since Losinga replaced these canons with a community of Benedictine monks, so that it became a monastic cathedral, the canons were not likely to be favourably inclined towards him.

The number of monks at Norwich seems originally to have been sixty, and even after the Black Death there were still fifty monks left in 1381. By 1441 the number had risen again to fifty-six, but in the last century of its existence as a monastery numbers gradually declined—to forty-seven in 1499, thirty-nine in 1514, and thirty-one on the eve of the Dissolution in 1538–9. Of the life lived by the monks at Norwich we are unusually well-informed, for no less than 3,500 rolls of accounts and other documents from the 12th to the 16th cs. have survived, showing, for instance, that the community sometimes bought up to 10,000 eggs a week; normally distributed the same number of loaves of bread each year in alms; ran a grammar school attached to the monastery; and often financed its grand rebuilding projects (e.g., the cloisters, burnt by the citizens during a riot in 1272 and gradually reconstructed over the next 150 years) by foregoing their extra food allowances on feast days. The riot of 1272 was not the only disaster to befall the cathedral: in 1362 a severe storm brought down the spire, which fell on the chancel and destroyed the Norman clerestory, and in 1463, almost exactly one hundred years later, lightning struck the new spire during another storm and the timber roof of the nave was burnt down along with those choir stalls which stood under the tower. The priory was dissolved on 6 April 1539. Although some of the monastic buildings were destroyed, Norwich remained a cathedral of Reformation England, with a dean, six prebendaries, and sixteen minor canons, most of them former monks from the priory.

The church is basically early 12th c., roughly contemporary with Durham, and must rank with the latter as one of the greatest Romanesque churches in England, although the visual effect created by Norwich is very different from that created by Durham. Norwich has little of the massive weightiness of Durham, largely because of the treatment of the piers. At Durham the incised markings on the piers serve to emphasise their size and solidity; at Norwich the surfaces of the piers are broken up by slender attached columns and long vaulting-shafts which stress the vertical. The nave consists of fourteen bays (the largest number of any medieval English church), the eastern two of which form part of the quire, with aisles on both sides. By the time of his death in 1119, Bishop Losinga had probably already completed the chancel, transepts, and four eastern bays of the nave, the rest of the nave being built by his successor Bishop Everard Montgomery (the west doorway is a later replacement of about 1430). Apart from the west window and the vault, which were added by Bishop Lyhart after the collapse of the spire in 1463, the rest of the nave is much as it was constructed during the first half of the 12th c., with a high triforium supporting the clerestory and

low north and south aisles. The nave aisles, roofed with a typically Norman groin-vault, seem crude compared with the excellent 15th-c. lierne-vault down the main part of the nave. Particularly fine are the roof bosses of this vault, those of the seven eastern bays illustrating scenes from the Old Testament, and those of the seven western bays scenes from the New Testament.

The chancel is the finest surviving example of the more ambitious type of Norman plan for the east ends of churches, with a presbytery of four bays followed by an apse round which the aisles were carried to form a processional ambulatory from which project three chapels to the north, south and east. The north and south chapels are still as built, but the eastern chapel was replaced by a new chapel of St Saviour in the 20th c. The foundations of the Norman chapel, also dedicated to St Saviour, and the Anglo-Saxon chapel (mid-eleventh century) beneath it can still be seen. The arcade and triforium stages of the elevation in the chancel date, like the nave, from the first half of the 12th c., but the clerestory stage was rebuilt by Bishop Thomas Percy, the brother of the Earl of Northumberland, after the spire collapsed in 1362. Its proportions are perfect, and make the apse in particular one of the most visually delightful east ends in Europe. The chancel and transepts were still roofed with timber, however, and it was not until the late 15th and early 16th cs. that they received their stone vaults. Bishop James Goldwell (1472–99) built the vault of the chancel, also erecting flying buttresses outside to support it; the bosses of the vault are decorated with golden wells, a pun on his name. He also built the stone spire, which is 315 ft. high, the second highest in England, and has proved sturdier than its predecessors. His successor Bishop Richard Nykke (1501–36) erected the vaults in the transepts, the bosses of which illustrate in the north transept the childhood of Jesus and the life of the Virgin, and in the south transept Jesus's ministry.

The only surviving major structural alterations made to the church at ground level after the 12th c. are the reliquary arch in the north quire aisle, built in 1424 to provide a place where relics could be kept safe from fires, the west doorway of 1430, and the Bauchon chapel of 1330, which projects southwards from the angle of the south quire aisle and the south transept; it is used today as a Consistory Court, and contains a set of roof bosses

illustrating the story of an empress falsely accused by her brother who had tried in vain to seduce her, but saved by the intercession of the Virgin. The choir stalls, containing some excellently carved misericords, were added by Bishop John Wakering (1416–25), and the hawks depicted on some of the canopies represent his arms. Of the other furnishings in this superbly embellished cathedral, the most notable are the bishop's throne, the Despenser Retable of 1381, given to the church by the warlike Bishop Henry Despenser in 1381 and illustrating scenes from the death and resurrection of Christ (it is now in the chapel of St Luke, which projects south from the apse); and the effigy of Bishop Goldwell on the south side of the presbytery, unique among English episcopal effigies because it shows the bishop wearing a cope instead of the usual chasuble over eucharistic vestments.

Of the monastic buildings, the finest survival is the cloisters. After the original cloisters had been destroyed in the riot of 1272, it was twenty-five years before rebuilding began, and a further 130 years before the new cloisters were completed. First came the east walk, rebuilt between 1297 and 1318, then the south walk between 1318 and 1330. The west walk was begun in 1338, but the Black Death intervened and reconstruction dragged on spasmodically to completion in the early 15th c.; in 1410 the north walk was begun, and in 1430 the whole task was at last finished. Although the general design is remarkably unified for work spread over such a long period, the development of the vaults and the tracery in the windows, from Geometrical to Perpendicular, clearly mark the main stages of English architectural progress from the late 13th to early 15th cs. The existence of an upper storey, used today for storage of documents, a library, and choristers' rooms, is most unusual; probably it was built for winter use, a rare luxury. The roof-bosses around the cloister include a hundred consecutive scenes from the Book of Revelation as well as a great variety of other happenings, from Henry II doing penance at the tomb of Thomas Becket to a woman bringing a sack of corn to a windmill. As a full series, they are among the finest roof-bosses in the world.

Of the remaining monastic buildings little need be said, although the plan of the buildings is clear. To the south of the south transept came a parlour followed by the chapter-house, some of the foundations of which can still be seen, and the

dorter. A road now runs over parts of this eastern range. To the east of the southern end of the dorter, at right-angles to it, the undercroft of the reredorter is visible, and beyond it stands the modern Deanery on the site of the old prior's house. The south range of the cloister contained the frater, several of the walls of which stand to a good height, and at its eastern end a passage known as the Dark Entry; this dates from 1125 and led through the range to the infirmary, unusually positioned on an east–west axis to the south of the frater. A few of its pillars are still *in situ*. West of this, some distance from the south-west corner of the cloisters, is the long, low and much remodelled cellarer's range, originally built in the late 14th c. The west range, which contained the guest house, has almost entirely disappeared, but at the north end of the range can be seen the outer parlour of the monastery, where business with tradesmen was transacted, and to the north of the church the bishop's palace built by Herbert Losinga early in the 12th c. still stands, though it has been so drastically renovated and remodelled that it no longer resembles a medieval building.

To the west of the church stands the Erpingham gate, built in 1420 and leading directly into the cathedral, while some distance to the north of the church, by the River Wensum, is the Pull's Ferry Water Gate, through which ran the canal leading from the river to the cathedral. It was along this canal that bargemen brought the stone with which one of England's finest cathedrals was built.

Peterborough Cathedral

ORDER: Benedictine monks
COUNTY: Cambridgeshire
ROUTE: In town centre
OS REF: 142:6037

Before the 10th c., Peterborough was known as Medeshamstede. Here, in 656, a monastery was founded by Peada, King of Mercia, the son of the heathen King Penda, who had renounced his father's paganism and accepted Christianity even before his father's death. The first abbot was the nobleman Saxulf, who was appointed Bishop of Mercia in 675 by Archbishop Theodore of Canterbury, and then in 679, when Mercia was divided into five sees, he became Bishop of Lichfield. Medeshamstede grew to be the most important monastery in Mercia, but in 870 it was sacked and totally destroyed by the Danes; the Peterborough version of the *Anglo-Saxon Chronicle* states that St Aethelwold, Bishop of Winchester, 'came to the monastery called Medeshamstede ... and found there nothing but old walls and wild woods ... Medeshamstede too he restored'. This was in 966, and the new monastery which Aethelwold founded was a Benedictine abbey dedicated to St. Peter.

This monastery too became one of the most important in the midlands, and is now remembered chiefly for the fact that it was the home of the longest-running version of the *Anglo-Saxon Chronicle*. Its entries continue down to the year 1154. In 1116, however, the Saxon church and monastery had been almost totally destroyed in a fire. Building began again in 1118, under Abbot John de Seez, and continued well into the 13th c., by which time almost the whole church as we now see it was complete. From the 12th to the 14th cs. the number of monks seems to have remained at about sixty-five. After the Black Death the figure fell to thirty-two, rising to forty-seven in 1437 before declining again to thirty-eight at the Dissolution. Its position on the great north road ensured that it remained constantly in the mainstream of the country's life, while the abbey's extensive flocks of sheep ensured its continuing prosperity. The abbey was dissolved on 29 November 1539, only to be refounded two years later as one of the new cathedrals of Reformation England, with provision for a dean and six prebendaries.

The church is 481 ft. long, and consists of a nave of ten bays terminating in western transepts and a west front as deep as a bay, north and south transepts with eastern aisles, and a chancel which consists of a quire of four Norman bays and a retroquire added about 1500. The original plan was that the nave should be only nine bays long. These nine bays were completed by about 1175. During the next twenty years the western transepts were added, and by 1238 the west front had been completed too. The west front was planned on a grand scale, and it is a powerful composition, but it lacks order. It consists of three huge entrance arches, each of six orders, flanked by slender towers with narrow spires and pinnacles, and surmounted by gables, pinnacles, and a short square tower with yet more pinnacles. The resulting impression is clustered and untidy. It is unfortunate that the two outer arches are broader than the central arch (the original plan was for the central arch to be broader), and even more unfortunate that a Perpendicular porch was inserted in the central arch in the late 14th c. It means that little emphasis is placed on the main entrance, and the composition is unbalanced.

With the exception of the retro-quire, the interior of the cathedral dates from the 12th c. The rhythm of the bays remains uniform, although details such as capitals and mouldings change, becoming more advanced as the west end is reached. The western transepts are Transitional, with occasional pointed arches and more slender shafts. East of this point all the arches are rounded, the piers are large and sturdy, and the elevation is standardised at a ratio of 5:4:3 for arcade, triforium and clerestory. The triforium has twin openings within a super-arch for each bay; the clerestory has three stepped arches to each bay, as at Durham and Ely. The aisles of both nave and chancel are rib-vaulted in stone, but all the central areas of the church are vaulted in timber. The vault of the nave is canted and decorated with diamond-shaped patterns in which are painted figures of kings, queens, saints, animals and monsters. Much of the painting here is original. Under the tower is a lierne-vault with a central boss of Christ in Majesty. Along the west wall of the south transept is the vestry, added in the late 12th c. On the floor of the crossing and the south transept the outlines of the Saxon church are marked.

The vault of the quire was erected in the 15th c.

PETERBOROUGH: *aerial view from the west*

to replace the 12th-c. vault. It is again of timber panelling and displays bosses at the intersections, including a series from the New Testament. The Norman church ended in three stepped apses at the east end, but about 1500 Abbot Robert Kirkton (1496–1528) erected the present retro-quire, demolishing the two outer apses which terminated the chancel aisles and building a square east end around the central apse, which was also squared off. The retro-quire may have been designed by John Wastell, the architect of King's College Chapel, Cambridge, and Bell Harry tower at Canterbury. It is of two bays (with tongues projecting into the aisles), and is beautifully fan-vaulted, as at King's College Chapel. The windows are of three and four lights, with panel tracery.

The monastic buildings stood to the south of the church, but they are now mostly ruined, and what does survive is interwoven with more modern work. The area of the cloister is easily recognisable, for it is still an open courtyard, but of the ranges which surrounded it only the east wall of the west range, which was the cellarium, and the north wall of the south range, which was the frater, are standing. South-east of the east range was the infirmary, built in the mid-13th c. It is divided into an aisled western part and an unaisled eastern part, and is covered with some fine blank arcading in two tiers around the walls. The arches are delicately moulded and carried on graceful, slender piers—a striking contrast to the work of the nave, for here is pure 13th-c. Gothic. South of the infirmary is the modern deanery, which was probably the monastic guest-house; it was heavily restored in the 19th c., but still contains a large fireplace and other medieval details inside. On the other (the west) side of the cloister there are more medieval buildings. The abbot's house, now the bishop's palace, is again mostly Victorian, but two 13th-c. undercrofts with rib-vaulting survive in its basements. The abbot's gate, the king's lodging, and the outer gate are all connected and set in with much later (mostly Victorian) work, but again there are many medieval details to see. The gateways have been little tampered with. The abbot's gate dates from the early 13th c. and still displays some of its original sculpture, while the outer gate was built in the late 12th c., but re-modelled about 1300. The outer gate is still the way through which the visitor enters the cathedral precinct.

Rievaulx Abbey

ORDER: Cistercian monks
COUNTY: North Yorkshire
ROUTE: On B1257, 2½ miles WNW of Helmsley.
OS REF: 100:5784

Rievaulx was not the first Cistercian Abbey to be founded in England, that distinction belonging to Waverley (1128), but it was the first of the celebrated group of northern Cistercian foundations, and for at least a century after its foundation it was the most famous. The ruins of the abbey are majestic and well preserved. Among Cistercian houses, only Fountains has left more extensive remains.

The site in the Rye Valley from which Rievaulx takes its name was granted to the original community by Walter l'Espec, lord of Helmsley, who nine years earlier had founded the Augustinian Priory at Kirkham. The grant was made in 1131, after Bernard of Clairvaux had carefully prepared the ground by writing to both King Henry I and the zealous Archbishop Thurstan of York, and the site was colonised directly by monks from Clairvaux, a group of thirteen headed by William, the first abbot, an Englishman. It was not until 1132, however, that the monks arrived, and the charter of foundation dates from 5 March of that year. The monastery grew with phenomenal speed. Within ten years the combined number of monks and lay-brothers at Rievaulx was said to be three hundred, and during the later years of the rule of St Ailred, the third abbot (1147–67), there were 140 monks and between five and six hundred lay-brothers.

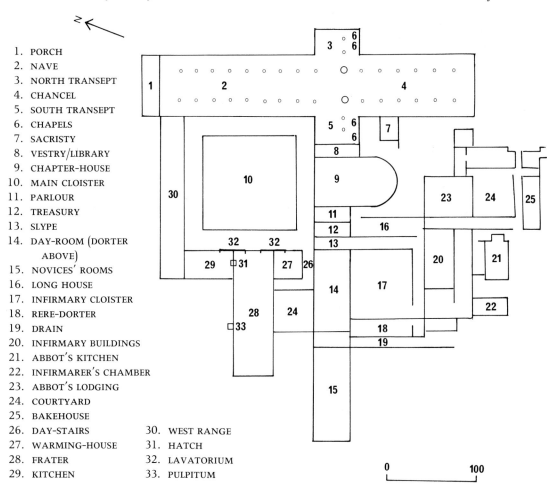

1. PORCH
2. NAVE
3. NORTH TRANSEPT
4. CHANCEL
5. SOUTH TRANSEPT
6. CHAPELS
7. SACRISTY
8. VESTRY/LIBRARY
9. CHAPTER-HOUSE
10. MAIN CLOISTER
11. PARLOUR
12. TREASURY
13. SLYPE
14. DAY-ROOM (DORTER ABOVE)
15. NOVICES' ROOMS
16. LONG HOUSE
17. INFIRMARY CLOISTER
18. RERE-DORTER
19. DRAIN
20. INFIRMARY BUILDINGS
21. ABBOT'S KITCHEN
22. INFIRMARER'S CHAMBER
23. ABBOT'S LODGING
24. COURTYARD
25. BAKEHOUSE
26. DAY-STAIRS
27. WARMING-HOUSE
28. FRATER
29. KITCHEN
30. WEST RANGE
31. HATCH
32. LAVATORIUM
33. PULPITUM

0   100

RIEVAULX: *aerial view from the (liturgical) south-*
west

Moreover, within eleven years of its foundation, Rievaulx had sent out colonies to found houses at Melrose, Warden, Dundrennan and Revesby. It was after being sent to Revesby as abbot that St Ailred, probably the greatest figure in English monastic life in the 12th c., returned after a few years to become Abbot of Rievaulx.

Although English by birth, Ailred had in his late boyhood joined the court circle of the Scottish kings, and rose to be steward in the household of King David I (1124–53), whose mother was the 'exquisite St Margaret', and who, it is said, had early singled Ailred out for the highest ecclesiastical preferment in the Scottish kingdom. In 1134, however, David sent Ailred south on a mission to Archbishop Thurstan of York. While there, Ailred heard of the white monks who had arrived at Rievaulx, and went to pass the night with Walter l'Espec at Helmsley. On the following day he visited Rievaulx, then returned to spend another night with l'Espec. Next morning he set off for Scotland again, but as he rode along the crest of the hill overlooking Rievaulx he found he could no longer resist the call; so, turning round, he rode down and presented himself at the door for the second time. This time he had come to stay. In 1142 Abbot William chose Ailred as his representative to Rome in the matter of the disputed archiepiscopal election at York. Within a few months of his return from Italy, Ailred was novice master at Rievaulx; a year later he became Abbot of Revesby, having already composed the *Mirror of Charity*, written at the behest of St Bernard, a deep analysis of the religious life. In 1147 he was chosen to be Abbot of Rievaulx. He was thirty-seven years old, and held office until his death on 11 January 1167. By that time his fame had spread far. He was the respected friend of King Henry II and was said to have greatly influenced that monarch's decision to support Pope Alexander III against the antipope Octavian in 1159. He corresponded regularly with popes, kings and bishops, and besides his spiritual writings he also wrote a *Genealogy of the Kings of England* and a life of Edward the Confessor. Under him, Rievaulx acquired a reputation for sanctity second to none, which was to stand it in good stead in later days when the initial enthusiasm had waned and its standing among the monasteries of England had fallen.

Along with the spiritual upsurge at Rievaulx came sustained building activity which lasted for over a century after the abbey's foundation, and although it left us the magnificent ruins we see today, it also left the monks heavily in debt. Indeed, from about 1300 onwards, although there is little recorded history of the abbey, the fortunes of Rievaulx appear to have declined. The Black Death and the changed labour conditions which resulted fell heavily on Rievaulx, and by 1380 the 140 monks and five or six hundred lay-brothers of Ailred's day had dwindled to a mere fifteen monks and three lay-brothers. In the late 15th or early 16th c., parts of the chapter-house, dorter and warming-house were taken down because they were too big for requirements. Nevertheless the house did not lose its esteem, and in 1464 its abbot ranked fourth in the list of dignitaries at the installation of the new Archbishop of York. In 1533 Abbot Kirkby was deposed by the royal commissioners for opposing the king's religious policy, but only seven out of the twenty-three monks would agree to a fresh election and a king's man, Richard Blyton, had to be imposed upon the community. The Dissolution came peacefully to Rievaulx on 3 December 1538, at which time there were twenty-one monks left with Abbot Blyton. Its clear annual income in 1535 was £278; when one remembers that at this time twenty-eight religious houses had incomes of £1,000 or more, it is clear how much Rievaulx had sunk from the heights it had once scaled.

The site on which Rievaulx was built slopes sharply to the west, making the construction of any major building on an east-west axis virtually impossible. Thus, although the builders of Rievaulx on the whole coped with the problems presented by this slope with remarkable ingenuity, it was at the expense of one almost universal convention: the church itself was built on a north–south axis, with the liturgical east end, i.e., the presbytery, in fact pointing almost due south, and the nave almost due north. In discussing Rievaulx, other writers have ignored the ninety-degree swing and discussed the architecture in liturgical terms, and their practice will be followed here. Thus the chancel is the 'east end', the nave is the 'west end', and the monastic buildings lie to the 'south' of the church.

The church as completed in the 13th c. was large, about 370 ft. in length. What remains of the nave, which is little more than the lower part of the walls and the square bases of most of the aisle piers,

RIEVAULX: *interior of the church, looking towards the nave*

dates from the earliest period of building, 1135–40; it is older than any large Cistercian nave standing in either France or Britain, and is plain, severe Romanesque in character, in accordance with the strict instructions regarding restraint of architectural design to which the earlier Cistercian houses adhered. The north, south and west walls of the transepts date from the same period, with the topmost stage added in the 13th c.

Looking down the nave from the west end of the church, the visitor sees one of the most perfect surviving comparisons between the practical restraint of 12th-c. monastic architecture and the embryonic splendour of English Gothic. The lower windows on the west walls of both transepts are pure Romanesque, as are the second pair of windows in the south transept, but in the north transept the 13th-c. reconstruction began lower down and the second row of windows have pointed arches. The upper windows on both sides are taller and broader shafted lancets, those in the north transepts being set within an arcade of blind lancets broken only by the central buttress. The transept east walls, the tower arch at the western end of the chancel, and the chancel itself combine to form one of the masterpieces of Early English Gothic. The 12th-c church extended only two bays east of the tower, but in about 1230 a new chancel of seven bays was added, two eastern chapels being built in each transept, and five chapels in the chancel's east bay. The aisle piers are shafted, five shafts to each face, and the arches are moulded accordingly; the triforium consists of two twin openings in each bay, shafted again, with ornate capitals and quatrefoils in the spandrels, and strangely in the western bay they are set within a round-headed super-arch. There was a North Country fashion for this motif at the time, for it also appears at Whitby, Hexham, and in the south transept of York minister. The clerestory has two narrow lancets flanked by two blank lancets, stepped to fit into the super-arch, in each bay. The east wall of the church is two-tiered, with three shafted lancets interspersed with two narrower blind lancets on the ground floor, and three stepped lancets set within a blind arch at the upper level; the eastern bay of the chancel's south aisle also stands in part, with an octagonal angle turret, but of the north aisle hardly anything remains. The two precarious flying buttresses on the north side of the chancel were added as a precaution in the

14th c. Dominating the view of the church from the west is the tower arch. With its massive shafted piers, it soars 75 ft. above the floor of the quire, and is topped by two short windows with pointed arches. The remains of the sacristy adjoin the south aisle two bays along from the south transept; this was a 14th c. addition.

Adjoining the south transept is a narrow vestry-cum-library dating from the 12th c. The next building to the south is the chapter-house, which differs greatly at Rievaulx from the normal rectangular Cistercian chapter-house. It is an oblong room with an eastern apse and a western vestibule, the latter being continued all the way round the building to form a vaulted aisle. The chapter-house itself could not be vaulted since the span of the vault would have been too wide and the dorter had to be situated above it. In the 15th c. the aisle running round the apse was pulled down and the arcade of the apse walled in; the walls then erected are still visible. Across the northern bay of the west wall is a most unusual shrine to William, first Abbot of Rievaulx, which once had a vaulted and gabled canopy under which the relics were kept. The empty coffin in the middle of the chapter-house may have been that of St Ailred.

South of the chapter-house are the parlour, the treasury, a narrow barrel-vaulted room over which were the monks' day-stairs to the dorter, and then a passage leading through the eastern range to the infirmary, which later became the abbot's hall. On the south side of this passage is the infirmary cloister, along the south wall of which ran the reredorter. The drain along the south side of the reredorter can still be seen. To the north of the infirmary are the remains of the abbot's lodging, which was connected to the church by a series of small rooms and courtyards. Continuing south from the passage through the eastern range are the monks' day room and the novices' rooms, above which, stretching 320 ft. to the south from the south transept of the church, was the monks' dorter. So steep was the fall of the ground that the last 100 ft. or so of the southern end of the dorter had to be built on three storeys, and the remains of several flying buttresses needed to support it can be seen on both sides of the building.

From east to west along the south range of the cloister are the warming-house, frater, and kitchen, all dating from the beginning of the 13th c. The warming-house originally had a south aisle with octagonal piers, but that was filled in in the 15th c.; the western wall includes a double fireplace 20 ft. wide, which must have given out all the heat the monks required. The frater, 124 ft. by 38 ft., is an excellent example of how the slope of the ground at Rievaulx was used to the best possible advantage, for it allowed the master mason to create the imposing height of an upper-floor type of refectory without having to insert a staircase leading from the cloister. What now appears as the floor was in fact the vault, used no doubt for cellarage, and the floor of the frater, which was tiled, was along the level between what seem to be the ground and first floors, the break being readily apparent. The frater walls were filled with a series of shafted lancets set in an arcade of blind lancets, except for the northern half of the west wall which contained the reader's pulpitum, reached by a flight of stairs set in the wall behind which were three continuous lancets. On either side of the frater door is a wall arcade, in which there were once lead-lined troughs to serve as a lavatorium. Little remains of the kitchen, or indeed of the lay-brothers' range along the west walk of the cloister, which is singularly small and inadequate. One can only wonder where the five or six hundred lay-brothers of Ailred's day were accommodated. There must have been much temporary wooden accom-modation around the abbey, for it is impossible that anything like five hundred lay-brothers could have stayed in the western range.

At the foot of the slope on which the abbey stands runs the river Rye, but it has not always run there. When the monks first moved into their new home at Rievaulx it ran down the centre of the valley, to the west (the true west) of the frater, but they diverted it and thus became owners of the lands now on its left bank, for the river had previously been the boundary between the lands of Walter l'Espec and Roger Mowbray, the founder of neighbouring Byland. The monks did not get their fresh water from the river. It was taken from springs on the hillside to a conduit house near the west end of the church and distributed from there, flowing also in a stone-built channel under the frater to the great drain on the south side of the rere-dorter—but the monks managed to use the old river to turn the abbey mill and to float the building stone which they needed on rafts down from Penny Piece quarry, constructing a wharf near the western end of the site. As at Fountains, the ways in which the available water-supply was used is one of the most remarkable features of the abbey's construction.

After the Dissolution the site was granted to Thomas, Earl of Rutland, and passed, along with the Helmsley estates, into the successive hands of the Manners, Villiers, and Duncombe families. It was Thomas Duncombe who constructed, about 1758, the famous Rievaulx Terraces in Duncombe Park, from which is obtained the most perfect view of Rievaulx. In 1918 the abbey site was placed in the hands of the Commissioners of Works, and is now in the care of English Heritage.

Roche Abbey

ORDER: Cistercian monks
COUNTY: South Yorkshire
ROUTE: Off A634, 1½ miles SE of Maltby.
OS REF: 111:5489

The Cistercian Abbey of St Mary of Roche is so called because of the white limestone rocks which jut out strikingly from the hillside on the north side of the site. The abbey was jointly founded in 1147 by Richard de Bully and Richard Fitz Turgis. They owned the land on either side of the stream which runs through the site and granted the monks permission to build their abbey on both sides of it. It was colonised from Newminster in Northumberland, itself a daughter-house of Fountains, and by the late 12th c. probably contained over twenty monks as well as sixty lay-brothers. Little of its history has been recorded, but it is known that by the late 14th c. the number of monks had declined to fourteen, with one lay-brother. In 1538 one of the monks was imprisoned at York on a charge of treason, but otherwise the dissolution of the house seems to have been peaceful, the house being surrendered to the crown on 23 June 1538 by eighteen monks and the abbot. Thirteen monks, four novices and the abbot received pensions.

Apart from the gatehouse to the north-west of the church, the only part of the monastic complex which stands to any great height is the east end of the church with its adjoining transept walls, yet so excellently has Roche been excavated and laid out that it is possible to follow the lines of the buildings over the whole site with the utmost clarity. The church's overall internal length is a little over 200 ft. Although there is no direct evidence by which to date it, it was almost certainly completed between 1160 and 1170. The nave of eight bays is broad and aisled; in the fifth bay from the west there were originally four chapels with eastern altars, and the remains of the screen walls which cut off this bay to both east and west can still be seen. The chancel is short and narrow, and the presbytery is placed between the twin eastern chapels of the transepts. The eastern parts of the Roche transepts, particularly of the south transept, are almost complete, and here one sees the importance of the church in the development of English Gothic. Not merely were the arches becoming more pointed, but much more impor-

1. NAVE
2. CHANCEL
3. NORTH TRANSEPT
4. SOUTH TRANSEPT
5. CHAPELS
6. SACRISTY/LIBRARY
7. CHAPTER-HOUSE
8. PARLOUR
9. UNDERCROFT OF DORTER
10. CLOISTER
11. WARMING-HOUSE
12. FRATER
13. KITCHEN
14. LAY-BROTHERS' FRATER,
    WITH LAY-BROTHERS'
    DORTER OVER
15. LAY-BROTHERS' INFIRMARY
16. ABBOT'S KITCHEN
17. ABBOT'S LODGING
18. INFIRMARER'S LODGING
19. RERE DORTER
20. MISERICORD (PROBABLE)

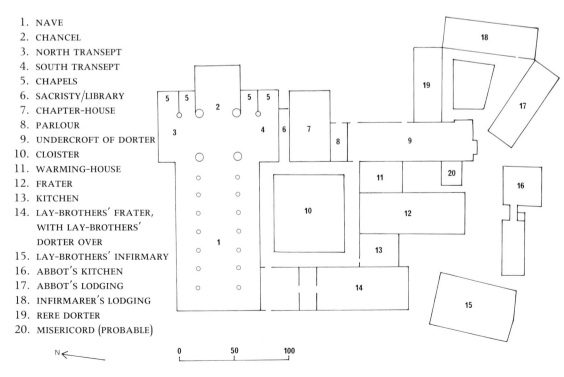

N ←

0   50   100

ROCHE: *aerial view from the west*

tantly, the decorative appearance of the church was becoming more closely allied to the structural problems involved in building it. The emphasis was gradually shifting away from massive and imposing forms towards a combination of windows, arches and walls which together create a far greater impression of spaciousness. Thus the piers are not massive squares or circles but groups of clustered shafts; the vaulting-shafts do not simply appear 'as from nowhere' at triforium or clerestory level, but run right up the walls from ground level. The transept chapels too are conceived in a different way, not as separate rooms divided by thick stone walls, but as related units in a vaulting system, like the bays of an aisle.

Indeed the whole church was vaulted in stone, which was the most 'Gothic' of all the innovations at Roche. Yet having said this, it remains true that Roche is not truly a Gothic church. Its walls are still thick, and the blind recesses of the triforium stage are too deep and too close to each other to suggest that the builders of Roche were intent on trying to create the lightness and spacious appearance of more developed Gothic work.

The monastic buildings approximate to a perfect late 12th c. Cistercian plan, but few walls stand above foundation level and there is little deserving of comment. The east claustral range contained, from north to south, a narrow library-cum-sacristy, the chapter-house, the parlour, and novices' rooms, with the monks' dorter on the first floor. The south range consisted of warming-house, frater on a north–south axis, and kitchen; all these were built in the 13th c. The western range, with the lay-brothers' frater and dorter over it, dates from the late 12th c. and is probably the oldest part of the complex, built to accommodate the builders of the church. Under the south end of the monks' dorter and frater runs the stream which served as the monastery's great drain, and across it running east from the dorter at right-angles is the rere-dorter. The floor of the frater above the stream has partly collapsed into it. There are more buildings on the south bank of the stream. The infirmarer's lodging and the lay-brothers' infirmary, which are the easternmost and westernmost buildings of this

ROCHE: *the transepts, from the west*

group, both date from the 13th c., but the central buildings, containing the abbot's lodging and his other private apartments, are 14th c. additions. The misericorde attached to the southern end of the dorter was built in the 15th c.

To the north-west of the church the fine gatehouse, rebuilt in the early 14th c., has one almost complete storey, including its vaulting. It has wide open arches at each end and a cross-wall in the middle divided into a wider part for horses and carriages and a narrower part for pedestrians. The second storey may have included a chapel for the laity, who were not allowed into the abbey church, but no trace of it survives. Another building attached to its south side, of which a few pieces of masonry remain, was probably an almonry.

Immediately after it was dissolved, Roche was plundered and largely destroyed by the people of the neighbourhood. 'All things of price', declared an Elizabethan writer whose father had been an eye-witness to the devastation, were 'either spoiled, carped away, or defaced to the uttermost . . . it seemeth that every person bent himself to filch and spoil what he could'. Possibly such an orgy of looting resulted as much from the townspeople's resentment of the abbey's formerly privileged position as from their desire to get their hands on all the lead, timber, building-stone and ornaments they could. In 1544 the site and what remained of the buildings were granted to Thomas Vavasour and William Ransden. They soon passed into the hands of Robert Saunderson of Fillingham, whose son was created Viscount Castleton in 1627. In 1720 the sixth viscount became Earl of Castleton, but died without issue and the abbey passed to Thomas Lumley, later Earl of Scarbrough. In the mid-18th c. it was landscaped by Lancelot 'Capability' Brown, It is now in the care of English Heritage.

Rochester Cathedral Priory

ORDER: Benedictine monks
COUNTY: Kent
ROUTE: In town centre, off High St.
OS REF: 178:7468

After Canterbury, Rochester is the second oldest episcopal see in England. The first religious house here was founded by King Ethelbert of Kent in 604, and the first bishop was Justus, who was consecrated by St. Augustine in the same year. The house attached to the cathedral was not a monastery, but a foundation for five secular canons. The Anglo-Saxon cathedral probably never flourished, but tended to remain in the shadow of Canterbury. The Danes raided Rochester on several occasions, and the 10th-c. revival of monasticism seems to have almost totally by-passed it. By 1075 the church was 'utterly forsaken, miserable and waste, from lack of all things within and without', and only four impecunious canons remained. In 1077, Archbishop Lanfranc consecrated the reformer Gundulf as Bishop, and the cathedral's fortunes revived. Gundulf began a massive new building operation and replaced the remaining canons with a community of Benedictine monks in 1080. By the time of his death in 1107 there were sixty monks. There were fires in 1137 and 1179, and the church was again rebuilt in the mid-12th c.

In 1201 occurred an event of great importance. A baker from Perth, William by name, who was said to be so charitable that he gave to the poor one out of every ten loaves which he baked, spent a night in the priory and was murdered by the roadside the following morning. His body was brought back to the cathedral for burial, and soon miracles began to occur at his tomb. Although the monks had to wait until 1256 for the official canonisation of St William of Perth, it seems that the fame of the charitable baker spread rapidly in the early years of the 13th c. and attracted numerous pilgrims. So Rochester, like its neighbour Canterbury and many other cathedrals and abbeys, had its own martyr's shrine to swell its income, and during the 13th c. funds were sufficient to allow the rebuilding of the whole east end of the church.

Still, however, there were setbacks. In 1215 King John's army pillaged the cathedral, and in 1264 Simon de Montfort stationed his forces here on Good Friday. What happened has been described by a contemporary: 'Armed knights on their horses coursing round the altars, dragging with impious hands some who fled for refuge hither, the gold and silver and other precious things being with violence carried off . . . The oratories, cloisters, chapter-house, infirmary and all the sacred buildings were turned into horses' stables, and everywhere filled with dung of animals and defilement of dead bodies.' In 1327 the citizens of Rochester themselves besieged and sacked the cathedral. In the later middle ages the history of the cathedral is less eventful. After the Black Death the number of monks declined to about thirty. The twenty remaining monks acknowledged the royal supremacy in 1534, and although Rochester's celebrated bishop, Cardinal John Fisher, was executed along with Thomas More on Tower Hill in 1535 for refusing to give the nod to Henry VIII's 'reforms', the monastery itself was surrendered without a struggle on 20 March 1540. In June 1541 it was reconstituted as a Protestant Cathedral, with provision for a Dean and six prebendaries.

Architecturally, Rochester is not one of the great cathedrals of England. It is 305 ft. in overall length, and consists of an aisled nave of eight bays, two sets of transepts, as at Canterbury, divided by a quire of four bays, and a narrow, aisleless chancel which culminates in a square east end. The west front is a well-balanced and harmonious composition. The four turrets with their mass of traditional Norman blank arcading below provide a strongly vertical effect which blends well with the eight-light perpendicular window, a 15th-c. insertion. The turrets themselves had to be reconstructed (from an original engraving) by J. L. Pearson in 1888. The west doorway of five orders is a noble piece of work and is enriched with some fine sculpture.

The nave is very horizontal, with broad, flat arches which place the minimum of emphasis on verticality. The spacing between the arches opens up the vistas into the aisles and tends to make of them an integral part of the structure, not isolated as in so many Norman and Gothic churches, and this again emphasises the lowness and flatness of the nave. Each pair of piers is shaped differently. The elevation follows the traditional Norman pattern of arcade, gallery, clerestory, the clerestory having been rebuilt along with the west window in the 15th c. In the angle between the nave and south

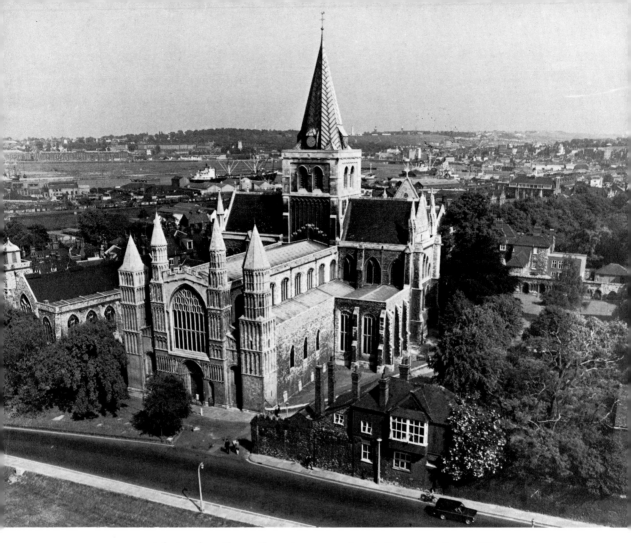

ROCHESTER : *aerial view from the south-west*

transept is the Lady Chapel, which was added in the first quarter of the 16th c. and stands with its three arches open to the south aisle. In the north-west corner of the nave is a half-circle marked in the paving; this shows the outline of the Saxon cathedral which preceded the Conquest, the lines of which have been recovered by excavation. Also in the nave is the episcopal throne, once the chair of Miles Coverdale, Bishop of Exeter and the first man single-handedly to translate the complete Bible into the English language; Coverdale died in 1551, and his chair was presented to the cathedral by the parish of Hadlow in 1954.

The eastern half of the church was built in the early 13th c., and as will be seen from the masonry joint and change of style, it was intended at that time to rebuild the nave as well, but presumably funds ran out and only the two eastern bays of the nave were rebuilt, the joint then being rather hurriedly patched up. The crossing tower was added in the mid-14th c. by Bishop Hamo Hythe, the former confessor of King Edward II; from its walls, large grotesque heads look down into the crossing. Both quire and chancel are Early English, with considerable amounts of Purbeck marble used, vaulting-shafts running from the floor to the roof, and sexpartite rib-vaults, but both also have peculiarly individual features. The quire has solid stone walls to separate it from its aisles, so that the latter are cut off from the main body of the church. The presbytery, on the other hand, has no aisles at all, only deep recesses to mark the bays between the vaulting-shafts and, even more unusual (indeed unique in an English cathedral), the elevation is of only two stages. Only a Purbeck marble string-course divides the arcade from the clerestory, the triforium being completely dispensed with.

Among the features of the eastern part of the cathedral are the 13th-c. wall-painting of the Wheel of Fortune in the quire, one of the finest

ROCHESTER: *the west doorway of the church*

surviving specimens of wall-painting of its period, and the remarkably sumptuous doorway to the chapter room, in the south-east corner of the eastern transept. Its rich decoration and figure-sculpture contrast strikingly with the sober and restrained architecture of the rest of the cathedral. Between the presbytery and the eastern chapel of the north-east transept is the tomb of Bishop John Northwood of Sheppey, who became treasurer of England, and behind it is a marble slab, all that remains of the shrine of St William of Perth, the Saint who was largely responsible for making the rebuilding of the eastern half of the church possible. Finally, below the east end is a crypt, which apart from its two Norman west bays dates from the early 13th c. It is spacious, although it cannot compare with Canterbury in size, and has slender, round piers with marble rings, which support a groin-vault throughout.

The monastic buildings lay to the south of the church, but unusually they adjoined the chancel, not the nave. They date from the episcopacy of Ernulf (1114–24), which is interesting because Gundulf too is said to have built monastic buildings some twenty-five years earlier. It may be that Gundulf built his cloister adjoining the nave, so that when Ernulf decided that new buildings were necessary he began reconstruction against the chancel so that the monks could go on using Gundulf's buildings until the new ones were ready. This is the usual explanation, although it is puzzling that no traces of an earlier cloister adjoining the nave have ever been found. The remains of the claustral ranges are heavily ruined, and only in the east range is anything distinguishable. Here the whole of the outer walk of the cloister stands, with the chapter-house and dorter undercroft behind it. The chapter-house has the usual triple entrance arches in two storeys, and blank arcading which continues along the rest of the wall. It was rectangular, with a vestibule in the western bay, over which a gallery carried the passage leading to the monks' night-stairs between chapter room and dorter. The doorway which led to these stairs is to the north of the entrance, and has an interesting tympanum with a relief sculpture of the Sacrifice of Isaac. The dorter undercroft lies to the south of this; when excavated (about 1900) it was found to be 91 ft. by 41 ft. The south side of the cloister was occupied by the frater, a building well over 100 ft. in length. Its entrance arch can still be seen, with the early 13th-c. lavatorium and towel recess behind a trefoil-headed arch next to it. At the south-west angle of the cloister is a gateway inserted in the 15th c., and at the southern end of the west range a square 12th-c. chamber, which presumably formed part of the undercroft of the cellarer's lodging, which usually occupied the west range. The only other medieval buildings of which remains can be seen are the 15th-c. prior's gate, a two-storeyed structure with an octopartite rib-vault, and, also on the north side of the church, the free-standing Gundulf's Tower, fitted into the space between the two northern transepts, but built of course before either of them. This was apparently the first building which Gundulf erected at Rochester, and must date from about 1080; originally it was a third as high again as it is now, and its purpose must surely have been defensive.

St Albans Cathedral

ORDER: Benedictine monks
COUNTY: Hertfordshire
ROUTE: In town centre
OS REF: 166:1407

Not until 1877 did St Albans become the see of a bishop, yet throughout the middle ages it was one of the greatest abbeys in England, and its abbots claimed, with some justification, to be the premier abbots of the kingdom. The abbey was built on the spot where St Alban, the proto-martyr of England, was said to have been martyred in 304 A.D., during the Diocletian persecution. Less than half a mile to the east is the site of Verulamium, one of the most important Roman towns in Britain. According to the tradition of the monks, St German of Auxerre visited the tomb of St Alban in 429. He left there the relics of other saints to rest with those of St Alban, and in 793 these were discovered by Offa, King of Mercia, who founded a monastery to preserve them. The monks were placed under the Benedictine rule, but this was apparently not strictly kept. In 968, St Oswald of Worcester and King Edgar introduced the strict Benedictine rule; it is from this time that the foundation of the abbey is usually dated. The abbey remained wealthy and influential: in 1077 Paul of Caen, who was rumoured to be the son of Archbishop Lanfranc of Canterbury, began to build the great Norman church which still forms the nucleus of the church we see today, and in 1154 the abbot was acknowledged as the first abbot of England. The abbey was exempted from episcopal control. The number of monks reached one hundred early in the 13th c., and remained at that level until the Black Death, when the abbot and forty-seven monks died.

During the 13th and 14th c. the fame of St Albans was at its height. More than any other British monastery, it was celebrated for its literary and artistic traditions: Matthew Paris and Thomas Walsingham, probably the two most famous chroniclers of medieval England, were both monks of St Albans. During the 14th c., St Albans was ruled by a succession of great abbots, of whom the last and greatest was Thomas de la Mare (1349–96), a builder and administrator whom the Black Prince was said to have 'loved as a brother', and whose influence was the equal at least of any contemporary ecclesiastic. That St Albans was not severely damaged during the Peasants Revolt of 1381 is usually attributed to his strength of character. From the late 14th c. until the Dissolution the number of monks remained at around 50. The abbey was dissolved on 5 December 1539.

The exterior length of the church, including the Lady Chapel, is nearly 550 ft. It consists of an aisled nave of twelve bays, north and south transepts with a tower over the crossing, and a chancel of seven bays with the Lady Chapel projecting from its east end. The west front is Victorian, built by the architect and lawyer Lord Grimthorpe in 1879 to replace the one built by Abbot John de Cella about 1200. Lord Grimthorpe paid for the work himself, and it is said to have cost him £130,000. The nave is long and narrow. The Norman nave built by Abbot Paul de Caen between 1077 and 1088 was nine bays long, but John de Cella decided to lengthen it by three bays. In the 14th c. the central six bays on the south side of the nave collapsed and were re-built (in the Early English style, to harmonise with the three western bays). Thus on the south side only the three eastern bays have survived from the Norman church, while on the north side all nine of the original bays have survived. The resulting impression is unbalanced, particularly at the lower stages where the pointed Early English arches reach several feet higher than the rounded Norman arches.

The sombre and weighty nature of the Norman work is best appreciated in the transepts and crossing. There is an almost total lack of decoration. The power of the architecture is emphasised by the tall crossing arches. Above them sits the squat and solid central tower, with tiers of twin-light openings surmounted by an embattled parapet. Many of the warm reddish stones here were taken by the monks from the site of Verulamium. The Norman chancel consisted of five bays with a trio of steeped apses at the east end, but this was replaced in the second half of the 13th c. In the bays next to the crossing some Norman work was allowed to remain, but the remaining bays are thoroughly Gothic. The aisles are rib-vaulted in stone. The central area of the chancel was also meant to be stone-vaulted, but in the event a timber roof was set up. It was recently re-painted in accordance with the medieval designs. The east window is of four lights surmounted by an octofoil, flanked by two narrow lancets. Above this group,

331

ST ALBANS: *the transepts*

visible from the exterior, is a charming sexfoil. The Lady Chapel, built in the first quarter of the 14th c., is in the Decorated style. Its windows have complex tracery and elaborate ornamentation. Like the chancel, the Lady Chapel was vaulted in timber, and the present stone vault was only erected in the 19th c.

The monastic buildings stood to the south of the church, but practically nothing has survived. To the south of the south transept is the slype, decorated with intersecting blank arcading. South

of this came the chapter-house, while the frater lay along the south range and the west range contained cellarage space, probably with the abbot's lodging above. Some of these buildings have been excavated. West of the church is the gatehouse, the only other building to have survived at St Albans. It was built by Thomas de la Mare in the late 14th c., and is divided into the usual broad and narrow arches, for carriages and pedestrians. It is a large and imposing structure, and no doubt served to remind many a medieval visitor that he was entering the precinct of one of the most illustrious English monasteries.

St Andrews Cathedral Priory

ORDER: Augustinian canons
COUNTY: Fife
ROUTE: In town centre, at E end of North St. and South St.
OS REF: 59:5116

St Andrews, the home of golf, Scotland's oldest university, and its archiepiscopal see, is steeped in history and legend. According to one of these legends, a Greek monk named St Regulus or Rule was warned in a vision about the year 345 that the emperor Constantine was about to remove the relics of the apostle St Andrew from their resting-place at Patras to his new capital Constantinople. Accordingly he went to the apostle's shrine and took an arm-bone, three fingers of the right hand, a tooth, and a knee-cap, and setting out by ship for western parts, arrived on the Scottish coast, still with the relics. There he established a religious house, and the town which grew up around it was called St Andrews. Other legends assign a similar story to the 8th c., when there seems certainly to have been a religious house here, and in 908 the one bishopric in Scotland was transferred from Abernethy to St Andrews. It was not until 1144, however, that the Augustinian priory to which the present ruins belonged was founded. The founder was the Bishop of St Andrews, Robert, who colonised it from Scone, the house of which he had formerly been prior. Three years later the Pope transferred the right to elect the bishop from the Culdees (the remains of whose church, St Mary of the Rock, can still be seen on the cliff-top to the east of the cathedral) to the new canons.

Bishop Robert built the church and tower of St Rule, which stands a few yards south-east of the cathedral, but his successor Bishop Arnold decided that a far grander church was necessary. In 1160 he began to build the great cathedral church of which the ruins still dominate the site. It was planned on an impressive scale, to be the second longest church in Britain after Norwich Cathedral, but in about 1275 the west end was destroyed in a storm, and when the new west end was erected, it was decided to shorten the nave by two bays. The 'new kyrk cathedralle' was consecrated in 1318 by Bishop Lamberton, a staunchly patriotic Scot who crowned Robert Bruce at Scone in 1306, and for his pains was seized by the English King, Edward I, and imprisoned in Winchester Castle for two years. After his release in 1308, secured with an oath of fealty to the new king, Edward II, he continued to support Bruce, and rebuilt the priory chapter-house and erected ten new churches in his diocese. About 1375 the roof of the church was destroyed in a fire, and in 1409 the gable of the south transept fell in a storm, but these misfortunes were overcome, and St Andrews became a mitred priory in 1418, and the archiepiscopal see of Scotland in 1472. From 1538 the priory was held by a series of commendators culminating with Ludovic, Duke of Lennox, for whom it was erected into a temporal lordship by Act of Parliament in 1592.

After the re-building of the west end in about 1280, the church consisted of an aisled nave of twelve bays, north and south transepts with eastern aisles containing three chapels on each side, and an aisled chancel of five bays from which projected an aisleless and square-ended sanctuary at the east end, bringing the total exterior length of the church to 375 ft. It was built during the second half of the 12th and early 13th cs., and apart from the re-building of the west end and necessary repair work to the upper stages after the various disasters recorded earlier, it remained largely unaltered. The main surviving parts are the ruined west front, the east end, the south wall of the nave, and the south and west walls of the south transept; but the foundations of the remaining parts of the church are clearly marked, and the bases of many of the piers are in situ, so that the arrangement of the whole church can be easily grasped.

The west front contains a small but deep-set doorway surmounted by a tier of blank arcading, above which were twin windows of three lights of which one survives. The solitary pinnacled turret which reaches upwards on the south side was undoubtedly matched by a similar one on the north side of the door, and between them was probably a wheel window. On the outside of the south wall of the nave can be seen several of the corbels which supported the lean-to roof of the north cloister walk, the windows having been set high enough to clear it; a change in the design of these windows can be seen after the fourth bay from the east, the western ones having probably been inserted in the late 13th c. after the collapse of the west front, which may have damaged them. Both doorways from the church to the cloister are now blocked.

ST ANDREWS: *the cathedral and precincts from the air, with the remains of the church of St Mary in the top right corner*

The west wall of the south transept is decorated with interlaced arcading, and in the south-west corner of the transept can be seen the canons' night-stairs to the dorter. The east end has lost its gable, but the pinnacles which flanked it can still be seen. The east wall now contains a row of three round-headed windows below a large three-light window which has lost its tracery, but as can be seen from the changes in masonry, this was not the original arrangement. When built, the east end contained two more rows of three round-headed windows above the surviving row; the large window was inserted during the first half of the 15th c., by Prior Haldenston.

The monastic buildings lay in their usual position on the south side of the church, around a large cloister the foundations of which can still be seen. To the south of the south transept came a slype which, to judge from the bench along the wall, was also used as a parlour. The entrance is decorated with pearl ornament on the capitals, and remains of a gutter can be seen in the floor. To the south of this in the east range came the original chapter-house, vaulted in nine bays from four central piers and with a fine triple-arched entrance. In the early 14th c. Bishop Lamberton built a new and large chapter-house projecting east from the range, and the old one was converted into a vestibule for the new. The wall-bench and blank arcading of the second chapter-house are visible along the south wall. The remainder of the range was taken up by the undercroft of the dorter, intersected about a third of the way down its length by the door which led to the canons' day-stairs to the dorter. The southern part of this undercroft was used as the warming-house, with a large fireplace in its east wall. The vaulting here has been excellently restored, and it is now used as a site museum, containing several grave-stones and other fragments found on the site as well as a

ST ANDREWS: *the Sarcophagus, probably tenth century*

magnificent sarcophagus of ninth or tenth century date which may have been made for King Constantine, the only early Scottish king who was not buried at Iona. It is one of the outstanding examples of Dark Age art to be found in Europe.

At the south end of the range are the ruins of the rere-dorter and its drain on an east–west axis, while to the east of the warming-house is another restored building which may have been the Prior's Lodging. This is now used as a museum for gravestones of post-Reformation date. Further east stands St Rule's Tower, which was constructed in the second quarter of the 12th c., probably as a reliquary church for the relics and shrine of St. Andrew. Until recently it was possible to climb the tower, but, at the time of writing, it has been closed for repairs until further notice. The south range contained the frater, with the kitchen adjoining it at the west end. The undercroft and its vaulting

have recently been restored, and along the south wall can be seen the semi-circular bulge where stood the pulpitum. In the centre of the south walk of the cloister are the remains of the lavatorium. The west range contained cellarage, perhaps with the guest-house above; a few barrel-vaulted cellars can still be seen.

The monastic precinct covered an area of about thirty acres, surrounded by a wall almost a mile long. Nearly all this wall still stands at St Andrews, and it is one of the finest examples of its type in Europe. It was probably first built in the 14th c., but was largely reconstructed early in the 16th c. by Prior John Hepburn, who was also responsible for most of the towers with which it is regularly punctuated. There are gates in the south and east walls, but the main entrance to the precinct was through the Pends, the 14th-c gateway which stands at the east end of South Street, just to the west of the west claustral range. Its roof and upper storey have gone, but the springers for the vaulting are still in place on the walls. So many cathedral

ST ANDREWS: *the Teinds Yett (southern gateway to the precincts)*

precincts and their walls have been superseded by the towns and cities which have grown up around them that St Andrews provides a rare opportunity to gain an impression of how extensive and securely isolated such precincts were.

St Andrews Cathedral Priory was granted to the Ministry of Works by Major M. D. D. Crichton-Stuart in 1946, and is now in the care of the Scottish Development Department.

St Augustine's Abbey, Canterbury

ORDER: Benedictine monks
COUNTY: Kent
ROUTE: Off Broad St., 100 yds. east of old city walls.
OS REF: 179:1557

The abbey founded by St Augustine and King Ethelbert of Kent on the east side of the city of Canterbury is one of the oldest monastic sites in the country. Canterbury was the first stop on Augustine's evangelizing mission of 597. This abbey was founded in the following year and dedicated to St Peter and St Paul, with the intention that all the bishops of Canterbury and kings of Kent should find a burial-place here, though this did not happen. The pre-Conquest monastery consisted of three small churches in a line from east to west, dedicated to St Pancras, St Mary, and St Peter and St Paul, while the monastic buildings lay to the north. They did not conform to a claustral pattern but, like other Dark Age monasteries, were free-standing buildings grouped together at random. The three churches have been excavated and in some cases the remains have been left exposed on the site, where they can still be seen. In the 7th c., under Abbot Adrian, Canterbury became the most important centre of learning in the country. In the 10th and 11th cs. the main church (that of St Peter and St Paul) was enlarged, and in 978 Archbishop St Dunstan extended the dedication to include St Augustine. These works were entirely superseded by the complete reconstruction of the abbey after the Norman Conquest, by Abbots Scotland and Guido. By the mid-12th c. there were sixty-one monks here, and in 1423 there were said to be eighty-four, although this seems unrealistically high and may well be an error. The abbey was surrendered on 30 July 1538. The number of monks then was thirty-one.

The church built at the end of the eleventh century by Scotland and Guido was never rebuilt, although a few minor additions and alterations were made to it through the centuries. It had an internal length of 349 ft. and consisted of a long and narrow aisled nave of eleven bays with two western towers, north and south transepts each with an apsidal eastern chapel, and an apsidal chancel ringed by an ambulatory from which radiated three chapels. In the 15th c., a Lady Chapel

of four bays was added to the east end. For the most part only foundations of the walls and piers of the church remain, but at the north-west corner can be seen the lower stages of the Ethelbert Tower, which collapsed in 1822, and a little east of it some five bays of the north wall of the nave stand to the level of the aisle roof. They are surmounted by Tudor brickwork, inserted when parts of the claustral range were converted into a 'King's House' after the Dissolution. At the east end of the nave are several of the piers of the Rotunda begun by Abbot Wulfric just before the Conquest. Octagonal outside and circular inside, it is of a design unique in this country, and was built to link the churches of St Peter and St. Paul and St Mary, but before it could be completed came the Conquest and the subsequent rebuilding of the whole site.

The chancel is entirely destroyed, but the crypt beneath it has been excavated. It represents faithfully the plan of the chancel above, even including the three radiating chapels. Originally the crypt was groin-vaulted, and although the original vaulting has fallen in, the vault of the eastern chapel (dedicated to Our Lady of the Angels) has been restored in plaster. Occasionally the chapel is still used by St Augustine's College. To the east of it are the remains of the Lady Chapel, while at a distance of about 70 ft. further east are the ruins of the free-standing chapel of St Pancras, which was probably erected in the 7th c. Although it received later alterations, the basic shape of the building, with rectangular nave, two side chapels, a western porch and an eastern apse (later replaced by a square-ended chancel), can still be seen. It is the oldest building still visible on the site.

The monastic buildings at St Augustine's lay to the north of the church, on the site of a fairly rudimentary claustral complex which may have been erected by St Dunstan towards the end of the 10th c. The cloister itself was 122 ft. by 117 ft., but only on the west side do its walls stand to any height; it was rebuilt in the thirteenth century. Most of the claustral buildings are visible only at foundation level. The east range consisted of a sacristy, of which the south wall is uncovered and contains a locker, followed by the chapter-house, in which many of the abbots were buried, then the usual slype through to the infirmary range, and finally the undercroft of the dorter. No more than the entrances to these rooms are now visible. The rere-dorter stood at the north end of the range,

ST AUGUSTINE'S, CANTERBURY: *the north wall of the nave, with Tudor brickwork above*

while the infirmary buildings were to the east. The north range contained the frater, and beyond it the hexagonal kitchen, both dating from the 13th c. also; the kitchen took four years to build (1287–91) and cost £414. The west range consisted of cellarage on the ground floor and the abbot's lodging on the first floor. These buildings were much altered when they were incorporated in the King's House after the Dissolution. In the north walk of the cloister, not built into the frater wall as usual but projecting into the garth, can be seen the foundations of the heptagonal lavatorium.

Finally, there are the two gatehouses to the abbey, the one known as Fyndon's Gate, which now forms the entrance to St Augustine's College, and further south the Cemetery Gate, opposite the end of what is now Church St. Fyndon's Gate was built by Abbot Thomas Fyndon at the beginning of the 14th c. Although it was damaged during the Second World War, it has been carefully restored and still retains its two original storeys. The front is decorated with octagonal turrets, the back with square turrets, and the entrance archway is rib-

vaulted in two bays. Ruins of the guest-house adjoin the gate to the south, and further to the south is the Museum with numerous finds from the excavations of the abbey, many dating from before the Conquest. The Cemetery Gate was built at the end of the 14th c., but its archways have been blocked and it is occupied as a dwelling.

After the Dissolution, most of the abbey buildings were promptly knocked down by crown agents, who sold the lead and other building materials to swell the royal coffers. The king was at this time establishing a chain of posting-houses on the route between London and Dover, and it was decided that the site of St Augustine's should be one of them. The 'King's House' was built over the west claustral range, using the west end of the north wall of the nave as its south wall. Elizabeth I stayed here for a fortnight in September 1573, and Charles II slept here on the night of 25 May 1660, on the way to his Restoration in London. Soon afterwards the house fell into disrepair. In the mid-19th c. the abbey ruins passed into the guardianship of St Augustine's College, and in 1939–40 they were placed in the hands of the Ministry of Works. St Augustine's Abbey is now in the care of English Heritage.

St Dogmael's Abbey

ORDER: Tironensian monks
COUNTY: Dyfed
ROUTE: On B4546, 1 mile W of Cardigan.
OS REF: 145:1645

St Dogmael's, the only Tironensian Abbey in Wales, was founded about 1113–15 by Robert fitz Martin, lord of Cemais, on the site of the ancient Celtic *clas* (or monastery) of Llandudoch. The first two centuries of its existence seem to have been troubled ones. The intermittent lawlessness of Welsh society probably delayed the completion of the original church until the 13th c., and during the wars which accompanied Edward I's conquest of Wales from 1277 to 1283, the abbey seems to have suffered further destruction which necessitated extensive rebuilding in the first quarter of the 14th c. The number of monks for whom the abbey was founded was thirteen, and it is doubtful if this figure ever increased greatly; in 1534 there were nine monks there, who subscribed to the Oath of Supremacy. St Dogmael's was suppressed in 1536.

The buildings are all heavily ruined, but their outlines for the most part have been recovered, and some of the walls still stand to an impressive height. The church was planned to consist of an aisled nave, north and south transepts each with apsidal chapels to the east, and a chancel with an eastern apse. Successive rebuildings have, however, almost entirely obliterated the original plan. The nave, built in the 13th c., was converted into the parish church of St Dogmael's after the Dissolution and there is consequently a considerable amount of 16th-c. masonry included in the structure, but the west and north walls, which stand almost to their original height, are medieval. The large west window has unfortunately lost all its tracery. There are two arched recesses for tombs in the north wall. The foundations of a wall at the east end of the nave mark the position of the monastic rood-screen, which was built up after the Dissolution to enclose the parish church.

Of the crossing piers and south transept only foundations remain, but the walls of the north transept are still standing. This was rebuilt at the beginning of the 16th c. and braced by four massive buttresses which marked the arrangement of the vaulting bays; the corbels from which the vaulting sprang were figure-sculpted and can still be seen in the north angles and on the west wall. The windows have again lost their tracery. Only low foundations of the chancel remain; the long wall which reaches east from the angle of chancel and north transept is of post-Dissolution date. The chancel was demolished and rebuilt with a crypt below the sanctuary in the 13th c., the 12th-c. apse being superseded by a square east end. A staircase built into the thickness of the north wall led down to the crypt, which was vaulted in two double bays

1. NAVE
2. NORTH TRANSEPT
3. SOUTH TRANSEPT
4. PRESBYTERY
5. CRYPT
6. SACRISTY
7. VESTIBULE
8. CHAPTER-HOUSE
9. INFIRMARY
10. CLOISTER
11. SITE OF DAY-ROOM
12. SITE OF FRATER
13. WEST RANGE
14. GUEST-HOUSE

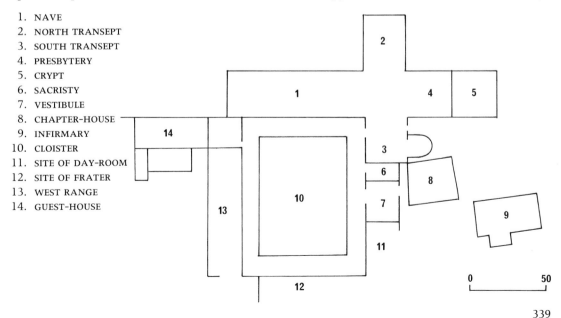

ST DOGMAEL'S: *view across the cloister, from the south-west*

with a simple quadripartite rib-vault; the wall-shafts and central pier from which the vaulting rose can still be seen.

The monastic buildings lay to the south of the church. Only low masonry remains of the buildings around the cloister itself, and they seem to have followed the normal plan; to the south of the south transept came a small sacristy followed by the vestibule to the chapter-house and then the undercroft of the dorter, which probably contained the warming-house. The dorter no doubt ran along the first floor of the range as usual. To the east of the range are two buildings of which more remains, the chapter-house and the infirmary. The chapter-house, next to the range and joined to the angle of the south transept, was built at a strange angle, slanting slightly to the north; erected in the 14th c., its position was determined by the infirmary to the south-east of it, which had been built in the previous century. Several tomb-recesses can be seen in the walls, and the south wall still stands close to its original height. Of the infirmary all the walls except the north wall still stand almost to roof level. It had an east window of three lights and a recessed chamber at the west end of its south wall, which may have been the infirmary chapel. The south and west claustral ranges were severely interfered with after the Dissolution, and only low masonry now remains. The south range contained the frater on an east-west axis; the exterior of its north wall still has the arched recess for the lavatorium, and in the centre of its west wall is another recess, probably the service hatch from the kitchen, which stood at the south-west angle of the cloister.

The west range is one of the oldest parts of St Dogmael's, dating from the late 12th c. The ground floor contained cellarage, while the Abbot's Lodging was probably on the first floor, but a rectory was built over the range after the Dissolution and little can be distinguished of the medieval buildings. The foundations which run west from the north end of the range are late 14th or early 15th-c., and probably represent a new guest-house erected at this time. New guest-houses are a feature of Welsh monasteries in the later middle ages.

After the Dissolution, Henry VIII granted the site to a royal agent, a man named Bradshaw, in whose family it remained until the 17th c. The nave became the parish church, and several of the other buildings were adapted for domestic purposes. At the Welsh Church Disestablishment the ruins passed to the Representative Body of the Church in Wales, which placed them in the hands of the Commissioners of Works in 1934. They are now in the care of Cadw: Welsh Historic Monuments.

St Frideswide's Priory (Christ Church Cathedral), Oxford

ORDER: Augustinian canons
COUNTY: Oxfordshire
ROUTE: In the buildings of Christ Church, Oxford
OS REF: 164:5106

In early English tradition, St Frideswide was the daughter of a local ruler in the Oxfordshire area, along the Thames, and the head of a community of nuns in the 8th c. Oxford itself did not exist before its foundation as a royal borough by King Edward the Elder in 912, but there was a monastery dedicated to St Frideswide within its walls in the tenth century. Burnt down by the Danes in 1002, restored for secular canons in 1004, it has entirely disappeared, and the continuous history of St Frideswide's begins with the priory founded on the spot by Henry I in 1122, apparently at the suggestion of his justiciar Roger, bishop of Salisbury. Originally intended for thirteen canons (who came from Holy Trinity, London), the priory expanded to house eighteen canons after 1160. In the early 16th c. there were nine in residence, a further six canons being absent serving parishes. In 1524 the priory was suppressed by Cardinal Wolsey, who always did things on the most lavish possible scale and who had decided to build an entirely new college chapel for his recently founded Cardinal College; but after Wolsey's fall in 1529, Henry VIII decided that the priory church should be retained as the chapel for the new college. In 1542 Oxford was made the see for a bishopric, and four years later St Frideswide's priory church was redesignated Oxford Cathedral, which it remains to this day.

For a cathedral, the church is remarkably small, about 160 ft. in overall length, but one must remember that about 50 ft. were knocked off by Wolsey's builders in the 1520s in order to make room for Tom Quad. The cathedral also underwent considerable alteration, notably at the hands of Sir Gilbert Scott, in the 1870s. The twin entrances of the west porch are a part of this restoration, and Scott also added a western bay to the nave. Apart from this nineteenth-century work, the church is relatively free from additions. It seems to have been built, in its entirety and with considerable rapidity, between 1190 and 1210, and throughout the following centuries no major structural revisions were undertaken. Both nave and chancel are aisled, and the north transept has aisles to east and west, although the south transept has only an eastern aisle because the cloister occupied the space into which a western aisle would have fitted. Throughout the church there is a structural peculiarity which, although not unique, is unusual: the triforium comes within the main arches of the arcade, and has to be supported by a second row of arches which, visually, does little to enhance St Frideswide's. Although the main arches are strongly moulded, the subsidiary arches are not moulded at all. The system is similar to that used at Romsey Abbey, but there the main arches are more strongly emphasised by long vaulting-shafts and the triforium arches themselves are more prominent, giving a clearer impression of an intermediate stage in the elevation. Here at St Frideswide's, it is almost as if the triforium was considered to be an embarrassment.

The nave has a timber roof, although the aisles are rib-vaulted, as are the transepts. The vaulting of the choir is much later, dating from the late 15th c. or early 16th, and consisting of a complicated system of lierne star-vaults with a profusion of bosses. The designer of this vault may have been William Orchard, who also designed the vault of the Oxford Divinity School and whose tomb is in St Frideswide's. The piers in the quire are round, while those in the nave alternate between round and octagonal; for the most part they have crocket capitals. To the north of the north quire aisle stands the later Lady Chapel. Leading off from the south transept is a tunnel-vaulted passage built in the twelfth century which must originally have connected with the monastic buildings, but after the rebuilding of the cloister in the early sixteenth century the level of the cloister was raised and the passage is now below that level and only accessible from the south transept.

Of the buildings around the cloister, the most impressive is the chapter-house, immediately to the south of this passage. Although the entrance dates from the 12th c., it is essentially a 13th-c. building. The east wall has five stepped lancets to the north and south and the ceiling is vaulted with a quadripartite rib-vault on which some excellent bosses are set (notably those of the Virgin and the four lions with one head). In the east wall the foundation stone of Cardinal Wolsey's college at

ST FRIDESWIDE'S, OXFORD: *the quire*

Ipswich has been re-set; it was founded in 1528, only a year before his fall, and was intended to serve Cardinal College as Wykeham founded Winchester to serve New College. The doorways in the south wall and on either side of the entrance from the cloister are modern additions. To the south of the chapter-house stands the priory house, on the site of the former monastic dorter, but the only visible survival of the dorter is a 15th-c.

doorway. The south range was largely rebuilt along with the cloister in the early 16th c., and contains an eastern passage followed by the frater. Although the latter in no way resembles a medieval building from the outside, it still has a 13th-c. rib-vault inside and along the south wall the remains of the pulpitum on two figure corbels can still be seen. Of the west range nothing survives, for it was all knocked down to make way for Tom Quad, and all the other outlying monastic buildings have also been superseded by college buildings.

Sawley Abbey

ORDER: Cistercian monks
COUNTY: Lancashire
ROUTE: Off A59, 3½ miles NNE of Clitheroe.
OS REF: 103:7746

The Cistercian Abbey of Sawley, or Sallay as it was called in the Middle Ages, stands on the left bank of the river Ribble. Founded by William de Percy in 1147, it was colonised by an abbot, twelve monks and ten lay-brothers from Newminster, and although it never became a particularly large or wealthy house, it developed a scholarly tradition. Stephen of Easton, abbot from 1224 to 1233, was a spiritual writer of some renown, and William of Rymyngton, who was prior at Sawley, was also chancellor of Oxford University in 1372–3. An unknown monk at Sawley translated into English verse a Latin work of the famous 13th-c. scholar-bishop, Robert Grosseteste. In 1381 there were fifteen monks and two lay-brothers at Sawley. In 1536 the abbey was suppressed, but during the Pilgrimage of Grace the monks were restored under a new abbot, William Trafford, which so incensed the king when he heard of it that he sent specific instructions to his commander in the north-west, the Earl of Derby, to proceed to the vicinity of Sawley and deal with the monks and their followers in the firmest possible way. As a result, Trafford was executed for treason on 10 March 1537, and Sawley, to which twenty-one monks and thirty-seven servants had returned, was once again suppressed.

Excavation has left the outlines of the buildings at Sawley clearly distinguishable, but few of the walls rise to any height above ground. The walls of the church stand higher than those of the monastic buildings, and they present a picture of a church of most unusual proportions, with an extremely short, aisleless nave stretching only about a third of the way along the north walk of the cloister, transepts with three eastern chapels each, and an aisled chancel considerably broader and longer than the nave. Naturally, this is not how the church was originally built: it had a longer, though equally narrow, nave which reached to the west end of the north cloister walk, and a shorter, aisleless chancel. In the 14th c. a narrow chapel was added along the north side of the nave, but later—possibly as late as the early 16th c.—the western part of the nave was considered superfluous and a wall put up across it only about a third of the way along its length from the crossing. This accounts for the modern impression of such a strangely small nave. At about the same time, or a little earlier, the chancel was lengthened and widened with the addition of aisles. The remains of the chancel's original side-walls can still be seen.

In the south-western corner of the south transept the remains of the monks' night-stairs to the dorter can still be seen, but little survives of the monastic buildings except for the foundations. The east range consisted as usual of a small sacristy-cum-library, a narrow chapter-house, a parlour, a passage, and the undercroft of the monks' dorter, which stretched over all these buildings. At the south end of the range the monks' rere-dorter ran at right-angles to the east, and its great drain is still clearly visible. The south range contained, from east to west, the warming-house, the frater on a north–south axis as was usual in second stage Cistercian plans, and the kitchen. The west range was originally given over to the lay-brothers, including their dorter and frater as well as cellarage space, but in the later middle ages, after the lay-brothers had dwindled in numbers, the abbots decided to convert part of the western range into a new lodging for themselves. The same was done at Hailes. At Sawley the new abbot's lodging was just to the west of the kitchen; two of its fireplaces can be seen, and other parts of it are incorporated in the more modern cottage immediately next to them. The squarish building with a chimney at the north end of the western range is probably a post-Dissolution addition.

The site was partly excavated by Lord de Grey in 1848, and he used material recovered from the scene to build the gateway across the main road about 250 yards north of the church. Sawley is now in the care of English Heritage.

Shap Abbey

ORDER: Premonstratensian canons
COUNTY: Cumbria
ROUTE: 1 mile W of A6, 10 miles SSE of Penrith.
OS REF: 90:5415

The white canons of the Premonstratensian order deliberately chose wild and desolate spots for their houses, but few remoter sites could be found than Shap Abbey. Founded by Thomas fitz Gospatrick and colonised from Cockersand, the community was originally settled some twenty miles further south, at Preston in Kendale, but within less than a decade the canons had moved to Shap, where they were established by 1201. At that time the place was known as 'Hepp' (i.e., a heap) on account of the heap of megaliths which had been part of a prehistoric stone circle, now known as Shap Stones; this changed to 'Hiap' and finally to Shap, by which name it has been known since about 1300. With the river Lowther to the east and Shap Fell summit only three miles to the south, the site combined the facilities and the solitude that were the ideal ingredients for a Premonstratensian house.

The history of the abbey, which was dedicated to St Mary Magdalene, is on the whole uneventful. During the 13th c. there were about twenty canons here, although by 1379 this figure had dropped to only six. Shap produced one outstanding dignitary of the late medieval church: Richard Redman, who became abbot about 1458, was appointed representative of the Premonstratensians in England, and became Bishop of St Asaph in 1471, of Exeter in 1496, and of Ely in 1501. Despite continual absences, he continued to hold the abbacy of Shap until his death in 1505 and he was responsible for the building of the great west tower which remains to this day the principal survival of the abbey buildings. Shap escaped dissolution in 1536 and was not finally suppressed until 14 January 1540, by which time the number of canons had risen again to fifteen.

The west tower, which dominates the ruins at Shap, is also the building through which the visitor enters the site. It dates from about 1500, following an unsuccessful attempt to build a tower over the crossing which had caused the collapse of the north-west crossing pier. Although it seems from the exterior to be only a two-storey building, it contained four storeys inside, and stands almost to its original height with the exception of the parapets. The great arch in the tower's west wall was originally two openings, with a traceried window of five lights above a doorway of four moulded orders, but in the 18th c. the masonry between them was knocked out to provide a vista right up the church. At each corner of the tower are two angle-buttresses, finely stepped and reaching right to the top of the building. In the south-west corner of the tower is a spiral staircase which ran up to the parapets. The small square flagstones on the floors are original. Above the archway leading into the nave on the east side of the tower, the eaves line of the church roof can still be seen.

The rest of the church, with the exception of the chancel which was lengthened in the 15th c., dates from the original period of building in the 12th c., but little remains above low foundation walls. Its overall length, even including the extended chancel and the tower, is only a little over 200 ft. internally, so clearly the original church was far from being a grand structure. It consists of a nave of six bays with a northern aisle, north and south transepts with eastern chapels, and a narrow, square-ended chancel. Several of the paving-stones of the nave survive, and on them, along the eastern half of the south wall and in the eastern bay of the north wall, several incised part-circles can be seen. These were the procession markers, which showed the monks exactly where to stand during processions. One other peculiarity has survived at Shap: in the north-east corner of the north transept there is a squint which gave direct view on to the altar, and was probably for lepers who had to be segregated from those attending services in the church. In this transept there are also two tombstones, one of which is incised with a crozier and must be of an abbot, and traces of a piscina and a wall-tomb in the south wall. In the south transept can be seen the foundations of the monks' night-stairs to the dorter.

The proximity of the site to the river made the monastic buildings grouped around the cloister both small and congested. Like the church, there is little left of them except for low foundation walls, but it is clear that they conformed fairly closely to the standard monastic plan. The east range consisted of a small sacristy adjacent to the south transept, followed by a large room the western half

1. TOWER
2. NAVE
3. NORTH AISLE
4. PORCH
5. CHAPELS
6. NORTH TRANSEPT
7. SOUTH TRANSEPT
8. CHANCEL
9. SACRISTY
10. CLOISTER
11. VESTIBULE AND PARLOUR
12. CHAPTER-HOUSE
13. SLYPE
14. WARMING-HOUSE, WITH
    DORTER OVER
15. LOBBY
16. RERE-DORTER
17. INFIRMARY
18. INFIRMARY CHAMBER WITH
    GARDEROBE
19. INFIRMARER'S DWELLING
    (probable)
20. FRATER UNDERCROFT
21. WEST RANGE
22. GARDEROBE PIT

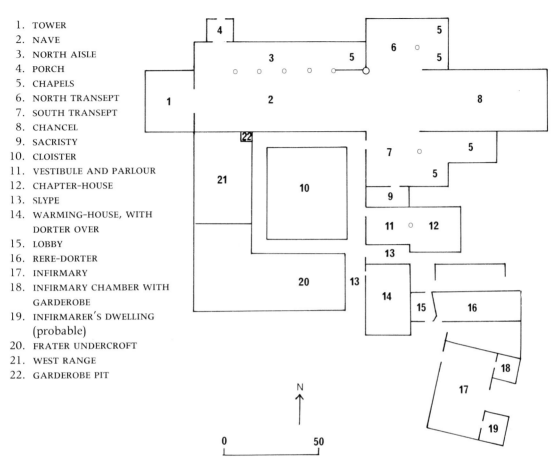

of which was used as a vestibule and parlour, and the eastern half as the monastic chapter-house; the bases of three central piers which supported a rib-vault can still be seen. South of this room came the warming-house, the fireplace of which is still visible, and over the whole range stretched the dorter. To the east of the warming-house, reaching right up to the bank of the river, is a long building which was the rere-dorter. Again there is little left of it, but several drains, the remains of channels cut in them, and the jamb of a penstock at the south end made it clear that here was something rather more efficient than the normal monastic rere-dorter. Some time in the later middle ages the two outfalls of the drain were blocked and it seems that from that time the building was used for a different purpose, but what purpose is obscure. South of the rere-dorter was the infirmary, originally vaulted in four bays but now almost totally ruined.

The south range contained the frater on an undercroft, while the west range was used for storage and cellarage, possibly with the abbot's lodging above. Originally built in the 13th c., this range was extensively remodelled in the 14th and divided into three barrel-vaulted apartments, the northern two of which have survived complete with their lobbies and parts of staircases to the first floor. In the north-eastern corner of the northern apartment is a square pit which formed the lower part of a garderobe coming down from the first floor, a clear indication that the first floor was used as accommodation, if not for the abbot then possibly as a guest-house.

After the Dissolution the site was sold to Sir Thomas Wharton, the Governor of Carlisle, and some of the monastic buildings seem to have been incorporated into a farmhouse. In 1729 the buildings were forfeited by his descendant, the Duke of Wharton, a nobleman of Jacobite sympathies, and were purchased by Richard Lowther

SHAP: *the west tower, with chapter-house in the foreground*

of Mauld's Meaburn Hall. Lowther Estates Ltd., the representatives of his descendant Lancelot Lowther 6th Earl of Lonsdale, placed the ruins in the care of the Ministry of Works in 1948, and during the next thirteen years the site was systematically excavated. In 1955 the bases of several of the nave and chapter-house piers were discovered at Lowther Castle and returned by the 7th Earl of Lonsdale to the abbey, where they have since been replaced in their rightful positions. The site is now in the care of English Heritage.

Strata Florida Abbey

ORDER: Cistercian monks
COUNTY: Dyfed
ROUTE: Off B4343, 1 mile ESE of Pontrhydfendigaid.
OS REF: 135:7465

The abbey of Strata Florida was originally founded some two miles to the south-west of the present ruins on the banks of the River Flur, from which the house took its name (Strata Florida = the valley of the Flur). The Norman baron Robert fitz Stephen founded the monastery in 1164; in the following year, however, fitz Stephen's estates were overrun by the Welsh Lord Rhys ap Gruffydd, who assumed the patronage of the monastery. The first site must have proved unsatisfactory, for in 1184 the monks moved to the present one on an important local route, and began to build again. Although it was consecrated in 1201, it was not for another seventy years that the church and monastic buildings were completed. Then came a series of disasters. In 1285 the church was severely damaged by fire after being struck by lightning, and in 1294, during the Welsh rebellion against Edward I, further destruction was caused. Over a century later, the monastery was to be vandalised, deserted, and then subjected to military occupation during the revolt of Owain Glyndwr. One of the main reasons why it suffered during these wars was that in the middle ages the track which was the main road between Rhayader and the coast passed close by the monastery, whereas nowadays the road lies several miles to the north.

This brought its compensations, though, for Strata Florida became one of the main centres of Welsh literature and culture. It was here that the scholar and writer Gerald of Wales left and lost his library, and here the national annals of Wales (*Brut y Tywysogion*) were written. The literary activities of the south Welsh house of Dinefwr were also concentrated here, and many of its members were buried in the abbey. The greatest of medieval Welsh poets, the 14th-c. Dafydd ap Gwilym, was buried here. In 1951 a memorial slab to him was erected in the north transept of the abbey church. Once wealthy on account of its extensive lands and flocks of sheep, by the 15th c. the prosperity of Strata Florida had dwindled away, and when it was

dissolved in 1539 there were only seven monks left here.

The ruins consist principally of the church, with the cloister, chapter house, and fragments of the western range to the south. The church had an aisled nave of seven bays, north and south transepts each with three eastern chapels, and a narrow, square-ended chancel; in other words, it was typically Cistercian. It dates from the late 12th and early 13th cs. apart from the eastern bay of the chancel, which was added in the third quarter of the 13th c. What remains now is mostly at ground level only, so presumably the misfortunes of 1285 and 1294 only necessitated rebuilding of the upper stages. The west front stands higher than any other part of the ruins and contains a fine doorway of four orders, richly decorated. In the south-west corner is the base of a spiral staircase which led into the western range. The nave is remarkable for its aisle arcades, which were not simply piers and arches but consisted of piers set on top of screen walls, which completely blocked off the aisles from the central part of the nave; such an arrangement

1. NAVE	8. SACRISTY
2. NORTH AISLE	9. CHAPTER-HOUSE
3. SOUTH AISLE	10. CLOISTER
4. NORTH TRANSEPT	11. WESTERN RANGE
5. SOUTH TRANSEPT	12. RECESS FOR
6. CHANCEL	COLLATION LECTERN
7. CHAPELS	

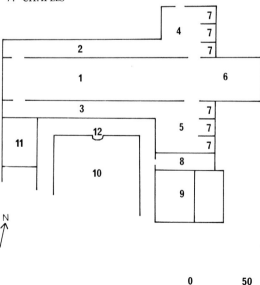

was unique in England and Wales, although some Irish churches were built with solid aisle walls instead of arcades. The transept chapels have recently been re-roofed with wood, to protect the medieval tiles which have been re-set in the chapel floors; originally the whole area of the transepts and crossing was laid with similar tiles. In the chancel a large oblong slab marks the position of the high altar, and a recess in the south wall marks the position of the sedilia. In the north-east corner of the north transept is the base of another spiral staircase, which led to the tower which originally stood over the crossing.

The cloister at Strata Florida contains one of only a few surviving examples of a recess for the Collation lectern, which projects into the garth in the centre of the north claustral walk (*see also* Tintern, where the recesses for both the abbot's Collation seat and the lectern can be seen). It was here that the lectern stood when the abbot read the Collation, or reading before Compline. From what survives, it seems that the monastic buildings followed the usual Cistercian pattern. To the south of the south transept is a narrow sacristy entered by doors from both the transept and the cloister,

suggesting that its western half may also have been used as a library. A solitary lancet is set in the east wall. The room to the south of the sacristy was originally the chapter house, built in the thirteenth century to project eastwards from the range; when this was destroyed, probably during the Welsh rebellion of 1294, it was decided to rebuild the warming-house on the site. It will be noticed that there is no entry from the cloister to the present room, which makes it extremely unlikely that it served as the chapter-house. The present building dates from the 14th c., while the ruins to the east of it are of the earlier chapter-house. This includes several medieval tombslabs, some of which probably belong to the house of Dinefwr. No doubt the eastern range continued with the dorter, and the south walk contained the frater and kitchen, but they have vanished. The western range, of which a few fragments may still be seen, was occupied by the lay-brothers. After the Dissolution the site passed to the Stedman family, who retained it until the 18th c. Later it was given to the Church of Wales, which in 1931 placed it in the hands of H. M. Commissioners of Works. It is now in the care of Cadw: Welsh Historic Monuments.

Sweetheart Abbey

ORDER: Cistercian monks
COUNTY: Dumfries and Galloway
ROUTE: In New Abbey, 7 miles S of Dumfries on A710.
OS REF: 84:9666

The Cistercian Abbey of Sweetheart acquired its name on account of its foundress, the remarkable Lady Devorguilla. She was the wife of John Balliol, the founder of Balliol College, Oxford, and the father of another John Balliol, who for a short time became King of Scots after being chosen by the English King Edward I to fill the vacant throne following the death of Alexander III and the Maid of Norway. After her husband's death, Devorguilla had his heart embalmed and placed in a casket of ivory and silver which she carried around with her everywhere, and which was buried with her in the abbey church when she died in 1289. She founded Sweetheart on 10 April 1273, and it took its name from her treasured relic; she also founded two houses for friars, and endowed Balliol College.

Colonised from Dundrennan, Sweetheart was apparently built quickly, but it can hardly have been completed when the War of Independence erupted; Edward I's army stopped at Sweetheart for a night during the last week of August 1300. Several years later the monks were to complain that the English soldiers damaged the abbey's lands and buildings to the extent of £5,000, for which they vainly petitioned for compensation. The church does not seem to have been seriously affected, however, for in style it dates clearly from the original building of the late 13th c. Towards the end of the 14th c. the abbey found a powerful patron in 'Black Archibald', Earl of Douglas, but in 1397 fire struck the abbey and necessitated a certain amount of re-modelling. In the following year, the abbot was granted the mitre

The last pre-Reformation abbot, John Brown, resigned in 1565, whereupon Gilbert Brown, one of the Browns of Carsluith, became commendator and titular abbot. This man was to prove an obstinate defender of the old faith. Exiled to France in 1587, he returned two years later and openly disputed with John Welsh, the brother-in-law of John Knox. In 1603 he was again arrested, imprisoned, and exiled to France; by 1608 he was back at Sweet-heart again. He was once more arrested, but on account of his old age he was permitted to remain at Sweetheart. In the following year he was found still to be saying the mass, so for the third time he was exiled to France, where he died in 1612. His obstinacy probably ensured that Sweetheart was the last British monastery at which mass continued to be said after its official abolition in Scotland in 1560. In 1624, the abbey and its lands were erected into a temporal lordship for Sir Robert Spottiswood.

The church, although it has lost its roof, still stands to eaves level and forms a beautiful ruin, because of the warmth of the red sandstone with which it is built. In style it is Early English. Its plan consists of an aisled nave of six bays, north and south transepts each with two eastern chapels, and an aisleless, square-ended chancel of two bays. The central tower still stands to the height of its gables and shows clearly the pitch of the roofs; only the aisles and transept chapels were rib-vaulted in stone, the remainder of the church being roofed with timber. The west front stands to its full height. Above the entrance doorway can be seen the corbels which supported the lean-to roof of a west porch which has long since disappeared, and above is the large west window. It is now in two parts, with three lights below and a rose window with trefoils set in the head, but the central band of masonry was only inserted at the end of the 14th c., probably as a result of the fire of 1397. The nave arcade rests on compound piers. There is no triforium, and the clerestory shows signs of having been remodelled at the end of the 14th c., for on the south side the rhythm of the windows changes from three-light to five-light set in a semicircle after the second bay from the east. The north transept window has been deprived of its tracery; at the north-western angle of the transept is a turret enclosing a newel staircase which gave access to the roof.

The south transept is the most interesting part of the church, for its chapels still retain their rib-vaulting (with heraldic shields dating from 1400 on the intersection bosses). Here is the 16th-c. effigy of Devorguilla. It replaced the lost 13th-c. original. It shows her dressed in gown and mantle, with her hands clasped round a representation of the casket which contained her husband's heart, which hangs from her neck. The effigy has lost its head, and the inscription wrongly gives Devorguilla's date of

SWEETHEART: *aerial view from the south-west*

death as 1284. The south wall of the transept includes an interesting three-quarter wheel window, the lowest quarter never having been constructed, to allow for the protruding gable against which the roof of the east range abutted. At the lowest level of the wall are an aumbrey and the door to the sacristy, and at the west end of the wall, on a slightly higher level, is the door through which the monks' night-stairs to the dorter passed. In the south wall of the chancel a sedilia and a piscina can be seen. The east window is an unadventurous composition of five lights surmounted by spherical trefoils of Geometric character; above is another window which has lost its seven-light tracery. On the floor of the chancel some of the original stone paving can be seen.

As far as can be gathered, the monastic buildings at Sweetheart conformed to the normal Cistercian plan (although the warming house, unusually, was in the east range), but only in the east range does

enough survive to indicate the layout of the buildings. To the south of the south transept came the sacristy-cum-library, entered from both the transept (for sacristy purposes) and the cloister (for library purposes). Then came the chapter-house, where the stone bench on which the monks sat can still be seen in parts; the window in the east wall is not original, having been taken from the old parish church when it was demolished in 1877. The narrow room to the south of the chapter-house was probably the abbey's treasury, followed by the parlour and then the strangely small warming-house, with the remains of the fireplace still visible in the east wall. To the south of this presumably was the novices' room beneath the dorter, with the rere-dorter projecting to the east. Of the south range only the cloister wall remains, with a few masonry projections showing the lines of attached buildings. At the east end were the day-stairs to the dorter, followed by the frater and the kitchen. The west range was presumably for the use of the lay-brothers. Only an isolated archway, the entrance from the cloister to the range, still stands, with a head and two figures carved on it. Outlying buildings such as the infirmary and abbot's lodging have disappeared, although considerable stretches of the precinct wall survive. They are remarkable for the size of the stones used. Nearly a mile to the north-east of the abbey is a ruined tower of 16th-c. date, traditionally known as the Abbot's Tower. Its purpose is unknown.

After the Reformation, the monastic frater was used as the parish church, but in 1731 it was demolished. A new parish church was erected on the site of the west range. This in turn was demolished when the present parish church was erected in 1877. Although the monastic buildings were systematically quarried for building stone, the local people clubbed together to save the abbey church from further destruction, considering it to be 'an ornament to that part of the country'. In 1928 the ruins were placed in the hands of the Ministry of Works; they are now in the care of English Heritage.

SWEETHEART: *effigy of Devorguilla the foundress clasping the casket containing her husband's heart (sixteenth century)*

Tewkesbury Abbey

ORDER: Benedictine monks
COUNTY: Gloucestershire
ROUTE: In town centre.
OS REF: 150:8832

The site on which Tewkesbury Abbey is built was apparently occupied by a hermit named Theokus in the 7th c. In 715 Dodo, a Saxon lord, founded a small monastery for four or five monks here, but it was severely damaged during the Danish raids and probably abandoned. In about 980 the abbey was re-founded as a cell of Cranborne Abbey. In 1102, however, the positions were reversed when Abbot Gerald of Cranborne transferred his abbey to Tewkesbury, making Cranborne a cell dependent on it. At the same time a massive new church was built, which was consecrated on 23 October 1123 in the presence of five bishops. By this time the nave, which still stands today, was probably complete, and there were over fifty monks at Tewkesbury. In the 13th c. the earldom of Gloucester, which included the patronage of Tewkesbury Abbey, passed to the de Clare family, and when Gilbert de Clare III was killed at Bannockburn in 1314, his sister and co-heiress Eleanor married Hugh Despenser and thus brought the patronage of the abbey into the hands of one of the most notorious characters of Edward II's tragic reign.

Despenser, a land-hungry courtier who was hated by the Queen and many of the leading nobles, was rumoured by his enemies to be the king's lover, and was accorded a traitor's death by Queen Isabella and her lover Roger Mortimer in 1326, shortly before Edward's deposition. His son Hugh, and his grandson Edward, were largely responsible for the re-building and adornment of the eastern parts of the church in the middle of the 14th c. On 4 May 1471, the Battle of Tewkesbury was fought just outside the town. When it became obvious to the Lancastrians that the Yorkists had defeated them, many of them fled to the abbey for sanctuary; the Yorkists pursued them, however, and some Lancastrians were said to have been slaughtered inside the church. Following this bloodshed, the church had to be closed for a month until it could be re-consecrated. By this time the number of monks at Tewkesbury had dropped to thirty-three, and although it rose again to fifty-eight in 1534, at the time of the Dissolution (9 January 1540), the number had dropped again to thirty-seven.

The west front and the nave are among the finest examples of Norman architecture in England. The enormous six-ordered arch of the west front is 65 ft. high and was built about 1150. The window which filled it collapsed in a storm in 1661 and was replaced by the present Perpendicular one in 1686. The original design also included a gable between the pinnacles, but this was later replaced by a plain parapet. The large round piers of the nave, reminiscent of those at Gloucester, support a tall arcade and a narrow twin-light triforium. The nave consists of eight bays, and is almost entirely undecorated. With the major exception of the vault, it is also largely unaltered since its completion in 1123. The aisles were rib-vaulted about 1300, and about 1340 Hugh Despenser (son of the notorious Hugh), replaced the old timber vault of the nave with the present lierne-vault. Although it diminishes the effect of the Norman architecture, it is a beautiful roof, with fifteen bosses depicting the life of Christ along the transverse ridge rib, and other bosses at the intersections of the liernes and the diagonal ribs. The Norman porch on the north side of the church is tunnel-vaulted.

Over the crossing is the largest, and one of the most impressive, of surviving Norman towers, completed about 1150 and extensively restored in 1935. The chancel was entirely remodelled in the mid-14th c. by Hugh Despenser and his wife Elizabeth Montacute, the daughter of the Earl of Salisbury. Although much of the Norman masonry was retained (including several of the piers), all the detail is in the Decorated style, with delicately moulded arches, stellar vaulting, and a superb set of windows around the altar, which were probably given by Hugh Despenser's mother, Eleanor de Clare, and contain some of the finest surviving medieval stained-glass in England.

Tewkesbury is also famed for the monuments in its chancel, particularly the Beauchamp and Despenser chantries. The Beauchamp chantry, begun in 1422 by Isabel Despenser in memory of her husband Richard Beauchamp, Earl of Worcester (her second husband was also called Richard Beauchamp, but he was Earl of Warwick), was not completed until 1438. It has an ornate and spiky canopy, and a lovely miniature fan-vault. The Despenser chantry, built in the late 1370s to

TEWKESBURY: *interior of the church, looking east*

TEWKESBURY: *the kneeling knight above the Despenser Chantry*

commemorate Edward Despenser (d. 1375) is remarkable for the unique figure of a kneeling knight above the canopy, the only known example of the use of such a device. The figure faces the high altar, and still retains much of its original gilding.

These two chantries are two of a series of five monuments which form a ring around the high altar. The others are the tombs of both Hugh Despensers, and the chantry of the founder of the abbey in 1102, Robert Fitz Hamon. Around these monuments, the chancel is ringed by a series of radiating chapels dedicated to St Margaret of Scotland, St Catherine, St Faith, and St Edmund and St Dunstan. At the entrance to the chapel of St Edmund and St Dunstan is another remarkable monument, to Abbot Wakeman. It depicts a decaying monk, over whose body are crawling a mouse, a frog, a worm, a snake and a beetle. Wakeman was the last abbot of Tewkesbury, and was made the first Bishop of Gloucester by Henry VIII. At the east end of the church there was a Lady Chapel. This was pulled down early in the 16th c., when it was intended to build a new one, but before it could be built, the Dissolution intervened.

Of the buildings around the cloister nothing remains, although it has been discovered by excavation that the cloister was 80 ft. square, and that the monastic buildings seem to have followed the usual Benedictine plan. To the west of the church stands Abbey House, a building dating from about 1520 which was either the abbot's lodging or the monastery's guest-house. The south front was completely re-fashioned in 1790, but the north front retains its medieval appearance and has a handsome oriel window, below which are a shield bearing the abbey's coat of arms and the initials of Abbot Henry Beoly (1509–31). The gatehouse which can be seen is not original, but a 19th-c., apparently exact, reconstruction of the original. It has triple entrance archways, one large one flanked by two smaller ones for pedestrians, sexpartite vaulting, and an embattled parapet.

After the Dissolution, the monastic buildings were almost entirely destroyed, but the townspeople of Tewkesbury claimed that the nave of the church had always been their parish church, and collected £453 in order to buy it from the crown. To this day it remains the parish church. It has undergone several restorations, notably the one instigated by Scott in 1875, which was to lead William Morris to found his Society for the Protection of Ancient Buildings in 1877, to protest against 'the threatened scraping and scouring of Tewkesbury Abbey'. On the whole, the restorations have done much to restore to Tewkesbury its ancient splendour.

Thetford Priory

ORDER: Cluniac monks
COUNTY: Norfolk
ROUTE: On the W fringe of Thetford, eleven miles N of Bury.
OS REF: 144:8683

The priory of St Mary at Thetford was founded in 1103–4 by Roger Bigod, an ageing warrior who had accompanied the Conqueror in the invasion of 1066. At first the monks occupied the old cathedral of St Mary in the heart of the town, which had been without a community to staff it since the East Anglian see had been moved to Norwich in 1095, but after three years the monks decided to move to the present site outside the town. On 1 September 1107 old Bigod himself laid the foundation stone of the new church, only to die a week later. Although he had asked to be buried at Thetford, the bishop seized his body and buried it in Norwich Cathedral.

The chief fame of the priory arose from a series of strange incidents which are reported to have occurred early in the 13th c. A local craftsman who suffered from an incurable disease prayed repeatedly to Our Lady to cure him. She thrice appeared to him in dreams and told him to ask the prior to erect a Lady Chapel to the north of the church. The prior, impressed by the man's dreams, proceeded to do so, but he built only a chapel of wood; when told by the craftsman that Our Lady wanted the chapel to be of stone, the prior took no notice, whereupon the Virgin appeared once again in a vision to a local woman, to make the same request. When the woman ignored her, her left arm was paralysed, so she promptly made her way to the priory to pass on Our Lady's request. This time the prior listened, and soon the wooden chapel was replaced with one built of stone. On completion of the chapel, it was decided that an old image of the Virgin which had stood in the cathedral at Thetford should be placed in it, but while the statue was being cleaned it was found to have a cavity in the head in which were hidden some holy relics. These were said to have miraculous powers of healing, and when word got around about this, the priory was soon inundated with sick pilgrims hoping for cures. The chronicler who tells the story says that there were indeed many miraculous cures following the discovery of these relics at Thetford.

Certainly the priory grew rich from the alms of visiting pilgrims, and in the 13th c. the east end of the church was rebuilt.

During the French wars of the 14th c. Thetford suffered, along with the other Cluniac priories, from being classed as an 'alien priory', but in 1376 the monks paid £100 for a charter of denization, and the priory was thenceforward exempt from the worst of the impositions. Numbers of monks seem

1. NAVE
2. NORTH TRANSEPT
3. SOUTH TRANSEPT
4. CHANCEL
5. LADY CHAPEL
6. LATER SACRISTY
7. EARLY SACRISTY
8. CHAPTER-HOUSE
9. CLOISTER
10. DAY-STAIRS
11. SLYPE
12. PARLOUR
13. WARMING-HOUSE, WITH DORTER ABOVE
14. RERE-DORTER
15. SITE OF INFIRMARY
16. SLYPE
17. FRATER
18. SITE OF EARLY KITCHEN
19. BUTTERY AND LATER KITCHEN
20. CELLARIUM
21. OUTER PARLOUR

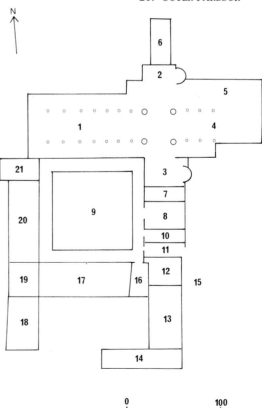

to have varied between twenty and twenty-four throughout most of the priory's history, although there was a severe (but temporary) drop after the plagues of the mid-14th c. The priory had powerful friends and patrons in the Bigods, Mowbrays and Howards, successive Earls and Dukes of Norfolk, and in 1539 Thomas, the third Howard Duke of Norfolk, tried to save Thetford from impending disaster by asking Henry VIII to convert it into a college of secular canons, pointing out not only that he was preparing his tomb in the church beside those of his ancestors, but also that the king's own natural son, the Duke of Richmond, was already buried there. The plea was unsuccessful. On 16 February 1540 Thetford went the way of all other English monasteries, the deed of surrender being signed by the abbot and the sixteen remaining monks.

As built in the 12th c., the church had an aisled nave of eight bays with two western towers, transepts with eastern apsidal chapels, and a short chancel of four bays ending in three stepped apses. The west end and the nave are now ruined and visible only in their outlines, but of the east end more remains. In the angle between the eastern bay of the nave and the north transept a small chapel was built in the late 15th c. to accommodate the tomb of the first Howard Duke of Norfolk, John, who died supporting Richard III at the Battle of Bosworth Field in 1485. The apse of the transept survives, and to the north of it is a ruined sacristy, also built in the late 15th c., which contains a small oven in which the sacramental wafers were baked. When the site was excavated, some fragments of tomb-sculpture were found here, and it may be that they were for the tomb which the third Howard Duke was preparing for himself in 1539.

In the 13th c., the east end of the church was rebuilt. First came the Lady Chapel on the north side (there is a spiral staircase at its west end, which led to a gallery from which a monk would be on duty during the pilgrims' visiting-hours), and then the chancel apse itself was knocked down and the east end extended to a line level with the east end of the Lady Chapel. The high altar has been reconstructed in stone, and a concrete slab marks the position of the tomb of Thomas, the second Howard Duke of Norfolk (d. 1524), famous for his exploits on the battlefield of Flodden. At the same time, the apse at the east end of the south aisle was squared off, and a chapel built in the bay between it and the

apse of the south transept. The south transept was also given a square end internally, so that of the five original apses only the apse of the north transept was left. Opening south from the south transept is the original sacristy, later replaced by the larger one to the north; at this time it was extended to the east by one bay.

The monastic buildings follow the standard layout and, apart from a few additions and reconstructions, they date like the church from the twelfth century. The cloister itself is about 110 ft. square, and along its east range, south of the sacristy, came the chapter-house, the monks' stairs to the dorter, the slype to the infirmary range, and then the undercroft of the dorter. These buildings are all ruined, but a good deal of the masonry still survives, and the plan is clear. The chapter-house was built with an eastern apse in the 12th c. Later, in the 14th c., the apse was pulled down and the east end squared off, but some of the Norman arcading from the apse was re-set in the new east wall. The undercroft of the dorter was partitioned at an early stage to form a small parlour to the north and a large warming-house of five bays to the south. The fireplace is in the east wall of the undercroft's central bay. To the east of the range is the infirmary block, most unusually and attractively arranged in the form of a monastery in miniature, with four ranges around a small cloister. Little of the masonry has survived, but remains of a serving-hatch and fireplaces can still be seen. The east end of its north range formed the infirmary chapel, with the base of its altar still visible against its east wall. At the south end of the east claustral range the rere-dorter runs at right-angles to it, with a drain along its south side. The bases of five of the shoots leading from privies into the drain can still be seen.

The south range had a passage at its east end followed by the frater along the rest of its length; both are mid 12th-c. The south wall of the frater includes a fascinating little detail: against its exterior are three large buttresses, erected in the 14th c. when it was obviously feared that the wall might collapse. Six centuries later the buttresses have sunk and detached themselves so that they no longer brace the wall, but the wall still stands as firm and upright as ever. The fears for its safety seem to have been unfounded. At the west end of the frater was the original buttery with the kitchen to the south of it and a well between them. In the

14th c. this plan was altered, however, the old kitchen being pulled down and the buttery being converted into the monastic kitchen; early in the 16th c. the two large double ovens were inserted in the fireplace in its south wall. The west range was the last part of the original monastery to be built, only being completed in the second half of the 12th c. Its undercroft, which contained cellarage with an outer parlour in the northern bay, can still be seen, but for the most part the masonry hardly reaches head-height, and the first floor has vanished entirely. If it followed the normal Cluniac plan, this would have included a guest-house, and possibly an early prior's lodging over the northern bays. To the west of the range stands a two-storeyed building known as the prior's lodge. Although some of the masonry here dates from the late 12th c., the building was so drastically restructured after the Dissolution that its medieval features are now hardly distinguishable.

The only other monastic survival is the gate-house, which stands some distance to the north-west of the church. A three-storeyed building, it is faced with knapped flint and still stands to the level of its octagonal turrets at the south angles, although the roof and parapets have vanished. It was built in the 14th c. The site is in the care of English Heritage.

Thornton Abbey

ORDER: Augustinian canons
COUNTY: Humberside
ROUTE: Off A1077, 6 miles ESE of Barton-upon-Humber.
OS REF: 113:1119

Founded as a priory from Kirkham by William le Gros, Count of Aumale, in 1139, Thornton was elevated to abbatial status in 1148. Le Gros himself, who was later to be made Earl of Yorkshire in recognition of his services at the Battle of the Standard, also founded the abbeys of Meaux and Vaudy, but it was at Thornton that he asked to be buried after his death in 1180. Its remote situation tended to cut Thornton off from the mainstream of events, and its history is uneventful. Numbers of canons are not easy to ascertain, but during the 13th c. there were probably at least thirty at Thornton. By 1377 there were twenty-nine, and during the next century and a half the figure fluctuated between twenty-four and twenty-eight. In 1518 Thornton became a mitred abbey. The last abbot, John Moor, was apparently implicated in the Pilgrimage of Grace and was accused of giving money to the rebels, but what happened to him is not clear; when the abbey was dissolved on 12 December 1539, the abbacy was vacant.

Two years later, Henry VIII decided that in addition to those former abbeys which he had raised to cathedral rank after the Dissolution, his new heirarchy for England should include two colleges of secular canons, and the two chosen sites were Burton-upon-Trent and Thornton. The foundation was made 'for the ministration of the sacraments, the observance of good manners, the care of the aged and those who had spent their lives in the service of the realm, and for the instruction of the young'. The experiment was unsuccessful, however: in 1545 Burton was dissolved, and in 1547, at the beginning of the reign of Edward VI, so was Thornton.

Since it is the most imposing survival from the monastic ruins and the normal point of entry for the visitor, the great gatehouse will be described first. This is the largest, and one of the finest, monastic gatehouses of England. Built at the end of the 14th c., it stands some distance to the west of the church and is constructed partly of stone, but largely of brick; this makes it one of the earliest large-scale brick buildings in the country, and it is likely that the bricks were made in nearby Hull and ferried across the Humber. Hull is one of the few English towns where brick-making is known to have flourished as early as the 14th c. What is also interesting about the gatehouse is that the abbots of Thornton seem to have used its upper floors as their lodging, an arrangement which ensured them a most luxurious set of apartments but which must have cut them off from the mainstream of monastic life in the ranges around the cloister. The front is a five-part composition with projecting turrets separating the bays, 68 ft. high and covered with canopies and niches for statuary, some of which has disappeared, but which was vividly described by Abraham de la Pryme in 1697: 'upon every exalted and turreted stone in the battlements . . . men with swords, shields, poll-axes, etc., in their hands looking downwards . . . so that, looking up, the battlements . . . seemed to be covered with armed men'. The archway is ribbed-vaulted, and above it is a large apartment which must have formed the main hall of the abbot's lodging. It is now used as a museum to house various carved-stone fragments found during the excavations of the site. Above it is a third storey which was probably sub-divided into chambers by wooden partitions during the time that the lodging was in use. Throughout the building is a system of wall-passages, fireplaces and garderobes. From the ends of the gatehouse the precinct walls project, and to the north of the entrance a barbican, probably added after the Dissolution, runs over the moat, which is now dry.

Of the church and monastic buildings little survives above ground, but the ruins have been methodically excavated and the plan is clearly marked out. The church, which was rebuilt in the late 13th and 14th cs., consisted of an aisled nave of eight bays (the original 12th-c. church was aisleless, at least on the south side), north and south transepts with eastern chapels, and an aisled chancel of six bays with a square east end. Abbot William Multon added the long Lady Chapel at the east end about 1400, and to the north of the chancel can be seen the foundations of another freestanding building which may have been a chapel to St Thomas of Canterbury. In the transepts and nave several mutilated grave-slabs and paving tiles can still be seen. The cloister was in its usual position to

the south of the nave, and was rebuilt in the early 14th c.

To the south of the south transept is the narrow parlour, with plain blank arcading and a rib-vault which has partially collapsed, while to the east of it is a small, dark room access to which was only by the spiral staircase leading down from the floor above. The purpose of this room is not certain, but it may have been the strong room in which the monastic plate and other valuables were kept. It is recorded that some time after the Dissolution one of the canons was found immured in a 'little hollow room' at Thornton, sitting at a table with a pen in his hand and a book open in front of him, though long since dead; the rush of fresh air into his walled-up tomb apparently caused the body to crumble to dust, just as happened to so many excavated Egyptian mummies. If the legend is true, it must surely be this room to which it refers.

To the south of these rooms comes the vestibule leading to the chapter-house, a lovely octagonal building dating from the early 14th c. which stands outside the range to the east. Its two surviving sides have some beautiful blank arcading, three trefoil-headed lancets surmounted by floriate quatrefoiled and cinquefoiled spheres, a pattern which was probably reproduced in the genuine windows which would have filled the upper stage of the destroyed sides. Of the remaining monastic buildings little has survived except low masonry. The east range continued with the undercroft of the dorter, with a slype running through it and a warming-house with fireplace at the southern end; this dates from the 12th c., and is the oldest part of the site. The south range contained the frater on an undercroft, while the west range contained cellarage. The farmyard to the south of the south range probably stands on the site of the infirmary, although this might have stood to the south-east of the east range. The rere-dorter was no doubt in its usual position at the south end of the east range.

After the Dissolution of the college in 1547, the site passed into the hands of Henry Randes, Bishop of Lincoln, whose son sold it to Sir Robert Tyrwhitt in 1575. Tyrwhitt's grandson in turn sold it to Sir Vincent Skinner in 1602. According to de la Pryme, Skinner pulled down the college and 'built a most stately hall out of the same on the west side of the Abbey plot within the moat, which hall when it was finished fell quite down to the bare ground, without any visible cause'. More successfully, Skinner is also said to have built the farmhouse to the south of the abbey. The site passed through several more hands before it was inherited in 1816 by Charles, 1st Lord Yarborough, whose descendant, 5th Earl of Yarborough, placed it in the hands of the Office of Works in 1938. It is now in the care of English Heritage.

Tintern Abbey

ORDER: Cistercian monks
COUNTY: Gwent
ROUTE: On A466, 5 miles N of Chepstow.
OS REF: 162:5300

The ruins of Tintern Abbey, set in lovely sur-roundings in a darkly-wooded valley of the Wye and celebrated by Wordsworth in a famous poem, represent what was a rather undistinguished medieval monastery. Founded in 1131 by Walter fitz Richard, Lord of Chepstow, it was the first Cistercian foundation in Wales and one of the earliest in Britain. No doubt the site was chosen for its remoteness and tranquillity. The first monks came from L'Aumône, near Chartres, and the number of monks probably reached twenty in the 13th c., towards the end of which the great rebuilding of the church began under the patronage of Roger Bigod, Earl of Norfolk, to whom

the lordship of Chepstow had passed. Since it was outside the area in which most of the fighting between English and Welsh took place, Tintern was more fortunate than many of the Welsh houses and suffered little at the hands of marauding armies and raiding parties. Edward II spent two nights in the abbey in 1326 when he was fleeing from the invading army of his wife Queen Isabella and her lover Roger Mortimer, but otherwise its history was largely uneventful. It was dissolved in 1536, at which time there were thirteen monks in residence.

Apart from its roof, and the north aisle arcade in the nave, the main fabric of the church stands almost complete; it completely dominates the ruins at Tintern, and because we are not nowadays accustomed to looking at such complete survivals, it seems much larger than it is. Its overall length is 228 ft. (compared with 350 ft. at Fountains, for instance, or 370 ft. at Rievaulx), and its shape is simple and cruciform, with an aisled nave of six bays, north and south transepts each with two eastern chapels, and a square-ended, aisled chancel

1. NAVE
2. NORTH TRANSEPT
3. SOUTH TRANSEPT
4. CHANCEL
5. CHAPELS
6. LIBRARY
7. VESTRY
8. CLOISTER
9. CHAPTER-HOUSE
10. PARLOUR
11. SLYPE
12. NOVICES' LODGING, WITH MONKS' DORTER ABOVE
13. WARMING-HOUSE
14. FRATER
15. KITCHEN
16. OUTER PARLOUR
17. PORCH
18. CELLAR
19. LAY-BROTHERS' FRATER, WITH LAY-BROTHERS' DORTER OVER
20. PULPITUM
21. INFIRMARY CLOISTER
22. INFIRMARY HALL
23. KITCHEN
24. ABBOT'S CHAMBER
25. ABBOT'S HALL ABOVE
26. RERE-DORTER
27. DAY-STAIRS
28. LAVATORIUM
29. INFIRMARY RERE-DORTER
30. ABBOT'S CHAPEL ABOVE
31. PANTRY

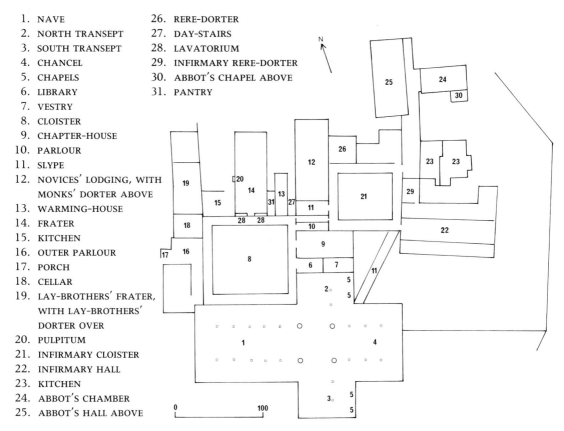

TINTERN: *aerial view from the north-east*

of four bays. Built in the last quarter of the 13th c., it replaced an earlier and smaller church which stood slightly to the north, and of which the lines are marked in the turf. The south transept wall of the 12th-c. church ran straight through the middle of the crossing of the later church.

The west front is a beautiful composition. The twin doorways have trefoiled heads and are contained within a super-arch filled with tracery and other decorative panels, while on either side of them are further panels. Above is the great west window of seven lights, with most of the reticulated tracery in its upper stages still intact, and a small circle in the head of the arch which has lost its tracery. The gable window above has also lost its tracery. At the south-west corner one of the delicate octagonal spirelets, which no doubt surmounted the other buttresses, as well has been preserved. Outside the west door are the bases of two columns, all that remains of an arcaded porch

added in the 15th c. The north aisle arcade does not stand, and the south arcade has only been saved from collapse by the insertion of steel reinforcing which has been partially concealed by the reconstruction of the south aisle roof. A break in building is clearly visible between the second and third bays from the west of the south aisle wall; the two western windows here are shorter than the four eastern windows in the aisle, and have quatrefoiled rather than sexfoiled heads. The north aisle windows are also shorter, thus allowing the sills to be heightened in order to clear the roof of the cloister. In the north-west corner of the church is a diagonal passage into the western range for the use of the lay-brothers, inserted at the same time as the south end of the west range was built, in the 14th c.; it is through this passage that the visitor enters the church.

The elevation throughout the church is standardised. There is no triforium, the aisle arcades being separated from the clerestory windows simply by two string-courses, and the triple vaulting-shafts

363

TINTERN: *interior of the church, looking west*

rise from the intersection of the arches rather than continuing down to the ground. The whole church was originally vaulted with a simple quadripartite rib-vault. A circular stair in the south-west angle of the south transept gave access to the roofs; the great window in the south transept was originally of six lights, but it has lost nearly all of its tracery. The north window of the north transept is interesting in that its lower stages did not clear the roof-line of the monks' dorter which abutted against the exterior of the transept, so these parts were simply filled in and treated as panelling. The window is of six lights and retains its tracery. Just to the west of it can be seen the monks' night-stairs to the dorter; the existing steps have been rebuilt in modern times, but on the original lines. The massive crossing arches used to support a low bell tower. The high altar stood in the second bay from the east wall, with four chapels to the east of it, on the raised platform which can still be seen. The east window was originally of eight lights; the central mullion and the rose in the head can still be seen, but the rest of the tracery has vanished. The original glass portrayed the arms of Roger Bigod, the man whose generosity enabled this second church to be built. In the east wall is another peculiarity, a low arch showing where the 'barrow-way' was, the entrance through which the workmen who constructed the church brought their building materials.

The cloister and monastic buildings lay unusually to the north of the church, probably in order to facilitate drainage into the Wye. Their outlines are almost perfectly preserved, and in some places the walls still stand to a considerable height although, like the church, they have lost their roofs. Excepting their position to the north of the church, they conform closely to the normal Cistercian plan. The cloister itself was built in the 12th c. and enlarged in the 13th; in the late 15th c. another rebuilding was begun, but this does not seem to have progressed very far before the Dissolution. The entrance to the cloister is through the east processional doorway, situated as usual in the angle of the nave and transept; it is a sumptuous 14th-c. insertion, with prominent moulding and a multi-foiled head. In the centre of the south walk can be seen the canopied recess for the seat where the prior sat while he was supervising the monks at their studies. Opposite is the base of his lectern.

The east range of the cloister contains, from south to north, the library-cum-vestry, the chapter-house, the parlour, a slype through to the infirmary range, and the undercroft of the dorter, with the monks' dorter extending over the whole range. The west part of the first room housed the library, the fine moulded and traceried doorway of which can still be seen; along with many of the monastic buildings it was rebuilt in the 13th c., but was still barrel-vaulted. The eastern part of the room contained the vestry, which was rib-vaulted in three small bays. The eastern bay still retains its vault. The vestry was entered only from the transept, for a screen wall divided the two parts of the room immediately to the west of the doorway from the transept. Various fragments of stone found in the church have been collected here, including an effigy of a knight in armour, dating from about 1200.

The chapter-house was rib-vaulted in three by five bays, and the bases of the piers supporting the vault as well as some of the medieval floor tiles can still be seen. The doorways of both this room and the parlour to the north of it still stand. The space to the north of the parlour probably contained the monks' day-stairs to the dorter, but no traces of the steps remain. The undercroft of the dorter was used as the novices' room at Tintern. Originally only three double bays in length, it was extended by a further three bays northwards at the end of the 12th c., a sure sign of expanding numbers at Tintern. The bases of the central piers are all *in situ*. The dorter which ran over the whole range has disappeared, but the line of its roof can be seen against the exterior wall of the north transept; it is noticeable how the rebuilding of the church in the 13th c. broadened the transept so that it overlapped the width of the buildings in the east range. Projecting east from the northern half of the range was the rere-dorter, through which the line of the main drain still runs.

To the east of the east range were a series of buildings comprising the infirmary and, a little to the north, the abbot's lodging. The infirmary buildings, built in the 13th c., were arranged around a second cloister of which the east claustral range formed the west range. They were connected to the cloister by the slype already mentioned, and to the church by a covered passageway leading to the angle of the chancel and north transept. The main infirmary building, the hall, occupied the southern half of the east range and overlapped it considerably further to the south. It is 107 ft. long and 54 ft. wide, with a central corridor on each side of which are 'aisles' which were divided up into cubicles by stone screen walls in the 15th c. Projecting from its north-west corner is the infirmary rere-dorter, with the drain still visible along its north wall. The use to which the other two buildings on the north range of the infirmary cloister was put is not certain; possibly they were chambers for corrodians. The building to the east of them, and to the north of the hall, was the infirmary kitchen, to the east of which a further kitchen was added in the 15th c.; fireplaces can still be seen in both of these kitchens.

Further north, abutting the precinct wall and close to the bank of the Wye, are the buildings comprising the abbot's lodging. They include the abbot's chamber to the east, built in the thirteenth century, and to the west his hall, added in the 14th c. Although little of this remains, it clearly contained cellarage below the hall, on the ground floor, and seems to have been built in the grand style.

Returning to the north walk of the monastic cloister, which was built in the early 13th c., it will be seen that the eastern part still stands to second-floor level. It contained the warming-house on the ground floor, the only room in the monastery where a fire was allowed apart from the kitchen and the infirmary. The central fireplace is unusual but practical, the arches on each side allowing all-round access to the warmth. The upper storeys above the warming-house contained the prior's lodging and another private chamber, but they are no longer accessible. In the middle of the north range, on a north–south axis, was the monastic frater, an early 13th-c. building 84 ft. by 29 ft. On either side of its entrance doorway are recesses, where the bowls and towels with which the monks washed and dried their hands before meals were kept. Several of its four-light windows, with plate tracery, can still be seen, as can the stairs leading up to the pulpit and the serving-hatch from the kitchen, both in the west wall. The kitchen completed the range, at the north end of which the main drain can again be seen, but the lines of a later cottage on the spot have much confused the outlines of the building.

The west range, as in other Cistercian houses, was largely for the use of the lay-brothers. The northern part of the range, from the line of the north walk of the cloister northwards, contained their frater on the ground floor and their dorter on the first floor. North of this was a cellar with no direct access to the cloister, followed by the outer parlour and porch, now converted into a ticket office, and the point at which the visitor enters the monastery. This was the room in which the monks could meet and converse with tradesmen and other visitors from the world outside. To the west of the abbey church the remains of the monastic guest-house can also be seen, while close to the inn, on the river, is the medieval gateway which led to the slipway for the ferry across the Wye; this ferry was still in use just after the first world war.

After the Dissolution the site and buildings were granted to Henry Somerset, Earl of Worcester (who was already the abbey's patron), and the buildings were systematically stripped of their roofs for lead. In the 17th c., a descendant of the Earl, Sir Thomas Herbert, may have occupied some of the buildings for a while; there are certainly signs (e.g., inserted windows and fireplaces) that some of the monastic buildings were converted into dwelling-houses at one time. In 1901, the Duke of Beaufort, Earl Henry's descendant, sold the site to the Crown, and in 1914 it was placed in the hands of the Office of Works. Tintern Abbey is now in the care of English Heritage.

Titchfield Abbey

ORDER: Premonstratensian canons
COUNTY: Hampshire
ROUTE: Off A27, 3 miles W of Fareham.
OS REF: 196:5406

Titchfield Abbey was founded in 1232–3 by Peter des Roches, Bishop of Winchester, and colonised from Halesowen, making it the second last Premonstratensian foundation in England. By the late 13th c., the number of canons had reached eighteen, but in the 14th c. the abbey fell into financial difficulties and by the late 15th c. the number was down to eleven. It was probably in Titchfield Abbey church that King Henry VI married Margaret of Anjou in 1445, but otherwise its history was uneventful. At the Dissolution in 1537, there were thirteen canons and the abbey was surrendered peacefully, Abbot John Sympson having been replaced in the previous year by the more obliging John Salisbury, who had already been consecrated as suffragan Bishop of Thetford. The site was granted to Thomas Wriothesley, to whom it had been promised even before the surrender, and who converted it into a magnificent Tudor residence, called Place House.

The church at Titchfield was 190 ft. in overall length and consisted of an aisleless nave of seven bays, north and south transepts each with three eastern chapels (the innermost chapel on each side projecting further east than the other two), and a square-ended, aisleless chancel. Only the foundations of the crossing, transepts and chancel remain, but the nave was used by Wriothesley as the gatehouse to Place House and, although it now looks most unlike the nave of a church, it still stands close to its original height. Originally Wriothesley's gatehouse also incorporated the crossing and chancel, but this eastern extension was demolished in about 1800. The nave walls were originally higher than they are now, and the roof was rib-vaulted, but Wriothesley lowered them and had them battlemented; then, screening off the central bay from the three bays on either side of it, he erected four towers, one at each corner, and completely rebuilt the walls in between, again battlementing them. The ranges on either side of the gatehouse, comprising the remaining six bays of the nave, were probably used as private apartments to the west and offices to the east. It will be noticed that the rebuilding and restoration carried out by Wriothesley here is considerably less careful, comprising much patchy brickwork. The two turrets in the western corners of the nave are monastic and contain original spiral staircases, but the south eastern turret is a 16th-c. addition.

The monastic buildings at Titchfield were, unusually, to the north of the church. The west range was completely rebuilt by Wriothesley, but has since been almost entirely demolished. The monastic frater, which occupied the north claustral range, was converted into the Great Hall of Place House; little more than the foundations can be seen, but what remains dates from the 13th c. Beyond the north transept, the east range consisted of the monastic library, chapter-house and warming-house, with the dorter over the whole range and extending considerably further to the north than the present ruins. Although it includes much 16th-c. restoration work, the east wall of the eastern range of the cloister survives. The triple-arched entrance to the chapter-house, although bricked in, is clearly distinguishable; it was originally vaulted in five bays, and the spots from which the eastern and western pairs of vaulting-shafts rose are clearly marked. The fireplace in the west wall of the warming-house is 16th-c.

Amazingly, Wriothesley's conversion of Titchfield into Place House took less than five years, being completed by 1542, and cost about £200. Wriothesley himself, who was a follower of Thomas Cromwell, continued to prosper after Cromwell's execution in 1540. In 1544 he became Lord Chancellor, and in 1547 he was appointed to the Council of State which governed for the young King Edward VI, and he became Earl of Southampton. His grandson Henry, the third Earl, is famous as a patron of Shakespeare, and it has been suggested (though with little evidence) that some of Shakespeare's plays may have received their first performances at Titchfield. In the 17th c. the property passed by marriage to the Noel family, Earls of Gainsborough, and in 1647, when Charles I escaped from Parliamentary custody on the Isle of Wight, it was to Titchfield that he made his way. In 1741 Place House passed to the Delme family, who demolished much of it, and early in the 20th c. it was sold by a descendant of the Delmes to the Ministry of Agriculture and Fisheries. It is now in the care of English Heritage.

TITCHFIELD: *aerial view from the west*

Tynemouth Priory

ORDER: Benedictine monks
COUNTY: Tyne and Wear
ROUTE: Off A193, 8½ miles ENE of Newcastle.
OS REF: 88:3769

The priory of St Mary and St Oswin at Tynemouth, with its almost impregnable position on a steep headland overlooking the North Sea, has always been as much a castle as a religious house. The monks were later to claim that the first monastery on the site was founded in 627 by King Edwin of Northumbria, but this seems unlikely as Bede states that Lindisfarne, founded in 634, was the earliest monastery in Northumbria. Tynemouth had certainly come into existence before 651, for in that year King Oswin, revered by his people for his saintliness but treacherously betrayed and slain by rivals for supremacy in the Northumbrian king-

dom, was brought here to be buried. Miracles were said to have been worked at his tomb, and the many pilgrims who flocked to his shrine were a constant source of income to the monks. From the year 800, however, the Danish raids on Tynemouth began, culminating in its destruction during the decade 865–875. Nevertheless, there seems to have been a revival here during the 10th c., and it was not until 1008 that the original monastery was eventually abandoned.

During the years immediately following the Norman Conquest, there were several attempts to refound Tynemouth, none of them successful until, in 1089–90, Robert Mowbray, newly-created Earl of Northumberland, refounded it as a house for Benedictine monks dependent on the great abbey of St Albans. Mowbray endowed the priory so lavishly that throughout its history it was one of the wealthiest of the black monk houses. In 1095 he rebelled against King William Rufus, however, and twice during the space of a few months Tynemouth

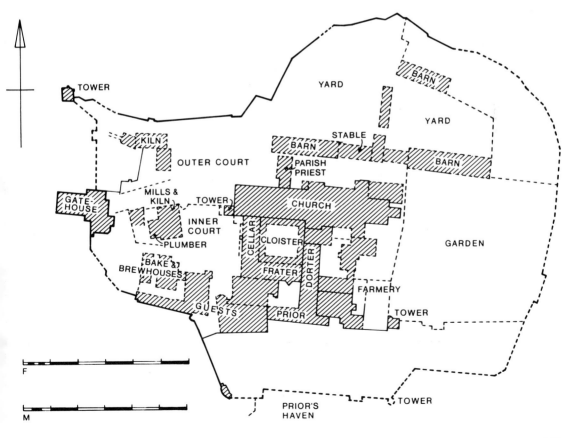

had to withstand sieges by royalist forces; on the first occasion the siege lasted for two months, on the second occasion only two days.

During the Scottish wars of the 14th c., the priory took on added military significance. The massive outer defensive walls were probably built by Edward I in 1296, and were continually maintained and improved by successive abbots and kings. Edward III regarded Tynemouth as one of his strongest northern fortresses and made continual demands on its resources, not only for frequent hospitality but also by insisting that an armed garrison be maintained at the priory. The result of this was financial disarray, made worse by Scottish raids on Tynemouth's estates. By the end of the century the walls had to be rebuilt. With the aid of generous grants from Richard II and John of Gaunt the new walls, including the now-ruined Gate Tower, were completed at the beginning of the 15th c. The perimeter of the outer walls was now 3,200 ft., making Tynemouth one of the largest fortified areas in England. The priory was surrendered to the king on 12 January 1539, at which time there were nineteen monks. The site was retained by Henry VIII as a royal castle.

The Norman church, built between 1090 and 1140, consisted of an aisled nave of seven bays, north and south transepts each with an apsidal eastern chapel, and an apsidal chancel with three radiating apsidal chapels, totalling 180 ft. in length. In about 1200, it was decided to build a new, much longer chancel, and as soon as this was completed work was begun on a new west end, extending the nave by two bays. In the 15th c. a Percy chantry was added to the east end. The result of all these additions was that the total exterior length of the church in its final form reached 310 ft. The total interior length of the church is only 295 ft.; Tynemouth is, not surprisingly, famed for the thickness of its walls.

This wall thickness can be seen around the west doorway of the church, which is of five moulded orders, none of them slender. Above it was a great traceried window inserted in the 15th c., but the tracery has disappeared, along with practically all the masonry above aisle arcade height throughout the nave. A large part of the nave's north wall has also disappeared, but of the south wall there is more left; eastwards from the second bay, this belongs to the first building period of 1090–1140. It will be noticed that a wall separates the nave from the crossing. It was inserted after the Dissolution, the nave continuing to be used as a parish church through to the 17th c. The transepts stand to a considerable height—indeed the further east one moves in the church, the higher the walls stand—and the arch leading through the east wall of the south transept into the south aisle of the chancel is particularly well-preserved. When the chancel was lengthened in the early 13th c., its east end was squared off and a further pair of transepts was added near this end. This accounts for the width of the arch in the south transept: in its final form the chancel consisted of four aisled bays containing the quire, then the two eastern transepts, and finally an aisleless presbytery of two bays which, because it was aisleless, was obviously narrower than the first four bays, which were even wider than the nave. It is the disappearance of the masonry between the central transepts and the east end which now makes it look as if these two parts of the church are out of alignment.

This east end soars to an impressive height and dominates the ruins at Tynemouth, in much the same way as does the east end of Guisborough Priory, although there is much less of the rest of the church there. Here the walls are over 7 ft. thick, and filled with massively tall lancets in place of the traditional great east window. Wall shafts run from the top of the lowest level of blank arcading up to corbels which supported the quadripartite vaulting, but it will be noticed that even above this there is a further series of windows. These lighted a large chamber which formed the highest stage of the east end at Tynemouth. It was only added in the late 14th c. and presumably served a defensive purpose. Certainly its addition must have demanded constructional skill of the highest order, but it is a most unusual feature to find in a monastic church and it hardly enhances Tynemouth's east end. The architecture at Tynemouth is powerful; whether it is beautiful is debatable, despite its magnificent setting.

In the middle of the 15th c. a further notable addition was made to the east end: the Percy chantry, named after the family of Earls of Northumberland who dominated Border politics for much of the later middle ages. It consists of three small bays and is less than 20 ft. in length, but is exceptionally well preserved and has a vaulting system of the greatest intricacy, with intersecting ribs joined by no fewer than thirty-three sculp-

tured bosses. There is a rose window at the east end, and beneath are the sculptured figures of the Virgin Mary and the angel. The figures over the door are St Oswin and, kneeling at his feet, the founder Roger Mowbray. There are no windows in the north wall, because there was a 14th c. Lady Chapel on the north side of the presbytery when the chantry was built which would have blocked the light coming into any windows here. Although the Lady Chapel has disappeared, windows have never been inserted here.

The monastic buildings at Tynemouth stood in their usual position to the south of the church, but little has survived above low foundation walls. The cloister itself is relatively small, 82 ft. by 79 ft., because it was not expanded when the church was lengthened, but retained its original Norman layout. Its west range contained a small outer parlour, where monks could converse with visitors from the world outside, followed by a long two-storeyed building which contained cellarage space on the ground floor and the 'common hall' on the first floor. Originally it was used by the lay-brothers, and later by the servants attached to the monastery. The south range contained the frater, with the kitchen south-west of it. A large oven can still be seen in the south wall of the buildings immediately south of the frater, which may have been a bakehouse or part of the kitchen. The east range is better preserved, but still little more than fragmentary. The oblong chapter-house adjoined the south transept, followed by the monks' day-stairs to the dorter, of which a few steps remain. The dorter stretched over the whole east claustral range, with the warming-house beneath it. Beyond this there was a narrow slype and then, returning

west at a slight angle, are the remains of the prior's lodging. Originally built in the early 13th c., this building came later to be known as the 'Lords' Lodging' on account of the number of guests of the monastery who were accommodated here; consequently the interior of the building was re-modelled by Prior de la Mare in the 14th c., so that distinguished guests could be entertained in the style to which they were accustomed. It was then that the two large windows, now blocked in, were inserted in the south wall, and the fireplace built.

At the south-east corner of the prior's lodging is his chapel, which has survived more completely than any of the other monastic buildings. It is rib-vaulted in two bays and dates from the early 13th c., with two tall lancet windows in the south wall. To the east of the prior's hall are the remains of the monks' rere-dorter. This was built about 1100 along with the original church, but in the 13th c. the thickness of its walls was increased on both sides, for what reason it is not certain. Outside the south-east corner of the rere-dorter are two remarkably well preserved drain chutes.

Clearly, there were further buildings at Tyne-mouth: the remains to the east of the rere-dorter can probably be identified as the monastic in-firmary, while those to the south and west of the claustral ranges probably contained more accom-modation for visitors. Many of the monastic buildings continued to be used after the Disso-lution, for Tynemouth castle was a military stronghold until the 20th c. Indeed parts of the site are still in military occupation and not accessible to the public, but all the medieval monastic buildings are in the care of English Heritage and open to visitors at the usual hours.

Ulverscroft Priory

ORDER: Augustinian canons
COUNTY: Leicestershire
ROUTE: Off B587, 10 miles NW of Leicester.
OS REF: 129:5012.

The priory of St Mary was founded about 1174 by Robert, Earl of Leicester, the chief justiciar of England and close friend of King Henry II. It was not the first foundation on the site, for a community of three hermits had begun to live here in 1134, but in 1174 the brethren were ordered by the Pope to observe the Augustinian rule, and it is from this year that the establishment of the house as a priory probably dates. The house never became large or influential, although in the later middle ages the canons acquired somewhat dubious fame for their fondness for hunting in surrounding Charnwood Forest. Despite this attraction, numbers at Ulverscroft remained small. In 1438 there were only eight canons, and in 1534, when the prior and canons took the oath of supremacy, there were ten. In 1536, possibly because the priory was noted as a hospitable resting-place for travellers and poor folk, the suppression was delayed for a while on payment of a fine, but on 15 September 1539 the prior and eleven canons finally surrendered the house.

The church, built in the late 12th c., was rebuilt in the 13th, and most of what remains dates from this rebuilding. The most conspicuous survival however, is the great west tower, added, within the west end of the nave, in the 15th c. It stands to the height of its parapets and has a massive west window. The church itself had neither transepts nor a south aisle, but it had a north aisle which, as can be seen, was almost as broad as the nave and only slightly shorter than it; the building of north aisles without south aisles was not uncommon in Augustinian houses. The south wall of the nave still stands to the height of the clerestory windows, and in various parts of the church, notably under the tower and in the aisle, the medieval floor-tiles can be seen.

Of the monastic buildings a fair amount remains, although much of it has been incorporated into more modern structures. The east range began as usual with the chapter-house, but this has vanished. However, remains can be seen of the parlour to the east of it and, further east, of the warming-house under the dorter and the sub-vault of the rere-dorter; they have been incorporated into a private house. The position of the prior's lodging at Ulverscroft is not certain: it may have been at the end of the east range, next to the dorter on the first floor, but more probably it was on the first floor of the west range, the west wall of which still stands and which is now used as a barn. The south wall of the frater, built in the 15th c., also stands. Around the oblong precinct can be detected traces of the moat by which it was surrounded on the north, south and east sides in the middle ages. The western wall of the precinct was bounded by a large fishpond.

Excavations which took place in the middle of the twentieth century cleared the site at Ulverscroft, and the ruins are now scheduled as an Ancient Monument.

Valle Crucis Abbey

ORDER: Cistercian monks
COUNTY: Clwyd
ROUTE: Off A542, 1½ miles NNW of Llangollen
OS REF: 117:2044

Valle Crucis was founded on 28 January 1201 by Madoc ap Gruffydd Maelor, ruler of the Welsh principality of Powys, and colonised by thirteen monks and several lay-brothers from the Abbey of Strata Marcella, near Welshpool. It took its name from its surroundings, for the vale in which it lies was known as the Valley of the Cross because the ninth-century Pillar of Eilseg, which stands a quarter of a mile north of the monastery as a monument to the former glories of the royal house of Powys, was formerly surmounted by a cross. Building began straight away, but some time during the first fifty years of its existence a disastrous fire occurred, necessitating considerable alterations. Traces of the fire can still be seen on some of the earliest masonry.

Within a few years of its foundation, the abbey was reprimanded by the general chapter at Cîteaux because it was reported that the abbot rarely celebrated mass or even received the Eucharist, but in general the history of the house was uneventful, and it is doubtful if the community ever numbered more than the original compliment of thirteen monks. There are indications, however, that by the 15th c. those thirteen were living a life of comfort bordering on luxury. The 15th-c. bard Guttyn Owain praised the hospitality of the abbots, remarking that their table was usually spread with four meat courses served in silver dishes and accompanied by 'sparkling claret'. In particular, the re-building of the upper floor of the eastern range towards the end of the century, creating separate chambers in which the abbots lived in semi-secular splendour, would have horrified the early fathers of Cîteaux. Valle Crucis was dissolved in 1538.

A feature of the buildings is the small scale on which they were planned. The church, most of which dates from the first period of building in the early 13th c., is a little less than 150 ft. long, with an aisled nave of five bays, north and south transepts each with twin eastern chapels, and a short, square-ended chancel which extends only to the width of the nave without the aisles. The upper parts of the church were mostly built after the fire. Both east and west fronts are well-preserved, the west front displaying a finely moulded door and, at the top, a rose window of eight trefoiled lights inserted when the top of the gable was renewed in the 14th c. A remarkable feature of the east end is the way in which the external buttresses are treated: the two outer ones are arched over the tops of the lower openings, while the two central ones are broadened to supply frames for the upper lancets, at the same time forming the impression of a blind lancet in the middle.

The door from the south aisle of the nave into the cloister shows clear evidence of the 13th-c fire and, together with the long barrel-vaulted sacristy immediately to the south of the south transept, it dates from the earliest period of building. To the

1. NAVE
2. NORTH TRANSEPT
3. SOUTH TRANSEPT
4. CHANCEL
5. SACRISTY, WITH (LATER) ABBOT'S CHAMBER ABOVE
6. CHAPTER-HOUSE WITH DORTER AND (LATER) ABBOT'S HALL ABOVE
7. SLYPE
8. RERE-DORTER
9. CLOISTER
10. FRATER
11. WEST RANGE

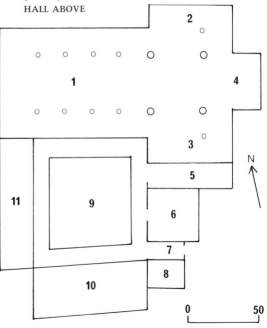

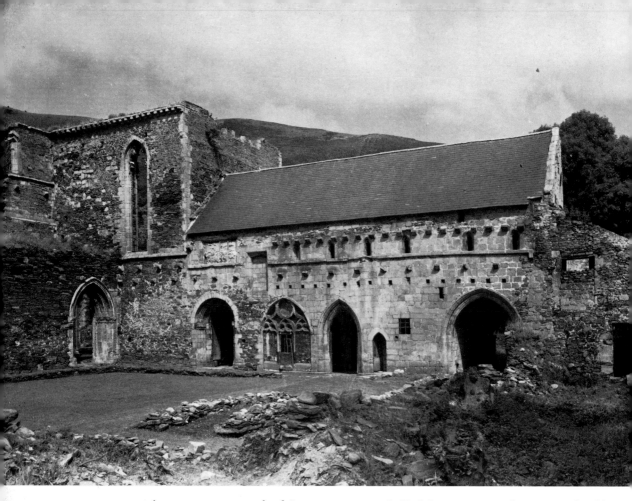

VALLE CRUCIS: *the east range, across the cloister*

south of the sacristy again is the late 14th- or early 15th-c. chapter-house, probably the most interesting architectural survival at Valle Crucis. It is a square building of nine bays with groined vaults, the ribs of which are supported by four central piers without capitals and by corbels set in the walls, and the whole is in fine condition. The east wall has three windows with reticulated tracery, while the west wall has an arched central doorway and a screen of elaborate tracery with a small doorway in the northern bay, enclosing a recess in the wall which was used as a book cupboard.

A small doorway in the exterior of the south-western bay leads to stairs which rise to the dorter. Now, as originally, the whole of the dorter forms one chamber, with rere-dorter forming a separate chamber attached to the southern end on both ground and first-floor level, but in the late 15th c. the northern end of the dorter was converted into an abbot's hall and a large fireplace inserted towards the northern end of the east wall. At the same time an abbot's chamber was added above the

eastern half of the sacristy, marking a considerable relaxation of monastic life at Valle Crucis. The long, narrow chamber above the eastern bay of the chapter-house was not added until after the Dissolution.

The cloister is only some 60 ft. square (it is not, in fact, quite square, the south wall inclining slightly to the north at its eastern end); and of the south range, which would have contained the frater and kitchen, and the west range, which housed the lay-brothers, there are only the scantiest remains.

After the Dissolution, the site passed to Sir William Pickering, and in the 17th c. to the Wootton family. In Elizabethan times the east range was converted into a dwelling-house, and in later times it was used as a farmhouse. Restoration was undertaken after the site came into the hands of the Coed Helen Estate, with Sir Gilbert Scott supervising the repair of the west front. In 1950 the Estate placed the abbey in the hands of the Ministry of Works; it is now in the care of Cadw: Welsh Historic Monuments, and is surrounded by a camping-site, which, however, does little to diminish the beauty of the ruins.

VALLE CRUCIS: *the west doorway of the church*

Walsingham Priory

ORDER: Augustinian canons
COUNTY: Norfolk
ROUTE: On B1105, five miles NNE of Fakenham.
OS REF: 132:9336

The priory of Our Lady of Walsingham, one of the most celebrated places of pilgrimage in medieval England, grew out of the chapel and shrine erected on the spot just before the Norman Conquest, after the miraculous appearance of the Virgin Mary here in 1051. The shrine itself, modelled on the Santa Casa at Nazareth, often led to the town being called either the second Nazareth or the second Bethlehem, and indeed this corner of England achieved such fame that it came to be known as England's Holy Land. Almost all the monarchs of later medieval England visited the shrine, leaving their shoes like other pilgrims at the Slipper Chapel a mile from the place of worship and completing the journey barefoot. The priory itself was not founded until over a century after the Virgin Mary's appearance, probably in 1169.

The founder was Geoffrey de Favarches who had visited the Holy Land and decided to add a house of Augustinian canons to the existing chapel. His priory grew to be one of the wealthiest and most important religious houses in East Anglia, with between thirty and forty canons in the 13th c. Although numbers dropped to twenty in 1377 and stayed around that level until the Dissolution, Walsingham remained an important and wealthy house, second only to Norwich in riches among the religious houses of Norfolk. In 1511 Henry VIII visited the shrine and left a candle burning there, but his youthful devotion did not prevent him from dissolving the priory later. In 1534 the last prior, Richard Vowell, and the twenty-one canons then resident, took the oath of supremacy. Although Vowell himself became a supporter of Cromwell and the royal agents in 1536–7, the subprior Nicholas Mileham and some of the other canons joined the uprising in Norfolk and were harshly dealt with. Mileham and another canon were executed for 'verbal treason', while several others received sentences of life imprisonment. In 1538 Prior Vowell removed the statue from the pilgrimage chapel, on the instructions of Cromwell, and on 4 August the priory was dissolved.

WALSINGHAM: *the healing wells, with the east end of the church in the background*

Of the church little remains above ground, although it is known to have consisted of an aisled nave with a western tower, north and south transepts with a tower over the crossing, and a chancel. The east wall of the chancel, with its large east window and twin turrets, still stands to its original height and dominates the ruins, as at Guisborough. Although originally built in the late 13th c., it was much altered in the second half of the 14th c. The east range contained as usual the chapter house, of which only two corner shafts remain, followed by a slype and then the undercroft of the dorter, of which three bays, vaulted

from octagonal piers, are intact. A late 18th-c. dwelling known as Abbey House has been built into the remainder of the east range. The south range contained the frater, and its late 13th-c. south wall still stands, complete with bar-tracery in the windows and the staircase leading to the pulpitum. By the entrance to the frater, at the south-west corner of the cloisters, can be seen the niche for the lavatorium. The west range, which probably contained cellarage on the ground floor and possibly the prior's lodging on the first floor, has almost entirely disappeared.

Of the shrine, which probably stood to the north of the church, there remains nothing. To the east of the church, however, stands a re-erected Norman doorway, beyond which are two healing wells to which the sick were brought in medieval times. Their proximity to the spot at which the Virgin appeared is supposed to have imbued the two wells with restorative powers. Close to the arch and the wells there stood also a chapel dedicated to St Lawrence but this, like the chapel of the shrine, has long since vanished. The only other medieval building standing is the gatehouse on the other side of the church. It has a fine four-centred arch on the outer side and was built in the 15th c.

After the Dissolution, Walsingham declined as a place of pilgrimage, but in recent years interest in the site has revived and in the 1930s a new Anglican shrine was built close to the ruins of the old priory. The ruins themselves are now scheduled as an Ancient Monument.

Westminster Abbey, London

ORDER: Benedictine monks
OS REF: 176:3079

Westminster Abbey is the royal and national church of England. For centuries its kings and queens have been crowned here, and many of them and their families have been buried here; it has also been the last resting-place of many of the most celebrated characters in our history. Architecturally, however, it is paradoxical that Westminster is the closest in style of any great English church to the ideals of the purest French Gothic.

The early history of the site is obscure. Archaeology has established that the site was used by the Romans, and there is a legend that a Christian church was built here in 184 which was turned into a temple of Apollo during the Diocletian persecution. At that time the site was known as Throney, or the Isle of Thorns, for it was a small island or peninsula among the marshes which flanked the Thames. More probably, the first church here was that erected by Sebert, King of the East Saxons, about 618; the foundation was said to be at the request of Bishop Mellitus, and there may have been a monastery attached to the church, although Bede does not mention it. It was some time after this that the name 'Westminster' (i.e., the minster or monastery to the west of London) began to be used. It was not until relatively modern times that the area known as Westminster was engulfed by London. Throughout the middle ages and beyond, the abbey was outside the city walls and there were open fields between Ludgate and Westminster.

Sebert's monastery or church was destroyed by the Danes in the 9th c., but during the 10th-c. monastic revival it was either rebuilt or restored, and in 959 that great reformer St Dunstan refounded it as a Benedictine Abbey for twelve monks. It was dedicated to St Peter, as Sebert's church had been. The first documented connection with royalty was when King Harold Harefoot (1035–40) was buried in the abbey precincts, but it was Edward the Confessor (1042–66) who made Westminster the royal church of England. He rebuilt the abbey on a grand scale and endowed it lavishly; the new church was consecrated on 28 December 1065, just one week before the Confessor

himself died. He was buried in his new church, and here too William the Conqueror came to be crowned once he had overcome Harold at Hastings. Since 1066, every sovereign of the kingdom, with the exception of Edward V (who never really ruled; he was the elder of the princes in the Tower) and Edward VIII, has been crowned in Westminster Abbey.

By the end of the eleventh century there were eighty monks at Westminster. Nothing now remains of the Confessor's church, for it was pulled down in the 13th c. to make way for the great new church begun by Henry III, but of the Norman monastic buildings various fragments are still visible, though these too were largely rebuilt in the 13th c. and later. During the second half of the 13th c. the number of monks at Westminster probably reached one hundred, but by the late 14th c. it had declined to twenty-eight. During the 15th c. numbers fluctuated between forty and fifty. At the suppression, which came to Westminster on 16 January 1540, the abbey was the richest religious house in England, with a net annual income of £2,470. Henry VIII converted the abbey into one of the new cathedrals of Reformation England, with provision for a Dean and twelve prebendaries. Although Queen Mary re-established the Benedictine Abbey in 1556, her sister Elizabeth dissolved it again in 1560 and made Westminster into the Collegiate church of St Peter, which it remains to this day. The Dean and twelve prebendaries were re-installed, and the church retained the independence from the Bishop of London which the medieval abbey had enjoyed. The sovereign, as Visitor, is still the supreme authority at Westminster Abbey.

The total exterior length of the church, including Henry VII's Chapel at the east end, is 531 ft.; without Henry VII's Chapel, it is 423½ ft. The width across the transepts is 203 ft. The width of the nave, excluding the aisles, is 38½ ft. The height of the vault varies between 101½ and 103 ft. Westminster is the most 'French' of our great churches, and in these proportions one finds one of the main factors in this stylistic similarity: the height of the vault in relation to the width of the nave. If the feeling of ascension is the essence of Gothic, it was the French rather than the English who took such ideas to their logical extreme. The height of the vault at Beauvais, the tallest Gothic church in Europe, is a staggering 158 ft. (although

WESTMINSTER: *interior of the church, looking east*

it did collapse in 1284, and took another forty years to re-build). Westminster is the tallest church in Great Britain, and is lower than many of the French churches (e.g., Amiens, Rheims, Bourges). More typical of English proportions is Lincoln, often considered the archetypal Gothic church of England, which has a vault height of 74 ft. and a width in the chancel 'nave' of 38 ft. Westminster is perhaps the one church in England where the 'heavenward thrust' which the architects of French Gothic strove to achieve is realized, and it is in some ways a surprise to find it, for by the mid-thirteenth century, when the chancel was begun, English architects had already developed a conspicuously anglicised Gothic which placed less emphasis on height (e.g., Salisbury, Wells, Lincoln), and one might have expected Henry III to build his new royal church in the 'national' style. The explanation is no doubt to be found in this king's well-known French sympathies.

Another French feature of Westminster is the flying buttresses, necessitated by the height of the vault; flying buttresses are common in France because architects there had to use them to support their immensely high vaults, whereas in England they are rare, partly because the lower vaults did not need them, and partly because they were considered distasteful. Thirdly there is the plan, which again is French and modelled in particular on Rheims: it consists of an aisled nave of eleven bays, north and south transepts with both eastern and western aisles (although the west aisle of the south transept is occupied by the east cloister walk), and the typically French chancel arrangement of a polygonal apse surrounded by an ambulatory with radiating chapels. Henry VII's Chapel was added to the east end at the beginning of the 16th c., replacing a much smaller chapel like the other four polygonal chapels around the chancel.

The foundation stone of the abbey was laid on 6 July 1245, and work proceeded very fast. On 13 October 1269 Henry III was present at the official opening of his new church, when the body of Edward the Confessor was translated to its new place behind the high altar. By this time the chancel, crossing, and eastern four bays of the nave had been completed. At this point building stopped for over a century. Edward the Confessor's Norman nave was still standing, and during the intervening period it would have continued in use.

In 1375 it was decided that the nave should be finished, and although most of it was built in the last quarter of the 14th c., the west front was not finished until 1520.

The first twenty years of the 16th c. also saw the erection of Henry VII's Chapel. The twin towers at the west end were added in the 18th c., and in the 19th c. Sir Gilbert Scott and John Loughborough Pearson virtually rebuilt the north transept front. Indeed, throughout its history, the abbey has been the victim of zealous restorers whose efforts have not always improved it. As a burial-place it has also had to endure the addition of numerous tombs, plaques and other monuments right up to the present day, so that it is a very overcrowded church, and a certain amount of the original architectural purity has been lost. Some of these monuments are beautiful, others are downright ugly. Yet if one takes the architecture of Westminster as a whole, it is a remarkably uniform building, and although the plan and proportions of the church are so French, much of the structural detail is unmistakably English. Purbeck marble, for instance, is used lavishly throughout; there is a gallery too, something with which French architects had almost unanimously dispensed with in favour of triforia by the beginning of the 13th c., to minimise the punctuation in the stages of the elevation and thus emphasise verticality; the vault has ridge-ribs as well as diagonal ribs. All these are 13th-c. English designs.

The uniformity of the church is startling when it is remembered that more than a century intervened between the building of its western and eastern halves. The architect who originally designed the church in 1245 was Henry de Reyns, almost certainly a Frenchman from Rheims, while the man responsible for the continuation of the nave at the end of the 14th c. was Henry Yevele, perhaps the greatest of medieval English architects. At Westminster, it seems that Yevele was content to follow the guide-lines set down by Reyns, a most unmedieval thing to do. The re-building of parts of churches nearly always incorporated the latest ideas and provided an opportunity for the architect to develop new themes within, or proceeding from, the current idiom. Thus, in the years 1375–1400 one would expect something Perpendicular from Yevele, but on this occasion he evidently decided to sacrifice progress to achieve uniformity, and with the exception of a few up-to-date details, he

built it as Reyns would have built it. To a Frenchman such modesty (or regression) would have been unthinkable; in England it was most unusual, although there are two other notable examples, Beverley Minster and Chester Cathedral.

The one part of Westminster Abbey which is completely different from the rest is Henry VII's Chapel, built by the king's master-masons Robert and William Vertue. It is one of the most over-powering buildings in England, a culmination of Perpendicular Gothic on which no expense was spared and of which hardly a square inch was left undecorated. It has been called vulgar and osten-tatious, but also a 'wonder of the world'. The vault, fan-traceried with stone pendents which seem to be suspended in mid-air, demanded stonemasonry of the highest order. The chapel also contains a wealth of figure-sculpture, some of which stands comparison with almost anything of contemporary date.

Of the medieval monuments in the abbey, the most notable are the Coronation Chair, which stands in the Chapel of St. Edward behind the high altar, the Retable on the south side of the ambulatory, and the tomb of Henry VII and Elizabeth of York behind the altar of Henry VII's Chapel. The shrine of Edward the Confessor, commissioned by Henry III and said by con-temporaries to be indescribably lovely, was unfortunately destroyed at the time of the Refor-mation and replaced by a wooden structure in 1557, on the original base. The Coronation Chair was made by Master Walter, King's Painter to Edward I, in 1301; it is of oak and was originally painted in bright colours which have now faded. It contains the Stone of Scone, the coronation seat of the Scottish kings, captured by Edward I in 1297. On the wooden seat above it, the sovereign sits to be crowned and annointed by the Archbishop of Canterbury. The Retable was probably the original reredos of the high altar; it dates from the last quarter of the 13th c., and although it is now badly faded, it is one of the finest panel-paintings to have survived from the middle ages. The tomb of Henry VII and his wife Elizabeth of York was made between 1512 and 1518 by Pietro Torrigiano, who once broke Michelangelo's nose, and Nicholas Ewen. It is a masterpiece of Renaissance sculpture, of black and white marble with figures of bronze gilt, surrounded by an elaborate bronze screen.

The monastic buildings lie to the south of the church, and although many of them have either vanished or been incorporated in more modern structures, a fair amount of medieval detail remains. The cloisters themselves date from the 13th and 14th cs. and are vaulted in stone with quadripartite rib-vaults and ridge-ribs in both directions; the later parts have tierceron-vaults and some fine reticulated tracery in the openings on to the garth. The bay immediately to the south of the south transept is occupied by the vestry and the chapel of St Faith, and is entered only from the south transept; it includes some fine wall-painting and, at the west (i.e., vestry) end, a gallery on a tunnel vault which led to the monks' night-stairs to the dorter. The first eastward opening from the cloister itself leads through two vestibules into the chapter-house, built in the mid-13th c. and restored by Scott in the 19th. The outer vestibule is small and low. The inner vestibule is higher and, because it is vaulted in two single instead of three double bays, also seems con-siderably wider, while the chapter-house itself is a tall octagonal room. The architect clearly intended to create a crescendo effect, passing from smaller to bigger rooms, thus emphasising the spaciousness of the chapter-house. The walls are filled with large four-light windows surmounted by quatrefoil and sexfoil motifs in spheres, while the vaulting springs from a graceful and slender central marble pier of eight clustered shafts. Both the vault and the pier were rebuilt by Scott. It was in the chapter-house that the Commons usually met during parliaments in the later middle ages.

Just south of the chapter-house are the day-stairs leading to the dorter, which ran over the east range. This is now the chapter library, while its undercroft contains the Pyx Chamber in its two northern bays and the museum in its five southern bays. The division of the undercroft was made in the mid-13th c., when the Pyx Chamber came to be used as a royal treasury; hence its name, for the money was kept in pyxes, or chests. The museum contains a fine 12th-c. capital from the cloister showing the Judgement of Solomon, as well as some medieval tiles, sculptured fragments, and effigies of monarchs and others. The whole dorter undercroft dates from the rebuilding of the abbey in the mid-11th c., and is the earliest surviving part of the buildings. To the south-east of the cloister is the little infirmary cloister; although it was almost entirely rebuilt in the 17th and later centuries, a

WESTMINSTER : *entrance to the chapter-house*

WESTMINSTER: *the Pyx chamber*

certain amount of 14th-c. work is incorporated, and the infirmary chapel, known as the chapel of St Katharine, is clearly recognisable.

Along the south walk of the cloister stood the frater, of which a few low walls remain; originally built in the eleventh century, it was largely restructured in the 14th. To the west of the cloister is the group of buildings which comprised the abbot's lodging, parlour, and cellarium, still incorporating medieval work. The parlour, at the south end of the walk, has a tierceron-vault, and from its north-west angle another tierceron-vaulted passage leads to the abbot's lodging, on the west side of an oblong courtyard; this is now College Hall. At the south end of the lodging is the kitchen, with a fireplace in its east wall, while at the north end of it is the Jerusalem chamber, so-called probably because of wall-paintings or tapestries depicting the Holy City which were once here. Henry IV died in this chapel in 1413; he had taken a vow to go on crusade, because he wanted to die in Jerusalem, so when he died here he was said to have fulfilled his vow. The north range of this courtyard contains the Jericho Parlour, erected early in the 16th c. by the penultimate abbot, John Islip. The east range of the courtyard contains the Deanery, built in the 17th c. and rebuilt after bomb damage in the Second World War. The abbey precincts extended to the north of the church as well, but of the remaining monastic buildings at Westminster nothing survives.

Whalley Abbey

ORDER: Cistercian monks
COUNTY: Lancashire
ROUTE: Off A59, 6 miles NNE of Blackburn.
OS REF: 103:7236

Whalley Abbey lies on the north bank of the River Calder one and a half miles above the point where it joins the Ribble. The house was founded by John Halton, Constable of Chester, in 1172, and was originally settled at Stanlaw in the Wirral, but the land around was marshy and inhospitable and, although the community remained there for over a century, by 1283 they had had enough and petitioned the Pope for permission to move to a better site. It still took them thirteen years to move, twenty monks eventually arriving at Whalley in 1296. Work on the new site progressed slowly: building stone and timber were hard to come by, and in 1316 it was almost decided to move site again, but the monks remained, and in 1330 work started on the church.

Throughout most of the 14th and 15th cs. the number of monks at Whalley seems to have been between twenty and thirty. The abbey had a violent end: the last abbot, John Paslew, and his community were sworn to the Pilgrimage of Grace only a few days before the rebellion collapsed, and for their 'treason' the king sent troops to Whalley with grim instructions concerning the way they were to be dealt with. Paslew and two other monks were tried at Lancaster and executed at Whalley early in March 1537, the remaining thirteen monks were ejected from the monastery without pensions, and the house was suppressed.

Of the church little remains above foundation walls, but the plan is clearly laid out and easy to distinguish. It was about 260 ft. in overall length, and consisted of an aisled nave of ten bays, north and south transepts each with three eastern chapels, and an aisled, square-ended chancel of three bays. A stone still marks the place of the high altar, and enough of the south transept remains to show that it was vaulted.

The monastic buildings are better preserved. The east range contained a sacristy to the south of the south transept followed by a vestibule leading to the chapter-house, which was a separate building to the east of the range and was octagonal in shape. Octagonal chapter-houses are an unusual elaboration in Cistercian houses, but there was a precedent in the twelve-sided chapter-house at Margam, dating from about 1200. South of the chapter-house vestibule came, as usual, a parlour, a slype leading to buildings east of the range, and then the undercroft of the dorter, with the dorter extending over the whole range. At the south-east corner of the dorter, almost overhanging the stream, are the remains of the monks' rere-dorter. The south claustral range contained the frater on an east-west axis.

From about 1150 the Cistercians had been building their fraters at right-angles to the south walk of the cloister, but towards the end of the middle ages this convention became more flexible; at both Croxden and Cleeve as well as here at Whalley there is evidence for late medieval Cistercian fraters on an east–west axis. The Whalley frater was not built until the 15th c. The western range was completed in 1415 and still stands, but by this time lay-brothers had all but disappeared from Cistercian monasteries, so the first floor was probably used as a guest house from the beginning, while the undercroft was used as usual for cellarage.

To the east of the eastern range there was a large complex of buildings, some of which have been incorporated into the Assheton mansion, a fine manor house originally built in the late 16th and 17th cs. but almost entirely rebuilt about 1840. The first foundations, just to the east of the southern part of the dorter, belonged to the abbot's lodging. To the east again are some much more substantial ruins. They formed the infirmary block, with chapel and hall, and were incorporated into a long gallery by Sir Ralph Assheton in 1664–5. The long gallery itself is now in ruins, and all the detail is 17th-c. Apart from these buildings there are also two fine gatehouses surviving at Whalley. The outer gateway to the west of the site is early 14th-c. and contains a fine archway rib-vaulted in eight bays. The vault is broken between the fifth and sixth bays, dividing the entrance into a narrow pedestrian way and a wider arch for horses and carriages. The inner gateway was built in 1480 and stands to the north-east of the church. It is battlemented along the parapet and has a wide arch with a pointed tunnel-vault to the north; the latter may have been remodelled after the Dissolution.

In the 17th c. the church and parts of the

WHALLEY: *aerial view from the north-west*

monastic buildings were dismantled, partly to provide building stone for the Assheton mansion, and partly to clear the views from that house. In 1922 the site came on the market and was sold in two lots, the western range passing into Catholic hands (it now contains a chapel). The rest was acquired by the Anglican diocesan authorities of Manchester. It is now used as a conference centre for the diocese of Blackburn, with a resident warden. It was the first warden of this house, Canon Lumb, who excavated the medieval abbey between 1930 and 1934 and gave it its present orderly appearance. The abbey is scheduled as an Ancient Monument.

Whitby Abbey

ORDER: Benedictine monks
COUNTY: North Yorkshire
ROUTE: On A171, on the E side of the town.
OS REF: 94:9011

Its splendid site, perched high on the summit of the East Cliff half a mile from the centre of the town, makes the Benedictine Abbey of Whitby one of the most picturesque of ruined monasteries. The first religious house here was founded in 657 when King Oswy of Northumbria, in celebration of his victory over the heathen King Penda of Mercia at Winwaed in 655 (on the eve of which he had vowed to found twelve monasteries if triumphant) summoned St Hilda from Hartlepool to be abbess of a double monastery for men and women on this site. Among others in the original community was Oswy's daughter Elfled, who herself became abbess before her death in about 714. In 663, only seven years after its foundation, Whitby was already famous enough to be the meeting-place for the Synod which marked a decisive new phase in British Christianity, deciding as it did in favour of the Roman rather than the Celtic dating of Easter and other matters of dispute between the two branches of the Christian religion in this country. Legends in abundance surround the early history of Whitby, and it figures prominently in Bede's *History*, but in 867 it was destroyed during the Danish devastation of the north, not to be re-founded until more than two centuries had passed.

In 1078 or thereabouts, three monks from the houses at Winchcombe in Gloucestershire and Evesham in Worcestershire travelled north to visit the ruined shrines of early Christianity, and one of them, Reinfrid of Evesham, settled with some companions on the site of the former monastery of Whitby, which had been given to them by the northern baron William Percy. Early in its history, the community fell out with its founder, but when William's brother, Serlo Percy, joined the monastery, relations improved, and after a while the founder's son, also called William, joined too, eventually becoming abbot.

Originally a priory, Whitby became an abbey in the first decade of the 12th c. and was soon the third wealthiest Benedictine house in Yorkshire, after Selby and St Mary's, York. In about 1153 the abbey and town were plundered by King Eystein Haroldson of Norway, but that does not seem to have greatly reduced the wealth of the house, and by the late twelfth century there were about forty monks at Whitby. In the first half of the thirteenth century the church was rebuilt, and what now stands of it, with the exception of the west end and the western half of the north wall of the nave, which were added in the 14th c., dates from this period. In the 14th c. Whitby became a mitred abbey, but after the Black Death numbers dropped and by the end of the century there were only twenty monks. The house was surrendered on 14th December 1539, at which time there were twenty-two monks.

The church built in the thirteenth century and completed in the 14th c. measures over 300 ft. in length, and one of its most remarkable features is that the walls of the chancel and nave do not form a continuous straight line, the nave walls inclining slightly to the north in relation to those of the chancel. The reason is not entirely clear, but the error seems to have occurred when the foundations were laid for the new chancel about 1220, for the outlines of the apsidal Norman chancel built in the late eleventh century have been excavated and can be seen to have been set axially with the later nave. The transepts, also dating from the 13th c., are set correctly at right-angles to the chancel rather than the nave. Extraordinary as the error—for presumably it was an error—appears, it does little to diminish the splendour of what remains.

Particularly striking is the north wall of the north transept, which survives to its full height along with its eastern aisle; its three tiers of lancet windows, topped by a rose-windowed gable flanked by turrets, dominate the view from almost any angle except due east and due west. The northern and eastern walls of the chancel also stand close to their full height, and along the north aisle there is some fine rib-vaulting. The east end is missing its south aisle, but its triple-tiered lancets, the top tier stepped to fit into the gable, and the row of arcading stretching south from it to form the inner wall of the chancel's south aisle, are fine examples of mid-13th c. building. The south transept and south wall of the nave have almost entirely disappeared, but the lower half of the north wall of the nave and the west end partly remain. The three eastern bays of the nave were built in the 13th c., the five western bays were

WHITBY: *the church from the north-west*

added in the 14th, and the difference is immediately clear in the windows of the nave north wall. The three eastern bays have slender lancets, while the next two have broader windows filled with geometric tracery. The next bay contains a fully-shafted doorway with trefoiled head, which once opened into a porch. The west front once contained a great window, probably of eight transomed lights, added in the 15th c., but what remains now dates from the 14th c.

Of the monastic buildings hardly anything remains apart from the foundations of a stepped passage in the southern part of what later became the south transept, but which would have adjoined the transept of the Norman church, and the outline of a parlour just to the south of the western end of the nave. In 1924–5 excavations were undertaken to the north of the church, and several remains of the Anglo-Saxon monastery were uncovered, but since then these have been buried once more.

After the Dissolution the site was leased to Richard Cholmley of Kingthorpe, in whose family it remained until 1791. The timber, lead and bells were stripped immediately, but the church structure was left intact, probably because it was a familiar landmark for mariners, and as late as the early 18th c. it was still substantially intact. In 1762 most of the nave fell, followed by the south transept in the next year and much of the west front in 1794. By this time the site had passed into the hands of the Fane family, by whom it was placed in the care of the Office of Works in 1920. Meanwhile, the central tower had crashed to the ground on 25 June 1830, the choir had been damaged by a storm in 1839, and the battered remains had received several direct hits from German cruisers shelling the north-eastern ports on 16 December 1914. Much of the stone from the vanished monastic buildings may have been used to build Abbey House, which stands to the south-east of the church and was built by Francis Cholmley in the late 16th c.

Whitby Abbey is now in the care of English Heritage.

Winchester Cathedral Priory

ORDER: Benedictine monks
COUNTY: Hampshire
ROUTE: In town centre
OS REF: 185:4829

The vast and magnificent cathedral at Winchester, which with its overall length of 556 ft. is the longest cathedral in England and second only to St Peter's, Rome (694 ft.) in Europe, dominates Hampshire's county town. Legend has placed a monastery here as early as the second century, but it seems more likely that the first religious foundation was the Old Minster begun by Cenwealh, son of Cynegils, King of Wessex, in 642–3. This was dedicated to the Holy Trinity and St Peter and St Paul, but after St. Swithun's episcopacy from 852 to 862 his name was added to the dedication, and the cathedral is now generally known as St. Swithun. Although plundered by the Danes in 860 and 879, the minster was repaired, and in 963 St. Ethelwold was chosen by King Edgar to be bishop; he was consecrated by Archbishop Dunstan, and in the following year he replaced the secular canons with Benedictine monks from Abingdon.

Work on the present cathedral was begun by Walkelin, the first Norman bishop, in 1079, and alterations and additions continued to be made until the early 16th c. Originally intended for seventy monks, the priory continued to maintain over sixty until the early 14th c., after which numbers gradually dropped, to twenty-nine in 1495, before rising again to forty-three just before the Dissolution. The monastery was surrendered on 15 November 1539, but the cathedral was retained as an episcopal see, as it still is.

It has been the scene of a multitude of royal occasions, notably the coronations of Egbert (827) and Edward the Confessor (1043), and the second coronations of William the Conqueror (1070) and Henry II (1172); the marriages of Cnut and Emma, the widow of Ethelred the Unready (1043), Henry I and Matilda (1101), Henry IV and Joan of Brittany (1403), and Mary Tudor and Philip of Spain (1554); and the famous visit of Henry VIII and the Holy Roman Emperor Charles V to St Swithun's shrine in 1522.

Perhaps the most remarkable story of all is how the cathedral was saved from collapse at the beginning of the 20th c. In 1905 it was reported that the south and east sides of the church were cracking and beginning to lean outwards, and it was discovered that the 11th c. timber foundation raft had begun to shrink and move as a result of a change of water level. All along the south and east sides shafts were sunk, some to a depth of 20 ft., and for six years a diver named William Walker, working in complete darkness, progressively cleared all the timber, marl and peat from underneath the walls until a new bed of cement sacks could be laid on the gravel below. Between these sacks and the base of the wall, nine courses of bricks and 6 ft. of cement were laid, and then ten flying buttresses were constructed to support the south wall of the nave. In 1912, King George V and Queen Mary attended a Thanksgiving Service for the preservation of the cathedral and a statue to William Walker, the man who 'saved this cathedral with his two hands', was designed by Sir Charles Wheeler and now stands to the north of the screen of Bishop Langton's Chapel.

The cathedral which William Walker saved has some of the finest examples of medieval church architecture, from Norman to Perpendicular, in the country. The earliest surviving parts of the present structure are the transepts and quire, and the crypt beneath the retro-quire. The oblong crypt is singularly well-preserved and has apses at both the east and the west end, the western apse having an ambulatory with flanking chapels; it probably corresponds to the layout of the original Norman east end. The transepts have both eastern and western aisles, the central eastern chapel of the south transept containing the grave of, and a window to, Isaac Walton. In the very centre of the crossing is the tomb of King William Rufus, who was struck dead by an arrow while hunting near Cadnam in the New Forest (whether it was deliberate or accidental could never be established) and carried on a cart to Winchester to be buried in 1100. It will be noticed that the stonework on the massive crossing piers is finer than that of the rest of the transepts; this is because the central tower built by Bishop Walkelin collapsed in 1107, and the present tower is of 12th-century date. Fear of the recurrence of such a disaster explains the size of the piers.

The transepts and crossing of Winchester cathedral are massive, heavy and powerful. The

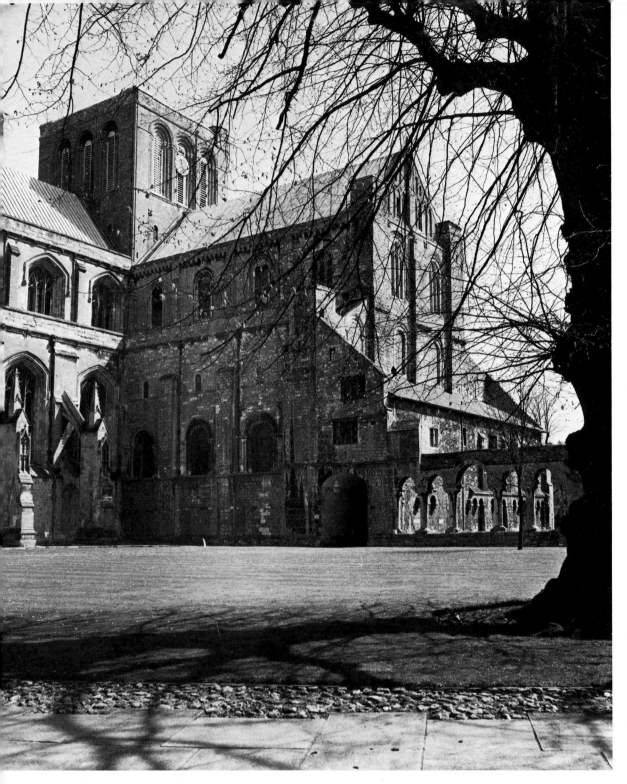

WINCHESTER: *the south transept and chapter-house arches*

WINCHESTER: *the nave*

rest of the church strikes a different note, with less emphasis on power and weight, more on grace and spaciousness. The retro-quire which forms the east end of the church was built by Bishops de Lucy (1189–1204) and des Roches (1204–38), and is now so filled with ornamentation that it is difficult to appreciate the beauty of the structure itself. It is rib-vaulted in three by three bays, the central ('nave') bays being rather wider than the flanking (aisle) bays, and has a projecting eastern Lady chapel flanked by two further chapels, the southern of which became the chantry chapel of Bishop Thomas Langton (d. 1500) after he had remodelled and extended the Lady Chapel. In the central bay of the retro-quire is the last site of St Swithun's shrine, marked by a monument erected in 1962, and just to the south of it is the fine chantry chapel of Henry Cardinal Beaufort, Bishop of Winchester.

The nave of the cathedral is twelve bays long and was rebuilt, or rather remodelled on the original Norman structure, by the two great 14th-c. Bishops of Winchester who also rose high in the royal administration and became Chancellors of England, William Edington (1346–66) and William Wykeham (1367–1404). The majority of this work was done by Wykeham, or, to be more precise, his master mason William Winford, an architect of outstanding ability who also collaborated with Wykeham at Winchester College and at New College, Oxford, as well as undertaking work for both Edward III and Richard II. Work on the west end of the cathedral was undertaken by Edington, but then there was a lull and most of Winford's work on the nave was done between 1394 and 1404. The Norman masonry was for the most part retained, but cut back and remodelled to form more slender piers, and a series of vaulting shafts inserted, as well as a complete new lierne-vaulting system. The result is visually satisfying, but perhaps (owing to the retention of the Norman masonry) a little too heavy to rank among the finest Perpendicular structures in the country.

Further additions were made in the late 15th c. when Bishop Courtenay (1486–92) built an eastern bay on to the Lady Chapel, at the same time extending the new lierne-vaulting to the western bay, and Bishop Langton (1493–1500) remodelled the chapel to the south of it and gave it a pseudo fan-vault. Finally, Bishop Fox (1500–28) remodelled the chancel from the gallery level upwards. The most remarkable feature of the chancel is the great screen, also erected by Fox, which cuts across it. Although despoiled of its figures at the Dissolution, it is now complete again, having been admirably restored at the end of the 19th c. Immediately to the west of it are the mortuary chests of Saxon kings and bishops. Among other monuments in a cathedral notable for its rich furnishings are the tomb of Jane Austen, in the seventh bay from the quire of the nave's north aisle, the chantry of William Wykeham set in the arcading of the nave's south aisle immediately opposite it, and the fine series of wall-paintings in the Guardian Angels' chapel just north of the Lady Chapel.

The monastic buildings at Winchester stood to the south of the church within the present Close, but little of them remains. South from the south transept stretches a row of arches which represent the entrances to the monks' night-stairs to the dorter, a slype, and the chapter-house. The arches of the chapter-house (one taller central doorway flanked by two arches on each side) are good examples of Early Norman arcading, with their solid round piers, heavy scalloped capitals, and fine stonework. Further south is the present Deanery, comprising the remains of the medieval Prior's lodging, which includes a 'cloister', in fact an open porch with 13th-c. Purbeck marble wall-shafts supporting rib-vaults. Further north are the remains of the kitchen, with its large fireplace, and a doorway which led from the cloister into the east range, probably into the undercroft of the dorter. Of the south and west claustral ranges there are no remains.

Worcester Cathedral Priory

ORDER: Benedictine monks
COUNTY: Hereford and Worcester
ROUTE: In the town, on the east bank of the Severn, off Deansway.
OS REF: 150:8554

Worcester became an episcopal see by direction of Archbishop Theodore of Canterbury, at the synod of Hatfield of 680. Soon after, the first cathedral, dedicated to St Peter, was built, and according to Bede it had a mixed community of monks and secular clerks, but by the early 10th c. monastic life was virtually extinct throughout England, and Worcester was no exception. In 969, however, one of the great figures of 10th-c. English monasticism, St Oswald, with support from the reforming King Edgar, re-founded the abbey for Benedictine monks and began to build a new church dedicated to St Mary. Along with neighbouring Pershore and Evesham, Worcester was in the forefront of the 10th c. monastic revival, but the church built by Oswald was largely destroyed by a Danish raiding army under Harthacnut in 1041.

In 1062 the great St Wulfstan became bishop of Worcester. Renowned particularly for his preaching against slavery, he was the only Anglo-Saxon bishop who was not eventually replaced by a Norman after the Conquest, and he began the construction of the present church in 1084 and increased the number of monks at Worcester from twelve to fifty. Although the number dropped to thirty-seven in the late 14th c., it rose to forty-five again in 1433 and remained fairly constant until the Dissolution. In 1218, fifteen years after the canonisation of Wulfstan, Henry III was present at a solemn re-dedication of the cathedral to St Mary, St Peter, St Oswald, and St Wulfstan. Two years earlier Henry's father, King John, had been buried in the cathedral, as he had requested. His tomb and effigy are in front of the high altar. The cathedral priory was dissolved on 18 January 1540. The monks were replaced by secular canons and Worcester retained its position as a cathedral of Reformation England.

The church is 425 ft. in overall length, and has a nave of nine bays with two northern projections (a porch in the fifth bay, and a Jesus Chapel in the second bay from the east), relatively small tran-

septs to the north and south, and a chancel of four bays followed by eastern transepts and a Lady Chapel; on the south side of the two western bays of the chancel another chapel projects. The west front of the church is basically a 19th-c. creation, with an eight-light window surmounted by a rose-window, and above that four pinnacles. The two western bays of the nave contain some of the earliest work in the cathedral; they are Transitional. The difference between these two bays and the rest of the nave is immediately noticeable, with the higher, more acutely pointed arcade, the narrower triforium, and more heavily-decorated capitals. These eastern seven bays were begun in 1320, but were a long time in the building; the north side came before the south side (no doubt so that the cloister could be left undisturbed as long as possible), and not until about 1370 was the vault erected. The Jesus Chapel dates from the same period and has some intricate floriated window tracery. With the north porch interior, which was built in 1386, the Perpendicular style has been reached, although its north front was almost entirely rebuilt during the 19th c.

The north and south transepts are the only parts of the church apart from the crypt which survive from the first half of the twelfth century. They were remodelled after the collapse of the Norman crossing tower in 1175, and several additions were also made in the 19th century. The crossing tower was not replaced until the last quarter of the 14th c. In the south transept is the entrance to the crypt, built in the last years of the eleventh century (naturally it was the first part of the cathedral to be built). It reveals what was probably the design of the original Norman chancel, that is, apsidal with an ambulatory running round the high altar but not apparently with radiating chapels. The ambulatory of the crypt has now been blocked off, but the remaining sturdy little pillars, block capitals, and groin vaults are typical of the best Early Norman work.

The chancel above it is the chief glory of Worcester cathedral. It was built in the mid-13th c. and is, along with the other great 13th-c. cathedrals of England (such as Lincoln and Salisbury), one of the lasting monuments of that 'classic century' of English Gothic. Throughout the chancel the emphasis is on verticality, with arches of many slender mouldings, tall windows, and above all the same lavish use of Purbeck marble columns as at

WORCESTER: *the chancel, looking into the north transept*

WORCESTER: *effigy of King John*

Canterbury and Lincoln. Purbeck marble too is used for the effigy of King John which was carved about 1230—an excellent example of 13th-c. English sculpture at its best; the elegant treatment of the drapery in particular is worth noting. Behind the sedilia on the south side of the high altar is the chantry of Prince Arthur, the elder brother of Henry VIII, who died in 1502, before their father, and thus never came to the throne. Had Arthur lived, his brother might never have become King of England, and there might not have been a Dissolution of the monasteries; or at least it might have been delayed for several years.

The monastic buildings at Worcester lay to the south of the church, but their arrangement was far from conventional. The cloisters were rebuilt in the 14th and early 15th centuries on to a Norman shell; they have windows with reticulated tracery and a lierne-vault with some fine roof bosses, particularly in the south walk. To the south of the south transept is the usual slype; although it has a 14th-c. doorway, the masonry and decoration are clearly Norman, dating from about 1100. Continuing to the south there are two recessed book-cupboards, followed by the chapter-house. This too has a 14th-c. doorway, but the interior is once again Norman, probably about 1120. The original shape was a simple circle, and from the inside this is still so, but in the 14th c. the exterior was re-cased and is now decagonal. The windows in the upper stage were also inserted at that time, but the blank arcading around the lower stage is clearly Norman. The central pier from which the semi-circular ribs of the vault spring is surprisingly slender for Norman, particularly early Norman, work. In the great majority of monastic plans, the dorter followed the chapter-house along the east range, but here at Worcester there was a problem with the water supply for the rere-dorter, adjoining the dorter, so the dorter was transferred to the west range. It was the absence of the dorter which allowed for such a sumptuous chapter-house.

WORCESTER: *the crypt*

To the east of the east range stood the guest-house, of which a ruined 14th-c. arcade with some excellent flowing tracery in the windows still stands. The south range of the cloister contained the frater on an undercroft. The undercroft is Norman, groin-vaulted on short round piers, but the frater itself was rebuilt in the mid-14th c. It has large windows with reticulated tracery, and in the east wall is an excellent, but sadly mutilated, Christ in Majesty, in a quatrefoiled niche. It dates from the first third of the 13th c., the rebuilders of the 14th century clearly considering it good enough to retain.

The west range displays the main irregularity of Worcester. To place the dorter here was unusual enough, but the monks went a step further and built it on an east–west axis, so that it reached out at right-angles from the west range towards the river. It must have proved too arduous a task to provide water for a rere-dorter in the east range, so the problem at Worcester was solved by extending the dorter range even further to the west with another block reaching right down to the Severn and containing the rere-dorter on the top floor and the infirmary on the lower two floors. The upper stages of this block, along with most of the dorter block itself, have disappeared, but the substantial ruins of the infirmary, built in the early twelfth century but largely rebuilt in the late 14th, still lie to the south-west of the church's west front, on the grassy slope running down to the Severn. Of the outlying buildings, the main survival is the gateway to the east of the cloister known as Edgar Tower, which was built in the 14th c. but largely remodelled, on the exterior at least, in the 19th. It is rib-vaulted, and has the usual double entrance, with a broad passage for carriages and a narrower one for pedestrians.

Monastic Sites in Britain not Described in the Text

This list is intended as a comprehensive guide to monastic sites in England, Scotland and Wales where remains of medieval buildings can be seen. The remains vary considerably in both nature and extent. They range from complete monastic churches, many of which were of great importance in the middle ages and are still splendid examples of the architecture of the period but which have since been almost totally shorn of their accompanying monastic buildings (e.g. Bath), to sites at which the medieval buildings have been incorporated in later work to the extent that their monastic nature is well-nigh impossible to appreciate (e.g. Welbeck), and those, the great majority, where the buildings are ruined but the ruins are less extensive than at those sites described in the text.

For further information on the location, history, and nature of the remains to be found at each site, the reader should refer respectively to the *Monastic Maps of Britain*, the two volumes of *Medieval Religious Houses (England and Wales*, and *Scotland)*, and the relevant volume of the *Buildings of England* series (See Bibliography).

The following abbreviations are used:

(1) Under Rank:

A = Abbey
CP Cathedral Priory
P = Priory
Pc Priory cell (cells not of priory rank are excluded)

(2) Under Order:

A   = Augustinian canons
Ac = Augustinian cannonesses
B   = Benedictine monks
Bn = Benedictine nuns
Bnf = Benedictine nuns, formerly of the order of Fontevrault

Br = Bridgettine nuns and priests
Ca = Carthusian monks
Ci = Cistercian monks
Cin = Cistercian nuns
CiS = Cistercian monks, formerly of the Savignac order
Cl = Cluniac monks
G   = Gilbertine nuns and canons
Gr = Grandmontine brothers
P   = Premonstratensian canons
T   = Tironensian monks
Tr = Trinitarian brothers
V   = Valliscaulian monks

	NAME	COUNTY	RANK	ORDER	DATE FOUNDED	DATE DISSOLVE
England	Abbey Dore	Hereford and Worcs.	A	Ci	1147	1536
	Abbotsbury	Dorset	A	B	1044	1539
	Abingdon	Oxford	A	B	954	1538
	Aconbury	Hereford and Worcs.	P	Ac	1237	1539
	Alberbury	Shropshire	P	Gr	1230	1441
	Alnwick	Northumberland	A	P	1148	1539
	Amesbury	Wiltshire	P	BnF	1177	1539
	Bamburgh	Northumberland	P	A	1121	1537
	Bardney	Lincoln	A	B	1087	1538
	Barking	London	A	Bn	975	1539
	Barlings	Lincoln	A	P	1155	1537
	Bath	Avon	CP	B	1090	1539
	Battle	East Sussex	A	B	1067	1538
	Beauchief	South Yorkshire	A	P	1176	1537
	Beeliegh	Essex	A	P	1180	1536
	Bindon	Dorset	A	Ci	1172	1539
	Birkenhead	Merseyside	P	B	1150	1536
	Bisham	Berkshire	P	A	1337	1536
	Blanchland	Northumberland	A	P	1165	1539
	Blyth	Nottingham	P	B	1088	1536
	Bourne	Lincoln	A	A	1138	1536
	Boxgrove	West Sussex	P	B	1105	1536
	Bridlington	Humberside	P	A	1113	1537
	Brinkburn	Northumberland	P	A	1135	1536
	Bromfield	Shropshire	P	B	1155	1540
	Broomholm	Norfolk	P	Cl	1195	1536
	Buckfast	Devon	A	CiS	1136	1535
	Buckland	Devon	A	Ci	1278	1539
	Bungay	Suffolk	P	Bn	1183	1536
	Burnham	Buckingham	A	Ac	1266	1539
	Bushmead	Bedford	P	A	1195	1536
	Butley	Suffolk	P	A	1171	1538
	Canons Ashby	Northampton	P	A	1151	1536
	Cartmel	Cumbria	P	A	1194	1536
	Cerne	Dorset	A	B	987	1539
	Chicksands	Bedford	P	G	1150	1538
	Chirbury	Shropshire	P	A	1195	1536
	Christchurch	Dorset	P	A	1150	1539
	Church Preen	Shropshire	Pc	Cl	1150	1539
	Cockersand	Lancashire	A	P	1190	1539
	Coggeshall	Essex	A	CiS	1140	1538
	Colchester, St. Botolph	Essex	P	A	1093	1536
	Colchester, St John	Essex	A	B	1096	1539
	Combe	Warwick	A	Ci	1150	1539
	Cornworthy	Devon	P	Ac	1238	1539
	Coventry	West Midlands	CP	B	1043	1539
	Coverham	North Yorks	A	P	1202	1536

NAME	COUNTY	RANK	ORDER	DATE FOUNDED	DATE DISSOLVED
Craswall	Hereford and Worcs.	P	Gr	1225	1462
Creake	Norfolk	A	A	1206	1506
Crowland	Lincoln	A	B	971	1539
Croxton	Leicester	A	P	1162	1538
Dale	Derby	A	P	1200	1538
Davington	Kent	P	Bn	1153	1535
Deeping St James	Lincoln	Pc	B	1139	1539
Deerhurst	Gloucester	P	B	1059	1540
Dieulacres	Stafford	A	Ci	1214	1538
Dorchester	Oxford	A	A	1140	1536
Dover, St Martin	Kent	P	B	1136	1535
Dover, St Radegund	Kent	A	P	1193	1536
Dudley	West Midlands	P	Cl	1160	1539
Dunkeswell	Devon	A	Ci	1201	1539
Dunstable	Bedford	P	A	1125	1540
Dunster	Somerset	P	B	1090	1539
Easebourne	West Sussex	P	Ac	1248	1536
Ellerton	North Yorks	P	Cin	1189	1537
Elstow	Bedford	A	Bn	1178	1539
Evesham	Hereford and Worcs.	A	B	995	1540
Exeter, St Nicholas	Devon	P	B	1087	1536
Flaxley	Gloucester	A	Ci	1151	1537
Forde	Dorset	A	Ci	1141	1539
Frithelstock	Devon	P	A	1220	1536
Gloucester, Lantony Secunda	Gloucester	P	A	1136	1539
Gloucester, St Oswald	Gloucester	P	A	1153	1536
Godstow	Oxford	A	Bn	1133	1539
Grace Dieu	Leicester	P	Ac	1239	1538
Great Bricett	Suffolk	P	A	1119	1444
Great Malvern	Hereford and Worcs.	P	B	1085	1540
Great Yarmouth	Norfolk	P	B	1101	1539
Halesowen	West Midlands	A	P	1218	1538
Hardham	West Sussex	P	A	1248	1534
Hartland	Devon	A	A	1169	1539
Healaugh	North Yorks	P	A	1218	1535
Herringfleet, St Olave	Suffolk	P	A	1216	1537
Hexham	Northumberland	P	A	1113	1537
Hinton	Avon	P	Ca	1232	1539
Holmcultren	Cumbria	A	Ci	1150	1538
Horsham, St Faith	Norfolk	P	B	1105	1536
Hurley	Berkshire	P	B	1087	1536
Ingham	Norfolk	P	Tr	1360	1536
Isleham	Cambridge	P	B	1100	1254

NAME	COUNTY	RANK	ORDER	DATE FOUNDED	DATE DISSOLVE
Jarrow	Tyne and Wear	P	B	1074	1536
Kenilworth	Warwick	A	A	1125	1539
Kersey	Suffolk	P	A	1218	1443
Kirklees	West Yorks	P	Cin	1138	1539
Kirkstead	Lincoln	A	Ci	1187	1537
Lacock	Wiltshire	A	Ac	1232	1539
Lancaster, St Mary	Lancashire	P	B	1094	1428
Langley	Norfolk	A	P	1195	1536
Lastingham	North Yorks	A	B	1078	1086
Launde	Leicester	P	A	1125	1539
Leominster	Hereford and Worcs.	P	B	1123	1539
Leonard Stanley	Gloucester	P	B	1146	1538
Letheringham	Suffolk	P	A	1200	1537
Lewes	East Sussex	P	Cl	1077	1537
Little Dunmow	Essex	P	A	1106	1536
Little Malvern	Hereford and Worcs.	P	B	1171	1537
Malmesbury	Wiltshire	A	B	970	1539
Mattersey	Nottingham	P	G	1185	1538
Maxstoke	Warwick	P	A	1337	1536
Michelham	East Sussex	P	A	1229	1536
Milton Abbas	Dorset	A	B	964	1539
Minster-in-Sheppey	Kent	P	Ac	1087	1536
Monk Sherborne	Hampshire	P	B	1130	1414
Monks Horton	Kent	P	Cl	1142	1536
Monkwearmouth	Tyne and Wear	Pc	B	1083	1536
Montacute	Somerset	P	Cl	1078	1539
Morville	Shropshire	Pc	B	1138	1540
Mottisfont	Hampshire	P	A	1201	1536
Newark	Surrey	P	A	1189	1538
Newminster	Northumberland	A	Ci	1138	1537
Newstead	Nottingham	P	A	1163	1539
Norton	Cheshire	A	A	1134	1536
Notley	Buckingham	A	A	1162	1538
Nuneaton	Warwick	P	BnF	1155	1539
Nun Monkton	North Yorks	P	Bn	1153	1536
Old Malton	North Yorks	P	G	1150	1539
Owston	Leicester	A	A	1161	1536
Pentney	Norfolk	P	A	1130	1537
Pershore	Hereford and Worcs.	A	B	970	1540
Peterborough	Cambridge	A	B	966	1539
Pilton	Devon	P	B	1200	1539
Pinley	Warwick	P	Cin	1135	1536
Plympton	Devon	P	A	1121	1539
Prittlewell	Essex	P	Cl	1121	1536

NAME	COUNTY	RANK	ORDER	DATE FOUNDED	DATE DISSOLVED
Quarr	Isle of Wight	A	CiS	1132	1536
Ramsey	Cambridge	A	B	969	1539
Reading	Berkshire	A	B	1121	1539
Repton	Derby	P	A	1139	1538
Richmond, St Martin	North Yorks	P	B	1137	1539
Robertsbridge	East Sussex	A	Ci	1176	1538
Romsey	Hampshire	A	Bn	967	1539
Rosedale	North Yorks	P	Cin	1158	1535
Royston	Hertford	P	A	1179	1537
Rufford	Nottingham	A	Ci	1146	1536
St Bees	Cumbria	P	B	1120	1538
St Benet of Hulme	Norfolk	A	B	1019	1539
St Germans	Cornwall	P	A	1184	1539
St Michael's Mount	Cornwall	P	B	1050	1414
St Osyth	Essex	A	A	1121	1539
Seaton-near-Bootle	Cumbria	P	Bn	1200	1540
Selby	North Yorks	A	B	1069	1539
Sempringham	Lincoln	P	G	1131	1538
Shaftesbury	Dorset	A	Bn	888	1539
Sherborne	Dorset	A	B	993	1539
Shrewsbury	Shropshire	A	B	1083	1540
Shulbred	West Sussex	P	A	1200	1536
Sibton	Suffolk	A	Ci	1150	1536
Smithfield, St Bartholomew the Great	London	P	A	1123	1539
Southwark Cathedral	London	P	A	1106	1539
Southwick	Hampshire	P	A	1153	1538
Steventon	Oxford	P	B	1135	1389
Stogursey	Somerset	P	B	1107	1442
Stoke-by-Clare	Suffolk	P	B	1124	1415
Stoneleigh	Warwick	A	Ci	1155	1536
Swavesey	Cambridge	P	B	1086	1411
Swine	Humberside	P	Cin	1153	1539
Syningthwaite	North Yorks	P	Cin	1160	1535
Syon House, Isleworth	London	A	Br	1431	1539
Tavistock	Devon	A	B	980	1539
Thame	Oxford	A	Ci	1140	1539
Thorney	Cambridge	A	B	973	1539
Thurgarton	Nottingham	P	A	1139	1538
Tilty	Essex	A	Ci	1153	1536
Tor	Devon	A	P	1196	1539
Tupholme	Lincoln	A	P	1166	1536
Upholland	Greater Manchester	P	B	1319	1536
Waltham	Essex	A	A	1177	1540

	NAME	COUNTY/REGION	RANK	ORDER	DATE FOUNDED	DATE DISSOLV
	Watton	Humberside	P	G	1150	1539
	Waverley	Surrey	A	Ci	1128	1536
	Welbeck	Nottingham	A	P	1154	1538
	West Acre	Norfolk	P	A	1135	1538
	West Malling	Kent	A	Bn	1090	1538
	Wetheral	Cumbria	P	B	1106	1538
	White Ladies	Shropshire	P	Ac	1199	1538
	Wigmore	Hereford and Worcs.	A	A	1179	1538
	Wilmington	East Sussex	P	B	1086	1414
	Winchester, Hyde	Hampshire	A	B	1110	1539
	Witham	Somerset	P	Ca	1179	1539
	Woodspring	Avon	P	A	1226	1536
	Worksop	Nottingham	P	A	1119	1538
	Wykeham	North Yorks	P	Cin	1153	1539
	Wymondham	Norfolk	A	B	1107	1538
	Yedingham	North Yorks	P	Bn	1163	1539
	York, Holy Trinity	North Yorks	P	B	1089	1538
	York, St Mary	North Yorks	A	B	1088	1539
Scotland	Ardchattan	Strathclyde	P	V	1230	1602
	Balmerino	Fife	A	Ci	1227	1603
	Beauly	Highland	P	V	1230	1634
	Cambuskenneth	Central	A	A	1140	1604
	Coldingham	Borders	P	B	1139	1606
	Coupar Angus	Tayside	A	Ci	1164	1606
	Culross	Fife	A	Ci	1217	1589
	Deer	Grampian	A	Ci	1219	1587
	Holyrood	Lothian	A	A	1128	1606
	Inchmahome	Central	P	A	1238	1604
	Iona	Strathclyde	A	B	1203	1588
	Kelso	Borders	A	T	1113	1607
	Kilwinning	Strathclyde	A	T	1162	1592
	Kinloss	Grampian	A	Ci	1150	1601
	Lindores	Fife	A	T	1191	1600
	May Island	Fife	P	B	1153	1550
	Newbattle	Lothian	A	Ci	1140	1587
	Paisley	Strathclyde	A	Cl	1169	1587
	Pluscarden	Grampian	P	V	1231	1454
	Restenneth	Tayside	P	A	1153	1606
	Saddell	Strathclyde	A	Ci	1207	1507
	Whithorn	Dumfries and Galloway	P	P	1175	1612
Wales	Abbey-Cwmhir	Powys	A	Ci	1176	1536
	Aberconway	Gwynedd	A	Ci	1190	1286
	Abergavenny	Gwent	P	B	1100	1536
	Bardsey	Gwynedd	A	A	1240	1537
	Beddgelert	Gwynedd	P	A	1240	1536

NAME	COUNTY	RANK	ORDER	DATE FOUNDED	DATE DISSOLVED
Brecon	Powys	P	B	1110	1538
Caldy	Dyfed	P	T	1115	1536
Chepstow	Gwent	P	B	1071	1536
Haverfordwest	Dyfed	P	A	1200	1536
Kidwelly	Dyfed	P	B	1114	1539
Llantarnam	Gwent	A	Ci	1179	1536
Margam	West Glamorgan	A	Ci	1147	1536
Monmouth	Gwent	P	B	1086	1540
Neath	West Glamorgan	A	Ci	1130	1539
Pembroke	Dyfed	P	B	1098	1539
Penmon	Gwynedd	P	A	1237	1536
Pill	Dyfed	P	T	1115	1536
Talley	Dyfed	A	P	1189	1536
Usk	Gwent	P	Bn	1236	1536
Whitland	Dyfed	A	Ci	1151	1539

Bibliographical Note

This selection includes only the most important authorities. The works cited have their own bibliographies which should be consulted by the reader who wishes to pursue the monastic story in depth.

To locate sites, reference should be made to the maps of *Monastic Britain* (North and South Sheets) published by the Ordnance Survey and available at HMSO bookshops. Architectural descriptions of all sites in England are found in *The Buildings of England* by Sir Nikolaus Pevsner (46 vols., 1951–1974). Brief descriptions of some Scottish sites are provided in *Scottish Abbeys* by S. Cruden (HMSO, 1960). This also includes a discussion on Scottish monastic buildings, while *Abbeys* by R. Gilyard-Beer (HMSO, 2nd ed., 1976) does the same for English and Welsh monasteries. English Heritage, Cadw: Welsh Historic Monuments, and the Scottish Development Department publish guide books to many of the sites in their care, which include architectural descriptions, and these are available from the publishers direct or at the sites.

For the history of monasticism in England, the great standard works are *The Monastic Order in England* by Dom David Knowles (1940), and *The Religious Orders in England* (3 vols., 1948–1959). Excellent shorter books are *Monastic Life in Medieval England* by J. C. Dickinson (1961), *Medieval English Nunneries* by E. Power (1922), and *The Monastic Achievement* by G. Zarnecki (1972), which is an introduction to European as well as British monasticism.

A comprehensive catalogue of religious foundations in Great Britain is provided by *Medieval Religious Houses: England and Wales* by Dom David Knowles and R. Neville Hadcock (1971), and *Medieval Religious Houses: Scotland* by I. B. Cowan and D. E. Easson (1976).

Some further reading

(ed.) H. E. Butler, *The Chronicle of Jocelin of Brakelond* (1949)

H. M. Colvin, *The White Canons in England* (1951)

F. G. Cowley, *The Monastic Order in South Wales, 1066–1349* (1977)

J. C. Dickinson, *The Origins of the Austin Canons* (1950)

J. C. Dickinson, *An Ecclesiastical History of England: The Later Middle Ages* (1979)

R. B. Dobson, *Durham Priory, 1400–1450* (1973)

F. R. H. Du Boulay, *The Lordship of Canterbury* (1966)

M. Gibson, *Lanfranc of Bec* (1977)

R. Graham, *St. Gilbert of Sempringham and the Gilbertines* (1901)

B. Harvey, *Westminster Abbey and its Estates* (1978)

(ed.) A. Hudson, *Selections from English Wycliffite Writings* (1978)

E. Miller, *The Abbey and Bishopric of Ely* (1951)

J. R. H. Moorman, *The Franciscans in England* (1974)

(ed. and trans.) F. M. Powicke, *The Life of Ailred of Rievaulx* by Walter Daniel (1950)

C. Platt, *The Monastic Grange in Medieval England* (1969)

G. W. O. Woodward, *The Dissolution of the Monasteries* (1966)

J. Youings, *The Dissolution of the Monasteries* (1973)

Index

412